TOWARDS BALANCED INTERNATIONAL GROWTH

TOWARDS BALANCED

INTERNATIONAL GROWTH

Essays presented to J. TINBERGEN

Editor H. C. BOS

1972
NORTH-HOLLAND PUBLISHING COMPANY
AMSTERDAM · LONDON

Library of Congress Catalog Card Number: 69-20411
North-Holland ISBN 0 7204 3036 4

Publishers:
NORTH-HOLLAND PUBLISHING COMPANY – AMSTERDAM
NORTH-HOLLAND PUBLISHING COMPANY, LTD. – LONDON
Sole distributors for the U.S.A. and Canada
AMERICAN ELSEVIER PUBLISHING COMPANY, INC.
52 VANDERBILT AVENUE
NEW YORK, N.Y. 10017

First Edition 1969
Second Printing 1972

PRINTED IN THE NETHERLANDS

EDITOR'S PREFACE

This volume of essays is dedicated to Professor Jan Tinbergen on the occasion of his retirement as Director of the Netherlands Economic Institute in the summer of 1968.

The contributors to the volume are colleagues and staff of the Institute and other Dutch and foreign colleagues or pupils who have worked on development problems since 1955 for shorter or longer periods at the Institute under Tinbergen's inspiring guidance.

In contrast with Tinbergen's wide range of activities since his appointment as Director of the Institute in 1933, the scope of this volume is a modest one, both with regard to the subject it covers – theory and policy of development – and to the selection of its contributors. It seemed appropriate to pose these limitations on this occasion, however, because Tinbergen's retirement as Director of the Institute does not mark the end of, nor even a reduction in his active life; it rather signifies the concentration of his creative energy on a narrower field which he feels deserves the highest priority: the design of a global development strategy and, a still more fundamental issue, the organisation of peace.

This volume is not, therefore, commemorative of an occasion such as is commonly the object of the traditional Festschrift. It is the expression of the affection, esteem and gratitude to Tinbergen upon his entry into another important stage of his life by those who are, or have been, more or less closely associated with Tinbergen's Division of Balanced International Growth of the Netherlands Economic Institute and of whom the contributors to this volume are but a small and to some extent arbitrary representation. They know that a volume of this kind can in no way return to Tinbergen what he has given them through his intellectual inspiration and human interest.

The editor's requests for cooperation in preparing this volume have been met with a warm response – who wonders! The Netherlands Economic Institute is grateful to the North-Holland Publishing Company who without hesitation accepted to publish this book. The editor would like to thank all those who have assisted him by way of their advice or otherwise in organising this volume. In particular, he would like to thank Mr. W. Kirwan from Dublin who did much more than carefully editing the English and Miss J. J. Bokhove and Mrs. S. van Willigenburg who typed the manuscripts untiringly in the short time left for their indispensable contribution to this collective enterprise in honour of Jan Tinbergen.

Rotterdam

H. C. Bos
Editor

CONTRIBUTORS

Gerard K. Boon
UNIDO Industry Advisor, Mexico

H. C. Bos
Professor of Development Planning, Netherlands School of Economics, Rotterdam

S. Chakravarty
Professor of Economics, Delhi School of Economics, Delhi University, New Delhi

Peter A. Cornelisse
Netherlands Economic Institute, Division of Balanced International Growth

B. Herman
Netherlands Economic Institute, Division of Balanced International Growth

M. Inagaki
Professor of Economics, Sir George Williams University, Montreal

Nurul Islam
Director, Pakistan Institute of Development Economics, Karachi

F. P. Jansen
Development Research Institute, Catholic School of Economics, Tilburg

L. H. Janssen
Professor of Economics, Catholic School of Economics, Tilburg

L. H. Klaassen
Professor of Regional and Socio-economic Research, Netherlands School of Economics, Rotterdam; Director Netherlands Economic Institute

A. Kuyvenhoven
Netherlands School of Economics, Centre for Development Planning, Rotterdam

Hans Linnemann

Professor of Economics, Institute of Social Studies, The Hague, and Professor of Development Economics at the Free University, Amsterdam

L. B. M. Mennes

Netherlands Economic Institute, Division of Balanced International Growth

J. P. Pronk

Netherlands Economic Institute, Division of Balanced International Growth

A. Qayum

Visiting Professor of Economics, Indiana University, International Development Research Center

J. C. Ramaer

Deputy Managing Director, Financial Department of N.V. Philips' Gloeilampen Fabrieken

J. C. Saigal

U.N. African Institute for Economic Development and Planning, Dakar

E. J. Schreuel

Netherlands Economic Institute, Division of Balanced International Growth

Jan Serck-Hanssen

Professor of Economics, University of Oslo

Jan Versluis

Netherlands Economic Institute, Division of Balanced International Growth

J. G. Waardenburg

Netherlands Economic Institute, Division of Balanced International Growth

A. C. van Wickeren

Netherlands Economic Institute

Y. B. de Wit

Institute for the Socio-economic Study of Less Developed Areas, University of Amsterdam

CONTENTS

SOME ASPECTS OF OPTIMAL INVESTMENT POLICY IN AN UNDERDEVELOPED ECONOMY*

S. CHAKRAVARTY

1. The Nature of the Problem

In recent years, a great deal of discussion has been devoted to deriving optimal investment policies for an underdeveloped economy. An underdeveloped economy for this purpose is defined as one which has insufficient capital stock to employ its current labour power. Clearly not all underdeveloped economies defined in the sense of low-income countries belong to this category. In particular, this leaves out economies where labour unassisted by capital or assisted by very small quantities of capital can produce commodities which are desired by the economy. A favourable land–man ratio would appear to be essential for such economies. There are examples of such economies in Africa or even Asia. But most of the Asian economies, which include some very large underdeveloped ones, fit my description and we define our problem only with respect to these economies. For these countries the derivation of the optimal amount and composition of investment raises some special problems which a capital-rich, fully-employed economy need not be particularly concerned with.

One of these special problems is connected with the 'nonshiftability' of the capital stock between the different commodity producing sectors of the economy. While such nonshiftability is an important factor in any economy, its degree of importance is clearly much greater for an underdeveloped economy with a relatively inadequate capital base. For some small-sized

*) In writing the second section of this paper, I have made use of some of the material contained in my unpublished paper 'Optimal Paths of Capital Accumulation in a Model with Nonshiftable Capital' (mimeographed), D.S.E. Working Paper No. 17, October 1966 (revised January 1967) [1]. I am also indebted to Dr. A. Bhaduri and Mr. R. K. Das for helpful discussions in writing the present paper.

underdeveloped countries with specially favourable foreign trade situations, nonshiftability is again a feature of relative unimportance. However, for a very large number of underdeveloped countries, foreign trade positions seem to be difficult enough to make 'nonshiftability' a matter of relative concern from the planning point of view.

The recognition that nonshiftability of capital stock between the sectors is a strategic factor in the growth process of an underdeveloped economy gives the Feldman–Mahalanobis–Domar [3, 6] two-sector growth model a degree of relevance which many other two-sector growth models do not enjoy. The relative difference in factor intensities between the consumer goods and capital goods industries which alone would otherwise justify two-sector growth exercises does not seem to be empirically very important.

The Feldman–Mahalanobis model was not, however, developed in the context of deriving utility maximizing growth paths. The allocation ratio of investment that would go to the total investment goods industry was determined there on a once-for-all basis. While it was shown that a higher share of investment devoted to the investment goods industry would eventually mean a higher output level, the calculus of comparing present costs with future benefits was not introduced excepting as an implicit 'time series' criterion which was rather crude in terms of economic logic. Stoleru [9] has given a more satisfactory formulation of the model in choice theoretic terms but since he does not consider utility functions which show diminishing marginal utility, he cannot capture the intergenerational equity problem which in the context of development planning was first rightly emphasized by Professor Tinbergen in his papers dealing with optimum savings [10, 11].

In this paper we show what explicit utility maximizing growth paths look like when developed in the context of a two-sector model of the Feldman–Mahalanobis type. It will be shown that in this 'nonshiftable' model, the utility maximizing growth paths for an infinite planning horizon will, in almost all cases, fail to possess an optimal growth path of the classical Ramsey type with a smoothly rising consumption level from the very initial period. Since our analysis rests here on the usual Ramsey assumption of a bounded utility function, this result is entirely due to rigidity on the side of production alone, a phenomenon which one-sector Ramsey models cannot exhibit.

In demonstrating this proposition we proceed on the assumption of a utility function of the Frisch–Tinbergen type, which postulates a constant elasticity marginal utility schedule. More general utility functions would lead to a more complicated algebraic discussion and change some points of detail, but so long as the usual diminishing marginal utility assumption is retained, the basic qualitative point is not going to change. We also assume that the technology is linear, e.g. the two sectors are each marked by constant capital–output ratios. Whether this constitutes a genuine limitation of our analysis is taken up for discussion later. In setting up our problem as one of utility maximization, as well as in our derivation of the basic result, we follow the Valentine extension of the classical Bolza problem in the calculus of variations.[1]) Alternative techniques are applicable to this problem. But I believe that the treatment adopted here is essentially simpler than the alternative techniques that may be applied. For an intuitive understanding of the problem, it is enough to know the classical technique of Lagrange multipliers, so familiar from the host of calculus problems one encounters in economics.

We devote the second section of the paper to the derivation of the basic result and then proceed to discuss in some detail the policy significance of the optimal growth paths obtained earlier. Those who are unwilling to go through the detailed mathematics and would be willing to accept the result as true may proceed to the policy discussion.

2. The Derivation of the Optimal Time Shape of Consumption

2.1. *The necessary conditions for an optimum*

The objective function of the planner is represented here by a utility function $\int_0^T U(C)\,\mathrm{d}t$. Here T may be assumed to be fixed and finite or put at infinity. We shall consider both cases. The problem now is to maximize this expression subject to the constraints of the problem. The constraints are as follows:

(i) $\dot{C}(t) = b_c \dot{K}_c(t)$

(ii) $\dot{K}_c(t) = b_i K_i(t) - \dot{K}_i(t)$

(iii) $\dot{C} \geqslant 0$

(iv) $\dot{K}_i \geqslant 0$.

---

[1]) For reaching conclusions, somewhat similar to the ones obtained in section 2, see the very recent article by L. Johansen in *Review of Economic Studies*, January 1967 [4]. The technique of analysis employed by Johansen is very different from the one employed in the present paper.

Here $\dot{C}(t)$ stands for the rate of change of consumption, $\dot{K}_i(t)$ and $\dot{K}_c(t)$ stand for capital formation in the capital and the consumer goods industry respectively. There are several things to be noted here. First, we note that because of non-transferability of capital in this case, the rate of change of consumption is related in this case to the capital formation in the consumption goods industry. Also, note that (i) and (ii) both rule out excess capacity. In fact, if we have a one-factor model, and there is no satiation of utility or production, there is no economic reason why we should have excess capacity. Equation (i) is self-explanatory. In (ii) we state that the increase of capital in the consumption goods industry is equal to the total output of investment goods industry *minus* the part of investment that goes to capital goods industry to create its own extra capital. The conditions embodied in (iii) and (iv) reflect the nonshiftability of capital engaged in consumer goods production and capital goods production respectively.

Mathematically, our problem now is to maximize $\int_0^T U(C)\,dt$ subject to the above restrictions and whatever boundary conditions we choose for our problem. Since the side conditions consist of differential equalities and inequalities, we have a non-classical problem of the Bolza type.[2] Assuming that the constraint qualifications[3] are satisfied, we begin our search for it by looking for the time functions $C(t)$, $K_c(t)$, $K_i(t)$, $\lambda_1(t)$, $\lambda_2(t)$, $\eta(t)$, $\varepsilon(t)$ which satisfy the Euler–Lagrange equations for $\int_0^T F\,dt$, where

$$\begin{aligned} F = U(C(t)) &+ \lambda_1(t)\,[\dot{C}(t) - b_c\dot{K}_c(t)] \\ &+ \lambda_2(t)\,[\dot{K}_c(t) - b_i K_i(t) + \dot{K}_i(t)] \\ &+ \lambda_3(t)\,[\dot{C} - \dot{\eta}^2] + \lambda_4(t)\,[\dot{K}_i - \dot{\varepsilon}^2]. \end{aligned}$$

[2] This is precisely the type of problem dealt with by Valentine and recently generalized further by Berkovitz. See Saaty and Brams: *Nonlinear Mathematics*, pp. 292–302 [8].

[3] The constraint qualifications are satisfied provided the following equations are mutually consistent and linearly independent.

(a) $\dot{C} - b_c\dot{K}_c = 0$

(b) $\dot{K}_c(t) - b_i K_i(t) + \dot{K}_i(t) = 0$

(c) $\dot{C} - \dot{\eta}^2 = 0$

(d) $\dot{K}_i - \dot{\varepsilon}^2 = 0$.

Matrix of partial derivatives of these equations with respect to $\dot{C}$, $\dot{K}_c$, $\dot{K}_i$, $\dot{\eta}$, $\dot{\varepsilon}$ is of rank '4' provided that $\dot{\eta}$ and $\dot{\varepsilon}$ do not vanish simultaneously. Since the case where $\dot{\eta}$ and $\dot{\varepsilon}$ both vanish (since it implies that capital stocks do not grow in either sector) is obviously non-optimal, we have no worry that 'an abnormal' solution may exist.

The Euler equations are:

$$\text{(i)}\quad \frac{\partial F}{\partial C} = \frac{\mathrm{d}}{\mathrm{d}t}\left(\frac{\partial F}{\partial \dot{C}}\right)$$

$$\text{(ii)}\quad \frac{\partial F}{\partial K_{\mathrm{c}}} = \frac{\mathrm{d}}{\mathrm{d}t}\left(\frac{\partial F}{\partial \dot{K}_{\mathrm{c}}}\right)$$

$$\text{(iii)}\quad \frac{\partial F}{\partial K_{\mathrm{i}}} = \frac{\mathrm{d}}{\mathrm{d}t}\left(\frac{\partial F}{\partial \dot{K}_{\mathrm{i}}}\right)$$

$$\text{(iv)}\quad \frac{\partial F}{\partial \eta} = \frac{\mathrm{d}}{\mathrm{d}t}\left(\frac{\partial F}{\partial \dot{\eta}}\right)$$

$$\text{(v)}\quad \frac{\partial F}{\partial \varepsilon} = \frac{\mathrm{d}}{\mathrm{d}t}\left(\frac{\partial F}{\partial \dot{\varepsilon}}\right).$$

Equation (i) gives $U_{\mathrm{c}} = \dot{\lambda}_1 + \dot{\lambda}_3$
Equation (ii) gives $-\dot{\lambda}_1 b_{\mathrm{c}} + \dot{\lambda}_2 = 0$
Equation (iii) gives $-\lambda_2 b_{\mathrm{i}} = \dot{\lambda}_2 + \dot{\lambda}_4$
Equation (iv) and (v) give $\dot{\eta}\lambda_3 = P$,
and $\dot{\varepsilon}\lambda_4 = Q$ where P and Q are arbitrary constants.

Now from the transversality conditions it follows immediately that $(\partial F/\partial\dot{\eta})_{t=T}$ and $(\partial F/\partial\dot{\varepsilon})_{t=T} = 0$. Since $\partial F/\partial\dot{\eta}$ and $\partial F/\partial\dot{\varepsilon}$ are constant over time, $\lambda_3\dot{\eta}$ and $\lambda_4\dot{\varepsilon}$ must vanish along an arc. If we have a sequence of arcs then the Weierstrass–Erdmann condition implies $F_{\dot{\eta}}|_+ = F_{\dot{\eta}}|_-$, $F_{\dot{\varepsilon}}|_+ = F_{\dot{\varepsilon}}|_-$ whenever a switchover takes place from one arc to another. This would also guarantee that the above bilinear expressions vanish for all values of t.

From this we deduce that either $\lambda_3 \neq 0$, or $\dot{\eta} \neq 0$; similarly for λ_4 and $\dot{\varepsilon}$. From Valentine's corollary 1 to Theorem 2, one would get $\lambda_3 \geqslant 0$, $\lambda_4 \geqslant 0$. We, therefore, have four classes of 'pure' solutions in a sequential manner provided the corner conditions are satisfied and the second order Legendre–Clebsch conditions are satisfied. Thus, if the solutions do not belong to any of these categories, we have to synthesize a solution consisting of a sequence of pure solutions. We first have to show that for the present problem unlike the shiftable case, there would in general be no pure solution. We then show how the synthesis is done for the infinite horizon case. For the finite horizon case no general synthesizing rule can be immediately obtained since it would depend on what sorts of terminal conditions are imposed.

Thus four classes of solutions are as follows:

(a) $\lambda_3=0$, $\lambda_4=0$. This is the classical case where nonshiftability constraints are ineffective in both the sectors;
(b) $\dot{\eta}=0$, $\dot{\varepsilon}=0$. This is obviously non-optimal since $\dot{K}_i=0$, $\dot{K}_c=0$ even though $b_c>0$, $b_i>0$;
(c) $\dot{\eta}=0$, $\lambda_4=0$. Only the rate of growth of consumption is constrained to be zero. But here $\dot{K}_i>0$. This is the case of investment specialization;
(d) $\lambda_3=0$, $\dot{\varepsilon}=0$. Here $\dot{C}>0$, but $\dot{K}_i=0$. In this case we have specialization in consumption.

2.2. *The case where both the nonshiftability constraints are ineffective and the planning horizon is finite*

Let us first explore the solutions in class 'a'. We want to know whether with arbitrary boundary conditions the solution would lie in this class for all 't'. If we would get an answer in the affirmative, we would have a timepath which is somewhat similar to the shiftable case. We shall comment on the economic significance of a solution of this type in our conclusion.

Here we have only the following equations to consider:

(i) $$U_c = \dot{\lambda}_1(t)$$

(ii) $$0 = \frac{d}{dt}(-b_c\lambda_1(t) + \lambda_2(t)) = -b_c\dot{\lambda}_1(t) + \dot{\lambda}_2(t)$$

(iii) $$-\lambda_2(t)\,b_i = \frac{d}{dt}(\lambda_2(t)) = \dot{\lambda}_2$$

From (iii) we get $\lambda_2(t)=Ae^{-b_it}$ where A is an arbitrary constant. From (ii) we get $+b_c\dot{\lambda}_1(t)=+\dot{\lambda}_2(t)$

Now, $b_c\dot{\lambda}_1(t)=-b_iAe^{-b_it}$ or $\dot{\lambda}_1(t)=-\dfrac{b_i}{b_c}Ae^{-b_it}$

Now, $U_c=-\dfrac{b_i}{b_c}Ae^{-b_it}$ from equation (i).

Assume in particular that $U_c=c^{-v}$, we get

$$C(t) = A'e^{(b_i/v)t}$$

where A' is an arbitrary constant. This gives us the timepath for consumption. Now, from the equations of constraint (i) and (ii)

$$\frac{1}{b_c}\frac{b_i}{v}A'e^{(b_i/v)t} = \dot{K}_c(t) = b_iK_i(t) - \dot{K}_i(t).$$

This is a linear non-homogeneous equation of the first order. Hence, we have as the complete solution

$$K_i(t) = Be^{b_i t} + \frac{A'b_i}{vb_c}\frac{1}{(b_i - b_i/v)}e^{(b_i/v)t}, \; v \neq 1 .$$

This is an expression having only two arbitrary constants, B and A'.

If our problem is formulated as one with fixed boundary conditions, then there cannot exist in general a solution belonging to class 'a'. This is mathematically quite clear since the final solution for our system of differential equations possesses only two arbitrary constants, which represent the only degrees of freedom that we have in the present case. Clearly, therefore, no solution in this class can exist if the two boundary conditions are given in *fixed* and *separated* forms.

Let us now consider whether a solution would exist satisfying the *non-negativity* restrictions if we have the endpoint variable for a given horizon T. We can, however, show that the set of solutions satisfying the nonnegativity constraint may very well be empty even when we allow the system's behaviour to be determined unambiguously by the Euler equation and the initial conditions. To show this we demonstrate that for arbitrary initial conditions and arbitrary values of the elasticity coefficient, the conditions that $\dot{K}_i(t) \geqslant 0$ for all t may be violated. This is shown below by the following simple algebraic analysis, which proves that unless an inequality constraint on 'v' is satisfied, even $\dot{K}_i(0)$ may turn out to be negative.

We have, $\dot{K}_i = b_i K_i - \dfrac{b_i}{vb_c} A'e^{(b_i/v)t}$

Now, $A' = b_c K_c(0)$

Hence, $\dot{K}_i(0) = b_i K_i(0) - \dfrac{b_i K_c(0)}{v}$

$$= b_i\left(\frac{vK_i(0) - K_c(0)}{v}\right)$$

Now $\dot{K}_i(0) \geqslant 0$ if $vK_i(0) - K_c(0) \geqslant 0$

This implies that $\boxed{v \geqslant \dfrac{K_c(0)}{K_i(0)}}$

It is clear that the above condition is merely necessary to show that $\dot{K}_i(t) \geqq 0$ for all t, but by itself it does not guarantee that it would be satisfied for all 't'. Now

$$\dot{K}_i(t) = b_i B e^{b_i t} + \frac{b_i}{v} \frac{A' b_i}{v b_c} \frac{1}{b_i \dfrac{(v-1)}{(v)}} e^{(b_i/v)t}$$

This implies,

$$\dot{K}_i(t) = b_i B e^{b_i t} + \frac{A' b_i}{(v-1) v b_c} e^{(b_i/v)t}$$

Now we can show that $B = K_i(0) - \dfrac{K_c(0)}{(v-1)}$.

Hence we have $\dot{K}_i(t) \geqslant 0$ provided

$$b_i \left[K_i(0) - \frac{K_c(0)}{(v-1)} \right] e^{b_i t} + \frac{K_c(0)\, b_i}{v(v-1)} e^{(b_i/v)t} \geqq 0 .$$

It does not seem possible to say that such an expression will necessarily be one signed for all values of 't'. Hence for a given finite horizon the set of solutions may very well be empty.

2.3. *An infinite horizon with ineffective inequality constraints*

We now turn to the discussion of an infinite horizon, where a clear negative result may be deduced. We may show that with both the inequality constraints ineffective, there does not exist any solution for the infinite horizon case even when the Ramsey boundedness condition on the utility function is satisfied.

When the nonshiftability constraints are ineffective, the problem of constrained maximization of $\int_0^\infty U(C) \mathrm{d}t$ may be replaced by an unconstrained maximization of a functional $\int_0^\infty F(Z, \dot{Z})\, \mathrm{d}t$ where $Z = \int_0^t K_i(S)\, \mathrm{d}S$. We, however, know that when our integrand is of the form $\int_0^\infty F(Z, \dot{Z})\, \mathrm{d}t$, then the conditions are that as $T \to \infty$, $F_{\dot{z}} \to 0$ and $F - \dot{Z} F_{\dot{z}} \to 0$. Since F is independent of time we must have $F - \dot{Z} F_{\dot{z}} = 0$ for all 't'. This condition is an obvious conclusion from the fact that when F is time-independent, the Euler equation admits a first integral. Further $F = U(C)$.

With our $U(C) = \frac{1}{1-v} C^{1-v}$, we then get

$$K_i = \frac{\frac{1}{1-v} C^{1-v}}{-C^{-v} b_i} = \frac{-\frac{1}{1-v} C}{b_i}.$$

Hence $K_i = \frac{1}{v-1} K_c$.

Hence $\frac{K_i}{K_c} = +\frac{1}{v-1}$.

With $v>1$, we get a solution which is economically meaningful. This is, of course, none other than the boundedness requirement on v, familiar from the usual discussion on optimal savings.[4])

Further, in this case $K_i = \mu K_c$ for all t, including $t=0$. This, however, contradicts the information given in the form of initial conditions which prescribes the ratio $(K_i(0))/(K_c(0))$ exogenously. Except by coincidence there is no reason why this exogenous ratio would equal the ratio $1/(v-1)$ even for $v>1$. Thus for an infinite horizon, no solution exists in class (a) except by chance.

2.4. *The case where one or the other inequality constraint is effective for an infinite horizon*

However, if we relax the requirement that $\dot{C}(t)>0$, and merely postulate that $\dot{C}(t) \geqq 0$, then our solution would lie either in (b) or (c). (b) would be evidently nonoptimal. If we are in (c), we have $\dot{C}(t)=0$ and hence $C(t)= b_c K_c(0)$.

Hence $K_i(t) = K_i(0)\, e^{b_i t}$. Clearly behaviour in phase (c) cannot be optimal for all 't'. Such an arc would violate the Legendre second order condition of the problem. This is economically evident from diminishing marginal utility considerations.

Let us now consider whether the optimal path can lie in phase (d) for all t. In phase (d), $\dot{K}_i=0$, $\dot{C}>0$ for all t. Here consumption grows linearly over time and hence there is no a priori reason why it cannot be optimal. However, with our present formulation of the utility function, we can show that

---

[4]) Instead of the Ramsey bliss assumption, we could have used a terminal condition based on the golden rule. This would be similar to the procedure used by Stoleru.

a solution in class (d) is dominated by a combination of solutions in (a) and (c), e.g., $\dot{C}=0$, $\dot{K}_i>0$ for an initial period of time and then $\dot{K}_i>0, \dot{K}_c>0$ subsequently. This is because if our solution is in class (d), consumption is merely growing *linearly* whereas by following a mixed policy of first letting consumption remain constant for *finite* 't', and then following an exponential timepath for consumption, we shall have a higher integral of utility for $\int_0^\infty U(C)\mathrm{d}t$ than by sticking all the way to a solution in 'd'.

Hence, the solution of the form (i) $\dot{K}_i>0$, $\dot{C}_i=0$ for an initial period followed by a solution where $\dot{K}>0$, $\dot{C}>0$, is better than following a policy of $\dot{K}_i=0$, $\dot{C}_i>0$ for all t. We now show that this policy is indeed optimal. To show this all we need to show is that the sequence $\dot{K}_i=0$, $\dot{C}>0$ cannot constitute the optimal *initial* policy for cases where there is no 'initial surplus' of capital in the capital goods industry.

This is because when $\dot{K}_i=0$, $\dot{C}_i>0$, the system can never switch over to phase (a) $\dot{K}_i>0$, $\dot{C}_i>0$. Because to be in phase (a), transversality condition and the existence of an invariant first integral would imply as we have seen a certain specific composition of capital. Hence, unless we have initially a relative surplus of $\dot{K}_i$, we would not move in the direction of the specific composition by keeping $K_i=0$. This is none other than one of the Weierstrass–Erdmann corner conditions that the *first integral* of the system must be the same whenever a switchover takes place. Thus if M is the first integral then $M_-=M_+$ at any junction point of two arcs. This is impossible in the present case for the reason menti oned earlier.

We can state the above argument in somewhat greater detail. The 'first integral' of the above problem is the following:

$$F-(\dot{K}_i F_{\dot{K}_i}+\dot{K}_c F_{\dot{K}_c}+\dot{\eta} F_{\dot{\eta}}+\dot{\varepsilon} F_{\dot{\varepsilon}})=M, \text{ where } M \text{ is a constant.}$$

Now the transversality condition and the invariance of the first integral jointly imply that

$$F-(\dot{K}_i F_{\dot{K}_i}+\dot{K}_c F_{\dot{K}_c}+\dot{\eta} F_{\dot{\eta}}+\dot{\varepsilon} F_{\dot{\varepsilon}})=0.$$

Invariance of the first integral follows from the fact that time does not enter the problem explicitly. Further we have seen on p. 5 that $\dot{\eta}F_{\dot{\eta}}=0$, $\dot{\varepsilon}F_{\dot{\varepsilon}}=0$ throughout in an optimizing solution. Hence we have $F-(\dot{K}_i F_{\dot{K}_i}+\dot{K}_c F_{\dot{K}_c})=0$ for all t. Now let t^* be the time point for switchover to the regime (a). This is a regime where both constraints $\dot{K}_c \geqslant 0$, $\dot{K}_i \geqslant 0$ hold as strict inequalities.

Hence the argument in Section 2.3 applies. Thus, it must be the case that

$$\frac{K_i(t^*)}{K_c(t^*)} = \frac{1}{v-1}.$$

Consider now a situation in particular where $v=2$.

Then, $\dfrac{K_i(t^*)}{K_c(t^*)} = 1$.

Now if initially $\dfrac{K_i(t^0)}{K_c(t^0)} < 1$,

then, if we follow an initial policy where $\dot{K}_i(t)=0$ and $\dot{K}_c(t)>0$, we shall have $(\dot{K}_i(t))/(K_c(t))$ falling over time and no value of t^* will exist for which $(K_i(t^*))/(K_c(t^*))=1$. Thus corner conditions cannot be satisfied with $\dot{K}_i=0$, and $\dot{K}_c>0$. On the other hand, when $\dot{K}_i>0$ and $\dot{K}_c=0$, we shall get a policy such that $(K_i(t))/(K_c(t))$ will steadily rise over time such that a switchover can take place for some value t^*. Further, such a policy will also satisfy the remaining corner conditions which require that

$$F_{\dot{K}_i}\Big|_{t^*+0} = F_{\dot{K}_i}\Big|_{t^*-0} \quad \text{and} \quad F_{\dot{K}_c}\Big|_{t^*+0} = F_{\dot{K}_c}\Big|_{t^*-0}.$$

Since $F_{\dot{\eta}}=0$ and $F_{\dot{\varepsilon}}=0$, we shall necessarily have $F_{\dot{\eta}}|_+ = F_{\dot{\eta}}|_-$ and $F_{\dot{\varepsilon}}|_+ = F_{\dot{\varepsilon}}|_-$.
Now

$$F_{\dot{K}_i}\Big|_{t^*-0} = \lambda_2 + \lambda_4\Big|_{t^*-0} \quad \text{and} \quad F_{\dot{K}_i}\Big|_{t^*+0} = \lambda_2 + \lambda_4\Big|_{t^*+0}.$$

Since $\lambda_4=0$ in both phases we require

$$\lambda_2\Big|_{t^*-0} = \lambda_2\Big|_{t^*+0}.$$

This condition would be satisfied if $\lambda_2(t)$ is continuous.
Now, from the transversality condition and the existence of the first integral, we know that

$$\lambda_2(t) = \frac{\frac{1}{1-v}\,[b_c K_c(0)]^{1-v}}{K_i(0)}\, \mathrm{e}^{-b_i t}$$

in the initial phase and

$$\lambda_2(t) = A\mathrm{e}^{-b_i t}$$

in the second phase, where A is an arbitrary constant. Putting

$$A = \frac{\frac{1}{1-v}[b_c K_c(0)]^{1-v}}{K_i(0)},$$

we get a continuous function $\lambda_2(t)$ which satisfies our corner condition. Similarly we can show that $\lambda_1(t)$ is also continuous.

Hence, our optimal policy for the infinite horizon would consist of the sequence of subarcs:

$$\dot{K}_i > 0, \dot{C} = 0 \quad \text{and} \quad \dot{K}_i > 0, \dot{C}_i > 0.$$[5]

The switching time t^* takes place when

$$\frac{K_i(t^*)}{K_c(t^*)} = \frac{1}{v-1}$$

In this case this takes place for a finite value of 't'. It is easy to see that there cannot be multiple switching points since the $K_i(t)$ is an exponential function for all 't'.[6]

2.5. *Finite horizon with effective inequality constraints*

For finite horizon problems, the choice of boundary conditions is more or less arbitrary. We may first consider the case where the horizon T is fixed and $K_c(T)$ and $K_i(T)$ are also fixed. From our discussion earlier, it is clear that there would not exist any solution in class (a) for the entire time $0 \leqslant t \leqslant T$. This is because we have shown that the Euler equation for this case is

$$K_i(t) = Be^{b_i t} + \frac{A' b_i}{v b_c} \frac{1}{(b_i - b_i/v)} e^{(b_i/v)t}$$

[5]) If we assume on purely theoretical consideration that we have an initial surplus of capital relative to the composition dictated by the transversality conditions, then it would be optimal to follow the rule $\dot{K}_i = 0$, $\dot{C}_i > 0$ for an initial period of time. This would be the case when $(K_i(0))/(K_c(0)) > 1/(v-1)$. In this case, the reverse of the case discussed earlier would follow. The argument is, however, quite similar. Initial conditions would, therefore, determine whether investment specialization or consumption specialization is optimal.

[6]) The explicit formula for the switching time that we obtain here rests on the assumption of a constant elasticity marginal utility schedule. Further, the absence of multiple switching points also depends on the assumption of a constant elasticity marginal utility schedule.

and this admits of only two boundary restrictions $K_i(0)$ and $K_c(0)$. Hence there cannot be a Euler trajectory connecting $K_i(0)$ and $K_c(0)$ with $K_c(T)$ and $K_i(T)$. Thus, for this case we have no pure solution in class (a). What about a solution in class (b)? That is clearly non-optimal nor does it necessarily fit the boundary conditions. Any solution in class (c) and (d) may be optimal but would not necessarily fit the boundary condition.

Hence, in general 'pure' solutions would not exist. But what about the mixture of pure solutions? Here the solution synthesized earlier would not apply since the transversality conditions for the infinite horizon case are totally inapplicable here.

We, therefore, cannot exclude the possibility that along some stretch of time $\dot{K}_i(t)=0$ and we merely accumulate in the consumption sector. We have, therefore, in general a mixture of all the three solutions belonging to classes (a), (c) and (d) respectively. In special cases one of the phases may be absent.

However, we can assume a more general form of a boundary condition where $K_c(T)$ and $K_i(T)$ instead of being fixed, lie in a certain set S where S consists of all pairs $K_c(T)$, $K_i(T)$ where $K_c(0) \leqslant K_c(T) \leqslant \mathrm{b}$ and $K_i(0) \leqslant K_i(T) \leqslant \mathrm{d}$. The numbers b and d are determined by solving max $K_c(T)$ subject to $K_c(0)$ and $K_i(0)$ and the constraint given earlier whereas d is equal to $K_i(0)\mathrm{e}^{b_i T}$, which is the maximum for $K_i(T)$. To solve the problem of determining maximum $K_c(T)$, we have to solve a linear maximization problem over time and we have to rely on the Pontryagin version of the maximum principle. If all that we require is that the final $K_i(T)$ and $K_i(T)$ should lie strictly inside the rectangular region given earlier, then

$$F_{\dot{K}_c(T)} = 0 \quad \text{and} \quad F_{\dot{K}_i(T)} = 0. \text{ Thus, } (\lambda_2 + \lambda_4)_T = 0 \text{ and}$$

$(-\lambda_1 b_c + \lambda_2)_T = 0$. If $\lambda_4 = 0$, at T, then $\lambda_2(T) = 0$; this would imply $\lambda_1 b_c|_T = 0$. This would imply $\lambda_1|_T = 0$. This is not possible for finite C for our form of the utility function. Hence $\lambda_4 > 0$ for T, imply that $\dot{K}_i(T) = 0$ for terminal T.

This demonstrates that we may get consumption specialization at the final instant T, thus showing that a solution in class (d) would generally form a part of an optimal policy for this problem.

3. The Policy Significance of the Present Model

We have derived the conclusion that for a whole class of very plausible utility functions, the optimal growth path for an underdeveloped economy would involve investment specialization. This is a result of some policy significance. It would be, therefore, worth our while to analyze in some detail how much value we can attach to such a conclusion. This would require an evaluation of the simplifying assumptions on which our analysis rests.

We should first point out that the exclusion of 'foreign trade' from our model does restrict the relevance of the analysis for some underdeveloped economies for which favourable foreign trade possibilities exist. However, the widespread discussion in the recent literature on underdeveloped economies dealing with the 'foreign exchange bottleneck' is an indication that such favourable conditions rarely exist. In fact, the existence of a 'foreign exchange bottleneck' is in many ways a symptom of the difficulty that faces an underdeveloped economy in raising its savings rate even when it has the will to reduce current consumption. Such difficulty often stems from the limited capacity to produce capital goods domestically. A persistent foreign exchange bottleneck may in some cases be regarded as an indication of the failure to step up allocation to investment goods, sufficiently ahead of time in keeping with the growth objectives of the economy. Thus, one implication of our analysis is that the foreign exchange bottleneck is, in some cases, an indication of the difficulties caused by the combination of nonshiftability of capital together with the shortsightedness of the policy-making agencies.

We now consider in succession the modifications that may be entailed in our analysis if we have to meet the following additional considerations. These considerations stem from several sources. First there is the basic requirement of maintaining per capita consumption constant in the face of rising population. There is, secondly, the problem that sometimes for political reasons, but also occasionally on grounds of nutrition, consumption per worker may have to be higher than consumption per capita. This may be an additional constraint on the growth process. Finally, if there is a choice of techniques of production and the government is unable or unwilling to interfere with the autonomous savings propensities of workers and capitalists then that may even imply a feedback effect on the optimal growth process. As compared with the first requirement or the second where it is based on nutritional grounds, I consider all the other considerations as relevant for defining 'second best' optima only. I shall take up these considerations one by one.

Let us first note that if our basic policy of investment specialization is taken literally, consumption in the initial period would not increase at all.

With a growing population, this would involve a decline in the per capita availability of consumer goods. This is a factor which would create special problems for development planning, although such declines may have taken place historically in the context of some industrialization experiences. A simple way out would be to impose a rising exogenous subsistence floor on consumption in keeping with population growth. Such a constraint, when *effective*, would imply that a part of investment would go into the additional production of consumer goods which would not have otherwise gone in that sector. But the basic policy conclusion would, however, remain unaltered.

There are several ways in which our mathematical analysis could be changed to take into account the requirement of a rising subsistence floor on consumption. Let $\bar{c}=C_0/L_0=b_c K_c(0)/L_0$ be our subsistence floor. The $C(t)\geqslant \bar{c}L_0 e^{nt}$ for all t. Our Lagrange function would now be modified to

$$F^* = F + \lambda_s\left[C(t) - \bar{c}L_0\, e^{nt} - \chi^2\right].$$

Clearly our previous analysis could proceed as before. We shall now have a phase along which $C(t)=\bar{c}L_0 e^{nt}$ which would imply a different allocation of $\dot{K}$ between $\dot{K}_c$ and $\dot{K}_i$. We should note, however, that when population is growing, the Ramsey transversality condition would not apply unless we redefine consumption in per capita terms. Thus, we would need to put all the relevant variables on a per capita basis. The period of switchover to the phase which is marked by ineffective inequality constraints would now be different in the light of this additional requirement.

A much more important limitation of our analysis stems from the implicit assumption that 'labour' is a free factor. For an overpopulated economy, there is an important sense in which one can maintain that 'labour' is a free factor. But there are two important problems here which we should explicitly discuss. One is that even though labour is 'free' in the sense that it is not a technological bottleneck to production, real wages may be inflexible in the sense that consumption per *worker* as distinct from consumption *per capita* may have to be higher. This would sometimes be due to the presence of trade union pressure by the organized workers in industries. In some cases, the justification for higher consumption per worker may be due to greater nutritional requirements. In that case, we should have an explicit constraint showing that the output of consumption goods industry should be greater than or equal to the wage bill. If this constraint is effective, then this would imply an endogenously rising consumption demand quite irrespective of utility considerations. And, therefore, the investment allocation ratio between the two sectors would be affected. But the change that would be brought about in this manner would be due to the operation of the wage goods constraint in the initial phase of planning. But the optimizing mechanism will still be guided by the nonshiftability considerations. The wage goods constraint would differ from the constraint of maintaining per capita consumption in the face of a rapidly rising population in being an endogenous constraint in the sense that the expansion of consumption is a direct result of the process of capital accumulation where capital accumulation is essentially of the capital widening type.

Finally, we come to a consideration which introduces a more difficult point of principle. This arises when we consider the possibility that there may exist different methods of production in both the sectors. We have so far assumed fixed capital–output ratios. Now, even if there were different methods of production, so long as labour is free, we would go in for techniques with the least capital–output ratios. Thus, it may be said that our use of fixed capital coefficients is quite justified irrespective of the possibility of choice in techniques of production. However, if real wages are inflexible and the government is unable to control consumption out of wage income, then it would no longer follow that when there is a choice of techniques, we shall necessarily go in for the least capital-intensive method of production. [7]) Thus, in such a situation our analysis based on linear technologies would be modified. This would mean that our formal model would be replaced by more general non-linear or piece-wise linear production functions. The resulting change in the optimum configuration over time should, however, be interpreted with some caution. The optimum so obtained is clearly of a 'second-best' type in the sense that it reflects neither technology nor social welfare considerations, but arises from the assumed inflexibility of real wages and/or the government's inability to achieve what would otherwise be the optimum savings rate. The second-best nature of the optimum would arise because in this modified analysis, some output is being lost in either sector while the implicit social price of output in every sector is non-zero.

We may make the above considerations somewhat more specific by considering the following formal model: as before we want to maximize the

---

[7]) See the contributions by Lefeber and Marglin [5, 7].

utility integral $\int_0^\infty U\,\mathrm{d}t$. If our technology is, say, of the Cobb–Douglas type[8]) and the utility schedule is of the constant elasticity form, then we have

(a) $U(C) = \dfrac{1}{1-v} C^{1-v}$

(b) $C = K_c^\alpha L_c^\beta \qquad \alpha > 0, \beta > 0, \alpha + \beta = 1$

(c) $\dot{K} = K_i^{\alpha'} L_i^{\beta'} = \dot{K}_i + \dot{K}_c, \quad \alpha' > 0, \beta' > 0, \alpha' + \beta' = 1$

(d) $C \geqslant \bar{w}(L_c + L_i)$

(e) $\dot{K}_i \geqslant 0$

(f) $\dot{K}_c \geqslant 0$.

Since labour is not a constraint so long as wage goods are made available, we may assume full utilization of capacity in both the sectors. We may set up the associated Lagrangian expression and easily obtain the necessary optimizing conditions.

As compared with our earlier analysis, we shall have three additional phases. These can be shown schematically as follows. If '1' indicates that a constraint is effective and '0' denotes its ineffectiveness, we have the following patterns of 1's and 0's. Thus we have the following table:

Wage constraint:	1	0	1	0	0	1	0	1
Nonshiftability constraint in capital goods sector:	1	0	0	1	0	1	1	0
Nonshiftability constraint in consumer goods sector:	1	0	0	0	1	0	1	1

Of these patterns, the first combination can be easily seen to be impossible. The second combination is the classical Ramsey case and raises no new points of principle. The patterns fourth, fifth and seventh have already been analyzed since the wage constraint is ineffective in each case. We are thus left with three additional possibilities which could not be considered earlier. From the necessary conditions for the optimum, we can easily work out the timepaths for the different variables where either of these cases prevails. What we cannot do so easily is to work out the exact ordering of the phases

[8]) We have chosen the Cobb–Douglas case merely for concreteness and possible simplicity of computation. Nothing would be lost from the qualitative point of view by choosing a more general first-degree homogeneous production function with 'well behaved' isoquants.

in time given a set of arbitrary initial conditions and parameters. We should, however, note that in both these models the final phase of the optimal programme would conform to the classical Ramsey path. The two models would differ with respect to the time when the Ramsey phase begins, and in the sequence of phases preceding this Ramsey phase. It would be worthwhile to work out numerically on the basis of at least a piece-wise linear objective function the extent of 'welfare' loss entailed by the model involving a non-linear production function and the additional constraint on wages. Such work, in order to be most useful, ought to be done for a specific economy where the numerical values for the parameters would have operational significance. Since none of the existing multisectoral planning models incorporate the basic qualitative features discussed in this paper, this would indeed appear to be an area for much further exploration.

References

[1] S. CHAKRAVARTY, Optimal Paths of Capital Accumulation in a Model with Non-shiftable Capital (Delhi School of Economics, Working Paper no. 17).

[2] M. DOBB, *An Essay on Economic Growth and Planning*, Kegan Paul, London, 1960.

[3] E. D. DOMAR, 'A Soviet Model of Growth', in *Essays in the Theory of Economic Growth*, Oxford University Press, 1957.

[4] L. JOHANSEN, 'Some Theoretical Properties of Two-Sector Growth Models', *Review of Economic Studies*, January 1967.

[5] L. LEFEBER, Industrial Planning in a Labour Surplus Economy (mimeographed).

[6] P. C. MAHALANOBIS, Some Observations on the Process of Growth of National Income', *Sankhya*, 1953.

[7] S. A. MARGLIN, Industrial Development in a Labour Surplus Economy (mimeographed).

[8] T. SAATY and L. BRAMS, *Nonlinear Mathematics*, McGrawHill, New York, 1964.

[9] L. G. STOLERU, 'An Optimal Policy for Economic Growth', *Econometrica*, April 1965.

[10] J. TINBERGEN, 'Optimum Savings and Utility Maximization over Time', *Econometrica*, April 1960.

[11] J. TINBERGEN and H. C. BOS, *Mathematical Models of Economic Growth*, McGraw Hill, New York, 1962.

OPTIMUM SAVINGS PROGRAMME: A NOTE

J. C. SAIGAL*)

1. Introduction

The origin of discussion on the problem of optimizing saving rate is to be found in the 1928 paper of Ramsey on the mathematical theory of savings [9]. Subsequently, there have been noteworthy contributions to the problem by Chakravarty [1, 2], Koopmans [6], Meade [8], Samuelson and Solow [11], and Tinbergen [12, 13]. Chakravarty's Econometrica article [1] contains an admirable analysis of the one-commodity-capital models of Ramsey and Tinbergen and sheds light on the nature of difficulties involved in selecting for a nation the best consumption profile over infinite time.[1]) These difficulties, he shows, arise from the crucial dependence on certain arbitrary assumptions of the unique solution to an optimal infinite savings programme. In Ramsey's model the assumption necessary for the determination of the optimal infinite savings programme is that 'Bliss' – defined as the maximum conceivable state of satisfaction – is attained for a finite level of consumption.[2]) In Tinbergen's model the relevant assumption is that the combined effects of diminishing marginal utility and social time preference relative to the rate of growth of consumption are such as to make the maximand

*) The views expressed in this paper are the author's personal views and do not reflect those of the United Nations or its African Institute for Economic Development and Planning.

1) Professor Sen in his Economic Journal article [10] spells out social and technical factors that limit the range from which the choice of the optimum rate of saving can be made.

2) It may be noted that the contributions of Meade [8] and Samuelson and Solow [11] are strictly based on Ramsey-type assumptions. Meade in his paper examines policy implications for aggregative, but more specific, situations, characterized by explicit production and utility functions, whereas the work of Samuelson and Solow is essentially an extension of Ramsey's analysis to a multiple-capital-goods economy.

$\int_0^\infty e^{-\rho t}\, U(C(t))\mathrm{d}t$ [3]) (i.e. the sum of utility derived by the society from consumption over infinite time) converge.

To sidetrack the difficulties involved in the infinite horizon models of Ramsey and Tinbergen, Chakravarty in his International Economic Review article [2] analyses a nation's optimum saving path with a finite but sufficiently distant planning horizon. [4]) The validity of this procedure has been questioned by Maneschi in his recent article [7]. Maneschi bases his criticisms against finite-horizon models on two statements made by Chakravarty, that the optimal consumption paths (obtained with appropriate initial and terminal conditions) are 'insensitive' to changes in terminal capital equipment for any fixed choice of the horizon 'T'; and that under certain conditions the optimum consumption profile shows invariance with respect to T. The condition is that $b(1-v)<\rho$, where b is the constant marginal output–capital ratio, v the constant elasticity of marginal utility with respect to consumption and ρ the constant time discount rate. Maneschi tries to show that the former statement is valid only if we grant an inappropriate terminal condition, namely, that the average rate of capital accumulation, g, during the plan period should be so low as to produce a drastic decumulation of capital towards the end of the plan. The invariance of the optimum consumption profile with respect to 'T' when $b(1-v)<\rho$, he shows, is in general not found; it occurs in the special case when the average rate of capital accumulation during the plan period coincides with the rate of growth which is optimal in the infinite horizon case. He argues further that if such invariance is in general not found, inconsistency in planner's decision-making will emerge, when the need to lengthen the horizon of welfare maximization is felt.

In this paper it will be shown that the criticisms levelled by Maneschi against finite-horizon models are trivial. If we use a more appropriate method of setting terminal conditions than the one used by Chakravarty in his model, Maneschi's criticisms, which are based on Chakravarty's statements regarding 'insensitivity' etc., remain no longer valid. This will be demonstrated in the next section. Finally in section 3 of this paper it will

---

[3]) ρ is time discount rate and $U(C(t))$ is social utility-consumption function.

[4]) Chakravarty also argues that for practical purposes a finite horizon is more appropriate in view of the fact that the planning authorities in many countries work on the implicit or explicit assumption of a finite planning horizon.

be shown that if the analysis of the optimum savings programme is to provide some sort of a criterion or guideline for the planner, reformulation of the consumption-utility function employed by Chakravarty, Tinbergen and others in their analysis, and relaxation of the assumption of an output-capital ratio constant over time are necessary.

2. The Choice of the Planning Horizon

Consider a one-commodity economy (the commodity being either consumed or invested) where the average and marginal output-capital ratios are assumed to be equal to a constant b, and the society's marginal utility of consumption function is $U'(C) = C^{-v}$ (or, in other words, consumption–utility function is $U(C) = 1/(1-v)\, C^{1-v}$). Now, the problem of optimum saving path with a finite planning horizon, T, can be presented as follows:
Maximize

$$\int_0^T e^{-\rho t} U(C(t))\, dt \tag{1}$$

subject to the balance equation

$$C = bK - \dot{K} \tag{2}$$

where C and K represent consumption and capital respectively. $\dot{K}$ is the first derivative with respect to time t (i.e. investment).

To solve the problem of variation contained in the above model we need a boundary or terminal condition, which Chakravarty specifies as follows:

$$K(T) = K(0)\, e^{gT} \tag{3}$$

where $K(0)$ is the initial stock of capital and g the average rate of capital accumulation during the plan period. This method of setting the terminal condition is based on the notion that some amount of capital should be bequeathed at the end of the plan to take care of the post-plan era. Thus, there is an ample degree of freedom in prescribing a value, within a wide range, to $K(T)$ (or g). The correctness of this method obviously depends on whether the optimum consumption profile (obtained with this terminal condition) is 'insensitive' to changes in terminal equipment (i.e. g) or not. If it is not, arbitrariness is certainly introduced into our analysis. This is what has been demonstrated by Maneschi. He finds that the insensitivity of optimum consumption profiles with respect to changes in $K(T)$ holds only when the range of numerical values of g is restricted to $g = 0.15$ approximately, and that these low values of g give rise to a 'decumulation phenomenon' towards the end of the plan. For higher values of g, (which make greater economic sense) he shows, the sensitivity increases rapidly.[5]) Since Maneschi also finds that the contention of Chakravarty regarding invariance of the optimum consumption profile with respect to T is not valid in general, he concludes that the optimization of the rate of saving is not justifiable over a finite horizon.[6]) This conclusion of Maneschi is questionable, because both the points raised by him regarding 'insensitivity' etc. are the product of the inadequate method of setting terminal conditions used by Chakravarty, and hence should not be taken as refutation of finite-horizon models in general. It will be shown below that if we adopt an alternative procedure of setting terminal conditions, the 'decumulation phenomenon' to which Maneschi objects disappears, and also, if T is sufficiently large, the optimum saving path remains invariant with respect to T.

Let us replace the terminal condition (3) by the following:

$$\begin{aligned} C(t') &= C(T)\, e^{r(t'-T)} \\ K(t') &= K(T)\, e^{r(t'-T)} \end{aligned} \quad (\text{For } t' \geqq T) \tag{4}$$

that is, output, consumption and capital beyond the plan horizon grow at a prescribed steady rate r (warranted by the rates of population growth and technical progress). The assumption underlying this method of setting terminal conditions is that the optimum path is in the long run asymptotic to the steady rate of growth.

Now, we can present our reformulated optimum savings problem as follows:

Maximize

$$\int_0^T e^{-\rho t} U(C(t))\, dt \tag{1a}$$

[5]) See [7] table 1, p. 114. The measure of sensitivity employed is $s = (C(t, 0) - C(t, g)/C(t, 0)$ where, $C(t, g)$ denotes the optimum consumption profile when capital is assumed to accumulate over the plan at an average exponential rate g.

[6]) See [7] pp. 116–118.

subject to

$$C = bK - \dot{K}\,(\text{balance equation}) \tag{2a}$$
$$C(t') = C(T)\,\mathrm{e}^{r(t'-T)} \tag{3a}$$
$$K(t') = K(T)\,\mathrm{e}^{r(t'-T)}\ \text{for}\ t' \geqq T\,(\text{terminal conditions}). \tag{4}$$

For this specific problem we get the following extreme paths for K and C by conventional variational procedure:

$$\begin{aligned} K(t) &= A\,\mathrm{e}^{bt} + B\,\mathrm{e}^{\frac{b-\rho}{v}} \\ C(t) &= \left(b - \frac{b-\rho}{v}\right) B\,\mathrm{e}^{\frac{b-\rho}{v}t}, \end{aligned} \tag{5}$$

where A and B are constants to be determined by applying initial and terminal conditions. From the initial and terminal conditions we obtain the following set of four equations in four unknowns A, B, $C(T)$ and $K(T)$.

$$\begin{aligned} A + B &= K(0) \\ A\,\mathrm{e}^{bT} + B\,\mathrm{e}^{\frac{b-\rho}{v}T} &= K(T) \\ K(T) &= \frac{1}{b-r}\,C(T) \\ C(T) &= \left(b - \frac{b-\rho}{v}\right) B\,\mathrm{e}^{\frac{b-\rho}{v}T} \end{aligned} \tag{6}$$

The simultaneous solution of (6) determines the four unknowns A, B, $C(T)$, and $K(T)$. The solution to the optimum consumption path with a finite horizon T is

$$C^T(t) = \frac{K(0)\left(b - \dfrac{b-\rho}{v}\right)}{1 - \left[\mathrm{e}^{\left(\frac{b-\rho}{v}\right)T}\left(1 - \dfrac{b - \dfrac{b-\rho}{v}}{b-r}\right)\right]}\,\mathrm{e}^{\frac{b-\rho}{v}t} \tag{7}$$

One would observe that the method of setting terminal conditions is such that the terminal capital $K(T)$ and the optimum consumption in the final year of the plan $C(T)$ are unknowns to be determined simultaneously with the particular solution of the extreme paths of consumption and capital. Thus, the arbitrariness involved in prescribing a value to $K(T)$ is eliminated and the alleged 'decumulation phenomenon', which Maneschi points to in finite horizon models, disappears.

We now turn to examine whether the optimal consumption programme $C^T(t)$ (obtained with new terminal conditions) shows invariance with respect to T when non-negative values of ρ and v satisfy the inequality $b(1-v)<\rho$.[7])

For this we should consider first the optimal consumption programme with an infinite horizon, that is, maximization over an infinite horizon of the integral of discounted utilities $\int_0^\infty e^{-\rho t} U(C(t))\, dt$. As stated earlier, this integral is convergent only when $b(1-v)<\rho$. The optimum consumption profile over an infinite horizon, denoted by $C^\infty(t)$ can be found by conventional variational procedure to be

$$C^\infty(t) = K(0)\left(b - \frac{b-\rho}{v}\right) e^{\frac{b-\rho}{v}t}. \tag{8}$$

If the optimum consumption programme with finite planning horizon is invariant with respect to T, the ratio of $C^\infty(t)$ to $C^T(t)$ for non-negative values of ρ, v and b which satisfy the inequality $b(1-v)<\rho$ (or, $b>(b-\rho)/v$) should show 'insensitivity' with respect to T. It will be shown below that such 'insensitivity' exists, provided T is sufficiently large.

From (7) and (8) we get

$$\frac{C^\infty(t)}{C^T(t)} = 1 - \left[e^{\left(\frac{b-\rho}{v}-b\right)T}\left(1 - \frac{b - \frac{b-\rho}{v}}{b-r}\right)\right] \tag{9}$$

since $\frac{b-\rho}{v} - b < 0$, the term

$$\left[e^{\left(\frac{b-\rho}{v}-b\right)T}\left(1 - \frac{b - \frac{b-\rho}{v}}{b-r}\right)\right]$$

would be a very small quantity if T is sufficiently large. In other words,

---

[7]) It may be pointed out here that generally for realistic values of b and v relatively high values of ρ will satisfy this inequality. For example, when $b=0.33$ and $v=0.6$, it will be satisfied if the time discount rate ρ is greater than 13.2%, which is rather a high value.

$C^{\infty}(t)/C^{T}(t)$ is very close to unity for $T \geqq T^*$. Thus, when $b\,(1-v) < \rho$, an appropriate choice of the plan horizon $T \geqq T^*$ can always assure invariance of the optimum consumption programme with respect to T.

3. The Assumptions of the Theory of the Optimum Rate of Savings

Since the contemporary interest of economists in the search for the optimum rate of saving is mainly with the intent of providing some sort of criterion for the planner's decisions, it would be pertinent to discuss here some questions regarding the social utility–consumption function employed in the analysis of the optimum savings programme and the assumption of an output–capital ratio constant over time.

Social utility–consumption function: The utility function employed by Chakravarty and Tinbergen defines a relationship between utility or welfare of the society and total consumption (i.e. $U = U(C)$), with the restriction of diminishing marginal utility of total consumption

$$\left(\frac{\mathrm{d}U}{\mathrm{d}C} > 0, \frac{\mathrm{d}^2U}{\mathrm{d}C^2} < 0\right).$$

The adequacy of this relationship can be questioned, because it implies that social welfare increases with an increase in total consumption, irrespective of whether consumption per capita remains constant, declines or increases. Both Chakravarty and Tinbergen would not deny that social utility depends, among other things, upon consumption per capita. Thus a more appropriate social utility–consumption function for analysing the inter-temporal allocation problem would be one which reflects both total and per capita consumption.[8]) More explicitly, $U = U(P, C/P)$[9]); where U is social utility, C is total consumption and P is population. An alternative way of taking into account per capita consumption in the social utility function of Tinbergen and Chakravarty would be to add a constraint to the utility–consumption function $U(t) = U(C(t))$ that the per capita consumption does not decline over time. In other words,

$$C(t) \geqq C(0)\,\mathrm{e}^{\lambda t} \tag{10}$$

where $C(0)$ is initial level of total consumption and λ is the exogeneously

---

8) See [4] pp. 371–72.

9) With the restrictions $\mathrm{d}U/\mathrm{d}P > 0$ and $\mathrm{d}U/(\mathrm{d}C/P) > 0$.

given rate of population growth. It is interesting to note that the above constraint takes care of one of the points raised by Sen, that there is a lower limit (set by the rate of growth of population) to the range from which the choice of the optimum rate of saving can be made [10]. Thus, we find that in order to bring greater realism into the formulation of the optimum savings problem the constraint (10) must be included in the variational problem of the previous section.

Output–capital ratio: The calculus of the search for the optimum savings programme is based on a rather restrictive hypothesis that the output–capital ratio for the economy as a whole remains constant over time. Implicit in this hypothesis is the assumption that over time shifts in production from less mechanized techniques to more mechanized ones do not take place and that the technological innovations incorporated in production methods are of a 'neutral'[10] character.

Such an assumption is not realistic for developing countries, where production processes in practically all branches are carried out with a very low degree of mechanization; in many cases methods of production are rather primitive. The initial phase of development of these economies is characterized by rapid changes in the structure and methods of production. New investments are in general more capital–intensive, and reflect both incorporation of technological innovations and shifts from less mechanized techniques of production to more mechanized ones. In other words, during the initial phase of transformation which is often quite long, the capital–output ratio increases through time. Therefore, if the search for the optimum savings programmes is meant to provide some sort of guideline for the policy-maker, a technical relationship between factor inputs and flow of output of a more realistic nature should be used in our variational problem of the previous section.[11]

4. Conclusions

Two substantive points advanced by Maneschi against optimizing a savings programme over a finite horizon are that 'insensitivity' of the optimal

[10] 'Neutral' technological progress is meant here as defined by R. F. Harrod [5].

[11] The author is not sure whether the generalization suggested in this section will need complete reformulation of our variational problem or whether it can be accommodated within the framework used in section 2.

consumption paths to changes in terminal capital is found only if we grant an inappropriate terminal condition, leading to drastic decumulation of capital towards the end of the plan; and that invariance of the optimum consumption path is in general not found. Both these points, it has been shown, arise from inadequacy of the terminal conditions used in Chakravarty's model and should not be taken as refutation of finite-horizon models. With a more appropriate terminal condition, it has been demonstrated that the 'decumulation phenomenon' to which Maneschi objects disappears and that when $b(1-v)<\rho$ the optimum consumption profile is invariant with respect to T for $T \geqq T^*$.

While optimization of a savings programme over a finite horizon is justifiable, greater realism has to be brought in our hypotheses regarding the social utility–consumption function and output–capital ratio, if the exercise on optimum savings is to aid the planner in deciding on a nation's optimal savings.

References

[1] S. Chakravarty, 'Existence of an Optimal Savings Programme', *Econometrica*, January 1962.

[2] S. Chakravarty, 'Optimal Savings with Finite Horizon', *International Economic Review*, September 1962.

[3] S. Chakravarty, 'Optimal Savings with Finite Horizon: A Reply', *International Economic Review*, January 1966.

[4] M. S. Feldstein, 'The Social Time Preference Discount Rate in Cost–Benefit Analysis', *The Economic Journal*, June 1964.

[5] R. F. Harrod, *Towards a Dynamic Economics*, London, Macmillan, 1948.

[6] T. C. Koopmans, 'Utility and Impatience', *Econometrica*, April 1960.

[7] A. Maneschi, 'Optimal Savings with Finite Planning Horizon: A Note', and 'A Rejoinder', *International Economic Review*, January 1966.

[8] J. E. Meade, *Trade and Welfare, Mathematical Appendix*, Oxford, Oxford University Press, 1955.

[9] F. P. Ramsey, 'A Mathematical Theory of Savings', *The Economic Journal*, December 1928.

[10] A. K. Sen, 'On Optimizing the Rate of Saving', *The Economic Journal*, September 1961.

[11] P. A. Samuelson and R. M. Solow, 'A Complete Capital Model Involving Heterogeneous Capital Goods', *Quarterly Journal of Economics*, November 1956.

[12] J. Tinbergen, 'The Optimum Rate of Savings', *The Economic Journal*, December 1956.

[13] J. Tinbergen, 'Maximization of Utility Over Time', *Econometrica*, April 1960.

EFFICIENT, INEFFICIENT, AND CRITICAL GROWTH*

M. INAGAKI

1. Introduction

The object of the theory of *dynamic efficiency* is to determine under which conditions a feasible growth path is or is not *consumption-dominated* by another one. The theoretical importance of this theory resides in the fact that it constitutes the common basis of all possible theories of *consumption-optimal* growth. However, in contrast to the concept of optimality, the concept of efficiency calls for a universal consensus. The practical interest of the theory is that it may give, it is hoped, some clue to the long-term value of the savings ratio which an economy cannot efficiently exceed.

The development of the theory of dynamic efficiency has hitherto been essentially directed to the establishment of *necessary* conditions for efficient growth.[1]) Little attention has been paid to *sufficient* efficiency conditions. The present paper tries to remedy this situation.

For this purpose, it first introduces the new concept of *critical growth*. More precisely, it defines the two concepts of a critical growth path and a critical growth strategy. Both are perfectly symmetrical with respect to what is and is not efficient; they constitute a sort of dividing-line between efficient and inefficient growth, which, however, leaves some feasible growth paths (or growth strategies) unclassified.

It is then shown that the famous *Golden Rule* or GR path is a critical path. This fact is used to generalize the GR path so as to include the case of models which are only 'asymptotically' capable of golden age growth. The resulting generalization is called *Relatively Attainable Golden Rule* or RAGR path. It is, like the original GR path, both a critical path and consumption-dominant

---

*) This paper is a revised version of Publication 33/36 of the Netherlands Economic Institute.

[1]) To the best of my knowledge.

with respect to a set of exponential growth paths. Moreover, it coincides with the GR path whenever the latter exists.

Finally, a critical strategy related to the GR concept is defined and called *Golden Rule Strategy*. The latter is interesting because it provides a rule for efficient growth which does not refer to any given growth path.

2. Basic Concepts

A *growth path* is here defined as a 3-dimensional time path

$$G(t) = (K(t), Y(t), C(t)), \quad 0 < K, Y, C < +\infty,$$

where K, Y and C denote respectively capital, production and consumption. We require $K(t)$ and $Y(t)$ to be continuous, and $C(t)$ to be piece-wise continuous. We only consider growth paths which extend over the whole of the positive time axis, $0 \leqslant t < +\infty$.

A growth path may or may not be feasible. It is (indefinitely) *feasible* if it satisfies the initial condition $K(0) = K_0$ and the given growth model. The *set of feasible paths* starting from the initial capital stock K_0 is denoted by $\{G(t), K_0\}$. It is furthermore convenient to call *'a priori' feasible* any path which is feasible for some unspecified initial capital stock.

In this paper we assume two classes of growth models, respectively called *Exponential Growth* or EG and *Quasi-Exponential Growth* or Q-EG models. The first class is a sub-class of the second. Both are characterized by a twice continuously differentiable neoclassical production function

$$Y = F(K, t), \quad 0 \leqslant K, t < +\infty,$$

which vanishes for $K = 0$ and is strictly increasing with respect to t and strictly concave with respect to K,

$$\frac{\partial F}{\partial t} > 0, \quad \frac{\partial F}{\partial K} > 0, \quad \frac{\partial^2 F}{\partial K^2} < 0, \quad 0 \leqslant K, t < +\infty.$$

In other words, we always assume the necessity of capital for production, positive marginal products, the law of diminishing returns, and, implicitly, positive technological progress and/or a strictly increasing autonomous labour force.

In addition, an EG model satisfies the condition

$$F(K_0 \, e^{gt}, t) = F(K_0, 0) \, e^{gt}, \quad 0 \leqslant t < +\infty,$$

for one and only one number $g>0$, and every K_0 in $0<K_0<F(K_0, 0)/g$. A Q-EG model only satisfies the weaker condition that there is a number $g>0$ and a strictly concave and twice continuously differentiable function $H(K)$, defined for $0<K\leqslant H(K)/g$, such that both

$$\lim_{t\to+\infty} \frac{F(K_0\, e^{gt}, t)}{H(K_0)\, e^{gt}} = 1$$

and

$$\lim_{t\to+\infty} \frac{\partial F}{\partial K}(K_0\, e^{gt}, t) = \frac{\partial H(K_0)}{\partial K_0}$$

uniformly on $0<K_0\leqslant H(K_0)/g$. Moreover, given any $K_0>0$, $F(K_0 e^{gt}, t)/e^{gt}$ does not converge to a positive number for any other positive value of g.[2])

Finally, we assume for both models that consumption is the difference between production and investment, i.e. that the economy is either closed or in balance of payments equilibrium,

$$C = Y - \dot{K}, \quad 0\leqslant t<+\infty .$$

A growth path $G^*(t)$ may thus be feasible, 'a priori' feasible or neither. In the latter case, it may still be *relatively attainable*, i.e. such that there is a feasible path $G(t)$ which satisfies

$$\lim_{t\to+\infty} \frac{K}{K^*} = \lim_{t\to+\infty} \frac{Y}{Y^*} = \lim_{t\to+\infty} \frac{C}{C^*} = 1 .$$

We are particularly interested in growth paths which are *exponential*, i.e. satisfy the condition

$$\frac{\dot{K}}{K} = \frac{\dot{Y}}{Y} = \frac{\dot{C}}{C} = g , \quad 0\leqslant t<+\infty ,$$

for some positive number g. Exponential paths which are 'a priori' feasible are indicated by an upper bar ($^-$) and those which are relatively attainable by a tilde ($^\sim$). Accordingly, their respective sets are denoted by $\{\bar{G}(t)\}$ and $\{\tilde{G}(t)\}$. Notice that the first is necessarily a sub-set of the second.

We now turn to the concepts which are specific to the theory of dynamic efficiency. We first recall the definition of *consumption-dominance*. A growth path dominates another one with respect to consumption if it yields never

[2]) Though mathematically stronger than necessary, these conditions are very weak from the point of view of the neoclassical theory of growth.

less, but sometimes more consumption. Mathematically, it means that $G_1(t)$ dominates $G_2(t)$ if both $G_1(t) \geqslant G_2(t)$ over $0 \leqslant t < +\infty$ and $G_1(t') > G_2(t')$ for some $t' \geqslant 0$. A member of a set of growth paths which dominates all other members of the set, is *dominant* in this set. Both sets of 'a priori' feasible and relatively attainable exponential paths may contain a dominant member, but the set of *all* feasible growth paths $\{G(t), K_0\}$ never does.

This does not mean that a feasible path never dominates any other. There are generally an infinite number of feasible paths which are dominated by other feasible paths. Any feasible path which is dominated by another feasible path is called *inefficient*, and any which is not is called *efficient*.

We next define a *critical path* as a path $\hat{G}(t)$, itself not necessarily feasible, such that:
i. Every feasible path $G(t)$ is efficient if it satisfies

$$K(t) \leqslant (1-\varepsilon)\,\hat{K}(t), \quad T \leqslant t < +\infty, \tag{1}$$

for some $T \geqslant 0$ and $\varepsilon > 0$.
ii. Every feasible path $G(t)$ is inefficient if it satisfies

$$K(t) \geqslant (1+\varepsilon)\,\hat{K}(t), \quad T \leqslant t < +\infty, \tag{2}$$

for some $T \geqslant 0$ and $\varepsilon > 0$.

Similarly, we define a *critical growth strategy* as a piece-wise continuous function $\hat{S}(K, t)$, $0 \leqslant K, t < +\infty$, such that:
i. Every feasible $G(t)$ is efficient if it satisfies at all points of continuity

$$\dot{K} \leqslant (1-\varepsilon)\,\hat{S}Y, \quad T \leqslant t < +\infty, \tag{3}$$

for some $T \geqslant 0$ and $\varepsilon > 0$.
ii. Every feasible $G(t)$ is inefficient if it satisfies

$$\dot{K} \geqslant (1+\varepsilon)\,\hat{S}Y, \quad T \leqslant t < +\infty, \tag{4}$$

for some $T \geqslant 0$ and $\varepsilon > 0$.

Notice that both a critical path and a critical strategy are always defined with respect to a given growth model or class of growth models. Notice also that one may want to distinguish between growth which is *relatively* critical and *absolutely* critical. All the foregoing definitions refer to relatively critical growth paths and strategies. To define absolutely critical growth paths and strategies, it is sufficient to replace respectively ε by $\varepsilon/\hat{K}(t)$ and $\varepsilon/\hat{S}(K, t)$ in these definitions. Thus, absolutely critical growth constitutes a much more stringent requirement than relatively critical growth.

3. Definition and Critical Properties of the Golden Rule Path

E. S. Phelps, one of the several economists[3]) who independently discovered the *Golden Rule* or GR path, introduced the Golden terminology [3], and has since developed and extended the application of the GR concept [4]. As already mentioned, nobody[4]) has hitherto put forth the critical properties of the GR path. Moreover, the GR concept has been unnecessarily restricted to constant returns to scale and labour-augmenting technological progress.[5]) The purpose of the present analysis is to fill this lacuna.

Definition 1: The Golden Rule path is the consumption-dominant member of the set $\{\bar{G}(t)\}$ of all 'a priori' feasible exponential growth paths.

Notice that, depending on the specification of $F(K, t)$, the set $\{\bar{G}(t)\}$ may be empty and in this case the GR path does not exist. Traditionally, the GR path is only defined with respect to EG models.

Theorem 1: Given an EG model, $\hat{K}_0\, e^{gt} > 0$ is the GR path if and only if

$$\frac{\partial F}{\partial K}(\hat{K}_0, 0) = g\,. \tag{5}$$

(Proof in the Appendix.)

E. S. Phelps has stressed the importance of

Theorem 2: Given an EG model and the existence of the GR path $\hat{G}(t)$, any feasible path $G(t)$ is inefficient if it satisfies $K(t) \geqslant (1+\varepsilon)\,\hat{K}(t)$, $T \leqslant t < +\infty$, for some $\varepsilon > 0$ and $T \geqslant 0$. (Proof in the Appendix.)

We complement Theorem 2 by

Theorem 3: Given an EG model and the existence of the GR path $\hat{G}(t)$, any feasible path $G(t)$ is efficient if it satisfies $K(t) \leqslant (1-\varepsilon)\,\hat{K}(t)$, $T \leqslant t < +\infty$, for some $\varepsilon > 0$ and $T \geqslant 0$. (Proof in the Appendix.)

Theorems 2 and 3 establish together:

Theorem 4: Given an EG model, the GR path is a critical path.

---

[3]) E. S. Phelps cites Maurice Allais, Jacques Desrousseaux, Joan Robinson, Trevor Swan, and Christian Weizsäcker. See [4] footnote 3 on p. 3.

[4]) To the best of my knowledge.

[5]) Labour-augmenting technological progress is a necessary condition for the existence of a GR path under, *but only under*, constant returns to scale. See [2].

4. The Generalized Golden Rule Path and the Golden Rule Strategy

It is Theorem 4 which makes the GR path so interesting. If the GR path satisfied only Theorem 2 or only Theorem 3, it would lose much of its importance. Indeed, whenever the GR path exists, there is an infinite number of 'a priori' feasible exponential growth paths which satisfy either Theorem 2 or 3. There is only one such path, however, which satisfies both theorems, i.e. which is critical. This is the GR path.

Any true generalization of the GR path should therefore retain this critical property. It should also be consumption-dominant with respect to some set of growth paths, preferably exponential. Finally, it should be uniquely defined and coincide with the GR path, whenever the latter exists. The following generalization satisfies these conditions.

Definition 2: The Relatively Attainable GR or RAGR path is the 'consumption-dominant'[6]) member of the set $\{\tilde{G}(t)\}$ of all relatively attainable exponential growth paths.

Theorems 5, 6, 7, and 8 correspond to Theorems 1, 2, 3, and 4. They reveal the close analogy which exists between the properties of the GR and RAGR paths.

Theorem 5: Given a Q-EG model, $\hat{K}_0 \, e^{gt}$ is the RAGR path if and only if

$$\frac{\partial H}{\partial K_0}(\hat{K}_0) = g . \qquad \text{(Proof in the Appendix.)} \tag{6}$$

Theorem 6: Given a Q-EG model and the existence of the RAGR path $\hat{G}(t)$, any feasible path $G(t)$ is inefficient if it satisfies $K(t) \geqslant (1+\varepsilon)\,\hat{K}(t)$, $T \leqslant t < +\infty$, for some $\varepsilon > 0$ and $T \geqslant 0$. (Proof in the Appendix.)

Theorem 7: Given a Q-EG model and the existence of the RAGR path $\hat{G}(t)$, any feasible path $G(t)$ is efficient if it satisfies $K(t) \leqslant (1-\varepsilon)\,\hat{K}(t)$, $T \leqslant t < +\infty$, for some $\varepsilon > 0$ and $T \geqslant 0$. (Proof in the Appendix.)

The last two theorems together imply:

Theorem 8: Given a Q-EG model, the RAGR path is a critical path.

From the point of view of dynamic efficiency, the properties of the RAGR path are perfectly similar to those of the GR path. Moreover, both paths coincide whenever the GR path exists.

---

[6]) 'Consumption' along an exponential RAGR path is here defined as $C \equiv H(K_0)\,e^{gt} - gK_0\,e^{gt}$.

Up to this point, our analysis has only considered the generalization of the GR *path*. One may, however, generalize the GR concept in a different direction by concentrating on the fact that the GR path always equates the growth rate of capital with the marginal product of capital or, what is the same, the savings ratio with the elasticity of production. In other words, one may focus one's attention on the GR strategy, rather than on the GR path.

Definition 3: Given a Q-EG model, the GR strategy is

$$\hat{S}(K, t) = \frac{K}{F(K, t)} \frac{\partial F(K, t)}{\partial K}. \tag{7}$$

The GR strategy is of special interest because of

Theorem 9: Given a Q-EG model, the GR strategy is a critical strategy. (Proof in the Appendix.)

For every given initial capital stock, the GR strategy defines a feasible growth path, say the GRS *path*. Indeed, $\partial F/\partial K > 0$, $\partial^2 F/\partial K^2 < 0$ and $F(0, t) = 0$ imply

$$\frac{\dot{K}}{F} = \frac{K}{F} \frac{\partial F}{\partial K} < 1, \quad 0 < K, t < +\infty.$$

In other words, the GR strategy defines a whole set of 'a priori' feasible GRS paths for every given growth model. Whenever it exists, the GR path is necessarily one of these 'a priori' feasible GRS paths. It follows that the GR path coincides with the GRS path if and only if it is feasible. For this reason alone, the GRS path cannot be considered as a true generalization of the GR *path*.

It is likely that the GRS path is critical whenever the RAGR path exists, but then the latter is all we need for dynamic efficiency analysis. Moreover, the GRS paths generally have a complicated form and, therefore, do not constitute convenient reference paths.

The GR strategy concept, on the other hand, avoids all the defects of the GRS path. Theorem 9 is simple and its application does not require the knowledge of the GRS path, but only of the instantaneous values of the growth rate and the marginal product of capital. As a matter of fact, it does not even require an exact knowledge of the production function. This is certainly a great advantage, insofar as the theory of dynamic efficiency is to become a guide for actual development planning.

Appendix

Proof of Theorem 1: Maximization of $C=F-\dot{K}=[F(K_0, 0)-gK_0]\, e^{gt}$ with respect to K_0 gives (5). Moreover, (5) implies $g\hat{K}_0/F(\hat{K}_0, 0)<1$, i.e. the feasibility of $\hat{K}_0\, e^{gt}$. (Q.E.D.)

Proof of Theorem 2: We show that one can always find a feasible path $G^*(t)$ which dominates any given feasible path $G(t)$ satisfying (2) for some $\varepsilon>0$ and $T\geqslant 0$. We define $G^*(t)$ as follows:

$$K^*(t) = K(t), \quad 0 \leqslant t \leqslant T, \tag{8}$$

$$\dot{K}^*(t) = \dot{K}(T) - \delta, \quad T < t < T_1, \tag{9}$$

$$\frac{\dot{K}(t) - \dot{K}^*(t)}{K(t) - K^*(t)} = g, \quad T_1 < t < +\infty, \tag{10}$$

where $\delta>0$ and T_1 have been chosen such that both

$$K^*(T_1) > K(T_1) - \varepsilon\hat{K}(T_1) \tag{11}$$

and

$$C^*(t) > C(t), \quad T < t < T_1. \tag{12}$$

Now (2), (10), and (11) imply

$$\frac{K^*(t)}{\hat{K}(t)} > 1, \quad T_1 \leqslant t < +\infty.$$

Hence, by the strict concavity of F with respect to K,

$$\frac{\partial F^*}{\partial K} < \frac{\partial \hat{F}}{\partial K} = g, \quad T_1 \leqslant t < +\infty, \tag{13}$$

and, using (10),

$$\begin{aligned} C^* - C &= (F^* - F) - (\dot{K}^* - \dot{K}) \\ &> (K^* - K)\frac{\partial F^*}{\partial K} - (\dot{K}^* - \dot{K}) > 0, \quad T_1 < t < +\infty. \end{aligned}$$

In other words, $G^*(t)$ dominates $G(t)$, i.e. $G(t)$ is inefficient. (Q.E.D.)

Proof of Theorem 3: Assume that both $G(t)$ and $G^*(t)$ are feasible, that $G^*(t)$ dominates $G(t)$, and that $G(t)$ satisfies (1) for some $\varepsilon>0$ and $T\geqslant 0$. Then, there is a $T_1\geqslant 0$, such that

$$C^*(T_1) > C(T_1), \tag{14}$$

and

$$K^*(t) < K(t), \quad T_1 \leqslant t < +\infty. \tag{15}$$

On the other hand,

$$C^* - C = (F^* - F) - (\dot{K}^* - \dot{K}) \geqslant 0, \quad T_1 \leqslant t < +\infty. \tag{16}$$

where

$$F^* - F < (K^* - K)\frac{\partial F}{\partial K}, \quad T_1 \leqslant t < +\infty. \tag{17}$$

It follows from (15), (16), and (17) that

$$\frac{\dot{K} - \dot{K}^*}{K - K^*} > \frac{\partial F}{\partial K}, \quad T_1 \leqslant t < +\infty. \tag{18}$$

Writing $\bar{K}(t) = (1-\varepsilon)\,\hat{K}(t)$ one has, by the strict concavity of F with respect to K and Theorem 1,

$$\frac{\partial F}{\partial K} \geqslant \frac{\partial \bar{F}}{\partial K} > \frac{\partial \hat{F}}{\partial K} = g, \quad T \leqslant t < +\infty.$$

Now,

$$F(K_0\,e^{gt}, t) = F(K_0, 0)\,e^{gt}, \quad 0 \leqslant t < +\infty,$$

implies

$$\frac{\partial F}{\partial K_t} = \frac{\partial F}{\partial K_{t=0}}, \quad 0 \leqslant t < +\infty,$$

along any 'a priori' feasible balanced growth path, in particular along $\bar{G}(t)$ and $\hat{G}(t)$.
Hence, for some $\delta > 0$,

$$\frac{\partial \bar{F}}{\partial K} = (1 + \delta)\frac{\partial \hat{F}}{\partial K}, \quad 0 \leqslant t < +\infty,$$

and, consequently,

$$\frac{\dot{K} - \dot{K}^*}{K - K^*} > (1 + \delta)\,g, \quad T_1 \leqslant t < +\infty. \tag{19}$$

This implies, however, the absurd conclusion that $K^*(t) < 0$ after some finite period of time, i.e. that $G^*(t)$ is not feasible. (Q.E.D.)

Proof of Theorem 5: Condition (6) determines the maximum of $\hat{C}=[H(\hat{K}_0)-g\hat{K}_0]\,e^{gt}$. This path is relatively attainable since $g\hat{K}_0/H(\hat{K}_0)<1$, by (6) and the strict concavity of $H(K)$. (Q.E.D.)

Proof of Theorem 6: We first define $\tilde{K}(t)=(1+\varepsilon/2)\,\hat{K}(t)$. It follows, by a similar argument as used in the proof of Theorem 7 below, that there is a $T_\eta \geqslant T$, such that

$$\frac{\partial \tilde{F}}{\partial K} < g\,, \quad T_\eta \leqslant t < +\infty\,. \tag{20}$$

We then define a $G^*(t)$ as in the proof of Theorem 2, except for the fact that we use T_η instead of T in (8), (9) and (12) and replace (11) by

$$K^*(T_1) > K(T_1) - \frac{\varepsilon}{2}\,\hat{K}(T_1)\,. \tag{21}$$

Then, by (2), (10) and (21),

$$\frac{K^*(t)}{\tilde{K}(t)} > 1\,, \quad T_1 \leqslant t < +\infty\,. \tag{22}$$

Now (20), (22) and the strict concavity of F with respect to K imply

$$\frac{\partial F^*}{\partial K} < \frac{\partial \tilde{F}}{\partial K} < g\,, \quad T_\eta \leqslant t < +\infty\,,$$

and, using (10),

$$\begin{aligned} C^* - C &= (F^* - F) - (\dot{K}^* - \dot{K}) \\ &> (K^* - K)\,\frac{\partial F^*}{\partial K} - (\dot{K}^* - \dot{K}) \\ &> 0\,. \end{aligned}$$

In other words, $G^*(t)$ dominates $G(t)$, i.e. $G(t)$ is inefficient. (Q.E.D.)

Proof of Theorem 7: As in the proof of Theorem 3, assume that both $G(t)$ and $G^*(t)$ are feasible, that $G^*(t)$ dominates $G(t)$, and that $G(t)$ satisfies (1) for some $\varepsilon>0$ and $T\geqslant 0$. Up to (18) included, we argue exactly as before.

Writing $\tilde{K}(t)=(1-\varepsilon)\,\hat{K}(t)$, one has, by the strict concavity of F with respect to K,

$$\frac{\partial F}{\partial K} \geqslant \frac{\partial \tilde{F}}{\partial K} > \frac{\partial \hat{F}}{\partial K}\,, \quad T \leqslant t < +\infty\,. \tag{23}$$

By the definition of the Q-EG model,

$$\lim_{t\to+\infty} \frac{\partial F}{\partial K}(K_0 e^{gt}, t) = \frac{\partial H}{\partial K}(K_0).$$

This implies that

$$\lim_{t\to+\infty} \frac{\partial F}{\partial K}(\hat{K}_0\, e^{gt}, t) = g\,,$$

and, by the strict concavity of H with respect to K,

$$\lim_{t\to+\infty} \frac{\partial F}{\partial K}((1-\varepsilon)\,\hat{K}_0 e^{gt}, t) = g + \text{pos. const.}$$

Hence, for some $T_2 \geqslant T$, T_1, and $\eta > 0$,

$$\frac{\partial \tilde{F}}{\partial K} > (1+\eta)\frac{\partial \hat{F}}{\partial K}, \quad T_2 \leqslant t < +\infty\,. \tag{24}$$

Now (18), (23) and (24) imply again (19), i.e. the absurd conclusion that $K^*(t)<0$ after some finite period of time or, in other words, that $G^*(t)$ is not feasible. (Q.E.D.)

Proof of Theorem 9: We first prove that $G(t)$ is efficient if it satisfies (3) for some $\varepsilon > 0$ and $T \geqslant 0$. We argue exactly as in the proof of Theorem 3 up to (18) included. It then follows from (3) and (18) that

$$\frac{\dot{K}}{K} < (1-\varepsilon)\frac{\dot{K}-\dot{K}^*}{K-K^*}, \quad T_3 \leqslant t < +\infty\,, \tag{25}$$

for some $T_3 > T$, T_1. Now (25) implies the absurd conclusion that $K^*(t)<0$ after some finite period of time, i.e. that $G^*(t)$ is not feasible.

We next prove that $G(t)$ is inefficient if it satisfies (4) for some $\varepsilon > 0$ and $T \geqslant 0$. Assume first that the RAGR path does not exist. This will be the case if either

$$\frac{\partial H}{\partial K}(K) > g \quad \text{for all } K > 0\,, \tag{26}$$

or

$$\frac{\partial H}{\partial K}(K) < g \quad \text{for all } K > 0\,. \tag{27}$$

Let us show that no feasible $G(t)$ can satisfy (4) if (26) obtains. Notice first that (26) implies

$$\lim_{K \to +\infty} \frac{K}{H} \frac{\partial H}{\partial K} = 1,$$

and, consequently, a K_0^{**} such that

$$\frac{K_0}{H(K_0)} \frac{\partial H(K_0)}{\partial K} > 1 - \frac{1}{2} \frac{\varepsilon}{1+\varepsilon}, \; K_0 \geqslant K_0^{**}. \tag{28}$$

Notice next that, by the definition of the Q-EG model, there is a T_ε which does not depend on K_0 in $0 < K_0 < H(K_0)/g$ and is such that

$$\begin{aligned} &\left| \frac{K_0 \, e^{gt}}{F(K_0 \, e^{gt}, t)} \frac{\partial F}{\partial K}(K_0 \, e^{gt}, t) - \frac{K_0}{H(K_0)} \frac{\partial H(K_0)}{\partial K} \right| \\ &= \frac{K_0}{H(K_0)} \frac{\partial H(K_0)}{\partial K} \left| \frac{H(K_0) \, e^{gt}}{F(K_0 \, e^{gt}, t)} \frac{\frac{\partial F}{\partial K}(K_0 \, e^{gt})}{\frac{\partial H}{\partial K}(K_0)} - 1 \right| \\ &< \frac{K_0}{H(K_0)} \frac{\partial H}{\partial K}(K_0) \left(\frac{1}{2} \frac{\varepsilon}{1+\varepsilon} \right) \\ &< \frac{1}{2} \frac{\varepsilon}{1+\varepsilon}, \quad T_\varepsilon \leqslant t < +\infty. \end{aligned} \tag{29}$$

This implies with (28) that

$$\frac{K}{F(K, t)} \frac{\partial F(K, t)}{\partial K} > \frac{1}{1+\varepsilon} \tag{30}$$

for $t \geqslant T_\varepsilon$ and $K \geqslant K_0^{**} e^{gT_\varepsilon}$.

On the other hand, (4) implies that there is a $T_1 \geqslant T, T_\varepsilon$, such that

$$K(t) > K_0^{**} \, e^{gt}, \quad T_1 \leqslant t < +\infty. \tag{31}$$

Indeed, as long as $K(t) \leqslant K_0^{**} \, e^{gt}$, one has

$$\begin{aligned} \frac{\dot{K}}{K} &\geqslant (1+\varepsilon) \frac{\partial F}{\partial K}(K(t), t) \\ &\geqslant (1+\varepsilon) \frac{\partial F}{\partial K}(K_0^{**} \, e^{gt}, t), \end{aligned}$$

where

$$\lim_{t\to+\infty} \frac{\partial F}{\partial K}(K_0^{**}\,\mathrm{e}^{gt}, t) = g + \text{pos. const.}$$

It follows that T_1 must exist.

Now (4), (30) and (31) imply

$$\frac{\dot{K}}{F} > 1, \quad T_1 \leqslant t < +\infty,$$

which is obviously impossible under our assumption of a closed economy. Thus, no feasible $G(t)$ satisfies (4) if (26) holds true.

We next show that no feasible $G(t)$ satisfies (4) if (27) holds true. (4) and $\dot{K}/Y \leqslant 1$ imply

$$\frac{K}{F}\frac{\partial F}{\partial K} \leqslant \frac{1}{1+\varepsilon}, \quad T \leqslant t < +\infty. \tag{32}$$

On the other hand, we know from (29) that there is a T_ε such that

$$\begin{aligned}\frac{K\mathrm{e}^{-gt}}{H(K\mathrm{e}^{-gt})}\frac{\partial H}{\partial K}(K\mathrm{e}^{-gt}) &< \frac{K}{F}\frac{\partial F}{\partial K} + \frac{\varepsilon/2}{1+\varepsilon}\\ &\leqslant 1 - \frac{\varepsilon/2}{1+\varepsilon}, \text{ using (32)}, \quad T_\varepsilon \leqslant t < +\infty.\end{aligned}$$

It follows that

$$K > \bar{K}\mathrm{e}^{gt}, \quad T_\varepsilon \leqslant t < +\infty, \tag{33}$$

for some $\bar{K} > 0$. Indeed, (27) implies $\partial H(0)/\partial K \leqslant g$ and

$$\lim_{K\to 0} \frac{K}{H(K)}\frac{\partial H}{\partial K}(K) = 1.$$

Now, for $\delta > 0$ and $\eta > 0$ such that $\eta < g - (H(\bar{K})/\bar{K}) - \delta$, there is a T_η which satisfies

$$\begin{aligned}\frac{\dot{K}}{K} &\leqslant \frac{F}{K}\\ &< \frac{H(K\mathrm{e}^{-gt})}{K\mathrm{e}^{-gt}} + \eta\\ &< \frac{H(\bar{K})}{\bar{K}} + \eta\\ &< g - \delta, \quad T_\eta \leqslant t < +\infty.\end{aligned} \tag{34}$$

This follows from (33), and the uniform convergence of $F(K_0\, e^{gt}, t)/K_0\, e^{gt}$ to $H(K_0)/K_0$ (34) is, however, contrary to (33). The conditions (4) and (27) cannot, therefore, both be satisfied by a feasible $G(t)$.

The condition (4) can thus only be satisfied if an RAGR path exists. Denote the latter by $\hat{G}(t)$ and any given feasible path satisfying (4) by $G(t)$. Choose $\eta>0$ and $\delta>0$ such that

$$\frac{\partial H}{\partial K}((1+\eta)\,\hat{K}_0) > \frac{1+\varepsilon/2}{1+\varepsilon}\,g + \delta\,.$$

Then, by the uniform convergence assumptions on F, there is a $T_\delta \geqslant T$ such that

$$\begin{aligned}\frac{\dot{K}}{K} &\geqslant (1+\varepsilon)\frac{\partial F}{\partial K}(K, t)\\ &\geqslant (1+\varepsilon)\frac{\partial F}{\partial K}((1+\eta)\,\hat{K}, t)\\ &\geqslant (1+\varepsilon)\frac{\partial H}{\partial K}((1+\eta)\,\hat{K}_0) - \delta\\ &> (1+\varepsilon/2)\,g\,,\end{aligned}$$

whenever $K(t) \leqslant (1+\eta)\,\hat{K}(t)$ and $t \geqslant T_\delta$. It follows that there is a $T_1 \geqslant T_\delta$ such that

$$K(t) \geqslant (1+\eta)\,\hat{K}(t), \quad T_1 \leqslant t < +\infty\,.$$

Now this implies the inefficiency of $G(t)$ by Theorem 7. (Q.E.D.)

References

[1] M. INAGAKI, *Efficient, Inefficient and Critical Growth*, Publication 33/36, Netherlands Economic Institute.

[2] M. INAGAKI, 'Balanced Growth Under Factor-Augmenting Technological Progress', *Zeitschrift für die gesamte Staatswissenschaft*, 123 Bd/1 Heft, January 1967.

[3] E. S. PHELPS, 'The Golden Rule of Accumulation: A Fable of Growthmen', *American Economic Review*, Vol. 51, No. 4 (September 1961), pp. 638–643.

[4] E. S. PHELPS, *Golden Rules of Economic Growth. Studies of Efficient and Optimal Investment*, New York: W. W. Norton & Company, Inc., 1966.

MODELS OF BALANCED AND MAXIMUM GROWTH IN DUALISTIC ECONOMIES*)

A. QAYUM

1. Introduction

Much attention has been given to the study of dualistic economies in recent years. In this paper an economy is called dualistic if it can be broadly divided into two parts; a predominant rural and agricultural sector and a modern industrial sector. The first sector is assumed to absorb all the workers and their families which do not find employment in the second. The industrial sector is initially small and is run on commercial lines and employs only that number of workers it finds profitable to hire. The rural and agricultural sector absorbs up to 70 or 90 percent of the total population of the country. All rural persons in the main working ages and many below or above such ages are assumed to remain busy in partly or wholly gainful pursuits. The productivity of the marginal workers may be below what they consume or below the average consumption of the community but it is assumed not to be nil.[1]) However, the marginal productivity of workers in the agricultural sector is generally far below that in the industrial sector. The main reason is that most agricultural and other rural activities are conducted, not on commercial lines, but as family enterprises; where every member of the

*) I am grateful to Professor and Mrs. S. Y. Wu, Mrs. Carol Oliven and Mr. J. M. Heineke, all of University of Iowa, for their comments on an earlier version of this paper, and to the participants of the faculty research seminar of the Department of Economics of Indiana University where I presented this paper. Professor George J. Stolnitz, Director of the International Development Research Center at Indiana University has been very helpful in making detailed comments and giving encouragement.

[1]) It is also not true that if some of the workers are withdrawn from the agricultural sector, the total production will not be affected, given the techniques and organization of production and other conditions of work including peak periods. See [4].

family shares more or less equally in the output raised by the family unit, whatever the productivity of the marginal workers.

The purpose of this paper is to study the process of growth of such a dualistic economy under some specific conditions. Among the large number of studies that have dealt with the growth of an underdeveloped dualistic economy, two stand out as precursors of what follows. They are: (i) the so-called Mahalanobis model [3], and (ii) the Ranis-Fei model [5]. Since these provide a frame of reference and a proper perspective for the present paper, it is useful to review their contents briefly, emphasizing the basic points of interest. This is done in section 2. Section 3 lists and explains the assumptions underlying the present study. Section 4 discusses processes of balanced growth along Ranis–Fei lines and analyses its implications. Section 5 presents an alternative dynamic model of balanced growth and derives the so-called commercialization point at which employment in all sectors is determined by marginal labor productivity. Section 6 deals with paths of maximum rather than balanced growth, and section 7 reexamines the commercialization point under both sets of conditions. In section 8, an attempt is made to study the effect of technological progress on the growth of a dualistic economy. Section 9 winds up the discussion with some concluding remarks.

This paper extends the Mahalanobis and Ranis–Fei models by including both labor and capital explicitly. The allocation of both factors is first studied under conditions of balanced growth and then by relaxing one of the assumptions of balanced growth, their efficient allocation is worked out to yield maximum output in each period. However, as in the Mahalanobis and Ranis–Fei presentations, the discussion here does not concern itself with optimal allocation of resources over multiple time periods as a whole, whether finite or infinite. Besides the complexity and arbitrariness of such discussions, the main reason for limiting the scope of this paper to period by period balance or maximization is the assumption that in dualistic economies, the wage-rate and hence the per capita consumption is fixed by convention and remains constant till the commercialization point is reached.

2. Two Precursor Models

Mahalanobis has constructed a simple model of an economy in two broad sectors, one producing capital goods and the other consumption goods. Increase in investment in year t equals the product of investment in the capital goods sector in period $t-1$ and the output–capital ratio in that sector. This implies full utilization of capital and a production lag of one period, or

$$I_t - I_{t-1} = \gamma_i \beta_i I_{t-1} \tag{1}$$

I_t denotes investment in year t, γ_i is the proportion, assumed constant, of investment going to the capital goods sector and β_i is the output–capital ratio, also constant, in that sector. From eq. (1) we have,

$$I_t = I_0 (1 + \gamma_i \beta_i)^t \tag{2}$$

Similarly increase in consumption in year t is

$$C_t - C_{t-1} = \gamma_c \beta_c I_{t-1} \tag{3}$$

where γ_c and β_c are the corresponding constant parameters for the consumer goods sector. Eq. (3) using (2) leads to

$$C_t = C_0 + \gamma_c \beta_c \frac{(1 + \gamma_i \beta_i)^t - 1}{\gamma_i \beta_i} I_0 . \tag{4}$$

Since $Y_t = C_t + I_t$, it is easy to see that whatever the values of C_0 and I_0, γ_i will be the decisive element in the growth of income after a critical period in which its presence in the denominator in (4) is counteracted by the exponentials in (4) and (2).

Despite its analytical power, this model has serious short-comings for purposes of practical application. First, allocation of investment according to γ_i (or γ_c) cannot be effected without full control and operation of the economy by a central authority. Second, a higher γ_i will lead to a higher rate of growth of income in the long run, but this may involve a reduction in per capita consumption over an initial period. There is nothing in the model to prevent this. Third, the model does not allow any substitution possibilities. Labor is not considered explicitly and is treated as if redundant. It is a two-sectoral but one-factor model. Fourth, the model does not contain any elements or aspects of optimality or allocative efficiency. In fact it has been shown that the model is non-optimal [2].

Ranis and Fei divide an underdeveloped economy in two sectors, a predominant traditional sector containing all agriculture and allied rural activities and a modern industrial sector. The latter is very small or insignificant in the initial stages. The traditional sector produces the total consumption, mainly food, by workers and their families. Wages of the workers in the two sectors are the same, being determined by conventions and institutions, and remain constant so long as any underemployment of labor exists. The non-traditional industrial sector produces all tools and equipment. Its size of employed labor force is determined by the marginal productivity. The rest of the work force and population remain attached to the traditional sector, where marginal productivity of the workers may be far below the constant institutional wage-rate and may even be as low as zero. [2])

In the latter event, employment in the industrial sector can increase without lowering the total agricultural production so long as labor with zero marginal productivity is available in the traditional sector. *Ceteris paribus*, once such labor is exhausted, further movement of workers to the industrial sector must be accompanied by the decrease in agricultural production, due to the positive marginal productivity of the shifting labor force. At this stage, increases in the production of the traditional sector can only be brought about by a countervailing degree of investment in that sector.

The authors focus on the commercialization point, defined as the stage where the marginal productivities of the workers in the two sectors become equal to each other and to the wage rate. They identify this point on the basis of two restrictive and simplifying assumptions: (i) marginal productivity falls linearly at a constant rate and (ii) an increase in agricultural productivity shifts the entire total production upward by a constant proportion. Under these assumptions they deduce that the proportion of population remaining in agriculture at the commercialization point would be equal to: $V_t = 1+T-\sqrt{1-T^2}$. V_t is the proportion of the total population remaining in the agricultural sector at the commercialization point and T is the nonredundancy coefficient, i.e., the largest fraction or number by which the agricultural population could be multiplied without making marginal productivity equal to zero. It turns out that V_t is independent of the size of the economy, as reflected by either absolute size of the population or absolute amount of initial agricultural output.

In addition to using very restrictive assumptions, Ranis and Fei employ only a partial analysis. The industrial sector is mentioned, but plays no essential role, either in connection with allocation of resources or with the process of capital formation. Like the Mahalanobis model, the Ranis–Fei model is two-sectoral but with one factor, in this case labor. Their analysis

[2]) As noted earlier we do not allow for zero marginal productivity in this paper.

is at best comparative static. The independence of V_t is partly the result of the above two unrealistic assumptions.

3. Own Assumptions

We begin with an obvious point of general methodology. Since it is impossible to unravel the economic reality of dualistic underdeveloped processes in full intricacy, the most that can be done is to focus on major forces and tendencies which have predominant influence on the variables of interest here. In so doing, however, it is necessary to recognize that the dominant forces and tendencies are not self-contained, but intermingle and interact with others. These approaches to reality are covered by the following assumptions and specifications.

(A1) The dualistic economy to be considered is a typical one, in which the traditional agricultural sector is assumed to be paramount in terms of labor force but unprogressive, using age-old methods and tools of production. The industrial sector is small but embryonic, using modern methods of production.

(A2) Two factors of production, capital and labor, are to be considered. All units of these factors are employed and have positive marginal productivities. This is implicit in the use of Cobb–Douglas production function to be employed below.

(A3) Unless stated otherwise, all output of the agricultural sector is for consumption only and all output of the industrial sector is for investment only. [3]

(A4) Productive activity in each of the sectors is characterized by a linear homogeneous production function. However, the production elasticities of factors in the two sectors are different. We use the simple Cobb–Douglas function, but this could be replaced by any other linear homogeneous function or even by a non-linear function for most of the analysis.

(A5) A real wage-rate determined by institutional forces prevails throughout the economy (the theory is not intended to explain its level). It remains at a constant level so long as any underemployment of workers exists. A worker is called underemployed if his productivity is less than the constant institutional wage-rate.

[3]) This ignores the often modern, dynamic aspect of plantation or commercialized agriculture. We assume this sector to be primarily significant for exports and international trade, which will not be explicitly considered. Also some nonagricultural output intended for consumption is included here in the agricultural sector.

(A6) Terms of trade between sectors remain constant.
(A7) The industrial sector is operated along commercial lines, so that only that number of workers is employed which brings about an equality between their marginal productivity and the constant institutional wage-rate. All other workers are absorbed in the traditional sector, which consists mostly of family enterprises employing its own members (this assumption is relaxed in the maximum growth model).
(A8) Real savings by the labor force is zero in both sectors. Accordingly, per worker consumption of agricultural goods everywhere equals the constant institutional wage-rate.
(A9) Amounts of capital are expressed in net terms, to simplify the discussion.
(A10) The dualistic economy is closed, with no international transactions.
(A11) Profits, in the sense of a return for uninsurable uncertainties, can be ignored, as amplified below.
(A12) No change in technology in the sense of no change of production function.
(A13) Units of capital and labor are homogeneous throughout the economy.

This is a formidable list of assumptions, yet one which is less restrictive than those implicit in the precursor models discussed earlier. As noted earlier, the main gain in approximating reality is in the use of two factors. This raises the question why the present treatment should, like the Mahalanobis model, abstract from the rate of interest or the marginal productivity of capital. The question does not, of course, arise in the case of the Ranis–Fei model, which makes no explicit reference to capital. The approach here taken is that the size or share of returns to capital is fixed by the volume of consumption rather than being linked to, or derived directly from, the production functions as such. The movement of marginal productivity of capital is traced but neither it nor the rate of interest or profits is regarded as crucial in the allocation of resources between the two sectors. Though this may appear a serious omission, the situation in underdeveloped countries appears to warrant it. The traditional agricultural sectors of such countries typically have higher rates of interest than their industrial sectors, yet fail to attract capital. Apparently crucial here are the marketing risks and uncertainties, lack of organizational facilities, frictions arising from lack of information, inadequate means of transportation and communication, and so on, which are associated with investment in the agricultural sector. In short, rates of interest appear secondary in importance in determining capital allocation compared to the availability of food at institutionally set levels of consumption. This finds full play in the following discussion.

In contrast, the assumption that the marginal productivity of workers equals the constant institutional wage-rate in the industrial sector is examined more critically below, being used in the balanced growth model but relaxed in the optimal growth model.

4. Balanced Growth

The functioning of a dualistic economy can be described broadly by the following diagram. AB measures the total number of workers in the economy. The vertical axis AC on the right hand side measures marginal labor productivity in the agricultural sector, and the left-hand axis BD measures corresponding industrial magnitudes. AW is the constant wage-rate per worker, all of which is spent on consumption goods produced by agriculture alone and exhausts that output. Such output is depicted in two ways, first by the area AGYR, and second by the area of the rectangle AWW′B; both indicate the total consumption of all the workers and their families.

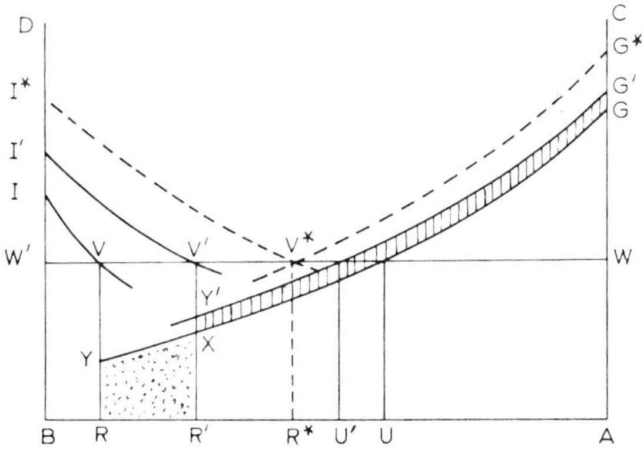

Fig. 1

Let initial marginal productivity in the agricultural sector be represented by GY and in the industrial sector by IV; the number of workers employed in the industrial sector is given by the intersection of the IV and WW′ line and is equal to BR. All the remaining workers, equal to AR, are absorbed in the agricultural sector. For AU of the workers engaged in agriculture, productivity is higher than the constant institutional wage-rate; the remaining UR workers have lower productivities. By definition, the latter represents the number of underemployed.

Area IVRB represents the production of capital goods. In the next period this amount of capital goods must be allocated to the two sectors. Assuming, for the moment, that the population does not increase in the next period, the allocation of labor and capital to the two sectors will have to be such that two conditions are fulfilled; (1) marginal productivity of workers in the industrial sector must continue to equal the constant institutional wage rate, and (2) total agricultural output must remain unchanged, since average consumption and population are both assumed to remain constant. As capital becomes allocated to the two sectors their marginal productivity curves will move upwards. Investment in the industrial sector will move the IV curve to the right and the GY curve to the left, the amounts of shift being interrelated through an appropriate allocation of capital. Such an allocation is determined by the requirements that the loss of agricultural production due to movement of workers from the agricultural sector is exactly compensated by the shift of this sector's marginal productivity curve and also that the labor force so shifted has the same marginal productivity under the new industry curve as before, or AW. In the figure IV shifts to I′V′, intersecting WW′ at V′ and indicating thereby a movement of RR′ workers from agriculture to industry. This causes a loss of agricultural production equal to YXR′R under GY, which must be made up through the gain in production by the shift from GY to G′Y′; the lined area covered by GG′Y′X must equal the dotted area covered by YXR′R. Thus the system is fully determined. At this stage, underemployment is reduced from UR to U′R′.

When the population increases the agricultural sector will have to produce an increased amount in proportion to the increase of population. As the population is exogenously given, the total requirement of agricultural output is predetermined, and hence the system is fully determined as before.

The movement of the dualistic economy along WW′ line can be labelled as a balanced growth path analogous to the Ranis–Fei concept. The explanation of such movement hinges on the constancy of the institutional wage-rate. If more capital is invested in one of the sectors, e.g., the industrial sector, than is warranted by balanced growth, food and other goods will be in short supply. This will necessitate some movement of capital to the agricultural sector, hence an upward shift of the marginal productivity curve for labor in agriculture and a downward shift of the industrial curve. The two curves must shift in the compensating fashion, till an equilibrium point like V′ is reached. So long as labor productivity remains below the constant institutional wage-rate, the latter will not tend to move up. Similarly if more capital goes to the agricultural sector than is warranted by the balanced growth path, there will be shortage of capital goods and excess of food supply and some labor and/or capital will move to the industrial sector. As labor moves in this adjustment process, its marginal productivity will rise in the agricultural sector, but here again so long as its marginal productivity at equilibrium remains below the constant institutional wage-rate, the latter will not be forced up. The corresponding capital shift from agriculture to industry in this case reduces the marginal productivity of labor in agriculture.

The sequence of such equilibrium-type allocations along the balanced growth path W′VV′ eventually comes to an end. With recurring increases of capital in the two sectors, the marginal productivity curve for workers in the agricultural sector will keep rising till a stage is reached where the marginal productivity of labor in the agricultural sector becomes equal to the constant institutional wage-rate. At this stage underemployment of workers will cease to exist, and the supply of labor will no longer be redundant. Any additional demand for labor due to further investment in either of the sectors will bid up the price of labor, and constancy of the institutional wage-rate can no longer be maintained. This is the commercialization point shown in the above diagram at V*. At the commercialization point, BR* represents the number of workers employed in the industrial sector and AR* the number of workers in the agricultural sector. Beyond this stage, the wage-rate will be determined by commercial considerations everywhere and will equal marginal productivity in the economy as a whole.

5. A Dynamic Model of Balanced Growth

The above diagrammatic outline of the dominant features of balanced growth in a progressive dualistic economy can now be developed in mathematical terms. Let the production function in the agricultural and industrial sectors be respectively[4])

$$A = L_A^{\alpha} K_A^{1-\alpha} \tag{5}$$

$$B = L_B^{\beta} K_B^{1-\beta}. \tag{6}$$

[4]) Units of A and B are assumed such that the need for the usual multiplicative constants is removed.

(5) and (6) are obviously linear homogeneous. The functions are assumed to hold for each period t; α and β do not change over time. In each period, total labor L_t and total capital K_t are fully allocated between the two sectors, but their proportions in the sectors must change to fulfill the requirements of balanced growth. Let g_t and h_t be the proportion of labor and capital going to the agricultural sector, so that the production functions of the two sectors in period t are, respectively,

$$A_t = (g_t L_t)^{\alpha} (h_t K_t)^{1-\alpha} \tag{7}$$

$$B_t = [(1 - g_t) L_t]^{\beta} [(1 - h_t) K_t]^{1-\beta}. \tag{8}$$

The basic requirements of balanced growth are (i) agricultural production should equal total consumption at the constant wage-rate, W, i.e.,

$$A_t = WL_t \tag{9}$$

and (ii) the marginal productivity of labor in industrial sector is also equal to W,

$$\frac{\partial B_t}{\partial (1 - g_t) L_t} = W. \tag{10}$$

Given the values of L_t, K_t and W, the values of g_t and h_t satisfying the balanced growth requirements can be derived. We assume that labor grows exogenously at the rate λ, so that

$$L_t = L_0 (1 + \lambda)^t. \tag{11}$$

Since only the industrial sector produces capital goods and equipment, the total capital stock in each period t is

$$K_t = K_{t-1} + B_{t-1} \tag{12}$$

Eqs. (9–12) complete the dynamic model of balanced growth.

An attempt at a general solution of the model meets with insurmountable difficulties as a rule. There is no doubt about the existence of the solution of the model, as the presence of the linear homogeneous production function guarantees it. Table 1 gives a numerical solution of the model for the selected values of variables and those of parameters.[5]) We assume[6]) $K_0 = 3$, $L_0 = 1$,

---

[5]) Substituting (9) in (7) and using the last and (10) to solve for g_t and h_t permits us to get B_t from (8), hence K_t from (12), for $t = 1, 2, \ldots$.

[6]) We have taken different values for λ and W in the tables to follow. This was done to suit the point of discussion in the following sections. For example, we have taken a lower value of W and n here, so that the commercialization point may be reached before too many years have passed.

TABLE 1

Balanced growth of a dualistic economy and the commercialization point. $A_t = (g_t L_t)^{\alpha} (h_t K_t)^{1-\alpha}$; $B_t = [(1 - g_t) L_t]^{\beta} [(1 - h_t) K_t]^{1-\beta}$; $K_0 = 3$, $L_0 = 1$, $L_t = L_0 (1 + \lambda)^t$, $\lambda = 0.02$, $\alpha = 0.80$, $\beta = 0.50$, $W = 1.15$.

t	K_t	L_t	g_t	h_t	$\Delta K_t = B_t$	A_t	$\frac{\partial A_t}{\partial g_t L_t}$	$\frac{\partial A_t}{\partial h_t K_t}$	$\frac{h_t K_t}{A_t}$	$\frac{\partial B_t}{\partial (1-g_t) L_t}$	$\frac{\partial B_t}{\partial (1-h_t) K_t}$	$\frac{(1-h_t) K_t}{B_t}$	$\frac{K_t}{Y_t}$	$\frac{\Delta K_t}{Y_t}$
0	3.00	1.00	0.93	0.88	0.15	1.15	0.99	0.09	2.30	1.15	0.22	2.31	2.30	0.11
5	3.94	1.10	0.90	0.85	0.22	1.27	1.02	0.08	2.65	1.15	0.22	2.29	2.59	0.15
10	5.47	1.22	0.86	0.83	0.37	1.40	1.07	0.06	3.24	1.15	0.22	2.30	3.03	0.20
15	7.87	1.35	0.80	0.82	0.56	1.55	1.14	0.05	4.18	1.15	0.22	2.30	3.65	0.26
16	8.48	1.37	0.79	0.82	0.61	1.58	1.16	0.05	4.42	1.15	0.22	2.30	3.80	0.27

$\lambda=0.02$, $W=1.15$, $\alpha=0.8$, $\beta=0.5$. For these values, table 1 traces the movement of the dualistic economy along the balanced growth path. The table gives the growth of capital and labor, the values of g_t and h_t showing the changing proportions of labor and capital going to the two sectors, the outputs in the sectors, marginal productivities of labor and capital, capital–output ratios in the two sectors, the over-all capital–output ratios, and the rate of savings, by quinquennial years through year 15.

It may be noted that agricultural marginal productivity of labor is 0.99 in year 0, less than either marginal productivity of labor in the industrial sector or the constant institutional wage-rate. It rises gradually to 1.14 in year 15 and to 1.16 in year 16. With the bench-mark value W at 1.15, this means that the commercialization point is reached in year 15. After this point, the level of wage-rate in the two sectors will tend to rise, for there will no longer exist any underemployment of labor in the agricultural sector to counteract the rises in the marginal productivity of workers as capital continues to be invested in the two sectors in successive periods.

6. Maximum Growth of a Dualistic Economy

In the previous model the growth of output depends upon the allocation of the two factors between the two sectors. But g and h, in turn, were completely determined by the two conditions (9) and (10), the two conditions of balanced growth. Hence there was no degree of freedom available to introduce any maximization criteria.

In order to introduce a maximization condition, therefore, one of the conditions (9) or (10) has to be relaxed. The first condition states in effect that the supply of food and necessary consumption must increase in proportion to population. Adequate supplies of food have been a major preoccupation of most dualistic economies in recent years. In underdeveloped countries where food supply has been neglected or slighted, the growth process has been considerably retarded. Hence we conclude that, on the grounds of realism, the first condition ought not to be relaxed, given the alternative of relaxing (10). It is doubtful that the marginal productivity of labor in industry equals the constant institutional wage-rate in underdeveloped areas. Accordingly, we replace this by the requirement that output of the industrial sector is to be maximized subject to the same (or unchanging) consumption condition of institutionally fixed consumption. As before, we abstract from policies and administrative arrangements that might be needed to launch a dualistic economy on a maximum growth path.

The key point to keep in mind in dealing with the maximum growth model just outlined is that only the output of the industrial sector needs to be maximized in order to maximize total output. This is because agricultural output is fixed exogeneously by the growth of population and constant rate of consumption. It can be rightly asked: why maximize capital goods indefinitely as if for its own sake? The answer, of course, is that such maximization would hasten the day when higher consumption might become feasible and self-sustaining. The solutions of the present model are, in this sense, ceiling levels of capital formation, a part of which could, at later periods, be reallocated for enhancing productivity in the consumer-goods sector or replaced by consumption itself. This is also the logic behind the Mahalanobis model, which abstracts similarly from rising consumption over an initial range of periods. Moreover, if we wished, we could easily allow for any given rate c of growth of per capita consumption, by replacing W in the present formulation by We^{ct}.

Our problem, then, is that of maximizing B_t in (8) subject to (9) as before, or maximize

$$B_t = [(1 - g_t) L_t]^\beta [(1 - h_t) K_t]^{1-\beta}, \text{ subject to} \tag{13}$$

$$A_t = (g_t L_t)^\alpha (h_t K_t)^{1-\alpha} = WL_t . \tag{14}$$

Solving the above equations we have,

$$\frac{g_t}{h_t} = \frac{1 - h_t}{1 - g_t} = \frac{1 - \beta}{1 - \alpha} \cdot \frac{\alpha}{\beta}, \tag{15}$$

$$h_t = W^{\frac{1}{1-\alpha}} \cdot g_t^{\frac{-\alpha}{1-\alpha}} \cdot \frac{L_t}{K_t} . \tag{16}$$

We solve (15) and (16) for g_t and h_t and substitute in

$$K_{t+1} - K_t = B_t = [(1 - g_t) L_t]^\beta [(1 - h_t) K_t]^{1-\beta}, \tag{17}$$

where $L_t = L_0(1 + \lambda)^t$ as before.
(17) is a non-linear differential equation, since g_t and h_t are functions of K_t, and it is not possible to find its general solution. Instead, we attempt a numerical solution for the following parameters and initial values of variables: $L_0 = 1$, $K_0 = 3$, $\lambda = 0.025$, $\alpha = 0.80$, $\beta = 0.50$, $W = 1.20$. Table 2 gives the values of variables by quinquennial years through 25 years.

TABLE 2

Optimal growth of a dualistic economy. $A_t = (g_t L_t)^{\alpha} (h_t K_t)^{1-\alpha}$; $B_t = [(1 - g_t) L_t]^{\beta} [(1 - h_t) K_t]^{1-\beta}$.
$K_0 = 3$, $L_0 = 1$, $L_t = L_0 (1 + \lambda)^t$, $\lambda = 0.025$, $\alpha = 0.80$, $\beta = 0.50$, $W = 1.20$.

t	K_t	L_t	g_t	h_t	$\Delta K_t = B_t$	A_t	$\frac{\partial A_t}{\partial g_t L_t}$	$\frac{\partial A_t}{\partial h_t K_t}$	$\frac{h_t K_t}{A_t}$	$\frac{\partial B_t}{\partial (1-g_t) L_t}$	$\frac{\partial B_t}{\partial (1-h_t) K_t}$	$\frac{(1-h_t) K_t}{B_t}$	$\frac{K_t}{Y_t}$	$\frac{\Delta K_t}{Y_t}$
0	3.00	1.00	0.98	0.91	0.08	1.20	0.98	0.09	2.28	1.69	0.15	3.39	2.35	0.06
5	3.42	1.13	0.98	0.91	0.09	1.36	0.98	0.09	2.29	1.69	0.15	3.39	2.36	0.06
10	3.92	1.28	0.97	0.90	0.11	1.54	0.99	0.09	2.31	1.69	0.15	3.38	2.38	0.07
15	4.54	1.45	0.97	0.89	0.14	1.74	0.99	0.09	2.33	1.70	0.15	3.40	2.41	0.07
20	5.34	1.64	0.97	0.88	0.18	1.97	0.99	0.08	2.38	1.71	0.15	3.43	2.48	0.08
25	6.45	1.85	0.96	0.85	0.25	2.23	1.00	0.08	2.46	1.76	0.14	3.52	2.58	0.10

TABLE 3

Balanced growth of a dualistic economy. $A_t = (g_t L_t)^\alpha (h_t K_t)^{1-\alpha}$; $B_t = [(1-g_t) L_t]^\beta [(1-h_t) K_t]^{1-\beta}$.
$K_0 = 3$, $L_0 = 1$, $L_t = L_0 (1+\lambda)^t$, $\lambda = 0.025$, $\alpha = 0.80$, $\beta = 0.50$, $W = 1.20$.

t	K_t	L_t	g_t	h_t	$\Delta K_t = B_t$	A_t	$\frac{\partial A_t}{\partial g_t L_t}$	$\frac{\partial A_t}{\partial h_t K_t}$	$\frac{h_t K_t}{A_t}$	$\frac{\partial B_t}{\partial (1-g_t) L_t}$	$\frac{\partial B_t}{\partial (1-h_t) K_t}$	$\frac{(1-h_t) K_t}{B_t}$	$\frac{K_t}{Y_t}$	$\frac{\Delta K_t}{Y_t}$
0	3.00	1.10	0.97	0.94	0.07	1.20	0.99	0.09	2.35	1.20	0.21	2.39	2.36	0.06
5	3.39	1.13	0.97	0.94	0.08	1.36	0.99	0.09	2.35	1.19	0.21	2.39	2.35	0.06
10	3.83	1.28	0.97	0.94	0.09	1.54	0.99	0.09	2.35	1.20	0.21	2.40	2.35	0.06
15	4.31	1.45	0.97	0.94	0.10	1.74	0.99	0.09	2.34	1.19	0.21	2.38	2.34	0.06
20	4.84	1.64	0.97	0.95	0.11	1.97	0.99	0.09	2.33	1.20	0.21	2.41	2.33	0.05
25	5.41	1.85	0.97	0.95	0.12	2.23	0.99	0.09	2.31	1.21	0.21	2.42	2.31	0.05

In order to make a comparison possible, we give in table 3 the values of the variables under the assumptions of balanced growth for the same boundary and parametric values. In table 2, the capital stock more than doubles in 25 years, while rate of savings increases from 6 to more than 10 per cent. Marginal productivity of labor in the agricultural sector is below constant average consumption, throughout the quarter century; in the industrial sector it is above the constant average consumption in the initial stages and increases in successive periods, though at a slow rate. Marginal productivity of capital in the agricultural sector is lower than in the industrial sector and decreases gradually in both sectors, as it should, since our initial values allow a higher rate of growth of capital than of labor.

Under the assumptions of balanced growth, the same initial values and the same values of parameters, capital stock is forced to increase at a lower rate, starting from 3 and rising to 5.4. in 25 years. Rate of savings decreases from 6 per cent to 5 per cent. Marginal productivity of labor in the agricultural sector is below average consumption in the initial stages and falls slightly over 25 years. Labor productivity in the industrial sector is, by assumption, equal to the wage-rate, apart from rounding errors.

In both tables 2 and 3, the capital–output ratio in each sector remains fairly stable, though it increases slightly in table 2 and decreases in table 3. This is due to the initial values and parameters assumed; for other sets of values it could decrease or increase at varying speeds.

7. The Commercialization Point

We have already described how the commercialization point is reached along a balanced growth path. If we now look at the commercialization point itself in terms of marginal productivity conditions as well as preceding consumption condition, we see that it is defined by the equations,

$$A_t = WL_t, \quad \frac{\partial B_t}{\partial(1 - g_t L_t)} = W = \frac{\partial A_t}{\partial g_t L_t}. \tag{18}$$

Equating the indicated partial derivatives of (7) and (8) to W and using the first equation of (18) we get

$$g_t = \alpha$$

$$\frac{h_t}{g_t} \cdot \frac{1 - g_t}{1 - h_t} = \left(\frac{W}{B}\right)^{\frac{1}{\beta - 1}} \cdot \left(\frac{W}{\alpha}\right)^{\frac{1}{1 - \alpha}}. \tag{19}$$

Eq. (19) shows that the proportion of labor remaining in the agricultural sector when the commercialization point is reached equals the production elasticity of labor in the agricultural sector, but that the proportion of capital going to the two sectors at this point depends upon the production elasticity of labor in the two sectors and the institutional wage-rate. This result, it will be noted, is independent of initial amounts of factors. In addition, we can find out the allocation of capital between the two sectors, a solution absent in the Ranis–Fei analysis. If $\alpha=0.8$, $\beta=0.50$, then $g_t=0.8$, and $h_t=0.82$ when $W=1.15$. This result can be checked from table 1, after allowing for the rounding involved. Table 4 gives the values of g and h at the commercialization point for some other values of α, β, and W. We could similarly work out the values of g and h, by eliminating W, in terms of the ratio of factors, i.e., K/L.

TABLE 4

$g=\alpha$	W	h		
		$\beta=0.45$	0.60	0.75
	1.05	0.524	0.559	0.572
0.55	1.10	0.529	0.556	0.552
	1.15	0.533	0.553	0.532
	1.20	0.538	0.550	0.514
	1.05	0.712	0.740	0.750
0.75	1.10	0.732	0.753	0.750
	1.15	0.751	0.765	0.750
	1.20	0.768	0.777	0.750
	1.05	0.832	0.851	0.858
0.85	1.10	0.862	0.874	0.872
	1.15	0.885	0.893	0.885
	1.20	0.905	0.908	0.896

A commercialization point can be derived from the above maximizing model of section 6, but under somewhat more realistic assumptions. We shall assume that only a proportion Φ of total wages is spent on the goods produced in the agricultural sector. Secondly, we shall assume that the commercialization point is defined not when the marginal productivity of labor in agriculture becomes exactly equal to the marginal productivity of labor in the industrial sector but when the ratio of the first to the second reaches a certain fraction Θ. This assumption seems realistic; thus not even in as mobile an economy as the United States is Θ equal to unity. Thirdly, we shall continue to assume that average wage is the same in the two sectors and equal to average consumption per worker, and that all of these magnitudes equal marginal labor productivity in industry. It should be noted that W is now a variable.

Under these assumptions, solution of the model involves maximization of (8), subject to:

$$A_t = \Phi W_t L_t \quad \text{and} \tag{20}$$

$$\frac{\partial A_t}{\partial g_t L_t} = \Theta W_t = \Theta \frac{\partial B_t}{\partial (1 - g_t) L_t}. \tag{21}$$

Solving the above we get

$$g_t = \left(\frac{\Phi}{\Theta}\right) \alpha \quad \text{and} \tag{22}$$

$$\frac{1 - \beta}{\beta} = \frac{\Theta (1 - h_t)(1 - \alpha) g_t + \Phi \alpha (1 - \beta) h_t}{\Theta (1 - g_t) \alpha h_t + \Phi \alpha (\beta - 1) h_t}. \tag{23}$$

The last equations show that g_t and h_t are constant and independent of the (initial and subsequent) amounts of the factors of production. The values of g and h can be easily obtained for various values of α, β, Θ and Φ.

8. Technological Progress in a Dualistic Economy

In recent years considerable theoretical work has been done on the questions of technological progress. We shall not enter here the discussion of contributions in this field, which has been mostly conjectural. However, we would like to mention that the theory to date is not far from what Professor J. Tinbergen established as far back as 1942 [6].

For this purpose, it may be interesting to see how the balanced growth model can be extended to allow for technological change. We shall use here what is known as factor-augmenting technological progress. This can be introduced in the production functions of our two sectors as follows:

$$A_t' = (g_t L_t \, e^{\rho_{LA}^t})^{\alpha} \, (h_t K_t \, e^{\rho_{KA}^t})^{1-\alpha}$$

$$B_t' = [(1 - g_t) L_t \, e^{\rho_{LB}^t}]^{\beta} \, [(1 - h_t) K_t \, e^{\rho_{KB}^t}]^{1-\beta}. \tag{24}$$

In (24) the exponentials attached to the factors of production in the two sectors are the coefficients of factor-augmentation. In the form of the Cobb–Douglas we are using here, factor augmentation can be represented in each equation by attaching exponentials to the factor inputs as in (24). For the sake of simplicity we confine our attention to capital-augmenting technological progress only, since it is commonly believed that this is more relevant in the context of underdeveloped countries with abundant supply of labor force [1]. Our approach will be to trace the growth of the dualistic economy, first under the assumption that capital-augmenting technological progress takes place in the agricultural sector only, and second under the assumption that equivalent progress takes place in the industrial sector only. This will allow for us to make comparisons between the two cases in order to draw some broad conclusions. We do this by considering a balanced growth path till the commercialization point is reached, and after that by allowing the wage-rate to equal marginal productivity of labor in both sectors.

In the first case, growth is traced on the basis of

$$A_t' = (g_t L_t)^\alpha \, (h_t K_t \, e^{\rho t})^{1-\alpha} = W L_t \quad \text{and}$$
$$\frac{\partial B_t}{\partial (1-g_t) \, L_t} = \beta \, [(1-g_t) \, L_t]^{\beta-1} \, [(1-h_t) \, K_t]^{1-\beta} = W. \tag{25}$$

In the second case, growth is traced according to:

$$A_t = (g_t L_t)^\alpha \, (h_t K_t)^{1-\alpha} = W L_t, \quad \text{and}$$
$$\frac{\partial B_t'}{\partial (1-g_t) \, L_t} = \beta \, [(1-g_t) \, L_t]^{\beta-1} \, [(1-h_t) \, K_t \, e^{\rho t}]^{1-\beta} = W. \tag{26}$$

Table 5 summarizes the growth of capital stock for the two cases over a 50-year period, using the following initial and parametric values: $L_0 = 1$, $K_0 = 3$, $\lambda = 0.025$, $\alpha = 0.80$, $\beta = 0.50$, $\rho = 0.01$, $W = 1.17$. The value of W has been reduced to reach the commercialization point well within 50 years.

It is seen that when capital-augmenting technical progress takes place in the agricultural sector, total capital stock and wages both grow at a higher rate than when such progress is concentrated in the industrial sector. This result is partly obvious, for the proportion of the stock of capital in the agricultural sector is higher than that in the industrial sector. However, this result is obtained even when the production elasticity of capital in the industrial sector is $2\frac{1}{2}$ times that in the agricultural sector. The table shows

TABLE 5

Year	First case				Second case			
	K	g	h	W	K	g	h	W
0	3.000				3.000			
5	3.502	0.932	0.882	1.17	3.727	0.930	0.889	1.17
10	4.925	0.886	0.837	1.17	4.845	0.903	0.873	1.17
15	6.539	0.843	0.815	1.17	6.190	0.873	0.862	1.17
20	9.697	0.800	0.812	1.17	9.355	0.818	0.857	1.17
25	13.818	0.800	0.828	1.24	13.318	0.800	0.874	1.20
30	18.748	0.800	0.845	1.32	18.106	0.800	0.891	1.25
35	24.589	0.800	0.854	1.38	23.728	0.800	0.905	1.30
40	32.975	0.800	0.865	1.44	28.891	0.800	0.914	1.33
45	41.280	0.800	0.868	1.49	37.879	0.800	0.924	1.36
50	50.964	0.800	0.872	1.53	46.653	0.800	0.931	1.39

that the commercialization point is reached in the 19th year in the first case and the 24th year in the second case. Wages and proportion of capital allocated to agriculture rises thereafter.

8. Concluding Remarks

This paper has dealt with a few growth aspects of dualistic economies under certain simplifying assumptions. Cobb–Douglas production functions of the ordinary type have been used throughout. Owing to the difficulty of expressing the variables to be solved as functions of boundary and parametric values, it has been necessary to find numerical solutions. These give a rough idea of the movement of the central variables and are not out of line with Professor Tinbergen's attitude 'to let the figures speak'. Perhaps by adapting the production functions, general solutions could have been obtained. This has not been attempted because it was felt that any further simplification of the production functions would deprive them completely of realistic values. We have used the same production elasticities everywhere except in section 7, but could readily have varied these by using any values between 0 and 1. Even the strict linear-homogeneity of the functions is not necessary for most of the above analysis. The allocation of resources and hence everything else in the models covered depend upon the production functions, average consumption per worker and the availability of resources in the initial period. The more precise and accurate estimates we have of these to start with and the more accurate information we have about the possible variations in the production functions and the size and per capita consumption of workers over time, the more reliable will be the results that have been arrived at.

References

[1] J. C. H. FEI and G. RANIS, 'Innovational Intensity and Factor Bias in the Theory of Growth', *International Economic Review*, Vol. 5, No. 2, May 1965, pp. 181–198.

[2] RYUTARO KOMIYA, 'A Note on Professor Mahalanobis' Model of Indian Economic Planning', *Review of Economics and Statistics*, Vol. XLI, February 1959, No. 1, pp. 29–35.

[3] P. C. MAHALANOBIS, 'Some Observations on the Process of Growth of National Income', *Sankhya*, Vol. XIV, December 1955, pp. 3–62.

[4] H. T. OSHIMA, 'Underemployment in Backward Economies – An Empirical Comment', *Journal of Political Economy*, Vol. LXVI, No. 3, June 1958.

[5] G. RANIS and H. C. FEI, *Development of the Labor Surplus Economy, Theory and Policy*, Richard D. Irwin, Inc., Homewood, Ill., 1964.

[6] J. TINBERGEN, *Zur Theorie der langfristigen Wirtschaftensentwicklung*, Weltwirtschaftliches Archiv, 55. Band (1942 1), pp. 511–549.

SOME EXERCISES WITH A SIMPLE MODEL FOR WORLD DEVELOPMENT PLANNING

B. HERMAN, L. B. M. MENNES and J. G. WAARDENBURG*)

1. Introduction

Now that we are nearing the end of the first Development Decade it becomes increasingly clear that we are in need of an indicative world development plan for the seventies, the second Development Decade. The arguments in favour of such a plan have been summarized by Professor Tinbergen as follows [6]:

(a) to avoid duplication in national planning;
(b) to supply market analysis materials for business;
(c) to contribute to the establishment of an international order;
(d) to specify the aims of international economic policies;
(e) to exert pressure on the developed countries.

Moreover the Secretary-General of the United Nations has been requested by the General Assembly to elaborate a preliminary framework of international development strategy for the 1970's which should concentrate on the elaboration of specific goals and targets for individual sectors and components.

In preparing this international development strategy a central role is played by the U.N. Centre for Development Planning, Projections and Policies. A number of specialized agencies like F.A.O., U.N.C.T.A.D., I.B.R.D., U.N.I.D.O., etc. will make contributions by providing partial plans at the sectoral level.

Partial plans at geographical level will be worked out by the U.N. Regional

*) The authors wish to express their sincere gratitude to Messrs. A. Kunstman M.A. and A. S. Louter of the Econometric Institute who have programmed and solved a number of the numerical exercises presented in this paper. Any errors are of course completely our responsibility.

Commissions. All these partial plans have to be integrated into a consistent world development plan by the Centre for Development Planning, Projections and Policies which for this purpose is assisted by a group of eighteen experts, the U.N. Committee for Development Planning whose chairman is Professor Tinbergen.

Evidently, drawing up such a world development plan involves a great number of technical and organizational problems which will be the topic of many discussions still to come. This article tries to make a small contribution to these discussions by presenting a simple model for world planning.

Essentially the main problem is to determine what products should be produced where and in what amounts. Account should be taken of at least three features:

(a) differences in production opportunities or production costs between different places;
(b) differences in transportability or transport costs between different products;
(c) different interests of different areas, to be taken account of as a reflection of a social policy.

The model to be presented here takes account of these features by

a) the introduction of different cost coefficients of the sectors at different places;
b) the distinction of different categories of mobility of the products and the corresponding sectors;
c) the introduction of income increase targets for the spatial units distinguished.

This type of model is dealt with elsewhere[1]) together with a discussion of its assumptions and more general formulations. The present model can be considered to be an extension of the models presented there, namely a closed economy model with a fourth order spatial subdivision and transportation costs implicit.

Here we will only elucidate the introduction of mobility classes of products and their corresponding sectors. Sectors are distinguished according to the mobility of their products as world, continental, national or regional sectors. For instance, regional sectors are those sectors of which the products can

---

[1]) In Mennes, Tinbergen and Waardenburg [4]. Cf. also Isard [2] and Leontief [3].

move (freely) within regions, but not at all from one region to another. To these four mobility categories correspond four types of spatial units hierarchically ordered: a world subdivided into continents, continents subdivided into countries and countries subdivided into regions. Within each spatial unit production of commodities of a corresponding mobility class must equal demand. For instance, within a region production of regional products must equal demand for them. Within a spatial unit a certain specialization is therefore possible only in sectors with a degree of mobility of their products higher than that corresponding to the spatial unit considered, e.g. countries can only specialize with regard to continental or world sectors. Classifying the sectors in this way we may neglect – as a first approximation – explicit transportation costs in determining the optimal spatial distribution of the production increases.

The model is an optimization model in the sense that the income (increase) targets for the lowest order spatial units (regions) are to be met at minimum total costs for the world at large. A different possible formulation of the problem of world planning will be mentioned at the end of this paper. The plan of the following sections of this paper is as follows. First, in section 2, a small example of the model is presented. While such a model could, in principle, be solved by a standard linear programming method, e.g. the simplex method, there are a few reasons against simply advocating such a procedure. If such a model were to be a realistic one, it might be so large as to make it difficult to solve it automatically even for large computers. In addition, with such a procedure the insight into the structure of the problem might get lost and politicians would have to trust the computer blindly. Finally it would be attractive, if it were possible, to build up an institutional or organizational structure having logical similarities with the solution method, thus structuring both the process of data collection and that of decision making.

For all these reasons we will introduce in sections 3 and 4 two simplified approximative solution methods which take account of some of these points. In section 5 the results of these approximative solution methods will be discussed and compared with each other together with the optimal solution. This is done with regard to (a) whether the sectors which are allocated to each spatial unit are the same in each solution; (b) the costs of the different solutions; (c) their implications from an organizational point of view.

The capital movements possibly implied by the optimal solution will also be discussed: section 6. Finally, section 7 will deal with an alternative formulation of the problem, some possible refinements, and will give a tentative conclusion.

2. The Model

In this section we will introduce our simplified example together with the numerical data. In it the world is divided into two continents; each continent consists of two countries and each country of two regions. The model distinguishes ten sectors: two regional, two national, three continental, and three world sectors. We assume the same input–output table for all regions.

It should be emphasized that this model is not only highly simplified, but also that it is a framework model in the sense that for a realistic application, however simplified, it should be refined. The most obvious refinement necessary is to add upper bounds to certain variables or groups of variables in order to avoid technically or economically infeasible rates of growth for certain sectors in certain regions or groups of regions. In this article we abstract, however, from such refinements necessary in practice. In addition, it should be noted that after the model has been solved the corresponding trade flows between the regions can be determined if for all products the increases in demand within each region are also known. They can even be determined optimally if transport costs in the widest sense per unit of each product transported between the regions are also known. All variables refer to increases in production over the planning period and are assumed to be non-negative.[2]) As the model is meant to be used for medium or long-term planning, we may assume equilibrium situations in the initial and final years so that e.g. the phenomenon of unused capacities can be neglected.

Increases in demand for investment goods are included in increases in final demand, which are proportional to increases in income, with the same demand coefficients in each region. Prices of the products are assumed to be constant and equal to 1. The costs of expanding a sector in a region are assumed to be proportional to the expansion. The total costs of expanding production are minimized, subject to appropriate balance equations for the several sectors and definition equations for the income increases (the targets) of the regions.

---

[2]) If one wants to allow for a possible decrease of a sector in a region, one could substitute for the corresponding variable ${}^r\tilde{x}^h - {}^r\bar{x}^h = {}^r x^h$, in which ${}^r\tilde{x}^h$ is the new non-negative variable, and ${}^r\bar{x}^h$ the maximum acceptable decrease of ${}^r x^h$.

In symbols the model is as follows:
Minimize

$$\sum_{r=1}^{8} \sum_{h=1}^{10} {}^{r}c^{h} \cdot {}^{r}x^{h} \tag{1}$$

subject to:

$$\sum_{h'=1}^{10} \varphi^{hh'} \cdot {}^{r}x^{h'} + \gamma^{h} \cdot {}^{r}y = {}^{r}x^{h} \qquad (h = 1, 2;\ r = 1, \ldots, 8) \tag{2}$$

(2 × 8 balance equations for the regional sectors),

$$\sum_{h'=1}^{10} \varphi^{hh'} ({}^{r}x^{h'} + {}^{r+1}x^{h'}) + \gamma^{h} ({}^{r}y + {}^{r+1}y) = {}^{r}x^{h} + {}^{r+1}x^{h} \qquad (h = 3, 4;\ r = 1, 3, 5, 7) \tag{3}$$

(2 × 4 balance equations for the national sectors),

$$\sum_{h'=1}^{10} \varphi^{hh'} ({}^{r}x^{h'} + \cdots + {}^{r+3}x^{h'}) + \gamma^{h} ({}^{r}y + \cdots + {}^{r+3}y) = {}^{r}x^{h} + \cdots + {}^{r+3}x^{h} \qquad (h = 5, 6, 7;\ r = 1, 5) \tag{4}$$

(3 × 2 balance equations for the continental sectors),

$$\sum_{h'=1}^{10} \varphi^{hh'} ({}^{1}x^{h'} + \cdots + {}^{8}x^{h'}) + \gamma^{h} ({}^{1}y + \cdots + {}^{8}y) = {}^{1}x^{h} + \cdots + {}^{8}x^{h} \qquad (h = 8, 9, 10) \tag{5}$$

(3 × 1 balance equations for the world sectors),

$$\sum_{h=1}^{10} \varphi^{oh} \cdot {}^{r}x^{h} = {}^{r}y \qquad (r = 1, \ldots, 8) \tag{6}$$

8 definition equations for the regional income increases.

$${}^{r}x^{h} \geqslant 0 \tag{7}$$

where

${}^{r}x^{h}$ = production increase of sector h in region r;
${}^{r}y$ = income increase target for region r;
γ^{h} = incremental final demand coefficient for sector h (the same in all regions);
$\varphi^{hh'}$ = input–output coefficients for deliveries from sector h to sector h';
${}^{r}c^{h}$ = total costs per unit of production increase ${}^{r}x^{h}$;

$$\varphi^{oh'} = 1 - \sum_{h=1}^{10} \varphi^{hh'} = \text{value added coefficient of sector } h'.$$

The model contains 8×10 variables which have to satisfy $16+8+6+3+8-1 = 40$ equations (one of the above restrictions is redundant).

Now we turn to the numerical data. They are all fictitious, but most of them display a remarkable similarity with reality. The model is meant to represent a world development planning model for the period 1970–1980. We assume world population in 1970 to be equal to 2,800 million people equally spread over the eight regions so that in each region 350 million people are living. The rate of growth of population is assumed to be the same everywhere, so that it can be neglected in the remainder of our exercise. Using per capita income data total income for each region has been estimated. Next we have set an income target for the poorest region's (region 1) income equal to an annual rate of growth of 7 per cent. This results in a doubling of income in ten years. The richer regions are assumed to grow more slowly: the richest region (region 8) by 4 per cent annually. The other regions show growth rates between 4 and 7 per cent: the higher the initial income, the lower the planned growth rate. Population and income data are summarized in table 1; the last column gives the data used directly in the model.

TABLE 1

Population, per capita income, total income, and planned income increase by region[a]).

Region	Population in mln. (1970)	Per capita income in U.S.$ (1970)	Total income in bln. U.S.$ (1970)	Income increase in bln. U.S.$ (1970–1980)
1	350	80	28.000	28.000
2	350	130	45.500	41.650
3	350	211	73.850	61.950
4	350	344	120.400	91.000
5	350	559	195.650	133.700
6	350	908	317.800	194.950
7	350	1,477	516.950	281.400
8	350	2,400	840.000	402.850

[a]) The data for 1970 are similar to those of [9].

The second set of numerical data is related to the sector classification. This classification has been derived from the Japanese 1951 input–output table. The 182 branches of this table have been condensed into the following ten sectors (table 2).

The corresponding input–output table and final demand coefficients can be found in the Appendix.

The third set of data are the cost coefficients. Obviously, these are rough estimates based on capital coefficients, value added–output ratios, and assumed shadow prices for capital and labour. They are summarized in table 3.

TABLE 2

Sector classification.

Sectors[a])		Activities
1	(R_1)	Trade, finance, real estate
2	(R_2)	Construction and maintenance
3	(N_1)	Transport and communication
4	(N_2)	Electricity and manufactured gas
5	(C_1)	Iron ore, non-ferrous metallic ores, non-metallic mineral ores
6	(C_2)	Coal and lignite, crude petroleum, natural gas, coal products
7	(C_3)	Agriculture, fishing, forestry, processed food
8	(W_1)	Non-metallic mineral products, iron and steel, non-ferrous metallic products, machinery and equipment, miscellaneous manufacturing
9	(W_2)	Chemicals and petrochemicals
10	(W_3)	Textiles, lumber, paper, rubber, and leather

[a]) The symbols between brackets indicate whether the sectors are regional (R), national (N), continental (C) or world sectors (W).

TABLE 3

Cost coefficients by sector and by region.

Sectors	Regions							
	1	2	3	4	5	6	7	8
1	0.250	0.245	0.240	0.235	0.230	0.225	0.220	0.215
2	0.160	0.160	0.160	0.160	0.160	0.160	0.160	0.160
3	0.290	0.285	0.280	0.275	0.270	0.265	0.260	0.255
4	0.350	0.345	0.340	0.335	0.330	0.325	0.320	0.315
5	0.150	0.155	0.160	0.165	0.170	0.175	0.180	0.185
6	0.200	0.205	0.210	0.215	0.220	0.225	0.230	0.235
7	0.125	0.135	0.145	0.155	0.165	0.175	0.185	0.195
8	0.095	0.090	0.085	0.080	0.075	0.070	0.065	0.060
9	0.135	0.130	0.125	0.120	0.115	0.110	0.105	0.100
10	0.075	0.080	0.085	0.090	0.095	0.100	0.105	0.110

In section 1 we have given already some reasons why we will not solve this model simply by one or another standard method of linear programming. Instead we will present in the next two sections two simplified solution methods, based on a few simplifying assumptions.

3. The Two-Stage Solution Method

One of the main difficulties in solving the model simultaneously by e.g. the simplex method is that at the same time account must be taken of three elements: the vertical interdependence between sectors, which arises from the interindustrial relationships, the horizontal interdependence between the sectors, which arises from the requirement that the regional income increase targets should be attained, and the costs which must be minimized. The simplification involved in the two solution methods is based on partly disentangling these elements by decomposing the problem into a number of problems, each of which is considerably simpler than the original problem. The cost of these simplifications is that the optimal solution is only approximately obtained as will be discussed in section 5.

The first simplified approximative solution method, which we call the *two-stage* solution method, is based on the assumption that for each sector's products the increases in intermediate, and, consequently, total demand in the largest spatial units within which the product is freely mobile, are proportional to the increases in income of those spatial units; in other words, that these increases in intermediate demand are independent of which particular sectors are expanded in those spatial units.[3]) The great simplification resulting from this assumption is that interindustry relations need only be taken into account at world level in a relatively simple aggregated problem in order to determine for each sector its demand and corresponding production increase for the world as a whole, the first problem.

The remaining second problem, namely to distribute these production increase totals over the regions in order to satisfy the regional income targets at minimum costs, turns out to be a simple classical transportation or Hitchcock problem, soluble by hand by means of the *transportation* or uv-method.[4]) For, according to the assumption just made, the increases in

[3]) This assumption is also used in Tinbergen [5].

[4]) See e.g. Dantzig [1], chapter 14. This solution method is indeed extremely simple in comparison with general linear programming solution methods and can be learned easily, without further knowledge of linear programming.

production (or demand) in the spatial units at appropriate levels can be calculated by distributing the corresponding increases in the world over these spatial units in proportion to the income increases in them; these production (or demand) increases should be expressed in value added terms, in the same way as the variables of the second problem.

The first problem can be expressed algebraically as follows: determine the x^h which satisfy

$$\sum_{h'=1} \varphi^{hh'} \cdot x^{h'} + \gamma^h \cdot y = x^h \qquad (h = 1, \ldots, 10) \qquad (8)$$

in which x^h is the increase in production of sector h in the world as a whole, and y is the increase in world income.

The solution of the first problem, expressed both in output and value added terms, is given in table 4.

TABLE 4

Total increase in world production (x^h) and income (y^h) per sector in bln. U.S.$.

Sec-tors	1	2	3	4	5	6	7	8	9	10
x^h	736.733	126.288	136.451	38.959	35.817	93.997	749.231	494.400	172.879	442.256
y^h	389.732	40.286	75.867	14.025	20.774	42.675	427.811	86.026	43.220	95.085

The second problem can be expressed in tabular form as in table 5.

The problem represented by table 5, is to find the non-negative values of the variables ${}^ry^h$ in such a way that they add up row-wise to the totals in the last column, and column-wise, together with the values of the regional sectors' variables, to the totals in the last row, and do so at minimum total costs expressed as

$$\sum_{r=1}^{8} \sum_{h=1}^{10} {}^r\tilde{c}^h \cdot {}^ry^h$$

in which ${}^r\tilde{c}^h$ are the cost coefficients which can be derived from table 3, by multiplying each cost figure ${}^rc^h$ given there by $1/\varphi^{oh}$.

The solution of the second problem computed by means of the uv-method is shown in section 5, table 7, where it is called solution I. As in all other solutions the variables are in terms of value added.

TABLE 5

Representation of the variables and data of the second (Hitchcock) problem in bln. U.S.$[a, b]).

Sectors	Regions								Sectoral production increases[c])
	1	2	3	4	5	6	7	8	
1 (R_1)	8,832	13.138	19.542	28.706	42.177	61.496	88.765	127.076	389.731
2 (R_2)	0.913	1.358	2.020	2.967	4.360	6.357	9.175	13.136	40.286
3 (N_1)	×	×							4.277
			×	×					9.392
					×	×			20.181
							×	×	42.017
4 (N_2)	×	×							0.791
			×	×					1.736
					×	×			3.731
							×	×	7.767
5 (C_1)	×	×	×	×					3.743
					×	×	×	×	17.031
6 (C_2)	×	×	×	×					7.689
					×	×	×	×	34.986
7 (C_3)	×	×	×	×					77.079
					×	×	×	×	350.733
8 (W_1)	×	×	×	×	×	×	×	×	86.026
9 (W_2)	×	×	×	×	×	×	×	×	43.220
10 (W_3)	×	×	×	×	×	×	×	×	95.085
Regional income increases	28.000	41.650	61.950	91.000	133.700	194.950	281.400	402.850	Total: 1,235.870

[a]) The cells with × indicate the variables ${}^r y^h$, $r = 1, \ldots, 8$; $h = 1, \ldots, 10$, which represent the production increases measured in value added terms of sector h in region r. The variables for regional sectors are left out of the table, as they are determined already by the given increase in demand for their products in each region and do not play any further role; their numerical values are given in the first two rows of the table, however.

[b]) In this and further tables figures may not add up precisely to the totals because of rounding.

[c]) The sectoral production (demand) increases in the appropriate spatial units in value added terms.

The number of positive variables in solution I of table 8 equals the number of positive variables which could be expected to appear in the optimal solution of the original problem, as the original and the second problem have the same number of restrictions. However, solution I in table 8 might not have the same variables with positive values as the optimal solution, nor need the given solution, if converted into output terms, be a feasible solution of the original problem at all, as the production increases might not balance with the increases in final and intermediate demand at lower than world level. In other words, the simplifying assumption made may not be correct. In order to find this out one could simply confront the production increases of the two-stage solution with the demand increases following from eqs. (2)–(4). Instead, however, we will compute the solution of the equations (2)–(6), after setting the same 40 variables equal to zero as in the two-stage solution, and will call this the corresponding consistent solution. Consistent is used here only in the sense that the input–output relations are now taken account of. This corresponding consistent solution, again in terms of value added, is also given in section 5, table 8 and is called solution II.

The comparison of the two-stage solution with its corresponding consistent solution shows that the assumption made does not give a good approximation of reality, as represented by this problem. The main difficulty involved is that agriculture (sector 7) requires relatively small inputs from regional sector 1, and as agriculture is a large sector, its figures in the solution are large. Therefore, the actual increase in intermediate demand for sector 1 products in a region depends heavily on whether agriculture is expanded in that region or not. If agriculture is increased considerably in a region, as in region 7, the increase of sector 1 is much lower in the corresponding consistent solution than in the two-stage solution, which has to be compensated for, mainly by an even larger increase in agricultural production in that region, at least if one retains the same 40 variables as possibly positive in the corresponding consistent solution.

However, in a more realistic model with upper bounds (and in some cases also lower bounds) for the variables, which would prevent increases of certain sectors in certain regions unacceptably high on technical or economic grounds and which would lead to less specialization of the regions especially with regard to the world and continental sectors, the same assumption would yield more satisfactory results.

In the example presented here, the corresponding consistent solution even turns out to be infeasible – sector 7 in region 8 shows a negative value –, which seems at first sight to be a very bad result. However, looking at it from another point of view, neither the two-stage solution nor the corresponding consistent solution is useless. If we want to find the optimal solution of the original problem, the essential computational problem is to find the optimal basis, that is, the group of variables which are positive in the optimal solution. It may turn out that the basis of the two-stage solution, although being non-feasible, actually differs very little from the optimal basis, which anyway must be feasible. If this is so, the basis of the two-stage solution could usefully be employed as a starting basis for the solution of the original problem by means of one or another more complicated standard method. Then the relatively simple calculations of the two-stage solution method may make the latter a useful method in order to find a good starting basis for the more complicated method. The comparison with the optimal solution will be made in section 5.

4. The Hierarchical Method

The second approximative or hierarchical method for solving our problem is again based on ideas used by Tinbergen, this time when discussing world planning [8] and developing his semi-input–output method [7]. One idea is that only the spatial allocation of production increases of world sectors needs to be done at world level; the other idea is that in determining comparative advantages between spatial units with regard to a sector's expansion of production, account should be taken of the complementary expansion of production in sectors whose products cannot be imported from other spatial units.

These ideas lead to the following approximation method which consists of four rounds. In the first round the increases in production of the world sectors in the world as a whole are allocated to the two continents; in the second round the resulting increases in production of the world and continental sectors in each continent are allocated to the two constituent countries of each continent; in the third round the resulting increases in production of the national, continental and world sectors in each country are allocated to the two regions into which it is divided; finally in the fourth round the resulting increases of production of the regional sectors in each region are also calculated. In the first three rounds (before the allocation problems are solved), the whole bunch of increases in sectors with a smaller mobility of their products, complementary to a unit increase of each sector to be allocated, is calculated, including the corresponding income increase and costs of each such bunch. In this case complementary increases are considered to comprise all increases in production necessary to meet the increase both in intermediate and final demand due to the production of the bunch. Thus starting from the spatial unit of highest order, within a spatial unit of higher order the corresponding bunches are distributed between the two spatial units of lower order of which it consists.

The allocation of the sectors (or bunches) in each round is done in such a way that the calculated total production increases in the relevant sectors expressed in value added terms are attained in both spatial units of lower order taken together, that the income increases of the bunches allocated to each spatial unit add up to each spatial unit's income increase target and that the increase in production costs of all bunches together is minimized. In calculating the costs of a bunch it is assumed that for each sector its smallest cost coefficient within a spatial unit is representative for its cost coefficient in the bunch. For instance, when calculating the costs of a bunch corresponding to a world sector in the first continent, the cost coefficient of continental sector C_1 is taken to be equal to the smallest cost coefficient of that sector C_1 within that first continent.

The typical problem which appears once in the first round, twice in the second round, and four times in the third round can be represented mathematically, in matrix notation as follows. At each round we distinguish between the mobile sectors (e.g. in the second round, the world and continental sectors) indicated by the index m to be allocated over the two spatial units indicated by the index $\bar{r}$ ($\bar{r}=1{,}2$) and the immobile sectors (e.g. in the second round the national and regional sectors) indicated by the index i.
Minimize

$$\sum_{\bar{r}=1}^{2} [\{{}^{\bar{r}}c^{i}_{\min}\}\,\{{}^{\bar{r}}x^{i}\} + \{{}^{\bar{r}}c^{m}_{\min}\}\,\{{}^{\bar{r}}x^{m}\}] \tag{9}$$

subject to

$$(A_{II})\,\{{}^{\bar{r}}x^{i}\} + (A_{IM})\,\{{}^{\bar{r}}x^{m}\} + \{y^{i}\}\,{}^{\bar{r}}y = \{{}^{\bar{r}}x^{i}\} \qquad (\bar{r}=1,2) \tag{10}$$

(the balance equations for the immobile sectors)

$$\sum_{\bar{r}=1}^{2} \{^{\bar{r}}x^{m}\} = \{x^{m}_{\text{tot}}\} \tag{11}$$

(a kind of balance equations for the mobile sectors)

$$\{\varphi_{oi}\}\{^{\bar{r}}x^{i}\} + \{\varphi_{om}\}\{^{\bar{r}}x^{m}\} = {}^{\bar{r}}y \qquad (\bar{r} = 1, 2) \tag{12}$$

(the equations defining income increases)

$$^{\bar{r}}x_{i}, {}^{\bar{r}}x_{m} \geqslant 0 \qquad \bar{r} = 1, 2;\ i = 1, \ldots, H_{i};\ m = H_{i} + 1, \ldots, 10 \tag{13}$$

The explanation of the symbols is as follows:

H_i : the number of immobile sectors.

$\{^{\bar{r}}x^{i}\}$ and $\{^{\bar{r}}x^{m}\}$, respectively: the $H_i \times 1$ and $(10-H_i)\times 1$, respectively vectors of production increases of the immobile and mobile sectors respectively in spatial unit $\bar{r}$.

$\{x^{m}_{\text{tot}}\}$: the $(10-H_i)\times 1$ vector of production increases in the mobile sectors in both spatial units of lower order together.

$\{^{\bar{r}}c^{i}_{\text{min}}\}$ and $\{^{\bar{r}}c^{m}_{\text{min}}\}$, respectively: the $1\times H_i$ and $1\times(10-H_i)$, respectively vectors of smallest cost coefficients of the sector concerned in spatial unit $\bar{r}$.

(A_{II}) : the $H_i \times H_i$ matrix of technical coefficients for the inputs of immobile sectors into immobile sectors.

(A_{IM}) : the $H_i \times (10-H_i)$ matrix of technical coefficients for the inputs of immobile sectors into mobile sectors.

$\{\gamma^{i}\}$: the $H_i \times 1$ vector of demand increase coefficients of the immobile sectors.

$\{\varphi_{oi}\}$ and $\{\varphi_{om}\}$, respectively: the $1\times H_i$ and $1\times(10-H_i)$, respectively vectors of value added coefficients of the immobile and mobile sectors, respectively.

$^{\bar{r}}y$: the income increase of spatial unit $\bar{r}$.

In determining the bunches, as defined above, which should relate values for the immobile sectors in a spatial unit to the variables $(^{\bar{r}}x^{m})$ of each mobile sector in the same spatial unit, and in calculating the income of the bunches per unit increase of the $^{\bar{r}}x^{m}$, one should express both the $^{\bar{r}}x^{i}$ and the $^{\bar{r}}y$ in terms of the $^{\bar{r}}x^{m}$. This can be done, using (10) and (12), which yields the expressions (14) and (15).

$$^{\bar{r}}y = \sum_{m=H_i+1}^{10} \bar{\varphi}_{om}\, {}^{\bar{r}}x^{m} \qquad (\bar{r} = 1, 2) \tag{14}$$

where

$$\bar{\varphi}_{om} = \frac{\{\varphi_{oi}\} \{I - A_{II}\}^{-1} (A_{IM})_m + \varphi_{om}}{1 - \{\varphi_{oi}\} \{I - A_{II}\}^{-1} \{\gamma^i\}} \qquad (m = H_i + 1, \ldots, 10)$$

in which $(A_{IM})_m$ indicates the column of (A_{IM}) corresponding to the variable ${}^{\bar{r}}x^m$, and

$$\{{}^{\bar{r}}x^i\} = \sum_{m=H_i+1}^{10} \{b^i_m\} \, {}^{\bar{r}}x^m \qquad (\bar{r} = 1, 2) \qquad (15)$$

where

$$\{b^i_m\} = (I - A_{II})^{-1} (A_{IM})_m + (I - A_{II})^{-1} \{\gamma^i\} \, \bar{\varphi}_{om},$$

$(A_{IM})_m$ again indicating the column of (A_{IM}) corresponding to the variable ${}^{\bar{r}}x^m$. In these formulas $\bar{\varphi}_{om}$ indicates the total income increase created by the bunch corresponding to sector m per unit of output increase of sector m and $\{b^i_m\}$ is the vector of production increases of the immobile sectors in the bunch corresponding to sector m, per unit of output increase of sector m.

The expression for $\bar{\varphi}_{om}$ can be made intuitively clear as follows. If production in sector m increases by one unit, it creates an income increase of φ_{om} units. The increase in intermediate demand for immobile products resulting from it makes it necessary for the immobile sectors to increase by $\{(I - A_{II})^{-1} (A_{IM})_m\}$ units as they must also satisfy their own increases in intermediate demand for immobile products, creating in this way an income increase of $\{\varphi_{oi}\} \{(I - A_{II})^{-1} (A_{IM})_m\} = p - \varphi_{om}$ units. These initial income increases $(=p)$ together, however, make final demand for immobile products increase by $\{\gamma^i\}p$, thus leading to a production increase of the immobile sectors by $(I - A_{II})^{-1} \{\gamma^i\}p$ which yields an initially additional income increase of $\{\varphi_{oi}\} (I - A_{II})^{-1} \{\gamma^i\}p = qp$ units. This additional income increase creates, however, a further increase in final demand for immobile products of $\{\gamma^i\} qp$ units, leading to a production increase of $(I - A_{II})^{-1} \{\gamma^i\} qp$ units, which gives a further additional income increase of $\{\varphi_{oi}\} (I - A_{II})^{-1} \{\gamma^i\} qp = q^2 p$ units. The reasoning can go on ad infinitum. Therefore, the total additional income increases add up to $(q + q^2 + q^3 + \cdots)p = [q/(1-q)]p$ units, and the total income increase of the bunch per unit of output increase of sector m is indeed $\bar{\varphi}_{om} = p + [q/(1-q)]p = p/(1-q)$ units.

The expression $\{b^i_m\}$ for the production increases of the immobile sectors per unit of output increase of sector m can be made intuitively clear as follows. The first term $(I - A_{II})^{-1} (A_{IM})_m$ gives the production increases necessary to meet the increase in intermediate demand for immobile products coming from sector m and consequently from the immobile sectors themselves, as a result of that. The second term represents the production increases necessary to meet the increases in final demand and the consequent increases in intermediate demand for immobile products.

The costs of each bunch per unit increase of its corresponding mobile sector (${}^{\bar{r}}\bar{c}^m$) can easily be calculated for each of the two spatial units of lower order separately by multiplying each production increase figure of the bunch by its corresponding cost coefficient in (9):

$$ {}^{\bar{r}}\bar{c}^m = \sum_{i=1}^{H_1} {}^{\bar{r}}c^h_{\min} \cdot b^i_m + {}^{r}c^m_{\min} \qquad (\bar{r} = 1, 2; m = H_i + 1, \ldots, 10) \qquad (16) $$

It remains to be discussed how the $\{x^m_{\text{tot}}\}$ in (11) are determined. In the first round one can either take them from the solution of (8) or calculate them from the three balance equations for the world sectors:

$$ \{\varphi_{oi}\} \left[\sum_{\bar{r}=1}^{r} \{{}^{\bar{r}}x^i\} \right] + (I - A_{MM}) \{x^m_t\} = \{\gamma^m\} \, y \, (m = H_i + 1, \ldots, 10) \quad (17) $$

in which A_{MM} indicates the matrix of technical coefficients for inputs from the mobile sectors into the mobile sectors, and using (15) to substitute for the $\{{}^{\bar{r}}x^i\}$. In the second and third round the $\{x^m_{\text{tot}}\}$ comprise terms of sectors which were also considered mobile in the previous round and terms of sectors which were considered immobile in the previous round. The values for these first terms are the direct results of the allocation problem expressed in output terms, while those for the other terms can be calculated with the aid of (15) from this result.

Using (14)–(16) the allocation problem (9)–(13) can be converted into the following problem.

Minimize

$$ \sum_{\bar{r}=1}^{2} \sum_{m=H_i+1}^{10} {}^{\bar{r}}\bar{c}^m \cdot {}^{\bar{r}}x^m \qquad \text{(replacing (9))} \qquad (18) $$

subject to

$$ \sum_{\bar{r}=1}^{2} {}^{\bar{r}}x^m = x^m_{\text{tot}} \qquad (m = H_i + 1, \ldots, 10) \text{ (the same as (11))} \qquad (19) $$

$$ \sum_{m=H_i+1}^{10} \bar{\varphi}_{om} \cdot {}^{\bar{r}}x^m = {}^{\bar{r}}y \qquad \text{(replacing (12))} \qquad (20) $$

$$ {}^{\bar{r}}x^m \geqslant 0 \qquad (\bar{r} = 1, 2; m = H_i + 1, \ldots, 10) \text{ (the same as (13))} \qquad (21) $$

The equations (10) are replaced by (15), but, assuming that all the b_m^i are non-negative which implies that the ${}^{\bar{r}}x^i$ are non-negative if the ${}^{\bar{r}}x^m$ are so, the equations (15) do not play a role in the allocation problem and can be omitted.

If we express the ${}^{\bar{r}}x^m$ and x_{tot}^m in terms of value added by applying the following substitution:

$$ {}^{\bar{r}}x^m = \frac{{}^{\bar{r}}y^m}{\bar{\varphi}_{om}} \qquad (\bar{r}=1,\ 2;\ m=H_i+1, \ldots, 10) \tag{22} $$

$$ x_{\text{tot}}^m = \frac{y_{\text{tot}}^m}{\bar{\varphi}_{om}} \qquad (m=H_i+1, \ldots, 10) \tag{23} $$

$$ \frac{{}^{\bar{r}}\bar{c}^m}{\bar{\bar{\varphi}}_{om}} = {}^{\bar{r}}\tilde{\bar{c}}^m \qquad (\bar{r}=1,\ 2;\ m=H_i+1, \ldots, 10) \tag{24} $$

the allocation problem (18)–(21) indeed reduces to a simple Hitchcock problem:
Minimize

$$ \sum_{\bar{r}=1}^{2} \sum_{m=H_i+1}^{10} {}^{\bar{r}}\tilde{\bar{c}}^m \cdot {}^{\bar{r}}y^m \tag{25} $$

subject to

$$ \sum_{\bar{r}=1}^{2} {}^{\bar{r}}y^m = y_{\text{tot}}^m \qquad (m=H_i+1, \ldots, 10) \tag{26} $$

$$ \sum_{m=H_i+1}^{10} {}^{\bar{r}}y^m = {}^{\bar{r}}y \qquad (\bar{r}=1, 2) \tag{27} $$

$$ {}^{\bar{r}}y^m \geqslant 0 \qquad (\bar{r}=1,\ 2;\ m=H_i+1, \ldots, 10) \tag{28} $$

Summarizing we find that at each of the first three rounds the $\{x_{\text{tot}}^m\}$, $\bar{\varphi}_{om}$, $\{b_m^i\}$, ${}^{\bar{r}}\bar{c}^m$, y_{tot}^m and ${}^{\bar{r}}\tilde{\bar{c}}^m$ need to be calculated and the Hitchcock problem(s) (25)–(28) need to be solved, after which in the last round only the output increases of the regional sectors need to be calculated from (15) and (22).

Now we turn to the actual calculations in applying the hierarchical method to our numerical example. In the first round the total increase in production of the world sectors was taken from table 4. The bunches, their incomes created and their costs in the two continents as calculated for the first round, are given for illustrative purposes in table 6.

The solutions of the typical allocation problems in the first and second round

TABLE 6

The bunches, their income coefficients, and their cost coefficients, per continent in the first round.

Bunch of sector	Production coefficients of the bunches								Income coefficients of the bunches	Cost coefficients			
										$^{r}\bar{c}^{m}$		$^{r}\tilde{\bar{c}}^{m}$	
	b_m^1	b_m^2	b_m^3	b_m^4	b_m^5	b_m^6	b_m^7	Mobile sectors	$\bar{\varphi}_{om}$	$\bar{r}=1$	$\bar{r}=2$	$\bar{r}=1$	$\bar{r}=2$
$m=8(W_1)$	0.653	0.097	0.110	0.033	0.042	0.083	0.479	1.000	0.959	0.373	0.359	0.389	0.374
$m=9(W_2)$	0.794	0.150	0.163	0.058	0.048	0.181	0.856	1.000	1.428	0.595	0.544	0.382	0.381
$m=10(W_3)$	0.625	0.118	0.122	0.029	0.016	0.049	0.824	1.000	1.164	0.399	0.438	0.343	0.376

TABLE 7

Solutions of the allocation problems in the first two rounds.

First round

Sector	Region 1, ..., 4	5, ..., 8	y_{tot}^m
$8(W_1)$	—	473.969	473.969
$9(W_2)$	—	246.955	246.955
$10(W_3)$	222.600	292.055	514.655
			Total:
$^{\bar{r}}y$	222.600	1,012.979	1,235.579*

* Difference with original figure due to roundings.

Second round

Sector	Region 1,2	3,4	y_{tot}^m
$5(C_1)$	—	2.963	2.963
$6(C_2)$	—	7.768	7.768
$7(C_3)$	69.650	67.043	136.693
$8(W_1)$	—	0	0
$9(W_2)$	—	0	0
$10(W_3)$	—**	75.176	75.176
			Total:
^{r}y	69.650	152.950	222.600

** This cell would sohw a non-zero figure in an alternative optimal solution.

Sector	Region 5,6	7,8	y_{tot}^m
$5(C_1)$	—	32.530	32.530
$6(C_2)$	—	70.052	70.052
$7(C_3)$	328.650	184.547	513.197
$8(W_1)$	—	214.185	214.185
$9(W_2)$	—	84.383	84.383
$10(W_3)$	—	98.632	98.632
			Total:
$^{\bar{r}}y$	328.650	684.329	1,012.979

can be found in table 7. In this table the $x^m_{tot}(m=5,..., 10)$ for both continents in the second round were calculated as indicated above. The results of the computations in the third and fourth round together are again given in section 5, table 8, where the full hierarchical solution is referred to as solution III.

This method gives a considerable simplification of the calculations, compared with the simplex method, especially as no square matrix of higher order than the number of immobile sectors needs to be inverted. The drawback of this method, however, is that, while the approximative solution found is always consistent and feasible, that is, satisfies all the constraints of the original problem, it is not necessarily optimal. The reason for this possible non-optimality is that in the allocation problems for each spatial unit and each sector the lowest cost coefficient of that sector in that spatial unit is taken as representative for the costs, while in the optimal solution the existence of the regional income increase targets may prevent several sectors from being expanded solely in their cheapest regions as far as the mobility of their products allows so at all. If that is so – and it will turn out to be so –, then the correct cost coefficient of a sector in a spatial unit is the weighted average of all its cost coefficients in that spatial unit, weighted by the production increases in the corresponding spatial subunits)[5].

However, whatever the computational advantages and the drawbacks with regard to optimality may be, the most attractive feature of this method seems to be its institutional counterpart which led us to name it the hierarchical method. Practically, this method reflects what could happen in an organizational scheme in which planning offices at different levels of spatial aggregation work together. The first round of the method reflects then the work which could be done at a planning office at world level. It results in giving control figures for the expansion only of world sectors to the continents. These control figures could also be stated in terms of trade flows of world products between continents. The second round reflects then the work of planning offices at continental level with regard to the distribution of the

[5]) This suggests that an improvement with regard to optimality of the solution found might be obtained by recomputing the solution after the ${}^rc^i_{min}$ and ${}^rc^m_{min}$ are replaced by their corresponding weighted averages, based on the production increases in the approximative solution. This method might even in general converge to the optimal solution. The extra work is limited as the $\bar{\varphi}_{om}$, $\{b^i_m\}$ and the first round $\{x^m_{tot}\}$ can be used unchanged in each new computation.

increases in production of continental and world sectors, leading to control figures for the countries, which still do not need to cover national and regional sectors. Planning offices at country level can use then these control figures as a starting point for their planning, corresponding to the third round. Regional authorities may do the rest corresponding to the fourth round. [6])

5. Comparison of the Solutions

In this section we will briefly compare the two-stage solution, its corresponding consistent solution, the hierarchical solution and the optimal solution. This last solution was obtained by the revised simplex method, using the basis of the hierarchical solution as the starting basis. They are represented in table 8, as respectively solution I, II, III, and IV. As we said before, all variables are in terms of value added. Any conclusions drawn from this comparison are, strictly speaking, only valid for the small numerical example of this paper. They may have, however, a more general validity, proofs for which are, however, outside the scope of this paper. In table 8 the sectoral totals of solution III deviate slightly from those of the other three solutions because of rounding.

As for *feasibility* of the solutions, solutions I and II are not feasible and their implementation would involve great difficulties. In the first one the supply increases do not equal the demand increases, while the second one requires production of sector 7 to decrease in region 8. The solutions III and IV, however, are both feasible and could be implemented, therefore, as far as consistency of the plans is concerned.

As for *optimality*, it does not make sense to compare the costs of infeasible solutions with those of the optimal solution. The costs of solution III differ only by roughly 0.03% from those of the optimal solution IV. However, if one checks by how much the bases of the first two and of the third solution differ from that of the optimal solution, it turns out that in the basis of the first solution only two variables of the optimal one are lacking, suggesting that the method could be computationally attractive in order to find a good starting basis for applying a more complicated method in order to find the optimal solution. In the basis of the third solution three variables of the

[6]) Cf. note 5. If the revision suggested there were to be institutionalized, this would imply the spatial units' planning offices sending revised cost figures to higher level planning offices.

TABLE 8

Solutions I, II, III and IV in bln. U.S.$ value added.

Sectors		Regions								Sectoral totals
		1	2	3	4	5	6	7	8	
1	I	8.831	13.138	19.543	28.706	42.177	61.496	88.765	127.076	389.732
	II	9.571	13.858	15.936	23.905	41.344	50.240	70.364	164.514	389.732
	III	7.003	10.688	21.176	24.412	33.437	50.037	79.528	163.473	389.753
	IV	9.571	10.755	18.959	23.986	41.344	50.240	71.412	163.465	389.732
2	I	0.913	1.358	2.020	2.967	4.360	6.357	9.175	13.136	40.286
	II	0.921	1.407	1.938	2.941	4.314	6.258	8.763	13.744	40.286
	III	0.872	1.332	2.038	2.967	4.166	6.236	9.030	13.659	40.300
	IV	0.921	1.340	1.995	2.951	4.314	6.258	8.857	13.650	40.286
3	I		4.277		9.392		20.181		42.017	75.867
	II		5.003		7.992		18.613		44.260	75.867
	III		3.494		9.508		16.487		46.418	75.906
	IV		4.186		8.809		18.613		44.260	75.867
4	I		0.791		1.736		3.731		7.767	14.025
	II		0.781		1.226		2.470		9.548	14.025
	III		0.414		1.596		1.951		10.075	14.036
	IV		0.582		1.425		2.470		9.548	14.025
5	I				3.743				17.031	20.774
	II				1.731				19.042	20.774
	III				1.737				19.068	20.804
	IV				1.731				19.042	20.774

Table 8 *(continued)*

Sectors		Regions 1	2	3	4	5	6	7	8	Sectoral totals
6	I				7.689				34.986	42.675
	II				4.262				38.413	42.675
	III				4.258			17.405	20.991	42.653
	IV				4.262			14.774	23.640	42.675
7	I			40.312	36.766	32.496	103.185	183.459	31.592	427.811
	II			41.041	48.943	34.101	117.370	202.273	−15.916	427.811
	III	20.125	25.723		44.132	96.097	120.240	121.480		427.796
	IV		24.788	17.360	47.836	34.101	117.370	186.357		427.811
8	I								86.026	86.026
	II								86.026	86.026
	III								86.026	86.026
	IV								86.026	86.026
9	I								43.220	43.220
	II								43.220	43.220
	III								43.220	43.220
	IV								43.220	43.220
10	I	18.256	22.087	0.075		54.667				95.085
	II	17.508	20.601	3.035		53.941				95.086
	III			38.735	2.391			53.958		95.085
	IV	17.508		23.636		53.941				95.085
Regional totals		28.000	41.650	61.950	91.000	133.700	194.900	281.400	402.850	Total: 1,235.500
Costs	I	11.007	17.934	20.156	35.214	54.090	74.065	100.974	165.756	479.194
	II	11.100	18.102	19.834	33.014	53.847	71.685	99.207	170.022	476.810
	III	8.158	13.902	25.976	34.039	44.408	70.986	112.186	167.434	477.089
	IV	11.100	14.232	23.378	33.343	53.847	71.685	102.024	167.339	476.948

optimal basis are lacking, suggesting that it could also be used as a good starting basis.[7]) However, in spite of the more complicated calculations of the hierarchical solution compared with the two-stage solution, its institutional implications set out in section 4, as well as the fact that it actually leads to a feasible solution make the hierarchical method decisively more attractive in our view than the two-stage method.

6. Implied Capital Flows

Another possibly interesting exercise can be done with regard to the implications of the optimal solution for investment, savings, and capital flows, these last being an important instrument for implementation of the plan. For this purpose we will calculate for the optimal production programme given in table 8, solution IV, the necessary investments to be made during the planning period. This is done for each country since we assume that the lowest level of our spatial hierarchy at which investment and savings decisions can be made is the country. Comparison of these investments with the savings to be expected yields the resulting capital flow between countries.

The net investments corresponding to the optimal development programme are computed by multiplying the income increases of each sector in each country by incremental capital–income ratios which have already been used in estimating the cost coefficients. Table 9 shows these capital coefficients.

Total income during the planning period can easily be calculated with the

TABLE 9

Incremental capital–income ratios by sector (1970–1980).

Sector	ICIR	Sector	ICIR
1(R_1)	4.5	6(C_2)	5.0
2(R_2)	5.0	7(C_3)	1.5
3(N_1)	5.0	8(W_1)	1.5
4(N_2)	6.0	9(W_2)	2.0
5(C_1)	2.5	10(W_3)	1.0

[7]) Following the suggestion of note 5 it might, however, be more efficient to go on with the hierarchical method itself, by recalculating it, using corrected cost coefficients, which would make it more attractive than the two-stage method. In that case no inversion of the matrix of coefficients corresponding to the starting basis is necessary.

aid of each country's initial income, its planned rate of growth and the formula for the sum of a geometrical series. In this way the following average net investment ratios have been calculated (table 10).

TABLE 10
Average net investment ratios by country (1970–1980).

Country	Average net investment ratio
1	18.09
2	16.54
3	13.38
4	13.58

We remind the reader that the first country consists of the two poorest regions while country 4 is composed of the two richest ones, the other countries between these two extremes being composed of increasingly richer regions. We see that the optimal development programme requires relatively considerable investments in the least developed areas while in the more developed regions the result is in conformity with the existing situation. If we assumed that each country should provide for its investments by domestic savings, too heavy a burden would clearly be laid upon the two poorer countries. We will, therefore, assume that the countries have agreed that the necessary investments will be financed by savings supplied by the four countries in such a way that each country saves the same percentage of its national income. In this case it would imply an overall net savings ratio of 14.00 per cent. This provides considerable relief from the savings burden of the less developed regions while the accompanying increase in the net savings ratio of the rich countries is negligible. The corresponding capital flows are summarized in table 11.[8])

TABLE 11
Capital flows 1970–1980 in bln. U.S.$.

Capital Imports		Capital Exports	
Country 1:	41.490	Country 3:	38.280
Country 2:	65.060	Country 4:	68.270
Total	106.550	Total	106.550

[8]) We neglect here the changes in the demand increases in the spatial units which may arise from such capital flows.

In terms of percentages the capital flows resulting from this savings policy of identical savings ratios in all countries are as follows. Countries 1 and 2, the poorest regions, will import 23 and 15 per cent respectively of their capital requirements during the planned period. Countries 3 and 4 then have to export 4 and 3 per cent, respectively, of their savings during the same period.

It is clear that many different exercises can be done, depending on the assumptions made with regard to the savings policy of the different countries.

7. Refinements, an Alternative and Conclusion

Obviously, the model presented in this paper needs to be refined before it ever could be used for planning. We want to mention here two such refinements. The first necessary refinement would be to restrict the values of the variables by introducing upper bounds for them and even in some cases lower bounds. Such upper bounds may account for the limited availability of appropriate natural resources in certain regions, the technical or social infeasibility of expanding appreciably some sectors in certain regions, the increasing unit costs when a sector expands too quickly somewhere, and the disadvantages of extreme specialization in certain regions, including the resulting transport costs. The bounds have to be determined very carefully as they influence especially the quantitative aspects of the optimal solution considerably. Large absolute values of the shadow prices for the bounds indicate a strong influence of them on total costs and may suggest a reconsideration of the values given to these bounds. The two-stage method, as well as the hierarchical method remain applicable with some adjustments[9]), but their performance with regard to feasibility or optimality has not yet been investigated. The two-stage method may perform better if bounds are introduced as far as feasibility is concerned, as argued in section 3.

The second refinement which could be introduced is to consider the costs of the resulting interregional transport flows in the model for a few 'heavy' sectors of which the unit costs of transport over an average distance are a sizeable part of the unit production costs. This may be the case e.g. with the continental sectors. Such explicit transport costs for heavy sectors have been dealt with elsewhere[10]), where for simple models it has been shown that it may be advantageous to calculate first the optimal solution without con-

[9]) Cf. Dantzig [1], chapter 18, and Mennes, Tinbergen, Waardenburg [4], chapter 4.
[10]) See Mennes, Tinbergen, Waardenburg [4], chapters 5 and 6.

sidering these transport costs explicitly and then to adjust the solution in a rather simple way. It has not yet been investigated whether and how far it would be efficient to use the ideas of either the two-stage or the hierarchical method when applying this decomposed solution method with explicit consideration of transport costs.

A more fundamental difficulty in using this type of models is that the cost coefficients either should be estimated indirectly by looking at the existing tariff structure, or directly by identifying scarce factors of production and weighting them with appropriate shadow or accounting prices. While the first method may lead to only very approximative estimates and insufficient coverage of the necessary data, the second method not only requires rather precise data on production functions but also estimates of accounting prices. The correct values of these prices, however, could be derived only after the optimal solution had been found. If the second method is used, after the optimal solution is known, it may be necessary to make new estimates of the cost coefficients and to recalculate the optimal solution with these new cost figures. This would lead to iterative approximations and obviously this raises problems of convergence which are outside the scope of this paper. However, an alternative formulation of the problem is possible which may solve this problem.

One could reverse the whole problem by maximizing the total world income increase under the constraints, firstly that the income increases in different regions must have fixed ratios to each other, secondly that fixed amounts of scarce production factors, with specified degrees of mobility, would be available, and finally, that the appropriate balance equations for sectors would hold.

If there is at least one not completely mobile factor of production or if there is more than one scarce factor of production, there will be in general more positive variables in the optimal solution than was the case in the model of this paper, and hence less specialization. It is again left open whether in such a reversed model two-stage or hierarchical solution methods would still be applicable. However, this seems to be the case at least for the hierarchical method. Such a reversed model could be useful for estimating the accounting prices for the scarce factors of production, which could be used in estimating the cost coefficients for the type of model presented in this paper, even if the latter model distinguished a considerable number of sectors (e.g. 200 or more) and the reversed version had only a limited number of sectors.

As a tentative conclusion the authors want to express their opinion that the hierarchical approach, as presented in section 4, appears to offer a very attractive scheme for planning, also in the case of a realistic exercise of world development planning, with many sectors and spatial units, a large number of bounds on the variables and may be explicit transport costs for a few heavy sectors. While for some time the related institutional arrangements have been suggested by Tinbergen, the mathematical formulation of the model as well as the outcome of the numerical exercise in this paper seems to confirm that such an approach is logical and much simpler than a simultaneous solution method, that it approaches well the optimal solution[11]) and that it can directly be implemented organizationally. Therefore, it appears worthwhile to investigate more extensively and deeply than could be done in this paper how the hierarchical approach will work out if one works with a more realistic model.

Appendix

In the numerical example of this paper the input–output coefficients of table 12 and the final demand increase coefficients of table 13, which describe which part of the income increase is spent on products of which sector, are used. They are assumed to be the same in all regions.

TABLE 12

Input–output coefficients.

Sectors	R_1	R_2	N_1	N_2	C_1	C_2	C_3	W_1	W_2	W_3
R_1	0.184	0.135	0.123	0.148	0.175	0.111	0.073	0.181	0.107	0.080
R_2	0.013	0.002	0.022	0.025	0.005	0.016	0.009	0.003	0.009	0.005
N_1	0.047	0.041	0.036	0.043	0.017	0.039	0.012	0.016	0.028	0.017
N_2	0.006		0.010	0.012	0.019	0.083	0.004	0.010	0.020	0.007
C_1	0.001	0.023	0.001				0.002	0.030	0.030	0.001
C_2	0.002		0.062	0.322	0.015	0.178	0.004	0.039	0.103	0.009
C_3	0.105	0.019	0.009	0.009	0.020	0.030	0.218	0.007	0.139	0.218
W_1	0.039	0.305	0.077	0.053	0.100	0.058	0.015	0.489	0.038	0.009
W_2	0.021	0.021	0.057	0.006	0.037	0.018	0.062	0.015	0.253	0.031
W_3	0.053	0.135	0.047	0.022	0.032	0.013	0.030	0.036	0.023	0.408
Value added coefficients	0.529	0.319	0.556	0.360	0.580	0.454	0.571	0.174	0.250	0.215

11) And might even reach it with a few iterations, as suggested in note 5.

TABLE 13

Final demand increase coefficients.

Sectors	R_1	R_2	N_1	N_2	C_1	C_2	C_3	W_1	W_2	W_3
	0.2807	0.0800	0.0458	0.0079	0.0082	0.0082	0.3052	0.1149	0.0262	0.1229

References

[1] G. B. DANTZIG, *Linear Programming and Extensions*, Princeton University Press, Princeton, New Jersey 1963.

[2] W. ISARD, *Methods of Regional Analysis: An Introduction to Regional Science*, The M.I.T. Press, Massachusetts–New York–London 1960.

[3] W. LEONTIEF et al., *Studies in the Structure of the American Economy*. Oxford University Press, New York 1953.

[4] L. B. M. MENNES, J. TINBERGEN and J. G. WAARDENBURG, *The Element of Space in Development Planning*. North-Holland Publishing Company, Amsterdam 1969.

[5] J. TINBERGEN, *Some Principles of Regional Planning*. Publication No. 29/65 of the Netherlands Economic Institute, Rotterdam 1965.

[6] J. TINBERGEN, 'Wanted: A World Development Plan', *International Organization*, Volume XXII, no. 2 (1968) pp. 417–431.

[7] J. TINBERGEN, 'Some Refinements of the Semi-Input–Output Method', *The Pakistan Development Review*, Vol. VI, no. 2 (1966), pp. 243–247.

[8] J. TINBERGEN, 'International Economic Planning', *Daedalus, Journal of the Academy of Arts and Sciences*, Spring 1966 – Issue: 'Conditions of World Order', pp. 530–557.

[9] *World Bank Atlas of Per Capita Product and Population*. International Bank for Reconstruction and Development. Washington D.C., September 1966.

ECONOMIC INTEGRATION AND THE OPTIMUM INTERNATIONAL DISTRIBUTION OF PRODUCTION

H. C. BOS and A. KUYVENHOVEN

1. Introduction

Economic integration has generally been recognized as an important device for promoting economic development, both for the developed and the developing countries, for the East and the West. Undoubtedly, however, the advantages of economic integration are particularly important for the developing countries. The necessity to diversify their economies makes industrialization a corner-stone of the development policy for most of the developing countries. The establishment of new industries, however, is economically justified only if they can operate at a scale at which efficient production is possible. For most industries and countries the domestic markets are not large enough to permit the operation of even one production unit of optimum size. New industries, therefore, are frequently set up in the hope or expectation that a satisfactory degree of capacity utilization can be achieved through exports to neighbouring countries where these industries do not yet exist. The possibility that these neighbouring countries will follow the same reasoning is not a theoretical one, and without international coordination of investment there is a real danger, which in many countries is already a fact, that overcapacity, high production cost and waste of investment resources will result.

This justification of economic integration is considered as conventional wisdom. Yet the implementation of policies aiming at such an international investment coordination has so far not been very successful. One of the reasons for the failures of integration schemes has been the inequitable distribution of the benefits which these schemes yield, or rather the expectation of an unequal distribution. Integration between countries in different stages of development or between large and small countries is often considered to favour the participating countries in an unequal way. On the other hand it is often suggested that where differences in comparative advantages do not exist, there is no basis for fruitful cooperation.

A satisfactory answer to these objections to integration can only be given through a systematic analysis of the impact of an integration scheme on the position of each partner. Very few such studies have been made so far. Most of the available studies are concerned with single industries or projects, such as the choice of the location of chemical plants in Latin American countries in the study by Vietorisz and Manne [6]. From a methodological point of view the sector studies by Manne [3] and Kendrick [2] are also important, although they consider only the choice of the location of plants within a single country. There is, however, a great similarity between the problems of choosing the location of plants between regions of a country and of choosing between countries. Chenery [1] has analyzed the interdependent investment decisions for several industries with economies of scale for an individual country. The only author who has, to the best of our knowledge, applied a multi-sectoral and multi-national model to study the impact of an integration policy has been P. J. Verdoorn in his study on the effects of measures of European integration [5]. His model, however, is less suitable for application in the conditions of the developing countries. In the European situation integration results primarily from a reduction in the barriers against a free movement of commodities, labour and capital and in particular through the reduction of trade tariffs. In the conditions of the developing countries trade liberalization is less important and an integration policy should concentrate on determining an optimum investment allocation between industries and countries.

One of the reasons why so few applied studies on international industrial integration are available must be the fact that the formulation of a model which is both suitable to analyze the problems typical of integration and manageable for computational purposes is no easy task.

Simple *linear programming* models do not meet the first requirement because of the economies of scale which are characteristic of most integration problems. The assumption of these models that all cost coefficients are independent of the level of output clearly conflicts with the presence of economies of scale.

Mixed integer programming techniques can be used to solve problems where consideration of indivisibilities causing economies of scale in the production process is essential. The available algorithms for solving this type of problems, however, do not meet the other requirement mentioned above: no easy computability of these models is possible.

The *classical* optimization method (Lagrangean multiplier method) has also well-known deficiencies. This method does not guarantee the finding of a global optimum, as distinguished from a local optimum and may yield results which have no economic meaning, for example, negative values for output levels.

This very brief survey of mathematical techniques shows that an ideal method does not exist and that in building models for the analysis of integration problems, as in other models, a compromise must be made between the requirements of realism and computability. Professor J. Tinbergen has shown the possibilities of applying the classical solution technique to solve investment planning problems involving indivisibilities [4]. The other authors mentioned above have applied simple linear programming, mixed integer programming or approximations to this method.

The *objective* of this paper is a very modest one. With the help of some simple models we will investigate a number of questions related to problems of integration. These models take account of economies of scale and transportation cost for all industries. Under very specific assumptions about investment coordination these models determine the optimum distribution of production between industries and countries for all industries simultaneously. The Lagrangean multiplier method is used in solving the optimization problems. This implies that in all cases to be studied the location of industries is given, but the levels of output have to be determined. The use of this technique does not permit to determine also the optimum location of the industries except through a comparison of all possible cases.

Chapter 2 gives a mathematical analysis of the optimum production structure. Chapter 3 gives a numerical illustration and further elaboration of these models.

The conclusions which can be drawn from this paper are at best that it seems worthwhile to pay sufficient attention to a careful formulation of the conditions in which integration takes place and that even for simple cases no easy generalizations are possible.

2. A Mathematical Analysis of the Optimum Production Structure

2.1. *General assumptions*

In this chapter we shall analyze in an algebraic way for a number of situations the optimum distribution of production between industries and countries, with and without investment coordination.

The general *assumptions* on which the analysis will be based are the following:
1. all industries are vertically integrated, i.e. they produce only final goods;
2. in the simple models capital is the only scarce factor; in other models labour is also introduced;
3. the planning objective is to minimize total investment cost under a number of side conditions;
4. one of these side conditions is that a given income level must be achieved for the country as a whole, or, in the case of international investment coordination, for a group of countries;
5. for each country total domestic demand equals total income, i.e. the balance of payments is in equilibrium;
6. all industries show economies of scale, but the geographical size of their markets is limited by transportation costs;
7. the location of industries is given, but the levels of output have to be determined.

2.2. *Production structure of a single country*

The first case to be studied concerns the allocation of investment between industries for a single country with free trade with the rest of the world. Capital is the only scarce factor.

The model describing this problem uses the following *variables*:
$\bar{Y}$: total income;
Y_h : net production of industry h ($h = 1, 2, \ldots H$);
K_h : total capital (investment) required by industry h;
X_h : domestic demand for product of industry h;
E_h : export surplus (exports minus imports) of industry h.

The *equations* of the model are the following:

$$K_h = \kappa_h^0 + \kappa_h^1 Y_h + \kappa_h^2 (Y_h)^2 . \tag{1}$$

This equation can be considered as a *production* or a *cost function* for industry h. The fixed (capital) cost κ_h^0 introduces the element of economies of scale; κ_h^1 can be considered as the marginal capital-output ratio. The first two terms together $(\kappa_h^0 + \kappa_h^1 Y_h)$ measure the capital requirements for the production process. Thus capital cost per unit of output will fall at a rate dependent on the value of the fixed cost. The last term $\kappa_h^2 (Y_h)^2$ is a rough approximation to transportation and distribution costs in terms of capital requirements. A larger output level will require a larger geographical market causing transport costs which increase more than proportionately with the output level.

$$\sum Y_h = \bar{Y}. \tag{2}$$

The total of the net production (value added) for all industries equals total income which is given.

$$X_h = \xi_h^1 \bar{Y} + \xi_h^0 \qquad \sum \xi_h^1 = 1 \quad \text{and} \quad \sum \xi_h^0 = 0. \tag{3}$$

Domestic demand for product h is a linear function of total income. The conditions for the coefficients guarantee balance of payments equilibrium.

$$Y_h = X_h + E_h. \tag{4}$$

These balance equations indicate the equality between the net output and total demand for each industry.

The *problem* to be solved with this model is to determine the composition of total income which minimizes total capital cost, or

$$\text{minimize} \sum K_h \tag{5}$$

subject to the side conditions (1) to (4). Since we shall impose no bounds on the values of the export surpluses, only the equations (1) and (2) are relevant in this minimization problem. Using the traditional Lagrangean multiplier method, we find the following optimal values for the Y_h's (the tilde $\tilde{}$ indicates optimal values of the variables):

$$\tilde{Y}_h = \eta_h^1 \bar{Y} + \eta_h^0, \tag{6}$$

where

$$\eta_h^1 = \frac{1}{2\kappa_h^2 \delta}, \quad \text{if } \delta = \sum \frac{1}{2\kappa_h^2} \quad \text{and}$$

$$\eta_h^0 = \frac{\varepsilon}{2\kappa_h^2 \delta} - \frac{\kappa_h^1}{2\kappa_h^2}, \quad \text{if } \varepsilon = \sum \frac{\kappa_h^1}{2\kappa_h^2}.$$

This result shows that the optimum composition of total production depends on the level of total income. The coefficients η_h^1 will always be positive, but the coefficients η_h^0 can be negative. Since negative values of Y_h cannot be accepted, the eqs. (6) hold only for values of $\bar{Y}$ larger than a certain miminum value.

An analysis of the coefficients η_h^1 and η_h^0 shows that $\tilde{Y}_h$ will be higher for lower values of κ_h^1 (capital–output ratio) and κ_h^2 (transportation cost).

Domestic demand is dependent only on $\bar{Y}$. The export surplus for each industry can, therefore, be derived from (3), (4) and (6). We find

$$\tilde{E}_h = \tilde{Y}_h - X_h = (\eta_h^1 - \xi_h^1)\,\bar{Y} + \eta_h^0 - \xi_h^0 . \tag{7}$$

The values of $\eta_h^1 - \xi_h^1$ and $\eta_h^0 - \xi_h^0$ can be either positive or negative. Consequently, the optimum value of the export surplus can increase or decrease, remain positive or negative, or change in sign with an increase in the level of total income. Because $\sum \tilde{E}_h = 0$, an increase in the export surplus for one industry must be accompanied by a decrease in this surplus for at least one other industry.

We conclude the discussion of this case with the remark that complete *autarky* for a single country does not allow an optimization of the investment allocation. In this case $E_h = 0$, and consequently, production for each sector has to meet domestic demand:

$$Y_h = X_h = \xi_h^1 \bar{Y} + \xi_h^0 . \tag{8}$$

2.3. *Production structure for a group of countries with investment coordination*

We shall now consider a case with investment coordination between N countries and in which capital remains the only scarce factor.

Investment coordination can be given various forms. Here we assume that such a coordination means that the cooperating countries in determining their production structure give up their national income targets, but accept an income target for the group of cooperating countries equal to the sum of the original income targets of these countries without cooperation. No restraints on foreign trade will be imposed.

The production functions for the same industry in different countries are assumed to show differences reflecting comparative advantages. Transport costs, however, are assumed to depend in the same way on the output level in all countries. An index $i = 1, 2, \dots N$ is given to all variables and coefficients which can differ between the countries.

The problem can now be formulated as follows:

$$\text{Minimize} \sum_i \sum_h {}^iK_h \tag{9}$$

subject to

$$ {}^iK_h = {}^i\kappa_h^0 + {}^i\kappa_h^{1\,i}Y_h + \kappa_h^2({}^iY_h)^2 , \tag{10}$$

$$ \sum_i \sum_h {}^iY_h = \sum_i {}^iY = \bar{Y} , \tag{11}$$

where $\bar{Y}$ is given.

The solution of this problem gives:

$$ {}^i\tilde{Y}_h = \frac{1}{2\kappa_h^2\delta}\frac{\bar{Y}}{N} + \frac{\bar{\varepsilon}}{2\kappa_h^2\delta} - \frac{{}^i\kappa_h^1}{2\kappa_h^2} , \tag{12}$$

where

$$ \bar{\varepsilon} = \frac{1}{N}\sum {}^i\varepsilon \quad \text{and} \quad {}^i\varepsilon = \sum_h \frac{{}^i\kappa_h^1}{2\kappa_h^2} . $$

The optimum level of production of industry h in country i is a linear function of the average income per country ($\bar{Y}/N$). Changes in this income affect all countries in the same way, as the coefficient corresponding to $\bar{Y}/N$ is the same for all countries. A low capital–output ratio for an industry in comparison to another country causes a relatively high optimal output level for this industry. More precisely, for two countries i and j:

$$ {}^i\tilde{Y}_h - {}^j\tilde{Y}_h = \frac{{}^j\kappa_h^1 - {}^i\kappa_h^1}{2\kappa_h^2} . \tag{13}$$

From (12) we can also derive the distribution of the income between the cooperating countries:

$$ \sum_h {}^i\tilde{Y}_h = {}^i\tilde{Y} = \frac{\bar{Y}}{N} + \bar{\varepsilon} - {}^i\varepsilon . \tag{14}$$

For two countries i and j:

$$ {}^i\tilde{Y} - {}^j\tilde{Y} = {}^j\varepsilon - {}^i\varepsilon = \sum_h \frac{({}^j\kappa_h^1 - {}^i\kappa_h^1)}{2\kappa_h^2} . \tag{15}$$

A lower average of the marginal capital–output ratios for all industries of country i in comparison to the average for country j leads to an optimal income for i which is higher than the optimal income for j.

If the production functions for each industry are the same for all countries, the optimal income will be the same for all countries. Comparative advantages cause deviations from this average pattern.

The strong tendency towards income equalization of this model seems logical for countries of equal population size, but is less acceptable for cooperation between countries of small and large population size. Equalization of total income between countries would in this case always lead to a higher per capita income in the small than in the large countries. A further generalization of this model which takes account of differences in size between countries is therefore necessary.

2.4. *The optimum production structure with capital and labour as scarce factors*

In this section we shall analyze the influence of the population size of the various cooperating countries on the choice of the optimum production structure. In order to be able to study this influence in isolation, we assume, in this section, that the production functions for each industry are the same for all countries.

The extension of the previous model with labour as a second scarce factor requires in addition a reformulation of the production function. We choose the simplest assumption possible: labour inputs are proportional to the output level. These inputs can be different between industries, but are assumed to be the same for each industry between the countries. The labour supply is given for each country.

The problem to be solved now is:

$$\text{Minimize} \sum_i \sum_h {}^iK_h \tag{16}$$

subject to

$${}^iK_h = \kappa_h^0 + \kappa_h^{1\,i}Y_h + \kappa_h^2({}^iY_h)^2, \tag{17}$$

$$\sum\sum {}^iY_h = \bar{Y}, \tag{18}$$

$$\sum_h \lambda_h {}^iY_h = {}^i\bar{L}, \tag{19}$$

where

${}^i\bar{L}$: given labour supply of country i

λ_h: labour input coefficient for industry h.

In writing out the solutions for the optimum values of the various variables, it is helpful to introduce a new variable ${}^iL$ indicating the deviation of the labour supply of country i from the average labour supply per country for the group:

$$^{i}L = {}^{i}\bar{L} - \frac{\bar{L}}{N} \tag{20}$$

if

$$\bar{L} = \sum {}^{i}\bar{L}.$$

For countries smaller than the average for the group $^{i}L < 0$ and for countries larger than the average $^{i}L > 0$. All ^{i}L's are given, since no labour migration is allowed.

The general form of the solution of $^{i}\tilde{Y}_h$ can now be written as follows:

$$^{i}\tilde{Y}_h = \mu_h^0 + \mu_h^1 \frac{\bar{Y}}{N} + \mu_h^2 \frac{\bar{L}}{N} - \mu_h^{3\,i}L. \tag{21}$$

The μ-coefficients depend in a rather complicated way on the coefficients λ_h, κ_h^1 and κ_h^2. We give only the values for μ_h^1, μ_h^2 and μ_h^3:

$$\mu_h^1 = \frac{\delta'' - \lambda_h \delta'}{2\kappa_h^2 \{\delta\delta'' - (\delta')^2\}}$$

$$\mu_h^2 = \frac{\lambda_h \delta - \delta'}{2\kappa_h^2 \{\delta\delta'' - (\delta')^2\}}$$

$$\mu_h^3 = \frac{\lambda_h}{2\kappa_h^2 \delta''}$$

where

$$\delta = \sum \frac{1}{2\kappa_h^2}; \quad \delta' = \sum \frac{\lambda_h}{2\kappa_h^2}; \quad \delta'' = \sum \frac{(\lambda_h)^2}{2\kappa_h^2}.$$

All these coefficients are independent of the κ_h^1's. These marginal capital–output ratios, however, determine with other coefficients the constant μ_h^0.

An analysis of eq. (21) and the values of the coefficients shows the influence of the size of the country on the production levels; since $\mu_h^3 > 0$ always holds, the production of industry h in country i will increase with the size of the country.

Summation of eq. (21) for all industries gives the total income of country i:

$$\sum_h {}^{i}\tilde{Y}_h = {}^{i}\tilde{Y} = \frac{\bar{Y}}{N} + \frac{\delta'}{\delta''}\,{}^{i}L. \tag{22}$$

This equation shows that there is no longer an equalization of the income between the countries, although they have identical production functions. Since δ'/δ'' is positive, large countries, i.e. countries larger than the average of the group, will have an income larger than the average income $\bar{Y}/N$.

More interesting than a comparison between the *absolute* incomes of the countries in the optimum situation, is a comparison between the *per capita income* of small and large countries. The per capita income for country i can be derived from the eqs. (20) and (22):

$$\frac{{}^iY}{{}^i\bar{L}} = \frac{\bar{Y}}{N^i\bar{L}} + \frac{\delta'}{\delta''}\left(1 - \frac{\bar{L}}{N^i\bar{L}}\right). \tag{23}$$

The properties of this equation can be shown more clearly with the help of the following example where $N=2$. In this case

$$\frac{{}^1Y}{{}^1\bar{L}} = \frac{1}{2}\left\{\frac{\bar{Y}}{{}^1\bar{L}} + \frac{\delta'}{\delta''}\left(1 - \frac{{}^2\bar{L}}{{}^1\bar{L}}\right)\right\} \tag{24}$$

$$\frac{{}^2Y}{{}^2\bar{L}} = \frac{1}{2}\left\{\frac{\bar{Y}}{{}^2\bar{L}} + \frac{\delta'}{\delta''}\left(1 - \frac{{}^1\bar{L}}{{}^2\bar{L}}\right)\right\}. \tag{25}$$

Now suppose $({}^2\bar{L}/{}^1\bar{L})>1$. Comparison of (24) and (25) shows that for *low* values of $\bar{Y}$ we have $({}^1Y/{}^1\bar{L})<({}^2Y/{}^2\bar{L})$ and for *high* values of $\bar{Y}$ we have $({}^1Y/{}^1\bar{L})>({}^2Y/{}^2\bar{L})$. In other words, at a low income level $\bar{Y}$ the larger countries will have a higher per capita income than the small countries; at a high income level the smaller countries will have a higher per capita income than the large countries. Further calculation shows that equality in per capita income is optimal only if

$$\bar{Y} = \frac{\delta'}{\delta''}\bar{L}. \tag{26}$$

The economic explanation of this result seems to be that at a low income level $\bar{Y}$ the transportation costs for a large country will be relatively less important than for a small country. The per capita income of the large country will therefore be higher than in the small country. On the other hand, at a high income level $\bar{Y}$ the small country will have relatively low transportation costs compared to a large country, because the transport costs increase more then proportionately with the output levels. Consequently, the per capita income of the small country will be higher than in the large country.

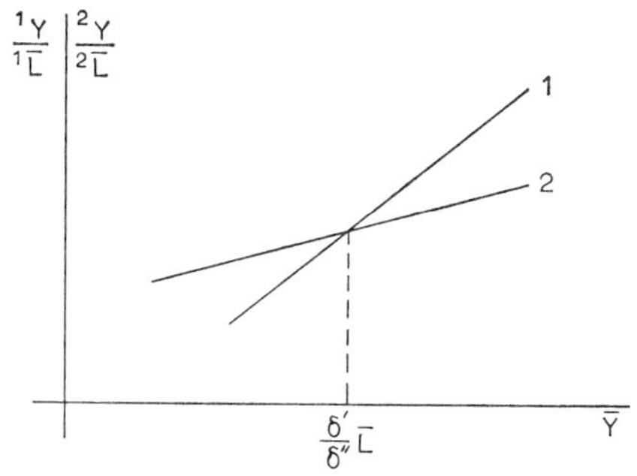

Fig. 1

Fig. 1 illustrates the situation here described for two countries.

If the two countries are of equal size, ${}^1\bar{L}={}^2\bar{L}$, the two lines for 1 and 2 will coincide and go through the origin with a slope equal to $1/2^1\bar{L}$.

2.5. *The optimum production structure with differentiation of the production functions between the countries*

A generalization of the model of the previous section can be obtained by allowing differences in the production functions between the countries. This differentiation will be introduced here only for the marginal capital–output ratios. They will now have to be indicated by ${}^i\kappa_h^1$. The other coefficients are assumed to be the same for all countries.

Using, with this exception, the same assumptions as in the previous section, we find that the output levels ${}^iY_h$ have the following optimum values:

$$ {}^i\tilde{Y}_h = {}^i\mu_h^0 + \mu_h^1 \frac{\bar{Y}}{N} + \mu_h^2 \frac{\bar{L}}{N} + \mu_h^{3\,i}L. \tag{27}$$

Comparison with eq. (21) shows that the only difference from our previous result is the value of the constant ${}^i\mu_h^0$ which depends in a rather complicated way on the various κ- and λ-coefficients.

An analysis of the factors which cause a difference in the optimum output levels between two countries i and j for industry h is given by the following equation:

$$ {}^i\tilde{Y}_h - {}^j\tilde{Y}_h = \frac{\lambda_h}{2\kappa_h^2\delta''}({}^iL - {}^jL) + \frac{\lambda_h}{2\kappa_h^2\delta''}({}^i\varepsilon' - {}^j\varepsilon') + \frac{{}^j\kappa_h^1 - {}^i\kappa_h^1}{2\kappa_h^2}, \tag{28}$$

where

$$^{i}\varepsilon' = \sum_h \frac{^{i}\kappa_h^1 \lambda_h}{2\kappa_h^2} \qquad i \neq j\,.$$

Eq. (28) shows that the difference in output level between the two countries is due to

a. the difference in population size $({}^{i}L - {}^{j}L)$;
b. the difference in comparative advantages for all industries $({}^{i}\varepsilon' - {}^{j}\varepsilon')$;
c. the difference in comparative advantages for industry h $({}^{j}\kappa_h^1 - {}^{i}\kappa_h^1)$.

3. A Numerical Illustration and Elaboration

3.1. *The optimum structure with identical production functions between countries*

This chapter gives a numerical elaboration and illustration of some of the cases discussed in the previous chapter.

We shall consider only cases where both labour and capital are scarce. First we assume *identical production functions* for all countries for each industry, and countries of different population size. Further we choose the number of industries $H = 3$ and the number of countries $N = 2$.

The coefficients have been given the following values:

$$\begin{array}{lll} \kappa_1^1 = 2 & \kappa_1^2 = 0.03 & \lambda_1 = 0.6 \\ \kappa_2^1 = 3 & \kappa_2^2 = 0.01 & \lambda_2 = 0.4 \\ \kappa_3^1 = 4 & \kappa_3^2 = 0.02 & \lambda_3 = 0.7 \end{array} \tag{29}$$

The problem discussed in section 2.4. gives according to the eq. (21) the following general solution for the optimum levels of output (in this section we shall drop the tilde to indicate optimum values):

$$\begin{aligned} {}^{i}Y_1 &= -\,0.250\,\frac{\bar{Y}}{N} + 0.833\,\frac{\bar{L}}{N} + 0.381\,{}^{i}L + 20.8 \\ {}^{i}Y_2 &= 2.417\,\frac{\bar{Y}}{N} - 3.611\,\frac{\bar{L}}{N} + 0.762\,{}^{i}L - 6.9 \\ {}^{i}Y_3 &= -\,1.167\,\frac{\bar{Y}}{N} + 2.778\,\frac{\bar{L}}{N} + 0.667\,{}^{i}L - 13.9\,. \end{aligned} \tag{30}$$

Adding these equations gives:

$$^{i}Y = \frac{\bar{Y}}{N} + 1.810\,^{i}L. \tag{31}$$

From these *general* solutions we derive specific solutions for the case where $N=2$, $\bar{L}=210$ and country 2 is two times the size of country 1, or $2\,^{1}\bar{L}={}^{2}\bar{L}$, or $^{1}\bar{L}=70$ and $^{2}\bar{L}=140$, and $^{1}L=-35$ and $^{2}L=35$.
We find

$$\begin{aligned} ^{1}Y_1 &= -\,0.125\,\bar{Y} + 95 \\ ^{1}Y_2 &= 1.208\,\bar{Y} - 412.7 \\ ^{1}Y_3 &= -\,0.583\,\bar{Y} + 254.4 \\ ^{1}Y &= 0.5\,\bar{Y} - 63.3 \end{aligned}$$

and

$$\begin{aligned} ^{2}Y_1 &= -\,0.125\,\bar{Y} + 121.7 \\ ^{2}Y_2 &= 1.208\,\bar{Y} - 359.5 \\ ^{2}Y_3 &= -\,0.583\,\bar{Y} + 301.1 \\ ^{2}Y &= 0.5\,\bar{Y} + 63.3\,. \end{aligned}$$

Inspection of these equations shows that they can only hold, i.e. give non-negative values for the $^{i}Y_h$'s, if $342 \leqslant \bar{Y} \leqslant 436$.

The critical income level at which the per capita incomes will be equal in the optimum situation is according to (26):

$$\bar{Y} = 1.81\bar{L} = 380\,.$$

This result can also be checked with the help of the equations expressing the per capita income as a function of the total income:

$$\frac{^{1}Y}{^{1}\bar{L}} = \frac{\bar{Y}}{140} - 0.904$$

$$\frac{^{2}Y}{^{2}\bar{L}} = \frac{\bar{Y}}{280} + 0.452\,.$$

As shown in section 2.4., we find for $\bar{Y}<380$ that $(^{1}Y/^{1}\bar{L})<(^{2}Y/^{2}\bar{L})$ and for $\bar{Y}>380$ that $(^{1}Y/^{1}\bar{L})>(^{2}Y/^{2}\bar{L})$.

A more detailed analysis of the economic structure of the two countries at different levels of total income is possible with the help of table 1. For

TABLE 1

Optimum structure of production, demand and foreign trade at alternative income levels.

	Production		Domestic demand		Net exports	
	$^{1}Y_h$	$^{2}Y_h$	$^{1}X_h$	$^{2}X_h$	$^{1}E_h$	$^{2}E_h$
A. Total income $\bar{Y}=350$						
Industry 1	51.3	77.9	41.2	83.8	10.1	−5.9
Industry 2	10.1	63.5	47.0	103.0	−36.9	−39.5
Industry 3	50.3	96.9	23.5	51.5	26.8	45.4
Total	111.7	238.3	111.7	238.3	0	0
Per capita income	1.60	1.70				
B. Total income $\bar{Y}=380$						
Industry 1	47.5	74.2	42.7	85.3	4.8	−11.2
Industry 2	46.4	99.7	56.0	112.0	−9.6	−12.3
Industry 3	32.8	79.4	28.0	56.0	4.8	23.4
Total	126.7	253.3	126.7	253.3	0	0
Per capita income	1.81	1.81				
C. Total income $\bar{Y}=430$						
Industry 1	41.3	67.9	45.2	87.8	−3.9	−19.9
Industry 2	106.8	160.1	71.0	127.0	35.8	33.1
Industry 3	3.6	50.3	35.5	63.5	−31.9	−13.2
Total	151.7	278.3	151.7	278.3	0	0
Per capita income	2.17	1.99				

three alternative values of $\bar{Y}$ the optimum production structures for countries 1 and 2 have been calculated. The income levels are, alternatively, smaller and greater than or equal to the critical income level 380.

In this table the values of the domestic demand and the export surpluses for each industry and country are also included for each of the three cases. For the calculation of domestic demand the following coefficients have been used:

$$\xi_1^1 = 0.1 \qquad {}^1\xi_1^0 = 30 \qquad {}^2\xi_1^0 = 60$$
$$\xi_2^1 = 0.6 \qquad {}^1\xi_2^0 = -20 \qquad {}^2\xi_2^0 = -40$$
$$\xi_3^1 = 0.3 \qquad {}^1\xi_3^0 = -10 \qquad {}^2\xi_3^0 = -20$$

The demand functions are assumed to be the same for both countries.

Differentiation of the constants ${}^{i}\xi_{h}$ between the two countries, however, is necessary in order to take account of the difference in population size.

An analysis of the results of the calculations included in table 1 leads to the following *conclusions*:

1. There is a marked difference in the production structure of both countries although identical production functions have been assumed.
2. The optimum industrial structure changes with the income level. These changes now show similarity to the changes in the structure of domestic demand.
3. The changes in the production structure imply not only *relative* increases and decreases of the various industries, but also decreases in the *absolute* levels of output of some industries.
4. The net exports of industries 1 and 3 decrease and surpluses change into deficits with an increase in total income. For industry 2 the net exports change from deficits into surpluses as a result of an increase in the optimum output level which increases much more rapidly than the domestic demand.
5. Although the countries have identical production functions, the export patterns offer possibilities for mutual trade between countries 1 and 2 in the cases A and B for industry 1. For the other industries and in case C both countries have positive or negative net exports.
6. The per capita income of the (small) country 1 increases more rapidly than for country 2.

Some final remarks should be made about the general interpretation of these results.

We have calculated in this example the levels of output for all industries in both countries which together minimize total capital cost, use the available (scarce) labour in each country and which realize an income target for both countries *together*. The income levels of the individual countries are *not* predetermined but result from the optimization. In other words, for a given total income for the countries together we determine the optimum distribution of this income between the two countries. This means that without the production and investment coordination of the kind we have assumed, and with the income targets for the individual countries set at fixed levels, the optimum distribution of the industries between the countries is generally not achieved. However, if the income distribution between the countries is optimal, international investment coordination would not be necessary: the choice by each country of production levels for its industries which minimize total capital cost for that country leads to the same production structure as with minimization of capital cost for all countries together.

3.2. *The influence of the population size and comparative advantages on the optimum production structure*

Our final numerical example enables to assess the influence of differences in population size and comparative advantages on the optimum structure of production, demand and foreign trade for two countries. We distinguish the following four cases:

I. Identical production functions; countries of equal size.
II. Identical production functions; countries of unequal size.
III. Differentiation of production functions; countries of equal size.
IV. Differentiation of production functions; countries of unequal size.

For each of these cases the values of the various variables have been calculated under the assumption of investment coordination as defined in chapter 2. The values of the marginal capital–output ratios have been chosen as follows:

Cases I and II	*Cases III and IV*	
$\kappa_1^1=2$	${}^1\kappa_1^1=2$	${}^2\kappa_1^1=2$
$\kappa_2^1=3$	${}^1\kappa_2^1=2.5$	${}^2\kappa_2^1=3$
$\kappa_3^1=4$	${}^1\kappa_3^1=4$	${}^2\kappa_3^1=3.5$

The numerical values of all other coefficients used in these calculations are the same as those in the example of section 3.1. For all cases we choose $\bar{Y}=380$ and $\bar{L}=210$.

The results of the calculations are given in table 2. The following are some of the conclusions which can be drawn from this table:

1. Equality in income and identical production structure are optimal under our assumption that each country can have free trade with the rest of the world if both countries are of equal size and have no comparative advantages with respect to each other.
2. Comparison between I and II shows that the countries have no longer identical structures if they differ in size, although their production functions are the same. In case II there is already a possibility of mutual trade between the countries in the products of industry 1.
3. Case III compared to I shows the impact of comparative advantages: the

TABLE 2

Optimum structure of production, domestic demand and foreign trade under alternative assumptions about relative population size and comparative advantages for $\bar{Y} = 380$ and $\bar{L} = 210$.

	Production		Domestic demand		Net exports	
	${}^1Y_h$	${}^2Y_h$	${}^1X_h$	${}^2X_h$	${}^1E_h$	${}^2E_h$
I. No comparative advantages; ${}^1L = {}^2L$						
Industry 1	60.8	60.8	64	64	−3.2	−3.2
Industry 2	73.1	73.1	84	84	−10.9	−10.9
Industry 3	56.1	56.1	42	42	14.1	14.1
Total	190	190	190	190	0	0
II. No comparative advantages; ${}^2L = 2{}^1L$						
Industry 1	47.5	74.2	42.7	85.3	4.8	−11.2
Industry 2	46.4	99.7	56.0	112.0	−9.6	−12.3
Industry 3	32.8	79.4	28.0	56.0	4.8	23.4
Total	126.7	253.3	126.7	253.3	0	0
III. With comparative advantages; ${}^1L = {}^2L$						
Industry 1	57.5	58.0	64.5	63.5	−7.0	−5.5
Industry 2	86.1	62.1	87.1	80.9	−1.0	−18.9
Industry 3	51.5	64.9	43.5	40.5	8.0	24.4
Total	195.1	184.9	195.1	184.9	0	0
IV. With comparative advantages; ${}^2L = 2{}^1L$						
Industry 1	44.1	71.3	43.2	84.8	1.0	−13.5
Industry 2	59.5	88.7	59.1	108.9	0.4	−20.2
Industry 3	28.2	88.2	29.5	54.5	−1.4	33.7
Total	131.8	248.2	131.8	248.2	0	0

relatively low value of the marginal capital–output ratio in country 1 for industry 2 and the relatively low value of this ratio in country 2 for industry 3 causes the relatively high levels of output of the industries 2 and 3 in the countries 1 and 2, respectively. The same impact is shown by a comparison between the cases II and IV.

4. Calculation of the per capita income shows no great discrepancies in the four cases between both countries:

	Case I	II	III	IV
Country 1	1.81	1.81	1.86	1.88
Country 2	1.81	1.81	1.76	1.77

References

[1] Hollis B. CHENERY, 'The Interdependence of Investment Decisions' in Moses Abramovitz et al. (eds.), *The Allocation of Economic Resources*. Stanford University Press, Stanford, California, 1959.

[2] David KENDRICK, 'Investment Planning and Economic Integration', *Economics of Planning*, Vol. 7, no. 1, 1967, pp. 48–72.

[3] Alan S. MANNE (ed.), *Investments for Capacity Expansion: Size, Location and Time-Phasing*, London, 1967.

[4] J. TINBERGEN, 'Economic Development and Investment Indivisibilities', in *Problems of Economic Dynamics and Planning*, Essays in Honour of M. Kalecki, Warsaw, 1964.

[5] P. J. VERDOORN, 'Welke zijn de achtergronden en vooruitzichten van de economische integratie in Europa en welke gevolgen zou deze integratie hebben, met name voor de welvaart in Nederland?', *Preadviezen* 1952 *van de Vereniging voor de Staatshuishoudkunde*, pp. 47–135 (in Dutch).

[6] T. VIETORISZ and A. S. MANNE, 'Chemical Processes, Plant Location and Economies of Scale' in A. S. Manne and H. M. Markowitz (eds.), *Studies in Process Analysis*, Cowles Foundation, Monograph 18, Wiley, New York, 1963, pp. 136–158.

TRADE FLOWS AND GEOGRAPHICAL DISTANCE,
OR THE IMPORTANCE OF BEING NEIGHBOURS*

HANS LINNEMANN

1. Trade Between Neighbour Countries

There is a saying that 'a near neighbour is better than a distant cousin'. This proverb may or may not be true in daily life; the reader may judge for himself. The present short article will deal with trade flows between nations, and, in particular, with the extent to which these trade flows are influenced by the fact that countries may be neighbours, or distant cousins, or just ordinary trade partners of each other. Unfortunately, there are also in the present-day world countries which are not (and sometimes indeed should not be) accepted as trade partners by other nations. From an economic point of view, there is not much to say about the absence of trade flows due to political considerations; in any case, we will presently focus our attention on the effect of neighbourhood on the value of trade between countries willing to accept each other as trade partners.

In this article, countries will be considered as neighbours when they have a common border, so that transport from one to another is possible without crossing another country or the sea. It is to be expected that trade will be stimulated by the existence of facility of communication and transportation between adjacent countries. What we want to establish is whether this stimulation exists indeed and, if so, what is its magnitude – in a number of individual cases and, if possible, in general. A first attempt in this direction has already been made by J. Tinbergen [6]. In point of fact, it is the stimulus of having been a working neighbour of this great economist that has induced the present author to follow Tinbergen's lead in the study of world trade

*) The author is indebted to Mr. B. S. M. Berendsen for his assistance in performing the necessary calculations.

patterns – another example of the importance of being neighbours, albeit in a different sense and with a one-way stimulation!

Tinbergen's approach can be summarized as follows. The trade flow from country i to country j primarily depends upon the economic size of the trade partners (measured by the GNP's of the countries) and the geographical distance between them. Additional explanatory variables, which play an active role only in certain cases, are the existence of preferential trade agreements between the two partners and the fact of their being neighbours. This type of explanatory variable is introduced in the form of a dummy variable that takes an arbitrary positive value if applicable, and the value zero in all other cases. Assuming a log-linear relationship, the trade-flow equation reads:

$$X_{ij} = \alpha_0 Y_i^{\alpha_1} Y_j^{\alpha_2} D_{ij}^{\alpha_3} N_{ij}^{\alpha_4} P_{ij}^{\alpha_5} \tag{1}$$

in which

X_{ij} = exports of country i to country j;
Y = gross national product;
D_{ij} = distance between country i and country j;
N_{ij} = dummy variable for neighbouring countries;
P_{ij} = dummy variable for preferential relations between countries.

Since no statistical information on trade in invisibles is available on a country-to-country basis, X_{ij} stands for commodity trade only. Application of least-squares regression analysis to the trade data of 18 countries for the year 1959 led to an estimate of α_4 which was just significantly different from zero at the 95 per cent probability level. The trade-increasing effect of adjacency was found to be very limited, however; neighbourhood increased trade by no more than 5 per cent. The sample comprised 15 developed and only 3 less-developed countries; instances of neighbourhood were found only in Europe and in the case U.S.–Canada. In a similar calculation for a sample of 42 countries (now with a majority of developing countries), α_4 was again found to be significant at the 2σ-level, but not at the 3σ-level. The trade-expanding effect of being neighbours, as implied by the estimated coefficient, was much stronger this time and amounted to about 75 per cent of the 'normal' trade value [6, p. 288].

Interesting as these results are, they nevertheless have not yet settled the issue. Very likely, trade flows are larger than usual if the partners are neighbouring countries, but the difference between 5 and 75 per cent is rather great. Also, the impact of the distance variable in determining the normal value of trade is very significant and carries a large weight; at the same time, the distance cannot always be measured accurately and is particularly hard to determine between neighbour countries. The procedure followed by the author in similar studies [3] was that for each country an economic centre or a 'centre of gravity' was chosen, from which the distances to other countries (centres) were measured. It is highly likely that the same was done in Tinbergen's analysis. It is obvious that the shorter are the distances (as in the case of neighbours), the greater the relative effect of uncertainties and errors in measurement. Without detailed analysis from case to case, the measurement of distance between adjacent countries is a matter of rough approximation only. For this reason, the interpretation of the results mentioned above is rather uncertain.

2. Normal or Proportionate Trade Flows

We shall try to approach the matter from another angle, disregarding for the moment the effect of the distance variable. Obviously, neighbour countries are always near to each other, and it might be found that in these cases it is not necessary to introduce the distance effect explicitly into the analysis. What we intend to do is, therefore, to make a comparison between actual and 'normal' levels of trade between pairs of neighbouring countries, without incorporating the distance effect in the calculation of the 'normal' trade level.

The most straightforward way of defining a 'normal' or 'proportionate' level of trade is to assume that each country's exports are distributed over all possible destinations in proportion to total imports of each country of destination. If we transform the international trade matrix expressed in absolute amounts into a matrix of trade propensities or trade shares – by dividing all elements by the value of total world trade –, a row total indicates a country's share in world exports and a column total a country's share in world imports. Writing $x_{i.}$ for the share of country i in world exports (with $x_{i.} = \sum_{j=1}^{n} x_{ij}$), and writing $x_{.j}$ for the share of country j in world imports, the normal trade share of the individual flow from i to j could be simply defined as

$$\bar{x}_{ij} = x_{i.}x_{.j}\,. \tag{2}$$

Multiplying $\bar{x}_{ij}$ by the value of total world trade would give the normal trade level in absolute terms. A good measure for the extent to which actual trade deviates from normal trade is the logarithm of the ratio $x_{ij}/\bar{x}_{ij}$. In his analysis of international trade patterns with the concepts developed in information theory, H. Theil [5] calls this logarithmic ratio the mutual information between the exporting country i and the importing country j. In the case of neighbour countries, the mutual information value is expected to be positive.

This extremely simple procedure is not satisfactory, however, because $\bar{x}_{ii}$ should be zero, while nevertheless $\sum_i \sum_j \bar{x}_{ij}=1$. The above procedure can be applied in the case of trade between *regions*, with intraregional trade flows included in the analysis, but not in our case of trade between individual *countries*. The total export and total import propensities $x_{i.}$ and $x_{.j}$ should be modified in such a way that the sum of their products (with $\bar{x}_{ii}=0$ *a priori*) equals unity. An iterative procedure for calculating trade propensities that meet this requirement has been proposed originally by Savage and Deutsch [4], and corrected and improved by Goodman [1, 2]. Starting with the column and row totals of the matrix of actual propensities, two vectors u and v (with $\sum_i u_i=\sum_j v_j=1$) can be calculated by successive approximation in such a way that

$$\bar{x}_{ij} = s u_i v_j \tag{3}$$

with $\sum_i \sum_j \bar{x}_{ij}=1$ $(i \neq j)$. Here s stands for the (constant) correction multiplier, which increases the trade propensity or trade share of each element not on the main diagonal of the trade matrix due to the exclusion of the possibility of importing into any country part of its own exports; $s=(1-\sum_i u_i v_i)^{-1}$.

This method of calculating normal or proportionally distributed trade flows has been applied to the 1964–1965 average flows of an 80 by 80 trade matrix, specifying 79 individual countries and a 'rest of the world'-row and column. The iteration process in computing the vectors u and v was continued until 6-digit accuracy was obtained. The resulting $\bar{x}_{ij}$ for all neighbouring countries in the sample are given in the Appendix, as are the corresponding ratios $x_{ij}/\bar{x}_{ij}$. With two exceptions, the countries included in the sample were the same as those for which a similar exercise was made earlier [3] for the average trade flows of 1958–1960; the results of the earlier analysis were not published in this form, however, and are, therefore, also given in the Appendix. It is interesting to compare the results for the different periods[1]), but for the present purpose we want to present the main findings

[1]) A striking development is the large relative increase in trade between neighbouring countries that are members of the Central American common market. Less marked relative increases are found in the case of LAFTA-member countries; the EFTA-effects, and, in par-

TABLE 1

Average level of trade stimulation between pairs of neighbouring countries, 1958–1960 and 1964–1965 (average ratio of actual over normal trade volume).

Afghanistan–Iran		1.1	Finland–Norway		1.6
Afghanistan–Pakistan		30	Finland–Sweden		3.8
Angola–Congo (Kinshasa)		7.0	France–Germany, F.R.		1.7
Argentina–Brazil		8.4	France–Italy		1.7
Argentina–Chile		7.0	France–Spain		1.9
Argentina–Paraguay		30	France–Switzerland		2.1
Argentina–Uruguay		4.8	Germany, F.R.–Netherlands		2.3
Austria–Germany, F.R.		3.8	Germany, F.R.–Switzerland		2.4
Austria–Italy		3.3	Greece–Turkey		1.1
Austria–Switzerland		3.2	Greece–Yugoslavia		6.8
Austria–Yugoslavia		4.7	Guatemala–Honduras		25
Belgium–France		2.4	Guatemala–Mexico		2.3
Belgium–Germany, F.R.		1.8	Guiana–Venezuela	[a])	0
Belgium–Netherlands		4.6	Honduras–Nicaragua		9.5
Brazil–Colombia	[a])	0.2	India–Pakistan		2.8
Brazil–Guiana	[a])	0	Iran–Iraq		0.7
Brazil–Paraguay		2.9	Iran–Pakistan		3.6
Brazil–Peru	[a])	0.9	Iran–Turkey		1.1
Brazil–Uruguay		6.4	Iraq–Jordan		16
Brazil–Venezuela	[a])	2.1	Iraq–Syria		9.0
Burma–India		7.9	Iraq–Turkey		1.1
Burma–Pakistan		13	Italy–Switzerland		2.7
Burma–Thailand		0.8	Italy–Yugoslavia		4.1
Cambodia–South Vietnam	[b])	27	Jordan–Syria		110
Cambodia–Thailand	[b])	3.0	Lebanon–Syria		92
Cameroun–Nigeria		2.0	Libya–Tunisia		9.6
Canada–United States		3.3	Libya–United Arab Republic		17
Chile–Peru		8.0	Malaysia–Thailand		24
Colombia–Peru	[a])	1.5	Mexico–United States		3.8
Colombia–Venezuela		0.3	Mozambique–Rhodesia		10
Costa Rica–Nicaragua		26	Mozambique–South Africa		12
Denmark–Germany, F.R.		2.1	Norway–Sweden		7.0
Denmark–Sweden		4.7	Portugal–Spain		2.3
El Salvador–Guatemala		63	Rhodesia–South Africa		21
El Salvador–Honduras		90	Sudan–United Arab Republic		17
Ethiopia–Sudan		15	Syria–Turkey		3.9

[a]) frontiers in inaccessible areas only.
[b]) 1958–1960 only.

ticular, the EEC-effects among neighbour countries are even less significant and cannot be found at all in several cases – at least not in the data of the Appendix.

in a more condensed form. This is done in table 1, where the arithmetic average of the four ratios of actual to normal trade pertaining to each pair of neighbour countries (i.e., two observations $x_{ij}/\bar{x}_{ij}$ and two observations $x_{ji}/\bar{x}_{ji}$) is given; a pair of neighbouring countries is listed under the name of the country that comes first in alphabetical order.

3. Actual and Normal Trade Flows Between Neighbour Countries

The figures of table 1 reveal that a large variation exists in the trade-promoting effect of neighbourhood, as measured on the basis of the normal or proportionate trade flows defined above. Some exceptionally low values can easily be explained; in several cases, the common borderline is situated in remote and inaccessible areas where virtually no economic activity takes place and where no sizeable transportation across the border is possible. A clear example of this situation is found in the case of the central part of South America, where Brazil's frontiers with Peru, Colombia and Venezuela lie in the 'empty' area of the basin of the Amazon river. Six cases of neighbourhood in South America have been excluded from further analysis, as, for geographical reasons, the existence of the common border had to be considered as devoid of significance. To be sure, there are other cases where at present the neighbourhood of countries may be largely or totally irrelevant from the point of view of economic geography (perhaps Burma–Thailand, or Cameroun–Nigeria, or Iraq–Turkey), but nowhere was the irrelevancy as obvious as in the case of the Amazon area. Therefore, no other instances of neighbourhood have been rejected in advance, although it is patently obvious from a look at the atlas maps of the various continents that there are large variations in the significance of being geographic neighbours.

If we take the results of table 1, in spite of all complications and inaccuracies, at their face value, a second conclusion to be drawn is that the trade-stimulating effect of being neighbours is presumably stronger between the (economically) smaller countries than between the larger countries. Another tendency, related to the first, is that of stronger trade stimulation between developing countries than between developed ones. Although the variations within one group are often quite large, and the average values therefore not too meaningful, table 2 tries to summarize the findings for different groups of countries.

The classification by continents and subcontinents shows, roughly speaking, three levels of trade stimulation on account of neighbourhood: (a)

TABLE 2

Average level of trade stimulation between neighbouring countries, for groups of countries.

Area	Number of cases	Arithmetic mean	Median
Europe	23	3.1	2.4
North America	2	3.6	
South America	8	8.5	6.7
Central America	6	36	26
Asia	10	11	5.8
Africa	6	11	11
Middle East (Arab partners only)	7	37	17
Middle East (other)	4	1.7	1.1

between developed, industrialized nations by a factor 3; (b) between developing countries usually by a factor 6 to 10; (c) between smaller developing countries, in particular in the context of regional cooperation schemes, by a factor 15 to 35. Trade flows with or between the non-Arab Middle East countries (Turkey, Iran) do not fit into this pattern; however, as observed before, the areas around the common frontiers of these countries are rather remote from the main centres of activity and poorly integrated into the transportation networks of these countries. It should also be stressed that the coverage of the sample is too limited in the cases of Asia and particularly Africa. Centrally planned economies are excluded altogether from the sample, except for Yugoslavia. For the period 1959–1960, Theil [5] found that intra-Communist trade was 5.4 times the normal or proportionate level (which he calls the independence level), and in the period 1951–1952 even 7.6 times.[2]) Thus, trade with immediate neighbours may well have been at 6 to 10 times the level of proportionately distributed trade.

A closer look at the detailed results as given in the Appendix suggests the importance of another systematic factor; the smaller the normal level of trade between a pair of neighbour countries, the stronger the trade-stimulating effect of neighbourhood. This relationship is illustrated in table 3, which gives the frequency distribution of the normal or proportionate trade flows included in the analysis (average of 1958–1960 and 1964–1965), and the corresponding average $x_{ij}/\bar{x}_{ij}$ ratios.

[2]) The findings are originally expressed in bits, a measure used in information theory; the figures are given in [5, p. 363].

TABLE 3

Ratio of actual over normal trade, between neighbouring countries, per frequency class of the normal trade volume.

Normal trade volume in mln. U.S.$	Frequency	Average $x_{ij}/\bar{x}_{ij}$ ratio
> 100	25	2.7
100 – > 10	20	4.0
10 – > 1	40	6.4
1 – > 0.1	36	15
0.1 – > 0.01	15	50

It is not difficult to find a partial explanation for the relationship shown in table 3. Trade stimulation between neighbours by a certain absolute amount (not dependent on the normal trade volume) would of course have a much greater relative impact if the normal trade were small, than if it were large. However, as a multiplication of the class mean by the ratio $x_{ij}/\bar{x}_{ij}$ immediately reveals, the class-to-class variation in absolute amount of trade increase is quite substantial – from \$2.5 mln. to about \$1,000 mln. for the two intervals at the extremities. The only conclusion that can be drawn from the analysis so far is a rather negative one; for the level of trade between two countries there is no simple and general way of expressing the significance of the fact of their being neighbours – certainly not by means of a single multiplicative of additive factor. This also explains why the Tinbergen results [6] described earlier are rather different for the two different samples of countries analysed by him. In the smaller sample, developed countries dominated; hence a much more limited neighbour-country effect was found than in the bigger sample which included a large number of developing countries, and therefore many trade flows of smaller volume.

The advantage of Professor Tinbergen's analysis over the approach followed here is that his method estimates a normal level of trade between a pair of countries taking into account the distance factor. As has been stated already, the distance variable turned out to be one of the most significant variables in explaining variations in the volume of trade between two nations. The neighbour-country effect operates, where applicable, in addition to the distance effect operating in all cases. We want to see now under what conditions it makes sense to try to tackle the problem in this manner, considering the margins of error involved in measuring the distance between neighbours.

4. The Effect of Being Neighbours, and Geographical Distance

The present method of normalising trade flows can be used to estimate the effect of geographical distance between trade partners on the level of trade. The ratio between actual and proportionate trade is compared with the distance, for twenty distance classes; for each distance class, ten observations are obtained by sampling methods. Class averages for $x_{ij}/\bar{x}_{ij}$ and D (for distance) are then correlated, on the basis of an assumed log-linear relationship comparable with equation (1):

$$\frac{x_{ij}}{\bar{x}_{ij}} = \beta_0 D^{\beta_1}. \tag{4}$$

This method has already been applied to 1958–1960 data in [3]; for this article it was applied to the 1964–1965 figures. For the latter period, another sample was made by choosing twenty countries (in a representative way) and selecting for each of these countries one observation per distance class. In all samples, the highest and the lowest observation for each class were rejected, in order to eliminate the influence of exceptional cases on the averages. The results of the regression analyses are given in table 4.

The important part played by the distance variable is again demonstrated

TABLE 4

The ratio between actual and normal trade, as explained by the distance between the trade partners; $\log(x_{ij}/\bar{x}_{ij}) = \log\beta_0 + \beta_1 \log D$. (Variable D is measured in 1,000 nautical miles.)

Sample	$\log\beta_0$	β_0	β_1	σ_{β_1}	r
A. 1958–1960:					
80 countries					
200 flows [a])	0.244	1.76	−0.70	0.12	0.81
B. 1964–1965:					
80 countries					
200 flows	0.653	4.50	−1.22	0.39	0.92
C. 1964–1965:					
20 countries					
242 flows	0.421	2.63	−0.87	0.28	0.92

a) See [3, p. 183].

by these results. The exponent of the variable D as estimated from A and C is quite similar to the earlier findings of Tinbergen [6] and of the present author [3]. The results of case B differ somewhat from these findings; the absolute values of the estimates for β_0 and β_1 are greater than in other cases. In the following section we will use the coefficients of cases A and C only.

Equation (4) will be used now, together with the parameter estimates given in table 4, to calculate the distances corresponding to some of the values of the ratio $x_{ij}/\bar{x}_{ij}$ that were found to exist between neighbour countries. Distances are originally measured in nautical miles, but are given also in kilometers; 1 nautical mile = 1.15 land miles = 1.852 kilometers. The constant-elasticity formula (4) offers us an easy way of estimating the consequences of a measurement error in D of, say, 10 per cent. The results have been brought together in table 5.

TABLE 5

Positive deviations in trade intensity, and the corresponding distances (if distances were the only determining factor).

$\frac{x_{ij}}{\bar{x}_{ij}}$	Case A; $\beta_1 = -0.7$			Case C; $\beta_1 = -0.87$		
	D	D (km)	Effect on ratio of 10% error in D	D	D (km)	Effect on ratio of 10% error in D
2	0.830	1,535	±0.14	1.375	2,544	±0.17
5	0.224	414	±0.35	0.479	886	±0.44
20	0.031	57	±1.4	0.100	185	±1.74
100	0.003	6	±7	0.015	28	±8.7

What do these figures tell us? Firstly, they show that trade-increasing effects of an order of magnitude of a factor 2 to 5 can be explained by the distance variable (without an additional neighbour-country effect), for distances varying between 1500 and 400 kilometers (case A), or between 2500 and 900 kilometers (case C). These values are high enough to encompass the 'distances' between most, if not all, neighbour countries. Moreover, in view of the margins of error involved in measuring these distances, an additional trade stimulation by 5 per cent on account of neighbourhood – Tinbergen's first case mentioned above – is not significant; a 10 per cent error in measurement has an impact on the trade volume of 7 to 9 per cent. In [3] the lowest value given to the distance variable was $D = 0.1$ (i.e. 185 kilometers), which is perhaps the shortest distance indeed between the economic centres of any pair of neighbouring countries. At this 'minimum distance', the value of the ratio $x_{ij}/\bar{x}_{ij}$ is almost 9 in case A, and 20 in case C. Higher values of the latter ratio could, therefore, be explained only in terms of an additional neighbour effect. Of course, this does not exclude the possibility of a neighbour-country effect in case of lower values of this ratio, because the distance between the neighbours may well be more than 185 kilometers. With an $x_{ij}/\bar{x}_{ij}$ ratio of less than 5, however, it is likely that the distance factor alone could account for the deviation from the normal or proportionate trade level.

This is about as far as the present analysis could bring us – which is admittedly not very far. We have found that it is impossible to come to a general conclusion about the intensity of trade stimulation between two neighbouring countries. This was found, first of all, when the distance factor was not introduced explicitly; deviations from a normal or independent pattern of trade varied tremendously. The general tendency found was for the trade-increasing factor operating between neighbouring countries to be stronger, the lower the normal level of trade (table 3). Then, secondly, the geographical distance between the trade partners was taken into account, which meant that the neighbour-country effect was considered purely as an extra factor, operating in addition to the trade-stimulating force of the short geographical distance between the neighbours. Here we had to conclude (a) that the distance variable plays a quite significant role in determining the actual levels of trade, (b) that a ratio of 5 between actual and normal (or proportionally distributed) trade between neighbours can be explained by the distance variable only, and (c) that an actual/normal trade ratio of more than 10 to 20 cannot be explained except by assuming a neighbour-country effect. But even in the latter case, it is next to impossible to quantify the intensity of the neighbour-country trade stimulation, because of the difficulties encountered in measuring with some accuracy the distance between neighbour countries. It may well be necessary to fall back on such crude methods of analysis as used in table 3, if one wants to estimate the actual trade level between neighbours when the normal or proportionate level is known.

5. The Effects of 'Neighbourhood' and 'Cousinhood' Compared

In the first paragraph of this article, we said something about neighbours and distant cousins. We may now compare, very roughly, the relative importance to trade of these two types of relations. By 'distant cousins' we mean the relationship between countries having special commercial and economic (and sometimes political) ties, usually based on colonial relations in the past – and also in the present, in some unfortunate instances. Disregarding the effect of distances on trade volumes, we compared actual and proportionately distributed trade flows for sixteen cases of cousinhood. Table 6 shows the results, as the averages of the ratios $x_{ij}/\bar{x}_{ij}$ and $x_{ji}/\bar{x}_{ji}$ for each pair of countries; the findings for 1958–1960 and 1964–1965 are reported separately so as to give an impression of the changes over time.

TABLE 6

Average level of trade stimulation between 'distant cousins', 1958–1960 and 1964–1965 (average ratio of actual over normal trade volume).

Pair of 'cousins'	1958–1960	1964–1965
Belgium–Congo (Kinshasa)	12	9.8
France–Cameroun	13	9.2
France–Ivory Coast	14 [a])	8.0
France–Morocco	7.6	6.9
France–Tunisia	11	7.0
Portugal–Angola	91	104
Portugal–Mozambique	84	77
United Kingdom–Australia	3.3	2.2
United Kingdom–Ghana	3.7	2.9
United Kingdom–Guiana	3.7	2.9
United Kingdom–India	2.6	1.7
United Kingdom–Jamaica	3.4	2.3
United Kingdom–Malaysia	2.2	1.8
United Kingdom–New Zealand	4.8	4.5
United Kingdom–Nigeria	4.6	3.5
United Kingdom–Pakistan	1.9	1.5

[a]) All countries of former French West Africa.

The figures of table 6 demonstrate that the order of magnitude of trade stimulation between distant cousins is about the same as that for neighbouring countries. The ratios have decreased in the five-year period that separates the two sets of observations; this may partly be due to the rapid expansion of trade between the European countries in these years, rather than to a weakening of the special relationship as such. The differences between the trade stimulation ratio of the Commonwealth cousins, of the francophone cousins, and of the other cases are remarkable. They are partly caused by differences in policies of 'economic cooperation' (no doubt an euphemism for colonial exploitation, in several instances) between these groups of countries; but we also find, as before, that the actual/normal trade ratio is higher for smaller normal or proportionate flows. This is illustrated by the figures of table 7, which have been calculated by classifying the table 6 data by the size of the corresponding proportionate trade flow.

TABLE 7

Ratio of actual over normal trade, between selected 'distant cousin' countries, per frequency class of the normal trade volume.

Normal trade volume in mln. U.S.$	Frequency	Average of $x_{ij}/\bar{x}_{ij}$ and $x_{ji}/\bar{x}_{ji}$
> 100	5	2.3
100 – > 10	18	5.5
10 – > 1	5	8.0
1 – > 0.1	4	89

Although the number of observations in the latter case is too low to permit firm conclusions, and although our concept of 'distant cousins' is vague and arbitrarily interpreted as referring to the trade relations between (former) metropolitan countries and their (former) colonies or dominions, it is still possible to conclude that this sort of special relationship – and the corresponding complementarity of the two economies involved – can apparently be made so strong and effective that a trade intensity is created which is as great as if the 'distant cousin' were a neighbour. We must emphasize once more that this analysis has not taken into account the effect of the distance between the partners on the trade volume; if this is done – as in [3], for instance – the effect of the special relations between the 'cousins' is of course much more pronounced, for the very reason that they are more 'distant' than neighbouring countries. The additional information contributed by the present article is that the special economic and political relations analysed here have resulted in trade levels of an intensity equal to those between neighbouring countries.

Appendix

Commodity trade between neighbouring countries.

	Volume of the normal (proportionate) trade flow, in mln. U.S.$		Ratio between actual and normal (proportionate) trade flow	
	1958–1960	1964–1965	1958–1960	1964–1965
United States to Canada	1136.9	1547.4	3.2	3.4
Mexico	240.4	274.3	3.4	4.0
Canada to United States	1037.0	1329.6	3.1	3.3
Costa Rica to Nicaragua	0.05	0.10	16	33
El Salvador to Guatemala	0.15	0.22	29	90
Honduras	0.07	0.11	54	111
Guatemala to El Salvador	0.11	0.19	35	97
Honduras	0.06	0.11	3.3	55
Mexico	1.31	1.49	0.4	0.1
Honduras to El Salvador	0.07	0.12	87	106
Guatemala	0.09	0.14	16	27
Nicaragua	0.04	0.09	2.5	8.9
Mexico to United States	140.0	169.1	4.0	3.7
Guatemala	0.99	1.34	5.2	3.6
Nicaragua to Costa Rica	0.06	0.12	25	30
Honduras	0.04	0.08	2.5	24
Argentina to Brazil	12.8	9.74	6.5	10
Chile	4.20	4.97	7.0	9.4
Paraguay	0.38	0.35	21	31
Uruguay	1.69	1.43	3.9	11
Brazil to Argentina	14.1	9.79	4.9	12
Colombia	5.14	4.45	0.0	0.6
Paraguay	0.47	0.37	2.3	6.5
Peru	3.93	5.30	0.1	1.3
Uruguay	2.09	1.49	9.6	10
Venezuela	16.8	9.87	0.1	0.4
Guiana	0.78	0.82	0	0
Chile to Argentina	5.45	4.22	5.8	5.6
Peru	1.52	2.28	2.0	1.9
Colombia to Brazil	5.93	3.63	0	0.1
Peru	1.47	1.89	1.4	2.1
Venezuela	6.30	3.53	0.2	0.6
Paraguay to Argentina	0.33	0.34	28	39
Brazil	0.37	0.36	0	2.7
Peru to Brazil	4.21	4.46	0.4	1.7
Chile	1.38	2.28	18	10
Colombia	1.37	1.96	0.8	1.8
Uruguay to Argentina	1.16	1.19	1.2	3.0
Brazil	1.30	1.23	2.8	3.0

Commodity trade between neighbouring countries (*continued*).

	Volume of the normal (proportionate) trade flow, in mln. U.S.$		Ratio between actual and normal (proportionate) trade flow	
	1958–1960	1964–1965	1958–1960	1964–1965
Venezuela to Brazil	23.9	18.5	3.7	4.3
Colombia	7.76	8.12	0.3	0.2
Guiana	1.18	1.49	0	0
Guiana to Brazil	0.79	0.64	0	0
Venezuela	0.84	0.62	0	0
Austria to Germany, F.R.	72.2	155.9	3.6	2.8
Italy	30.7	65.6	5.4	2.7
Switzerland	17.7	32.1	2.6	3.6
Yugoslavia	4.93	11.3	6.3	3.4
Belgium-Luxembourg to				
France	154.9	377.4	2.2	2.4
Germany, F.R.	277.7	628.3	1.7	2.0
Netherlands	146.6	262.2	4.9	5.1
Denmark to Germany, F.R.	110.1	228.3	2.5	1.5
Sweden	31.2	53.2	3.5	5.0
Finland to Norway	8.79	16.2	0.9	0.9
Sweden	15.9	32.4	1.9	2.7
France to				
Belgium-Luxembourg	166.4	361.8	2.4	2.6
Germany, F.R.	390.4	1026.3	1.9	1.7
Italy	165.9	432.0	1.7	1.7
Spain	40.0	149.9	1.9	2.0
Switzerland	95.6	211.0	2.6	2.7
Germany, F.R. to Austria	109.6	212.6	4.5	4.2
Belgium-Luxembourg	366.4	677.3	1.7	1.9
Denmark	151.0	293.1	2.4	1.9
France	479.6	1153.9	1.7	1.6
Netherlands	454.0	801.7	1.9	2.2
Switzerland	210.6	395.1	2.8	2.9
Greece to Turkey	0.82	1.01	0.5	0.3
Yugoslavia	1.01	2.35	9.5	5.2
Italy to Austria	30.4	76.9	2.9	2.0
France	133.1	417.4	1.5	1.7
Switzerland	58.4	142.9	3.7	2.6
Yugoslavia	16.3	50.5	4.8	3.1
Netherlands to				
Belgium-Luxembourg	126.1	227.2	4.2	4.0
Germany, F.R.	295.8	644.6	2.6	2.6
Norway to Finland	5.27	12.3	2.5	2.0
Sweden	18.3	32.7	4.7	6.3
Portugal to Spain	2.42	8.05	1.2	1.9

Commodity trade between neighbouring countries (*continued*).

	Volume of the normal (proportionate) trade flow, in mln. U.S.$		Ratio between actual and normal (proportionate) trade flow	
	1958–1960	1964–1965	1958–1960	1964–1965
Spain to France	24.9	59.3	1.8	1.8
Portugal	2.74	4.54	1.8	4.4
Sweden to Denmark	32.5	60.5	4.5	5.6
Finland	15.1	34.8	5.3	5.4
Norway	28.9	46.3	7.8	9.3
Switzerland to Austria	17.5	32.1	3.0	3.6
France	76.4	174.1	1.6	1.4
Germany, F.R.	137.0	289.8	2.2	1.6
Italy	58.2	122.0	2.4	1.9
Turkey to Greece	1.35	2.47	1.4	2.0
Syria	0.46	0.55	7.1	4.5
Iran	1.63	1.89	0.7	1.7
Iraq	0.81	1.05	1.1	0.5
Yugoslavia to Austria	3.56	11.2	6.5	2.7
Greece	1.71	5.66	8.9	3.4
Italy	11.9	42.6	5.2	3.3
United Arab Republic to				
Libya	0.33	0.99	6.6	1.8
Sudan	0.35	0.77	44	10
Syria to Turkey	0.30	0.54	1.0	2.8
Lebanon	0.18	0.42	83	84
Iraq	0.20	0.42	16	9.9
Jordan	0.06	0.14	113	48
Lebanon to Syria	0.05	0.09	124	77
Ethiopia to Sudan	0.08	0.15	25	5.3
Iran to Turkey	3.13	4.03	0.4	1.5
Iraq	2.05	3.10	1.0	0.8
Afghanistan	0.26	0.43	0	2.8
Pakistan	3.52	7.36	7.2	4.6
Iraq to Turkey	2.57	2.70	0	5.6
Syria	0.96	1.08	1.6	8.5
Iran	3.41	3.72	0.6	0.4
Jordan	0.52	0.72	1.4	1.4
Jordan to Syria	0.01	0.03	200	78
Iraq	0.02	0.06	30	33
Libya to				
United Arab Republic	0.06	3.76	58	3.2
Tunisia	0.02	0.98	10	4.2
Sudan to				
United Arab Republic	0.69	1.04	11	3.7
Ethiopia	0.10	0.15	20	7.7

Commodity trade between neighbouring countries (*continued*).

	Volume of the normal (proportionate) trade flow, in mln. U.S.$		Ratio between actual and normal (proportionate) trade flow	
	1958–1960	1964–1965	1958–1960	1964–1965
South Africa to Mozambique	1.19	1.39	17	18
Rhodesia	4.17*	2.72	40*	30
Angola to Congo (Kinshasa)	0.32	0.27	8.3	17
Congo (Kinshasa) to Angola	0.49	0.43	2.0	0.5
Cameroun to Nigeria	0.45	0.50	0.8	0.6
Mozambique to				
South Africa	1.09	1.75	5.2	6.5
Rhodesia	0.31*	0.22	9.3*	20
Nigeria to Cameroun	0.33	0.48	2.7	4.0
Rhodesia to South Africa	7.16*	5.91	5.9*	6.4
Mozambique	0.58*	0.38	4.2*	7.1
Tunisia to Lybia	0.18	0.22	6.0	18
Afghanistan to Iran	0.34	0.26	0.3	1.2
Pakistan	0.29	0.34	26	22
Burma to India	3.39	3.69	11	5.6
Pakistan	0.91	1.33	19	8.0
Thailand	0.57	0.92	0.2	0.5
India to Burma	2.07	2.54	9.2	5.7
Pakistan	5.91	9.99	2.8	1.8
Pakistan to Iran	1.82	2.22	1.3	1.1
Afghanistan	0.12	0.17	33	38
Burma	0.54	0.75	16	19
India	5.73	8.17	2.8	3.8
Cambodia to South Vietnam	0.09	0.18	14	1.9
Thailand	0.14	0.38	1.4	0
South Vietnam to Cambodia	0.03	0.02	40	7.5
Malaya to Thailand	1.71	4.77**	5.2	3.5**
Thailand to Burma	0.45	0.89	1.1	1.5
Cambodia	0.11	0.32	4.5	0
Malaya	0.93	4.09**	55	32**

* Federation of Rhodesia and Nyasaland;
** Malaysia–Singapore

References

[1] L. A. GOODMAN, 'A Short Computer Program for the Analysis of Transaction Flows', *Behavioral Science*, 9 (1964), pp. 176–186.

[2] L. A. GOODMAN, 'Statistical Methods for the Preliminary Analysis of Transaction Flows', *Econometrica*, 31 (1963), pp. 197–208.

[3] H. Linnemann, *An Econometric Study of International Trade Flows*; Amsterdam, North-Holland Publishing Company, 1966.
[4] I. R. Savage and K. W. Deutsch, 'A Statistical Model of the Gross Analysis of Transaction Flows', *Econometrica*, 28 (1960), pp. 551–572.
[5] H. Theil, *Economics and Information Theory*; Amsterdam, North-Holland Publishing Company, and Chicago, Rand McNally, 1967.
[6] J. Tinbergen, *Shaping the World Economy – Suggestions for an International Economic Policy*; New York, Twentieth Century Fund, 1962.

IMPORTS FROM DEVELOPING COUNTRIES: A COMPARISON BETWEEN EEC, EFTA AND USA

F. P. JANSEN and L. H. JANSSEN

1. The Problem

Export performance of developing countries is one of the important issues in applied development economics. The question has two sides; one, often overlooked, refers to supply conditions: the capability of developing countries to supply the right amounts of such commodities as are demanded by their customers under the present regime of international trade; the other side is demand: which factors govern demand on the part of importers. The present paper deals with this second aspect. More specifically, it attempts to explain the import behaviour, vis-à-vis developing countries, of the three major markets in the western world: the European Economic Community, the European Free Trade Association, and the United States.

The exclusion of other important trade partners such as Japan and the socialist countries, is not a matter of logic or of principle, but rather of sheer convenience. In fact, the upsurge of Japan as a major industrial power is felt throughout the underdeveloped world; and the fast growing trade with socialist countries seems to open new vistas for the export possibilities of developing countries. Nevertheless, the developed market economies of Western Europe and North America so far form the main outlet for developing countries' trade; and they are bound to retain this predominant position for some time to come. These circumstances may lend some justification to the geographical limitations adopted in this paper.

According to table 1, the annual growth rate of developing countries' exports to the world increased from about 3% in the second half of the 'fifties to 6% in the first half of the present decade. The difference is partly due to price movements. In 1966 and 1960 the average price levels of developing countries' exports were about equal, but in 1955 prices were some

TABLE 1

Exports by developing countries according to destination.

Destination	Billion $, f.o.b., current prices			Annual percentage change	
	1955	1960	1966	1955–1960	1960–1966
World	23.69	27.31	38.75	2.9	6.0
Intra-trade	5.75	6.03	8.03	1.0	4.9
EEC	5.19	6.25	9.50	3.8	7.2
EFTA	3.90	4.32	5.11	2.1	2.8
USA	5.55	5.86	7.58	1.1	4.4
Japan	0.97	1.40	3.13	7.6	14.4
Other developed market economies	1.50	1.95	2.50	5.4	4.2
Socialist countries	0.57	1.22	2.45	16.4	12.3
Unspecified	0.26	0.28	0.45	—	—

Sources: 1955, 1960: UN Statistical Yearbook 1966; 1966: GATT-report 1967.

6% higher. In real terms, therefore, the average annual growth rate between 1955 and 1960 was over 4%, thereafter climbing to 6%.

There are large differences as between the various markets. Mutual trade within the group of developing countries expanded rather slowly. At the other extreme, fastest growth was recorded in exports to Japan and to the socialist countries, but trade with these countries forms yet only a modest share of total exports, the bulk of interchange being with western market economies.

In 1966, EEC, EFTA and USA together took about 70% of exports by developing countries, excluding their intra-trade. The largest single customer of the developing countries is the EEC, accounting for over 30% of their exports to the outside world.

This predominant position of the EEC is partly due to the general resource position of Western Europe which, in terms of food, raw materials, fuels and base metals, is much more dependent on imports from developing countries than, for example, North America. As an average over the five years 1962 through 1966, both EFTA and EEC countries imported about $ 45 per head annually, excluding manufactures other than base metals, from developing countries. The corresponding figure for the United States, where per capita income is twice as high, amounted to only $ 30.

TABLE 2

Exports by developing countries to EEC, EFTA and USA.

	1955	1960	1966	1955–1960	1960–1966
	Billion \$, f.o.b., current prices			*Annual change, percent*	
EEC	5.19	6.25	9.50	3.8	7.2
EFTA	3.90	4.32	5.11	2.1	2.8
USA	5.55	5.86	7.58	1.1	4.4
	Prices indices, 1966 = 100				
EEC	106	95	100		
EFTA	106	95	100		
USA	106	98	100		
	Billion \$, f.o.b., 1966 prices				
EEC	4.90	6.62	9.50	6.2	6.2
EFTA	3.68	4.60	5.11	4.6	1.8
USA	5.23	6.01	7.58	2.8	3.9
				Annual growth of real GNP, percent	
EEC				5.0	4.9
EFTA				3.3	3.7
USA				2.2	4.8

Sources: exports in current prices: table 1.
price indices: weighted averages of price indices for food, raw materials, fuels and manufactures exported by developing countries to developed market economies, as given in UN Statistical Yearbook 1966.
real growth GNP: UN Yearbook of National Account Statistics 1966.

Apart from these differences in basic position, there is the striking fact that exports from developing countries to the EEC show a much more vigorous growth than exports to other western countries. In 1955 the USA was the largest single outlet for exports from developing countries, and the difference between EEC and EFTA was considerably smaller than it is today. As evidenced by table 2, developing countries' exports to the EEC increased nearly twice as rapidly as exports to both EFTA and USA. The difference would even be larger if manufactures were excluded.

Such divergences might be satisfactorily explained by differences in economic growth performance for the period 1955–1960, but certainly not for the period since 1960. Growth of GNP was highest in the EEC and lowest in the EFTA countries, but since 1960 the differences in the rate of expansion of imports from developing countries have been much larger than the differences in GNP growth rates. Indeed, in both EFTA and USA, imports from developing countries increased at a slower rate than GNP, whilst the reverse was true in the EEC. If import expansion were to be ascribed to income growth, a much higher response to income growth in the EEC should be reckoned with, the elasticity coefficient being about double the comparable EFTA and USA figures – and even two and a half to eight times as high if manufactures were excluded. It seems plausible to assume that the high-income development pattern of the United States will be less natural resource-oriented than the European pattern; this may partly explain the differences between the USA and Europe, but not the differences between EFTA and EEC.

Various general hypotheses in explanation of the differences between the EEC and the other western markets may be discarded offhand.

Firstly, the fast growth of imports from developing countries into the EEC cannot be attributed to the latter's preferential arrangements with the associated countries. This is unlikely on a priori grounds, since associated countries' exports compete mainly with other developing countries and much less so with other sources of supply. Moreover, the first adjustments to the common external tariff did not take place until 1962, whilst the maximum preferences came into force only halfway through 1964, and even then incompletely; the preferential system has thus hardly had time to prove its effectiveness. These considerations are confirmed by the facts: as shown in appendix table 8, EEC imports from associated countries during the period 1960–1966 expanded even less than imports from developing countries in general (5.3% per annum as against 7.2%). This was partly due to differences in commodity composition of exports but, as the table shows, growth was also below normal for most individual commodities.

Second, the expansion of EEC imports cannot be attributed to a liberal policy regarding imports of manufactures. Table 3, which gives a breakdown of relevant imports into a few broad categories, shows that imports of manufactures from developing countries into the EEC were rather insignificant. On a per capita basis such imports were over twice as high in the United States and over thrice as high in EFTA-countries.

Tariff levels for those manufactures which have been identified by GATT as being of especial interest to developing countries were about equal in the EEC and the UK (17–18%), with a somewhat lower level in

TABLE 3

Composition of imports from developing countries into EEC, EFTA, and USA; $ per caput per year, average 1962–1966; f.o.b.value.

Importer	Food	Raw materials	Base metals	Fuels	Manuf.	Total
EEC	15.6	9.4	3.2	15.8	2.2	46.2
EFTA	18.6	8.6	3.2	15.5	7.1	53.0
USA	13.8	5.6	2.2	8.8	4.9	35.3

Source: GATT-report 1967; c.i.f. values for EEC and EFTA converted into f.o.b. values by means of a flat deduction rate for all categories

the USA (15%).[1] But non-tariff restrictions are much more stringent in the EEC, especially for textiles, than in the USA and the UK. Moreover, Commonwealth preferences have much more substance than EEC preferences for associated countries because of the very low levels of development prevailing in the latter. These various elements together result in the EEC being effectively much less liberal than the others as regards imports of manufactures from developing countries.

Finally, trade and general economic policies in the EEC have not been particularly conducive to larger imports from developing countries. Internal taxes on tropical products (sometimes very high as in the case of coffee) have persisted. Agricultural policy is geared to a high degree of self-sufficiency which for some products, e.g. grains, fruits, sugar, militates against the interests of underdeveloped exporters. Moreover, there is no system by which underdeveloped countries are privileged vis-à-vis other outside suppliers; mention may be made for example of the large quantities of oilseeds and cotton supplied by the United States in direct competition with underdeveloped countries. By and large, it is nearer to the truth to contend that imports from developing countries increased in spite of, rather than thanks to, policies pursued by the Community. Up to now, increasing imports appear merely to reflect growing needs of the European economy; they are not induced by liberal measures in recognition of developing countries' interests.

1) Pre-Kennedy Round figures, quoted from: Sidney J. Wells, The EEC and Trade with Developing Countries, *Journal of Common Market Studies*, December 1965.

The problem of an unequal import behaviour between the major western markets thus remains, with no obvious general explanation at hand. It seemed useful, therefore, to go into more detail and to analyse the matter by way of a commodity by commodity comparison. Such an approach ideally opens the possibility for taking into account both factors affecting demand – income, prices, and more specific circumstances – and forces working on the supply side – to what extent competition exists by domestic or other developed sources to the exports of underdeveloped suppliers. The analysis should next enable a distinction between temporary phenomena and factors to be regarded as being of a more lasting nature, on which basis indications for future developments may be found. An approach along these lines will be attempted in the next section of this paper: an analysis of tendencies since 1960 in both demand and supply, and a tentative projection of likely developments between 1966 and 1975. A really thorough study for each commodity group admittedly was beyond the scope of the present paper; wherever available existing analyses and forecasts have been drawn upon, but in other cases rather simple trend extrapolations sometimes had to be relied upon. Results for the individual commodity groups should therefore be interpreted with due reservation; however, the authors hope that at least part of the errors in detail will cancel out in the aggregates.

2. Individual Commodity Groups

For the purposes of analysis, total commodity imports from developing countries into EEC, EFTA and USA have been broken down into 24 commodity groups, arranged under 4 main headings: food, beverages, tobacco (12 groups), raw materials and base metals (8 groups), fuels (2 groups), and manufactures (2 groups). The commodity breakdown, with corresponding SITC-numbers, is listed in appendix table 1.

Imports from developing countries into the three markets for the years 1960 through 1966, are indicated in appendix tables 2, 3 and 4; the figures are in current prices. For the sake of convenience, the last column of these tables gives projected figures for 1975 in 1966 prices. Appendix tables 5, 6 and 7 list corresponding imports from all sources, but exclude intra-EEC and intra-EFTA trade. All figures in these six tables, with the exception of the 1975 forecasts, are derived from the import statistics of the OECD (Foreign Trade Statistics Series B and C) and the EEC (Foreign Trade Statistics, Analytical Tables). It should be borne in mind that EEC and

EFTA figures are in c.i.f. terms, whilst USA statistics are on an f.o.b. basis, so that no direct comparison is possible.

Apart from these figures in current value terms, the analysis has been based on developments in real terms, either directly by comparing volume figures of main commodities or indirectly by making use of published price indices. Where appropriate, the results of such comparisons are indicated in the text below; no systematic listing of the underlying figures has been attempted.

As a framework for the projections, some pattern of future income growth in the importing countries had to be assumed. In order to eliminate possible influences of differences in economic growth performance, projections were based on the assumption that the rather vigorous growth of recent years would continue in the EEC and the USA, and that growth in EFTA-countries would catch up. More specifically, the following figures have been accepted (table 4).

TABLE 4

Annual growth of real GNP (%).

	EEC	EFTA	USA
Total GNP			
1960–1966	4.9	3.7	4.8
1966–1975	4.9	4.9	4.9
Population			
1960–1966	1.1	0.8	1.3
1966–1975	1.0	0.7	1.2
GNP per caput			
1960–1966	3.8	2.9	3.4
1966–1975	3.8	4.2	3.7

Food, beverages and tobacco

Meat (SITC 01). Meat imports into the EEC increased considerably after 1962; if a 27% price increase between 1960 and 1966 is allowed for, imports at the end of the period appear to have been some 80% larger than in 1960. Total demand for meat increased at a much slower rate. Meat imports into the EEC are marginal in comparison to total consumption, and the growth of imports seems largely due to a presumably temporary shift in the balance between domestic supply and demand.

FAO projections of demand and supply [2]) indicate for 1975 a deficit which, percentagewise, will be at about the same level as that of the early sixties. In 1966 prices, and assuming the same share in imports for developing countries as during 1960–1966, this would imply that the 1975 level of exports by developing countries would hardly differ from those of recent years.

The situation is different in EFTA. Over 40% of the UK's consumption is derived from imports; on the other hand, Denmark is a significant exporter. For EFTA as a whole, the net deficit is proportionally much higher than in the EEC, although it has been on the decline in recent years. FAO expects that increases in demand in the UK will be largely met from expanding home production; moreover, important production increases are expected for Denmark. In the aggregate, EFTA deficits are projected to decline by some 25% from the level of the early 'sixties. Taking into account price increases since then, and assuming an unchanged share in the trade for developing countries, a virtually unchanged level of imports from developing countries appears between 1966 and 1975.

In the USA, as in the EEC, growth of meat imports, also marginal in comparison to consumption, outstripped growth in total consumption. For 1975 FAO expects the deficit to rise by some 45% over the level of the early 'sixties. With an unchanged share for developing countries, this would lead to a projected figure some 35% over the 1966 figure.

Cereals (SITC 04). EEC cereal imports from developing countries consist largely of coarse grains for livestock feeding and, to a far lesser extent, of wheat and rice. Between 1960 and 1966 imports, both from developing countries and from the world, increased by some 40% in volume terms. Wheat imports into the EEC may be expected to be wiped out almost completely in the near future; rice imports will increase considerably but their share in the total is insignificant. As to coarse grains, FAO expects an increase of the net deficit by nearly 50% over the level of the early 'sixties.

In EFTA countries, imports of grains from developing countries are much less important than in the EEC. The coarse grain deficit is expected to decline by some 15%; wheat imports may decline even faster but rice imports may increase by some 25%. On balance, a level of cereal imports

[2]) Agricultural Commodities – Projections for 1975 and 1985 FAO, 1967 (hereafter called: FAO-projections). This comprehensive study of demand and supply developments has been drawn upon extensively for agricultural products.

from developing countries some 10% higher than in 1966 may be expected for 1975.

Imports of cereals into the USA are insignificant. The figure for 1975 is taken as equal to 1966.

Fruit (SITC 05). European imports of fruit from developing countries consist for some 50% of citrus and bananas. In the United States bananas account for 40%, citrus imports being negligible.

In the EEC total imports of citrus and bananas expanded at an annual rate of some 6% between 1960 and 1966; the imports of other fruits from developing countries increased at an annual rate of nearly 9%. As to citrus, developing countries have to compete with domestic suppliers (Italy) and with developed outside suppliers. For the period up to 1975, an income elasticity coefficient of 0.6 is assumed, but production in Italy is likely to rise faster than imports from outside sources. On balance, the projections result in a 43% increase over the 1961–1963 import level. Bananas are supplied exclusively by developing countries. FAO projections indicate a rise in EEC-consumption between 1965 and 1975 of 40%, indicating a slowing down of recent rates of increase. For other fruits a somewhat declining growth rate has been assumed, in line with the expectations for citrus and bananas. Total future fruit imports from developing countries would then increase at 3.8% per year, implying an overall elasticity coefficient of 0.75.

Developments in the EFTA-market have been rather similar to those in the EEC, and elasticity coefficients for bananas and citrus for the future may also be expected to be of the same order of magnitude. Projections for the EFTA-market are therefore based on an elasticity coefficient of 0.75, applied to total fruit imports from developing countries.

The income elasticity of demand for bananas is much lower for the United States than for Europe – some 0.2, which would give an annual rate of increase of imports in the order of 2%. For other fruits, a 50% increase between 1966 and 1975 has been assumed.

Sugar (SITC 06). The EEC is a net exporter of sugar and is expected to continue so. Gross imports, from developing countries and other sources alike, show large year-to-year fluctuations but no trend. It has therefore been assumed that imports from developing countries in 1975 will be at the average 1960–1966 level (measured in 1966 prices).

Sugar imports are of much more significance in EFTA countries than in the EEC, the UK covering about two-thirds of requirements by imports. Consumption increases very slowly and home production tends to expand faster. For the EFTA countries together, FAO expects about the same deficit in 1975 as in the early 'sixties.

Imports supply more than 50% of requirements in the USA. It is expected that the deficit in absolute figures will decrease by some 10%, measured from the level in 1961–63.

Coffee, cocoa, tea (SITC 071, 072, 073). The three regions show large differences in consumption habits and developments for these products. Per capita consumption of coffee is highest in the USA, having reached near saturation level; second is the EEC, with still appreciable reactions of consumption to income growth. Per capita tea consumption in EFTA countries is about 10 times as high as in the USA and nearly twenty times as high as in EEC countries; only in the EEC can a positive correlation between consumption and income be found. Cocoa consumption is at about equal level in EFTA and USA, and somewhat higher in the EEC, although the differences here are less pronounced than with the other tropical beverages.

Projections have been based on the following income elasticity coefficients derived from long-term trends, and thought to be applicable to the period 1966–1975:

	Coffee	Cocoa	Tea
EEC	0.4	0.25	0.35
EFTA	0.3	0.15	0.0
USA	0.1	0.1	0.0

Beverages (SITC 11). In trade with developing countries this item is significant only in the EEC, where it relates mainly to imports of wine from Algeria. There is a steady decrease in such imports, a trend which, it is assumed, will continue in the years to come.

Projections for EFTA and USA are based on simple trend extrapolation.

Tobacco (SITC 12). Imports from developing countries into the EEC during the last 4 years increased at an annual rate of 2%; in earlier years growth rates were higher. The FAO projections expect a 2% growth rate of consumption for the future; because of expected production increases in the southern EEC countries, however, a somewhat lower rate of increase for imports, viz. 1.5%, has been assumed here.

In EFTA there is hardly any growth in per capita demand; a significant fall in the developing countries' share in total imports in 1966 is deemed to have been incidental. Projections are based on an annual 1% growth, reckoned from the 1964–1965 basis.

In the USA imports are rather small; there is no growth in per caput consumption. Projections assume an annual rate of growth in imports of 1%.

Oilseeds and vegetable oils (SITC 22, 42). In western developed countries, vegetable oil consumption reacts only weakly to income growth. EFTA imports confirm this, but EEC imports of oils and oilseeds between 1960 and 1966 show much more significant increases. This may be attributed mainly to a shift in the direction of soy-beans with a low oil content, and a corresponding high yield in terms of oil cakes, for which there is an ever increasing demand in EEC countries. Translating imports of oilseeds into terms of oil equivalent, and discarding the exceptionally high imports of the single year 1966, EEC import demand seems reasonably in line with expectations based on income and population growth.

The USA is a net exporter of oilseeds, and gross imports are only marginal in comparison to production and consumption. Although imports have increased rather strongly in recent years, a development in accordance with population and income growth is assumed for the near future.

Projections, then, are based on the following average elasticities for the period 1966–1975:

EEC : 0.1
EFTA: 0.0
USA : 0.05

The question may be raised whether the pressure exercised by developing countries towards processing more agricultural products domestically, may lead to a shift in the trade pattern from oilseeds to oils. This possibility cannot be excluded but since, at present world market prices, the margin of the oils plus cakes over the value of unprocessed seeds is of the order of 10% only, and since the shift presumably would affect not more than part of the trade, it seemed justifiable to neglect the possible effects in our projections.

Other food (remainder of main group). This item shows a rather fast expansion in EEC and USA, and much weaker growth in EFTA. Projections which, because of the heterogeneity of this group, have to be nominal, are based on a linear extrapolation of the changes in the share of this item in total food imports from developing countries.

Summary of food, beverages and tobacco. Summing up, the following picture for food imports from developing countries appears (table 5).

TABLE 5

Imports of food, beverages and tobacco, 1960, 1966, and 1975 (projected).

	Million $			Annual percentage change	
	1960	1966	1975	1960–1966	1966–1975
EEC	2,716	3,595	4,390	4.8	2.2
EFTA	1,908	1,948	2,378	0.3	2.2
USA	2,396	2,787	3,428	2.5	2.3
Total [a]	7,020	8,330	10,196	2.9	2.3
Price index 1966 = 100	93	100			
Total [a] 1966 prices	7,548	8,330	10,196	1.7	2.3

[a]) Imports of EEC and EFTA are on a c.i.f. basis, US imports in f.o.b. terms; so strictly speaking no direct adding would be allowed.

Sources: Appendix tables 2, 3 and 4. Price index: index for 'food' exported from developing countries to developed market economies, as given in *UN Statistical Yearbook* 1966.

Two main conclusions may be drawn from table 5:

(1) Provided income growth rates in EEC and USA are kept at recent levels and growth rates in EFTA catch up, it seems likely that the real growth in food imports from developing countries into the three regions together will accelerate somewhat in the years to come.

(2) Growth rates of imports into the three regions would converge, which especially would mean a slowing down of imports into EEC and a corresponding stepping up of imports into EFTA. Differences in economic growth performance apart, it would seem that the recent divergences in import behaviour between the EEC and EFTA markets have been largely incidental.

Raw materials and base metals

Hides and skins (SITC 21). Imports of hides and skins from developing countries show neither an upward nor a downward trend in any of the three regions. Imports in 1975 have therefore been projected at the same average level as found for the years 1964–1966.

Rubber (SITC 23). The volume of imports of natural rubber is at best stagnating in all three regions. Moreover, during the period 1960–1966 prices were under heavy downward pressure, 1966 prices being 40% below the 1960 level. The FAO projections assume a further decline of the share of natural rubber in the growing demand for rubber. The outcome for 1975 would be a slight increase in imports over 1966 for EEC and USA, and a slight decrease for the EFTA market.

As with other products, the results are given in 1966 prices; however, with regard to this commodity in particular, it should be remembered that a further fall in prices is likely.

Wood (SITC 24). During the period 1960–1966, the growth in imports of tropical hardwoods was weak in the EFTA and somewhat stronger in the EEC. The rather small imports into the United States hardly changed between 1960 and 1965, but increased by 25% in 1966.

The constraint on the expansion of imports seems to lie with supply rather than with demand. During the 'fifties imports rose at an annual rate of 10%, slowing down to some 5–6% after 1960. For the future, an annual growth rate of 5.5% is assumed for each of the three regions; this is roughly in line with FAO projections. However, it is uncertain whether supply will expand sufficiently to meet this increase in demand.

Textile fibres (SITC 26). Demand for natural fibres grows slowly in all western countries. The FAO projections, taking into account the likely development of demand, home production, and competition from man-made fibres, expect the following decennial growth percentages for imports during 1965–1975:

	EEC	EFTA	USA
Wool	12	5	11
Cotton	20	8	0
Jute	−15	−15	0

Assuming the same development for the minor fibres as for the three products mentioned, and weighting according to shares in the total, the following growth for total fibre imports from developing countries between 1966 and 1975 is attained:

EEC : 12.5%
EFTA: 5 %
USA : 6 %

In the EEC and EFTA, the increase may be somewhat larger if the US share in world cotton exports is reduced, but the effects of such a change can never be spectacular.

Metalliferous ores (SITC 28). This item can be subdivided into iron ore and the nonferrous ores, for which two categories developments are rather dissimilar.

In the EEC the volume of iron ore imports from all sources in 1966 was about 50% above the 1960 level. The entire increase was due to expanded exports from developing countries, which more than doubled in the six-year period, increasing their share in total EEC imports from 40% to 60%. In fact, neither EEC home production of iron ore nor imports from outside developed countries, at present accounting together for 60% of total supply, increase, all growth in demand being met from imports from developing countries. This tendency is likely to persist in the future, which means that any increase in EEC ore requirements has, and will have, a much more than proportional effect on exports by developing countries. It is assumed that pig iron production will continue to expand at an annual rate of 5.5%, which is in accordance with the trend observed over the last ten years. This implies that between 1966 and 1975, iron ore imports from developing countries will have to expand by 150%. Demand expansion for the other ores is rather weak; a nominal 10% increase between 1966 and 1975 is assumed. In 1975, therefore, imports of all ores from developing countries will be some 85% above the 1966 level.

The present picture in EFTA countries is different. About one-third of iron ore requirements is supplied from developing countries, and this share shows no sign of increasing. Accompanying the weak growth in GNP, however, expansion of pig iron production has been sluggish, and it is to be expected that when overall growth in EFTA catches up with EEC growth rates – a basic assumption in our projections – iron and steel production will increase accordingly.

Under such conditions, it seems most likely that EFTA, like the EEC, will have to turn to developing countries in order to meet its expanding iron ore requirements. For this reason, we assume that EFTA imports from developing countries will develop similarly to EEC imports. Because of the relatively larger share of nonferrous ores, however, growth in total ore imports from developing countries will expand at a slower rate than in the EEC, namely, by some 60% between 1966 and 1975.

Pig iron production in the United States expands at the much lower rate of 1.5–2% annually. Home production of iron ore meets about two-thirds of requirements but production is constant and will possibly decline. Imports are about equally divided between developed (Canada) and developing countries. On the basis of these tendencies, a future annual growth of imports from developing countries of over 5% might be expected. With regard to nonferrous ores, there has been a sharp decline in copper ore imports, due partly to a shift from ore to refined copper. The other nonferrous ores exhibit an annual growth in the order of 5–6%. The projections assume an annual rate of growth of imports from developing countries of 5.5% between 1966 and 1975 for all ores together.

Base metals (SITC 67, 68 minus 681). In the three western regions, imports from developing countries of products of the iron and steel group are insignificant in comparison with nonferrous metals. In value terms, imports of the latter increased rapidly due largely to considerable price increases, especially for copper which represents the main product in the trade of all three regions. European consumption of copper expanded noticeably during the 'fifties, but slowed down after 1960. However, developing countries improved their share of the trade. Copper is under heavy competition from the side of substitutes, and it is difficult to foretell to what extent the recent very high copper prices will stimulate this process of substitution.

Copper consumption in the United States rose considerably after 1960 under influence of heavy military demand, which factor adds an element of uncertainty to any projection. Other hardly predictable developments include the expansion of domestic production and substitution by other materials, as in Europe.

A resumption of European demand and a dampening of the US war effort might bring future growth rates closer to each other. Future demand for copper is in general expected to be rather strong. The market may be considerably weaker for other metals, however. A rather nominal assumption has been made for the projections of a 4% annual rate of increase of imports of base metals from developing countries into each of the three regions.

Other raw materials. For the remaining items, growth of imports from developing countries is assumed to be equal to the average development of the whole main group.

Total raw materials and base metals. Aggregating the foregoing, the following results are obtained (table 6).

TABLE 6

Imports of raw materials and base metals, 1960, 1966, and 1975 (projected).

	Million $			Annual percentage change	
	1960	1966	1975	1960–1966	1966–1975
EEC	2,340	3,137	4,414	5.0	3.9
EFTA	1,401	1,433	1,885	0.3	3.1
USA	1,545	1,727	2,432	1.9	3.9
Total [a]	5,286	6.297	8,731	3.0	3.7
Price index, 1966 = 100					
Raw materials	105	100			
Base metals	56	100			
Total [a], 1966-prices	5,913	6,297	8,731	1.1	3.7

[a]) Total of c.i.f. values of EEC and EFTA and f.o.b. values of USA.
Sources: Appendix tables 2, 3 and 4. Price indices: raw materials: index for developing countries' exports to developed market economies, as given in *UN Statistical Yearbook* 1966; base metals: index for nonferrous metals exported by developing countries, as given in *UN Yearbook of International Trade Statistics* 1965.

When added, the projections for the detailed items appear to indicate a certain acceleration for the group as a whole. It should be borne in mind that the largest part of the projected growth will be due to metals and metal ores, growth in the remaining items being much slower.

The same remark applies to the comparison of growth rates between the regions. As with food, the projections point in the direction of convergence between growth rates. This again is largely due to the fact that projected growth rates for imports of metals and ores into the three regions are rather similar. If iron production in EFTA fails to catch up with the EEC, or if imports of nonferrous metals show diverging patterns, a possibility which certainly cannot be excluded, the differences in future growth rates for the group as a whole may be far greater than suggested by the results of the projections.

Fuels

In the trade between developing countries and the West, solid fuels and natural gas play hardly a role; the only commodities of significance in this group are mineral oils and products thereof (SITC 33).

Increases in consumption of mineral oil are large, especially in Europe. Import figures reflect the underlying trends rather imperfectly because of the different proportions of crude oil and refined products, both over time and as between areas. Figures on consumption, expressed in crude oil equivalent form a better basis for the analysis.[3] Expansion of inland oil consumption shows the following figures (annual percentage rates of growth) for EEC and EFTA:

	1955–1960	1960–1966
EEC	13.3	15.3
EFTA	10.4	9.2

Two factors cause these high rates of growth: fast growing energy requirements, and substitution of oil for other fuels (mainly coal).

EFTA per capita energy consumption is higher than that of the EEC; this may partly explain the somewhat slower expansion during the past decade. Other factors include the weaker growth of GNP and, especially, the fact that coal has so far retained a larger share of the energy market.

As to the future, taking into consideration the development of total energy requirements, competition from the side of domestic oil production, exploitation of natural gas deposits, and the introduction of nuclear energy, OECD expects a slowing down of oil imports which, according to the average of a high and a low projection, would increase at an annual rate of about 6.5% during the period 1966–1975. Assuming that EFTA's import requirements will continue to grow somewhat more slowly than EEC's because of

[3]) Sources used in this section are the following OECD publications: *Oil Today*, 1964. *Oil Statistics*, 1961–1966. *Energy Policy*, 1966. *OECD Observer*, October 1966.

slower expansion of total energy requirements and continuing larger protection for domestic coal production[4]), the EFTA annual figure has been put at 5.5%, and the figure for EEC at about 7%.
In the United States, substitution of oil for coal has approached closer to technical limits than in Europe. Energy demand grows more slowly. Domestic oil production is directly protected for reasons of national security. Taking these factors into account, the OECD projections indicate a growth rate of 3.25% per annum for the period 1966–1975.

It should be observed, however, that oil imports in the US are much more marginal than in Europe; so that rather modest changes in the basic assumptions regarding domestic production might cause fairly drastic changes in the rate of growth of imports.

Manufactures

Manufactures exhibit the highest growth rates of all imports from developing countries into the western markets. Taking into account an estimated 5% rise in prices between 1960 and 1966, real annual growth rates during the period were as follows:
EEC : 13.4%
EFTA: 10.6%
USA : 16.1%

It should be remarked, however, that in spite of these high growth rates in the past, present imports are minute by any standard: a few dollars per head, and less than one percent of total demand for industrial products in the three markets. Lowest and highest on the scale are EEC and EFTA, respectively. Textiles, including clothing, constitute about 50% of imports in EFTA and USA and one-third in EEC.

More than for any other product, future developments in manufactures will depend on trade policies, which makes projections very hazardous. Although, even with high future growth rates, imports will be rather small in 1975 as compared to total consumption of industrial products, the impact in specific sectors will be felt more and more heavily, and the chances of even more restrictive policies will grow correspondingly. On the other hand, the necessity for the developing countries to export will hopefully gain increasing recognition, and thus give rise to more liberal tendencies.

[4]) Although the opposite possibility of a pent-up demand for substitution becoming effective cannot be completely discarded.

It is tentatively assumed that present growth rates will persist, although a prognosis of this kind must necessarily be made with the greatest possible reservations.

3. Conclusions

The following results may be drawn from the foregoing analyses (table 7).

TABLE 7

Imports from developing countries in 1966 prices.

	Billion $			Annual percentage change		
	1960	1966	1975[a]	1955–1960	1960–1966	1966–1975
EEC (c.i.f.)						
Non-manufactures	7.53	10.60	15.84	...	5.9	4.6
Manufactures	0.29	0.62	1.93	...	13.4	13.4
Total	7.82	11.22	17.77	6.2	6.2	5.2
EFTA (c.i.f.)						
Non-manufactures	4.96	5.16	7.16	...	0.6	3.7
Manufactures	0.47	0.87	2.16	...	10.6	10.6
Total	5.43	6.03	9.32	4.6	1.8	5.0
USA (f.o.b.)						
Non-manufactures	5.51	6.29	8.23	...	2.2	3.0
Manufactures	0.50	1.29	4.93	...	16.1	16.1
Total	6.01	7.58	13.16	2.8	3.9	6.3
Three Regions combined[b])						
Non-manufactures	18.00	22.06	31.23	...	3.5	3.9
Manufactures	1.26	2.78	9.02	...	12.3	14.0
Total	19.26	24.84	40.25	4.5	4.3	5.5

a) Projected.
b) Adding c.i.f. values for EEC and EFTA to f.o.b. values for USA.

The main inferences to be drawn from table 7 are as follows. On the assumption that the rather strong expansion of the EEC and USA economies will be maintained and that GNP growth in EFTA countries will be lifted to the same level, the growth of imports of non-manufactures into the three regions combined might improve somewhat over past performance. If, at the same time, the high growth rates of imports of manufactures would remain at the same level, total imports from developing countries into the three markets might reach an annual rate of expansion in the order of 5.5%. However, the possibility cannot be excluded that positions regarding imports of manufactures from developing countries will harden once such imports start to make considerable inroads into specific sectors. By and large, therefore, it seems safer to anticipate that, under conditions of fairly vigorous GNP growth, total imports from developing countries might increase at a rate in the order of 5–5.5% per year, as compared with an annual rate in the order of 4.5% during the past decade.

The picture varies with regard to individual markets. The EEC will not maintain its high rate of expansion for imports of non-manufactures. Even with persistently high rates for manufactures, expansion of total imports will slow down from about 6% in the last decade to about 5% in the 1970's.

In EFTA, imports during the first part of the 'sixties were affected by weak economic expansion and a number of specific temporary factors, which together made for near-stagnation of imports of non-manufactures. The assumed resumption of economic expansion, and return to a more normal pattern of imports, would lead to growth rates definitely higher than in the past, but still below the rates anticipated for the EEC. The larger share of manufactures, for which trade is fast expanding, would lift the rate of growth for total imports from developing countries to the proximity of the projected EEC level.

In the United States, finally, imports of non-manufactures are expected to expand more slowly than in the European countries. The rather high share of manufactures in total imports from developing countries, however, would bring the total growth rate to a level of over 6%. Among other things, this would imply that in 1975 nearly 40% of all imports from developing countries would consist of manufactures.

Such developments might prove amenable to restrictive pressure, in which case total growth rates would be reduced, possibly to a level more in conformity with the rates projected for Western Europe.

APPENDIX TABLE 1

SITC numbers and definitions of commodity groups.

SITC numbers	Definitions
0, 1, 4, 22.	*Food, beverages, tobacco*
01	Meat and meat products
04	Cereals and cereal preparations
05	Fruit and vegetables
06	Sugar, sugar preparations, and honey
071	Coffee
072	Cocoa
073	Tea
11	Beverages
12	Tobacco and tobacco manufactures
22	Oil seeds, oil nuts, and oil kernels
42	Fixed vegetable oils and fats
Rest main group	Other food
2 minus 22, 67, 68 minus 681	*Raw materials and base metals.*
21	Hides, skins, and furs (dressed)
23	Crude rubber, including synthetic and reclaimed
24	Wood, lumber and cork
26	Textile fibres, not manufactured into yarn, thread or fabrics, and their waste
28	Metalliferous ores and metal scrap
67	Iron and steel
68 minus 681	Non-ferrous metals minus silver and platinum group metals
Rest main group	Other raw materials
3	*Fuels*
33	Petroleum and petroleum products
Rest main group	Other fuels
5, 6 (minus 67, 68, but including 681) 7, 8	*Manufactures*
65, 84	Textile yarn, fabrics, made up articles and related products and clothing
Rest main group	Other manufactures

APPENDIX TABLE 2

EEC imports from developing countries; million $ c.i.f. value; 1960–1966 in current prices, 1975 (projected) in 1966 prices.

Commodity	1960	1961	1962	1963	1964	1965	1966	1975
Food								
Meat	70	67	73	100	198	188	193	201
Cereals	281	172	348	276	314	370	369	326
Fruit	459	467	531	606	556	702	724	1010
Sugar	133	81	93	159	180	105	103	110
Coffee	493	494	501	508	645	665	677	846
Cocoa	198	186	181	189	195	173	178	214
Tea	14	14	20	25	30	28	27	33
Beverages	280	253	280	179	226	176	182	95
Tobacco	65	68	87	89	96	96	88	108
Oil seeds	308	318	301	331	316	337	371 }	685
Vegetable oil	176	176	186	211	207	229	235 }	
Other food	239	245	312	350	358	417	448	762
Total	2716	2540	2913	3012	3320	3485	3595	4390
Raw materials and base metals								
Hides and skins	110	116	108	116	99	100	140	113
Rubber	322	222	211	226	218	207	208	218
Wood	194	210	205	242	300	286	301	488
Textile fibres	538	577	642	673	620	582	668	752
Ores	422	403	345	380	579	657	587	1096
Iron and steel	3	4	4	15	17	24	28 }	1382
Nonferrous metals	558	553	547	503	590	683	945 }	
Other raw materials	194	176	182	210	235	248	259	365
Total	2340	2262	2253	2364	2658	2786	3137	4414
Fuels								
Petroleum	2080	2355	2591	2976	3370	3709	3853	–
Other fuels	1	1	5	4	4	5	7	–
Total	2082	2356	2596	2980	3374	3714	3860	7040
Manufactures								
Textiles	81	93	109	142	180	213	241	–
Other manufactures	190	213	202	242	266	286	382	–
Total	271	306	311	384	499	446	623	1931
Grand total	7409	7464	8073	8740	9798	10484	11215	17775

APPENDIX TABLE 3

EFTA imports from developing countries; million $ c.i.f. value; 1960–1966 in current prices, 1975 (projected) in 1966 prices.

Commodity	1960	1961	1962	1963	1964	1965	1966	1975
Food								
Meat	221	174	188	218	206	161	165	162
Cereals	85	66	122	68	63	104	79	85
Fruit	234	238	273	280	272	306	312	438
Sugar	179	139	130	333	292	205	219	170
Coffee	194	196	201	221	281	270	294	352
Cocoa	104	85	88	85	74	68	74	83
Tea	323	323	329	323	310	301	281	301
Beverages	8	9	10	10	13	11	13	25
Tobacco	130	132	123	140	122	134	74	141
Oil seeds	148	141	141	148	129	146	133 }	344
Vegetable oil	90	85	68	68	77	98	95 }	
Other food	192	169	198	204	219	219	209	277
Total	1908	1718	1848	2099	2058	2024	1948	2378
Raw materials and base metals								
Hides and skins	39	37	38	46	37	35	41	38
Rubber	229	210	175	150	138	136	128	122
Wood	112	112	98	116	138	136	130	211
Textile fibres	351	367	368	378	370	332	337	354
Ores	224	226	183	154	208	223	215	349
Iron and steel	5	6	2	3	5	5	2 }	640
Nonferrous metals	327	297	217	300	333	394	449 }	
Other raw materials	114	87	83	120	136	139	131	171
Total	1400	1343	1264	1266	1365	1399	1433	1885
Fuels								
Petroleum	1416	1435	1547	1647	1761	1757	1764	–
Other fuels	...	...	...	...	...	13	19	–
Total	1416	1435	1547	1647	1761	1770	1783	2890
Manufactures								
Textiles	214	217	242	288	341	300	326	–
Other manufactures	233	234	240	290	338	508	545	–
Total	447	451	482	578	679	808	871	2160
Grand total	5172	4947	5141	5590	5863	6001	6035	9313

APPENDIX TABLE 4

USA imports from developing countries; million $ f.o.b. value, 1960–1966 in current prices, 1975 (projected) in 1966 prices.

Commodity	1960	1961	1962	1963	1964	1965	1966	1975
Food								
Meat	61	76	80	35	73	81	107	144
Cereals	2	2	2	2	3	3	2	2
Fruit	227	206	208	242	312	359	415	559
Sugar	546	470	500	588	446	422	496	435
Coffee	1012	969	994	962	1206	1062	1076	1238
Cocoa	152	169	143	143	141	126	131	151
Tea	52	51	54	53	54	52	51	57
Beverages	3	3	3	4	5	6	6	16
Tobacco	38	35	27	24	30	27	19	28
Oil seeds	64	52	50	43	47	59	47	166
Vegetable oil	48	49	53	63	72	76	100	
Other food	191	190	244	309	248	278	337	632
Total	2396	2271	2358	2468	2636	2550	2787	3428
Raw materials and base metals								
Hides and skins	64	47	54	59	57	63	64	62
Rubber	326	221	232	202	209	194	184	212
Wood	35	32	39	36	34	35	47	76
Textile fibres	183	180	175	183	152	158	157	166
Ores	664	473	523	360	439	494	533	863
Iron and steel	14	23	9	23	34	33	34	812
Nonferrous metals	149	224	309	322	377	459	538	
Other raw materials	110	128	160	140	142	139	170	241
Total	1545	1328	1500	1324	1443	1575	1727	2432
Fuels								
Petroleum	1429	1427	1502	1520	1598	1798	1771	–
Other fuels	6	8	8	9	9	9	9	–
Total	1435	1435	1510	1529	1607	1808	1780	2373
Manufactures								
Textiles	258	258	328	381	400	486	565	–
Other manufactures	221	224	310	346	435	570	721	–
Total	479	482	638	727	835	1056	1286	4925
Grand total	5855	5516	6006	6048	6521	6989	7580	13158

APPENDIX TABLE 5

EEC imports from world, excluding EEC intra-trade; million $ c.i.f. value

Commodity	1960	1961	1962	1963	1964	1965	1966
Food							
Meat	271	252	282	405	575	602	644
Cereals	858	966	1171	1043	1023	1232	1343
Fruit	817	884	1043	1096	1110	1358	1398
Sugar	149	94	119	259	241	145	136
Coffee	499	498	505	515	651	671	682
Cocoa	201	188	182	193	203	179	185
Tea	26	27	29	26	31	31	30
Beverages	318	298	338	245	300	265	274
Tobacco	219	224	298	296	310	315	332
Oil seeds	553	543	562	591	651	688	816
Vegetable oil	320	285	269	327	283	306	316
Other food	963	939	1095	1232	1340	1552	1618
Total	5194	5198	5893	6228	6718	7346	7774
Raw materials and base metals							
Hides and skins	308	316	320	361	378	398	475
Rubber	435	329	307	306	300	290	299
Wood	727	803	796	880	1009	1002	987
Textile fibres	1609	1573	1545	1607	1674	1433	1561
Ores	969	992	851	844	1141	1285	1233
Iron and steel	465	564	524	602	561	504	548
Nonferrous metals	1129	1072	1063	1015	1211	1417	1849
Other raw materials	852	915	930	1016	1177	1252	1377
Total	6481	6465	6336	6631	7451	7581	8309
Fuels							
Petroleum	2371	2650	2957	3374	3748	4060	4262
Other fuels	299	298	349	536	507	450	411
Total	2670	2948	3306	3910	4255	4510	4673
Manufactures							
Textiles	499	548	588	704	800	886	984
Other manufactures	4601	5073	5779	6364	7039	7554	8245
Total	5050	5621	6367	7068	7839	8440	9229
Grand total	19395	20232	21902	23837	26263	27877	29985

APPENDIX TABLE 6

EFTA imports from world, excluding EFTA intra-trade; million $ c.i.f. value; current prices.

Commodity	1960	1961	1962	1963	1964	1965	1966
Food							
Meat	790	678	685	684	836	856	818
Cereals	891	813	967	844	893	941	946
Fruit	964	1008	1189	1171	1180	1258	1352
Sugar	279	268	240	568	490	349	366
Coffee	200	203	208	228	290	280	309
Cocoa	140	122	121	88	78	101	110
Tea	335	331	332	327	313	311	287
Beverages	158	177	182	207	227	221	230
Tobacco	388	384	334	392	381	356	362
Oil seeds	271	246	253	262	259	288	269
Vegetable oil	136	134	117	118	135	166	164
Other food	1108	1041	1148	1237	1470	1375	1355
Total	5660	5405	5775	6126	6552	6502	6569
Raw materials and base metals							
Hides and skins	162	153	151	193	202	193	233
Rubber	291	262	231	209	204	197	193
Wood	547	563	499	531	658	677	601
Textile fibres	986	949	919	1020	1066	922	882
Ores	501	537	444	448	573	662	664
Iron and steel	813	694	661	664	832	830	812
Nonferrous metals	021	819	813	798	1040	1241	1362
Other raw materials	550	584	560	597	669	723	741
Total	4871	4561	4278	4460	5244	5445	5488
Fuels							
Petroleum	2002	2047	2243	2427	2508	2582	2683
Other fuels	268	243	256	285	275	282	282
Total	2270	2290	2499	2712	2783	2864	2965
Manufactures							
Textiles	1013	1101	1147	1253	1441	1364	1426
Other manufactures	5605	6153	6597	7029	8438	9741	10564
Total	6618	7254	7744	8282	9879	11105	11990
Grand total	19419	19510	20296	21580	24458	25916	27012

APPENDIX TABLE 7

USA imports from the world, million $ f.o.b. value; current prices.

Commodity	1960	1961	1962	1963	1964	1965	1966
Food							
Meat	326	357	496	524	411	427	600
Cereals	54	59	43	43	50	40	43
Fruit	314	303	306	343	427	479	539
Sugar	570	508	564	682	520	492	559
Coffee	1012	969	994	964	1208	1064	1080
Cocoa	167	179	154	155	152	137	140
Tea	56	54	60	58	60	58	57
Beverages	257	291	320	338	379	427	498
Tobacco	121	119	105	103	115	127	144
Oil seeds	70	59	55	46	50	63	53
Vegetable oil	74	72	79	84	95	98	128
Other food	558	618	651	644	677	779	948
Total	3579	3588	3827	3984	4144	4191	4789
Raw materials and base metals							
Hides and skins	166	154	168	180	184	193	215
Rubber	333	229	240	212	225	215	207
Wood	357	358	379	402	398	409	438
Textile fibres	390	391	411	440	404	436	436
Ores	893	685	937	806	819	915	1020
Iron and steel	483	411	513	657	783	1235	1305
Nonferrous metals	637	711	844	868	960	1197	1468
Other raw materials	633	674	719	720	764	805	892
Total	3892	3613	4211	4285	4537	5405	5984
Fuels							
Petroleum	1547	1609	1732	1773	1873	2093	2127
Other fuels	30	53	97	110	123	129	135
Total	1579	1662	1829	1883	1996	2222	2262
Manufactures							
Textiles	846	790	1018	1072	1135	1342	1517
Other manufactures	4350	4273	4928	5236	6197	7476	10132
Total	5196	5063	5946	6308	7332	8818	11649
Grand total	14246	13926	15813	16460	18009	20636	24684

APPENDIX TABLE 8

E.E.C. imports from associated countries and Algeria: million $ c.i.f. value current prices: 1960–1966 actual and 1966 hypothetical value [a]

Commodity	1960	1961	1962	1963	1964	1965	1966	1966 hyp. [a]
Food								
Meat	5	4	3	4	5	6	5	13
Cereals	18	13	12	16	11	8	13	23
Fruit	174	184	197	203	156	198	194	276
Sugar	66	65	71	70	72	68	74	60
Coffee	120	118	122	125	167	138	155	165
Cocoa	65	62	65	80	83	83	78	59
Tea	...	...	...	...	...	...	...	...
Beverages	246	219	244	128	176	150	152	161
Tobacco	12	14	8	8	10	8	8	17
Oil seeds	102	97	105	100	97	87	93	122
Vegetable oil	83	78	81	84	99	94	92	111
Other food	29	30	38	42	37	41	42	54
Total	920	884	946	860	913	881	906	1061
Raw materials and base metals								
Hides and skins	15	15	11	13	12	11	18	19
Rubber	17	14	12	12	11	9	13	11
Wood	97	112	117	139	177	168	181	150
Textile fibres	48	45	40	43	44	33	38	60
Ores	108	94	75	84	118	137	134	151
Iron and steel	10	10	7	10	14	19	20	
Nonferrous metals	230	227	213	195	233	248	392	418
Other raw materials	20	19	24	29	25	30	34	28
Total	545	536	599	525	634	655	830	837
Fuels								
Petroleum	166	295	438	476	475	472	490	–
Other fuels	...	...	...	1	1	4	6	–
Total	166	295	438	477	476	476	496	307
Manufactures								
Textiles	2	3	2	3	4	4	5	–
Other manufactures	29	41	34	29	28	26	33	–
Total	31	44	36	32	32	30	38	72
Grand total	1662	1759	2019	1894	2055	2042	2270	2277

[a] Hypothetical value 1966: value imports would have had if share in total imports from developing countries would have remained at 1960 level.

Please indicate your specific field(s) and return this card to us. It will enable us to keep you informed about new publications of direct importance to you.

- ☐ Economic Planning, Statistics
- ☐ Economic Theory, Mathematical Economics
- ☐ Econometrics
- ☐ International Economics
- ☐ Economics of Developing Countries
- ☐ Public Economics
- ☐ Monetary Economics, Banking, Business Finance
- ☐ Industrial and Labour Economics
- ☐ Regional and Urban Economics, Transport Economics
- ☐ Distribution and Consumer Research, Marketing
- ☐ Managerial Economics, Business Economics
- ☐ Operations Research, Mathematical Programming

(Please print) Name: .... Title: ....

Institute or Company: ....

....

Full address: ....

....

....

PRINTED MATTER
IMPRIMÉS

Please
put
your
stamp
here

ELSEVIER/NORTH-HOLLAND SCIENTIFIC PUBLISHERS

BOOK DIVISION

305-311 KEIZERSGRACHT

P.O. BOX 3489

AMSTERDAM - The Netherlands

STAGES IN PLANNING. THE INDONESIAN CASE

Y. B. DE WIT

1. Introduction

The author has been confronted with problems of planning in Indonesia, a country that recently found itself in almost complete chaos. Planning in a chaotic situation raises special problems, that are rather different from those with which economic planning theory usually deals. A number of these problems will also exist in other developing countries at present although in most cases to a lesser degree.

It may be clear that under chaotic economic and administrative conditions application of advanced planning techniques and methods is not appropriate. With reference to the situation in Indonesia this article contains a number of reflections and suggestions on the type of planning activities that can put an end to the most serious aspects of chaos and at the same time will provide a basis for further development planning. It is a modest attempt to explore broadly but in a systematic way the logic in the sequence of planning activities and its interrelationship with the sequence of government activities in other fields. If we restrict the term planning to the formulation of more or less detailed quantitative coherent plans for national economic development this article may also be labelled as a contribution to pre-planning or, to put it in another way, as an inquiry into the prerequisites for planning.

The first section of this article is descriptive in character. It is intended to illustrate against the Indonesian background some features of the real nature of the problems arising in a totally chaotic situation. The second section deals with the case for planning in such a situation. How should planning be understood and can it be expected to make a useful contribution? The third section proposes with regard to the Indonesian case a rough classification of consecutive stages in planning and the way in which they might be related to certain stages in other fields of government activities.

2. Indonesia 1966

2.1. *Previous developments*

After an almost uninterrupted period of government lasting more than three centuries the Dutch in 1942 lost control in the Indonesian archipelago when Japan took over forcibly. Immediately following the Japanese surrender that ended World War II the Republik Indonesia was proclaimed on August 17, 1945. On this date for the first time in history an independent state covering practically the entire Indonesian territory was formed. During the first four years of its existence the young republic was in open conflict with the Dutch who at that time were not yet ready to accept the political reality of an independent Indonesia.

After the struggle for independence, one of the longer ones in the postwar decolonization process, the new state faced numerous political, administrative and economic problems. Domestic political life was still in an experimental stage characterized by lack of stability that was reflected in a rapid succession of cabinets. Even when President Sukarno replaced the constitutional form of democracy by his so-called guided democracy the political situation remained unstable. As a matter of fact Sukarno was the most permanent element during the republic's first two decades but not necessarily therefore the most stable one. In any case he survived several serious rebellions and managed to stay in power, despite ever continuing political intrigues, by shifting from one temporary equilibrium to another. The main opposing forces were the army, the communists, the Islamic extremists, the moderate pro-Western groups, and various regional interests.

Domestic disturbances were strongly interwoven with external politics which were dominated until 1963 by the efforts to realize the national claim to West-Irian, the only part of the former Netherlands East Indies still in the hands of the Dutch, and from 1963 on by the 'konfrontasi' movement against Malaysia. Economic and political relations with the Dutch, the English and the Americans were subsequently disrupted. This process reached a climax in large waves of nationalizations in 1958. These caused a sharp fall in production. Finally Indonesia even cut all ties with the international organizations.

These developments of course had their impact on an administration that was also suffering from a serious lack of experienced civil servants, a heritage of colonial times when Indonesians were allowed to play only a very modest role in the civil service.

Due to ruthless exploitation by the Japanese and the harmful effects of the revolutionary war the Indonesian economy badly needed a period of consolidation and recovery. Although in a number of fields some achievements could be recorded the overall economic performance was poor. Indonesia is probably one of the very few developing countries with no clearly discernible rise in the per capita income in the post-war period.

The task of reconstruction and development of the economy was a difficult one and was aggravated by the above-mentioned political developments. Although any general judgment on political and economic developments in Indonesia is of doubtful value, the author believes that in the long run 1966 will stand out as marking a turning point. This was the year in which the Indonesian economy touched rock bottom while at the same time signs of more encouraging developments became apparent. The political situation in 1966, however, was far from stable. The Suharto regime gradually superseded that of Sukarno and seemed to be tackling the numerous problems successively in a slow but extremely determined and prudent way. This approach contrasted sharply with that of the previous regime which was characterized by inconstancy and absence of a really purposeful policy especially in the economic domain.

In the opinion of the new leaders economic planning fitted well into their approach. A survey of the various economic and administrative factors bearing directly on planning may reveal the size and the nature of the problems the planners faced.

2.2. *Inflation*

Hyperinflation was by far the most striking feature of the Indonesian economy in 1966. Since independence there had been continuing inflationary pressure which has finally become almost an institution. The rate of inflation as measured by the increase in the Djakarta cost of living index, had accelerated dramatically from 1960 onwards and reached the high level of roughly 600% a year in 1965 and even more than that in the first quarter of 1966. In the latter stages of this monetary drama the increase in money supply could not always keep up with the rising prices, lagging behind partly for technical (printing) reasons.

The principal source of inflationary finance was the government. The major part was accounted for by the budget deficit and the remaining part resulted mainly from credits granted by state banks (all larger banks had been nationalized) to state enterprises. From 1963 on budget revenues were less than half the expenditures. This reflected the high military expenditures in connection with the West-Irian affair and the confrontation policy towards Malaysia, and the expenditure on some costly prestige projects.

Although the rupiah continued to serve as the monetary unit in which daily prices were expressed and as a medium of exchange, it had ceased to function normally as a yardstick of value and generally accepted means of payment. As a matter of fact confidence in the rupiah had already been lost years before, as was demonstrated by a flight into goods and an unwillingness to conclude transactions in rupiahs without immediate payment. This may be illustrated by the fact that government employees and other wage-earners were paid partly in kind (rice, textiles, housing).

2.3. *Foreign debts*

The most pressing economic problem in 1966, though not the most serious one, appeared to be the large foreign debt. In the first months of 1966 it became clear that Indonesia would no longer be able to meet her foreign obligations. In the past large credits had been obtained from Western countries for development purposes as well as from socialist countries, especially Russia, for military purposes in connection with the West-Irian and Malaysia policies.

A relatively large part of these credits consisted of short-term loans and this resulted in a sharp accumulation of debt maturities, arrears and interest obligations. For years Indonesia's imports of daily necessities had been financed by short-term credits on hard terms and in addition to the repayments of these short-term debts a beginning had to be made with the amortization of long-term debts.

It was estimated that for 1966 Indonesia had to fulfill foreign debt obligations totalling roughly $500 million against expected export earnings of about $430 million! Indonesia faced not only the task of obtaining a comprehensive rescheduling of its foreign debts; it was also clear that the country needed new credits for imports necessary in order to have any chance of curing its sick economy.

2.4. *Foreign trade and balance of payments*

The alarming foreign debt position had been caused by adverse developments in foreign trade and high imports for military purposes. Total official reserves had been decreasing for years. After stagnation in the late 1950's exports showed a disappointing decline in the sixties. The estimated 1966 level of export revenues amounted to only about 50% of the annual average for the period 1955–1960. This was due to a number of reasons: unfavourable price developments for major export products (especially rubber), the repercussions of the inflationary pressure on export production, lack of incentives for export caused by discouraging foreign exchange regulations, the disorderly take-overs of foreign-owned companies and the effects of rebellions in some of the major export regions. Part of this large fall in exports, however, may be more statistical than real as it was probably compensated by smuggling on a much larger scale than before.

Excluding imports for military purposes the current account from 1961 onwards showed deficits of the order of $200 million. A continuous flow of new foreign credits mostly consisting of short-term credits and so-called deferred payments was needed to finance necessary imports. In 1966 the extremely low level of expected export proceeds made it practically impossible to obtain new short-term credits; imports that had been falling steadily for several years had to be reduced to a dangerously low level. Rice imports were threatened and production levels were affected in all sectors dependent on imported materials including fertilizer for agriculture, cotton for the textile industry, spare parts for transport, etc.

2.5. *Production*

As rice is the biggest single item of consumption, accounting for about one quarter of total consumption, rice production is of overwhelming importance to the Indonesian economy. Moreover, rice is of high symbolic value in traditional as well as in modern Indonesian society. Notwithstanding a steadily increasing trend in rice production Indonesia has not been able to meet the needs of its rapidly growing population and to put an end to rice imports.

The overall national situation, however, conceals the acute problems which are to be found on Java. The total increase in production from 1956 to 1966 probably amounted to about 25% but while it was roughly more than 30% on the outer islands, on Java it was less than 20% so that it could not meet the estimated rate of population growth of approx. 2.6% per annum.

Some regions, especially in central and east Java, that are traditionally known for their precarious food situation faced a much more critical situation than others. By far the most serious conditions, however, prevailed in the larger urban districts especially in Djakarta Raya (greater Djakarta) but also in other 'giants' like Surabaya and Djokjakarta.

It was generally accepted that, from a social as well as a political point of view, the level of rice consumption in these areas should not be allowed to fall. This necessitated large-scale rice imports. The government itself had to be the principal importer in order to meet its obligations to the military, civil servants and employees of state enterprises and their dependents, a total of about 4 million people.

The growing gap between population growth and the increase in rice production combined with the shortage of foreign exchange for imports of rice and fertilizer made the food situation expressed in terms of rice prices the most important barometer of the economic and political situation.

Production in other parts of the agricultural sector including the export sector had either stagnated or declined since 1960. By contrast the development of fisheries, in particular of the sea-fishing industry, was demonstrated by a welcome increase in production of more than 60% in the period 1960–1965.

By 1966 industrial production had nearly come to a standstill. Various estimates indicate that probably only 20% to 30% of existing capacity was used. Apart from insufficient supplies of raw materials and spare parts this was largely due to factors such as lack of managerial skills, fear of direct requisitions and unfavourable price and tax policies.

In the mining sector oil production was maintained and nickel and bauxite production reached higher levels, but the output of tin ore continued its downward trend.

2.6. *Transport*

The geographical structure and position of Indonesia provide a direct explanation for the heavy dependence of the Indonesian economy on the condition of national and international transport facilities.

In the postwar period relatively few new facilities had been created. The important inter-island shipping traffic was hard hit when the fleet of the experienced Dutch KPM shipping company was barred from Indonesian waters. Despite serious efforts to build a national fleet, funds and above all experience were lacking.

In recent years existing facilities in almost all types of transport have been seriously neglected. Nearly all necessary maintenance and repair work on roads, harbours, railroads, rolling stock, trucks and ships was neglected for years. The transport volume declined and was reported to correspond to a use of original capacity of approx. 25% by the end of 1965. As a result of inadequate transport important flows of goods were disrupted. It is reported that in 1966 rice supplies available in some parts of Sulawesi could not be transferred to shortage areas for lack of shipping facilities. At the same time it proved to be easier to import rice as this could be handled by non-Indonesian shipping. During his visit to Indonesia at the end of 1966 the author was struck by seeing hundreds of abandoned trucks and buses along the roads near Djakarta. Moreover, this did not appear to be exceptional in other parts of Java.

2.7. *Government administration*

The deplorable economic conditions of Indonesia in 1966 were closely related to some aspects of the functioning of the government machinery. Some of these aspects that seem particularly relevant to economic policy will be reviewed below.

The most striking feature in the administrative field is the deep-rooted corruption that has penetrated all government sectors at all levels. Although corruption had existed before, it increased sharply in the years immediately prior to 1966.

Corruption on closer scrutiny is found to include a number of different phenomena. First, a distinction should be made between (a) fraud in the sense of unlawfully obtaining direct material gain, and (b) nepotism, i.e. the unjustifiable favouring of relatives, friends and political associates by providing them with jobs.

The causes and effects of these two kinds of corruption are different. Whereas fraud at least in the Indonesian case has been largely conditioned by the economic situation, nepotism is more closely connected with socio-political forces in a society where personal and political loyalties are accepted as prevailing over technical competence while the economy is suffering from serious lack of employment opportunities. Nepotic pressure resulted in overcrowding of government offices. This was fostered on the one hand and could be justified on the other by frequent changes of the government's organizational structure which was altered fundamentally after independence almost every 4 or 5 years and not less than four times between 1964 and 1966.

Fraudulent corruption in present-day Indonesia must be viewed against the background of the prolonged inflation. Rises in salaries of government employees for years lagged behind the spiralling cost of living. Two widely tolerated reactions to this are illegal out-of-office work and asking for illegal payments for services, approvals, licenses, etc. These two kinds of fraudulent corruption are almost completely institutionalized in Indonesia providing a functional system of compensatory effects. Although most Indonesians were never blind to these kinds of corruption and disapproved of them in principle, they acquiesced as long as the officials concerned practised them in a 'normal' way, i.e. without obtaining unusually large gains in this way. The more spectacular dimensions of corruption which had also increased greatly by 1966, producing a class of quick-rich profiteers known for their conspicuous consumption, aroused strong resentment.

Among the principal effects of corruption are the increasing administrative inefficiency and indecision. All affairs had to pass through the hands of an ever-increasing number of officials who could be found in their offices only at odd times often for no more than a few hours a week. Each of them tried to decline even the slightest responsibility thereby reinforcing the already endemic tendency for even the most insignificant decisions to await the ministers' personal attention.

Another important aspect of Indonesian government administration closely connected with the forementioned is the lack of effective controls on the implementation of laws and regulations. It is part of the political structure that government officials in all ranks are subject to all kinds of socio-political controls but these are exercised only to safeguard group interests and loyalties and in no way constitute a check on the correct implementation of official policies. As a matter of fact each official has a large degree of freedom of action as long as he is assured of political protection. Large discrepancies have arisen between official policies and actual government behaviour. Thus in many cases only a symbolic value, i.e. a statement of intentions, should be attributed to official measures. They were either announced simply to prove the government's high moral aims or to influence the people in the hope that thereby a successful implementation might be assured notwithstanding the lack of administrative power and efficiency. The inability to collect taxes according to official legislation or to implement the intricate foreign exchange regulations provide examples of these phenomena.

In some cases legal controls as far as they still existed had been invalidated by special decrees. Thus budget policy had been seriously undermined by the institution of a number of so-called special budgets that were not controlled by the Budget Service.

In addition to the above-mentioned aspects the Indonesian administration suffered from an inadequate organizational structure, characterized by a highly uncoordinated decentralization and numerous cases of overlapping. This was a result of extremely vague demarcation of areas of competence conditioned by the distribution of political power and the need for a growing bureaucracy to justify its existence. The same matters were often handled in several departments at the same time whereas others were not considered at all. The fact that the systems of communication and information were in no way adequately functioning only made matters worse. Some sections, departments and local authorities, partly for political reasons and partly to prove their own importance or indispensability, treated the official data under their control as more or less private secrets to be used only at their discretion.

This brings us to another important feature closely connected with the previous one i.e. the lack of reliable statistics and other data.

Of course Indonesia, like most other developing countries since independence, had to cope with a data problem of major importance. The statistical apparatus created by the Dutch, although partly lost during the Japanese occupation, constituted a valuable heritage and a good starting point for further development. Notwithstanding considerable efforts by those concerned with compiling and processing the basic material, results have been poor, especially in the years immediately prior to 1966. Apart from more general and well-known reasons applying in many developing countries we may point to some more specific ones for Indonesia. First, Indonesia as a country is exceptionally large and diversified and therefore subject to unusually strong fragmentation which hampers the easy communication and coherence that are necessary to build up a consistent statistical system.

Far more important, however, than this natural handicap was the influence of the major political and economic developments especially in the 1960's. Indonesian political leaders in those years disliked making decisions and designing policies on the basis of facts and figures. They were primarily concerned with symbols, ritual ceremonies, ideologies, with the Indonesian image and prestige, and with personal and political interests. This may be illustrated by the 'birth' of the 8-year plan. An unwieldy committee of seventy members, none of them economists, selected on the basis of political considerations and headed by the well-known poet and ideologist Prof. Yamin produced within the space of a few months a plan for social, cultural and economic development made up of exactly 17 volumes, 8 parts and 1945 clauses. These numerals spelled out the date of Indonesia's proclamation of independence! It is practically a foregone conclusion that this plan was based more on wishful thinking and exalted ideas than on reliable facts and figures.

The problems of data collection were aggravated by heavy and irregular inflation, smuggling, tax-evasion and wide-spread reluctance and inability to regularly provide basic data. All juggling with price-indices, simulated exchange rates and corrections for incompleteness could hardly counterbalance these shortcomings. Thus the practical value for policy-making of a number of figures available (on national income, production, investments, consumption and employment), even if we disregard methodological criticisms, should not be rated highly. Moreover, the sole more or less detailed and coherent post-war estimates of national accounts made by S. D. Neumark covered only the years 1951 and 1952. All other estimates are revisions, extrapolations and extensions of the Neumark figures but less precise and less detailed.

2.8. *Development plans*

If we leave out of consideration some programmes of a more limited scope like the emergency plan of 1951 and the recent plan for stabilization and rehabilitation, Indonesia has had two development plans so far; the First Five-Year Plan (1956–1961) and the Eight-Year Plan (1961–1969).

The First Five-Year Plan was not an economically consistent overall development plan but it was, nevertheless, a thoroughly prepared and carefully formulated document based on extensive economic research. Like many other development plans it contained a general macro-economic framework based on an aggregative model of the economy on the one hand and a list of suggested government projects on the other. As usual with this kind of plan, however, these two elements were only tenuously linked to one another. Basically it was no more than a rather modest five-year government investment programme against the background of a sophisticated overall projection of the economy. Under the given circumstances this lack of coherence had seemed unavoidable. By and large it did, however, offer a realistic approach that held out a promise for future planning. Had it not been for the disturbing events in 1957 and 1958 (the ousting of Dutch firms and the rebellion) this plan could have marked the beginning of Indonesia's era of development planning.

Unfortunately the emergency conditions not only led to the Plan being abandoned but also, as a result of political factors, to an incipient decline in the influence of the bureau and its competent staff. It also lost the interest of the government and finally ceased to function. The work accomplished and the experience gained by the staff were thus lost and had no noticeable effect on subsequent planning activities.

Mention has already been made above of the Eight-Year Plan's focus on symbolism and popular support. As a matter of fact these were probably its strongest points. From an economic point of view this plan was rather weak. Except for lessons in ideology it consisted of a long enumeration of 'projects' including investment projects as well as other items of government expenditure especially for spiritual, mental and cultural matters. Basic economic relations were almost completely ignored. No estimates were made of the expected overall effects on such important economic quantities as imports and exports, growth rate, government revenues and expenditure, national savings etc. Consequently the Plan never served as a serious guide to economic policy. The weakest points concerned the absence of any clear and detailed indications concerning proper implementation and sound financing of the Plan. Moreover few references were made to economic and technical complementarities between the various projects. The division into A and B projects, the latter to be financed and executed with foreign assistance to provide the foreign and domestic means needed for the former, was highly confusing. Approximately 200 of the 335 A projects were actually initiated during the first four years but as a result of lack of funds and organizing capacity only a few have been completed and many had to be abandoned at a halfway stage.

Probably the most harmful effect of the plan is that it caused many false ideas about the scope and the nature of development planning; in the eyes of the people it was completely associated with the ideology and the political visions and fantasies of the existing regime. By the end of 1966 the author could find hardly anybody at BAPPENAS (the planning office) who was able to think of planning in terms other than as a political system of listing all kinds of government activities and calling them projects. By and large, the reputation of planning in Indonesia by 1966 was not at all favourable; it had lost its image as a panacea for social and economic development.

The above description of the economic, administrative and political conditions in Indonesia in 1966 may impress upon the reader what is really meant by chaos, or, to put it in another way, how chaos 'works'. Although it is a rough and fragmentary picture it might be considered proportionately much too long in an article of such limited scope as the present one. In the author's opinion, however, this digression should be considered essential for the argument and not as an example of an unevenly composed article. In this way he wishes to focus attention on the vital importance, as a basis for any planning activity, of sound knowledge and comprehension of the actual situation. The original situation, of course, should be described in the usual terms of quantitative economic information but in the Indonesian case, and probably in many others, conditions relating to the *working* of the economy and the administrative machinery are much more relevant. Descriptions similar to the one given above of the Indonesian situation are necessary to provide the information required to decide what kind of planning fits the situation under review.

3. The Case for Planning in Indonesia

Considering Indonesia's experience with development plans it may at first sight seem surprising that the new government expressed its desire for a new start in planning. By means of many demonstrations and mass-meetings public feeling had expressed the need for measures to curb inflation, to combat excessive corruption, and to keep down rice prices, but certainly not for planning. On the contrary, to many people it seemed self-evident and in line with the new policies, that planning should be done away with as 'decontrol' was one of the basic principles of the *orde baru* (new order). In parliament it had even been suggested that planning be terminated by liquidating BAPPENAS.

The desire for planning can partly be explained by taking into consideration the background of the new leaders. Political power in 1966 was largely in the hands of the military. In matters of economic policy they were assisted by a group of capable advisers all of them professional economists and members of the economic faculty of the Universitas Indonesia. From the military point of view a transmission of the concept of planned action from the battlefront to the economic field might have seemed attractive; the economists on the other hand, mainly because of their scientific and unbiased approach to planning, were able to tackle the problems of planning without being prejudiced by experience in the previous period.

Moreover, on the international scene pressure was brought to bear on Indonesia to start planning in order to enable international organizations and donor countries to judge Indonesia's efforts and intentions in the field of economic policy with a view to rescheduling foreign debts and providing new assistance.

It is in this light that the desire for planning that was officially expressed in 1966 by the Indonesian government should be seen. But was planning possible in this chaotic situation? Was there a real need for planning under the prevailing circumstances? The answers depend on the kind of planning we have in mind.

Although there seems to be widespread confusion as to what planning in developing countries exactly is or should be, in practice most economists agree on the main principles. Two characteristic elements of planning in developing countries, as we usually understand it, may be pointed out.

First, since shortage of capital is one of the most striking problems in all poor countries, planning in these countries normally focuses on capital formation. Thus to a large extent it may be identified with investment planning. Second, emphasis has been laid on the formulation of a multi-year 'plan' consisting of a coherent set of figures indicating the most desirable development of the national economy over the period concerned. Thus, the quantitative aspects and the prognostic character of planning are stressed.

As the concept of planning in stages includes these elements and may also be considered representative for planning in many other respects, the question arises if this is the type of planning that fits the Indonesian situation. To answer this question we have to test whether planning in stages is *useful* and *possible*. We may consider a certain type of planning to be useful if there is a 'demand' for it and possible if it can be 'supplied'. For planning in stages to be useful and possible in a particular situation both the 'demand' and the 'supply' sides of planning have to meet a number of conditions. We will examine below to what extent these conditions are fulfilled in the Indonesian case.

The reader is assumed to be familiar with the concept of planning in stages. Here we only want to point out that the 'stages' refer to methodological steps in preparing a plan and not to a series of consecutive plans or policies.

As to the 'demand' for planning we may distinguish between objective demand or need on the one hand and subjective or effective demand on the other. The need for a certain type of planning refers to the nature of the economic policy that fits the particular economic situation. The effective demand for a certain type of planning depends on what the government expects from planning and on the government's intentions and policy aims.

For planning in stages to be useful the first condition to be fulfilled is that it sufficiently meets objective demand i.e. it must offer a solution to the specific problems of the actual situation. The reason for this condition is that the very essence of planning should be seen in a 'rehearsal' of the actual course of events. Section 1, above, should make it obvious that planning in stages is not immediately relevant to Indonesia's specific problems. Even when carried out in a rather simple and primitive way it would be premature.

The second condition, i.e. sufficient effective demand, implies a reasonable degree of correspondence between the government's intentions and the plan drawn up by the method of planning in stages. If there is no such correspondence the plan will soon become one of those documents that although skilfully drawn up, has no noticeable impact on actual economic policy. The type of planning and the government's views on planning can only be brought into line with each other through a process of mutual adaptation brought about by regular contacts between planners and policymakers.

Against the background of the political and economic conditions in Indonesia briefly described in section 2 it may be clear that the government had to give precedence to policies aimed at political consolidation and monetary stabilization. Planning in stages can certainly not provide the appropriate framework for the preparation of this kind of policies.

From the foregoing it may be inferred that the conditions for a useful application of planning in stages could not be met within the Indonesian case.

We now turn to the 'supply' side. How far the planning-in-stages-approach can be followed depends on the extent to which the country concerned can meet a number of essential prerequisites. These can be grouped into three categories:

a) Prerequisites for drafting the plan.
b) Prerequisites for the technical implementation of the plan.
c) Prerequisites with regard to the successful effect of the plan.

It is easy to see that it is impossible to give an exhaustive enumeration of all the prerequisites, even of the essential ones. Therefore, we shall only mention some of the major ones in each category.

ad a. A planning agency staffed with some competent economists and technicians is indispensable. They should have a certain minimum amount of statistical and other data at their disposal. Furthermore, for meaningful projections based on empirical coefficients (capital–output ratios, input–output coefficients, elasticities etc.) it is necessary that the economy should have shown a more or less regular pattern during the previous period. Finally a reasonable number of suggested projects and project studies should be available for incorporation into the sectoral and national plans.

ad b. First of all the administrative machinery should perform, with a tolerable degree of inefficiency, those tasks that bear directly on the execution of the proposed policies. Special attention should be paid to such matters as tax collection, credit policy, exchange control, agricultural extension, market regulations, issue of construction licenses and price and wage policies. Furthermore government services must be able to ensure the proper preparation, execution and operation of projects in the public sector. The governments must also meet some minimum requirements in such fields as legislation, preserving law and order, and collection of statistics. Although they may seem less directly connected with economic policy they should be considered indispensable for the proper implementation of a plan.

ad c. Even if the above-mentioned conditions were fulfilled the success of a plan cannot be guaranteed if there is not a minimum level of understanding and support both within and outside the government. Without the confidence and the cooperation of rather large groups in various strata of the population it is almost impossible to carry out a plan involving structural economic and social changes.

Does this mean that Indonesia would be better off without planning? If we adhere to the usual concept of planning in developing countries i.e. to planning in stages and to similar types of medium-term quantitative investment planning the answer is in the affirmative. But if a wider definition is adopted there is a strong case for planning even in the Indonesian situation.

Planning may then be defined as every systematic and coordinated preparation of government activities.

This definition covers a wide range of possible types of planning including planning in stages. The applicability of planning in stages is restricted as we have seen by a number of conditions that are not fulfilled in the Indonesian situation. It may, however, become the appropriate type of planning at some future time. Perhaps we could look at planning in stages as the final stage in a process of continuous adaptation of the type of planning to the changing situation. To the extent that the various conditions are fulfilled the type of planning may evolve so as to correspond at each stage with the demand for and supply of planning.

In the earlier stages the type of planning may consist merely of a coherent set of rather simple and comprehensive qualitative policies. These may be aimed at bringing order into the administrative apparatus, the monetary system and the pattern of public expenditure, as well as at stimulating investment and production, either in general or in some strategic sectors and regions. Provided such policies are well prepared and coordinated they may in the circumstances make a more direct and valuable contribution to economic development than might be expected from more sophisticated types of planning.

4. Stages in Planning

As may be clear from section 3 the type of planning has to be adapted to the particular stage of development in which the country finds itself. Thus, we may also speak of *stages in planning* corresponding to stages in development.

It must be pointed out that these stages are not automatically determined by a country's level of per capita income. A poor country like India may well be in the appropriate stage of development necessary for the successful application of planning in stages whereas a richer country like Brazil is probably not. Furthermore, although the stages determine the appropriate type of planning they do not necessarily determine the scope of planning. According to our definition planning may be comprehensive at any stage. There is no general case for gradually shifting from project planning to public sector planning and from this to comprehensive planning as has been suggested by Waterston [1].

The extent to which the above-mentioned conditions are fulfilled may be influenced at each stage by government action. We may also relate each of the conditions to a particular field of government activities. Thus the 'demand' conditions may be influenced by shaping and modifying government's intentions and objectives and by carrying out policies directly relevant to the actual economic situation. The 'supply' conditions may be influenced by creating the appropriate framework to draw up and to implement a plan and by creating a favourable political atmosphere to ensure widespread support.

The stages in planning shade off into one another logically through the application of more and more advanced techniques. How far these changes in the type of planning may continue will depend on the extent to which the government is able to ensure the fulfillment of the conditions essential for each type of planning.

The logical structure of the interrelationships between the various stages and the fields of government activities can be represented in tabular form. The rows show the fields of government activities and the columns the stages of planning corresponding to the actual situation.

The sole purpose of table 1 is to serve as an example. It gives a very rough and incomplete outline containing a few suggestions concerning the Indonesian case. In fact the proper construction of such a table in a more elaborate form may constitute the first step towards planning. It may then become a useful instrument to make clear to the planners as well as to the policy-makers the nature of the most pressing development problems and their mutual relations.

Any choice concerning the number of stages is arbitrary from a theoretical point of view. The three stages proposed in the table reflect the views of the Indonesian policy-makers on future development. At present (early 1968) Indonesia is still in the stabilization stage. Some of the activities listed in this stage are being carried out already whereas others still have to be prepared.

References

[1] A. Waterston, *Development Planning. Lessons of Experience.* Baltimore 1965, Chapter IV.

TABLE 1

Government activities	Stage of planning		
	Stabilization	Rehabilitation	Economic growth
Establishment and specification of objectives	Curbing inflation Preventing food shortages Settlement of foreign debt Decontrol	Sector priorities (food, textile, transport) Regional priorities Land tenure system Basic choice on the extent of the public sector	Rate of growth Employment objectives Income distribution Population growth
Economic policy	Balanced budget Credit restrictions Rescheduling foreign debt Rice imports by government	Public sector expenditure planning Rehabilitation of transport and irrigation Agricultural extension Tariff policies to protect industries in course of rehabilitation	Promotion of saving Refining tax and subsidy policies Investment act Birth control
Creation of the framework for drawing up plans	Planning act Planning bureau + staff Procedure of planning Collection and processing of data	Sector divisions Analysis of basic statistics Establishing project criteria Applied economic research	Projections Macro-models (Semi-)input–output tables
Creation of the framework for implementing plans	Improving tax collection Restoring administrative discipline Financial controls Improving extension serv.	Reorganization of civil service Project preparation Improvement of accounting systems	Raising efficiency Flexibility
Creation of favourable political atmosphere	Information to obtain understanding and confidence	Encouraging cooperation	

THE SEMI-INPUT–OUTPUT METHOD UNDER UPPER BOUNDS

PETER A. CORNELISSE and JAN VERSLUIS

1. Introduction

This paper seeks to compare sector evaluation procedures according to a linear programming formulation on the one hand and Tinbergen's semi-input–output method on the other. It will serve to demonstrate that, in the problem's most simple form, the semi-input–output method, which concentrates on a small part only of the input–output matrix, arrives at exactly the same result as a linear programming approach which embraces the entire matrix. It has been assumed here that the reader is familiar with the basic properties of the semi-input–output method; otherwise, for an exposé of this method the reader is referred to Tinbergen [2], Cornelisse and Tilanus [1], or Pronk and Schreuel (in the present collection).

The next section discusses the formulation of a problem of selecting the optimal sector applying linear programming. The model has been kept as simple as possible in order to avoid all complications that would divert attention from our principal aim. It has also been arranged in such a way that a direct comparison with the semi-input–output method should be possible. The confrontation of the two approaches is made in section 3.[1]) The last two sections investigate an issue that has recently entered into the discussion, namely the effects of an adaptation to reality in the form of upper bounds on production and exports. Whereas production bounds are neutral and do not affect the attractiveness of the sectors concerned, it will be shown that under export bounds the two approaches may give different outcomes with the result that a special provision must be made in the semi-input–output method in order that the optimal solution be in fact attained. Verbal inter-

[1]) A different approach to a similar problem has been described by Waardenburg [4].

pretations of the main findings are given more extensively in the last paragraphs of the relevant sections.

Due to the existence of an upper bound on the amount of space allocated to this article, it has been impossible to include full demonstrations of the realism of some of the assumptions made below. Though the assumptions – mainly concerning feasibility – are very important for the following arguments, they have, therefore, nevertheless been dealt with rather loosely. It seems to us, in any case, that the realism of the assumptions is not in doubt. This may further justify our focussing on the confrontation of the two approaches, the present subject of discussion.

2. The Selection of the Optimal Sector with Linear Programming

2.1. In the linear programming formulation of our selection problem we shall also distinguish between national and international sectors as the semi-input–output method does. The production equation of an international sector may be written as:

$$\sum_m d_{fm} v_m + \sum_m i_{fm} - x_f + q_f = v_f , \quad f = 1, \ldots, F; \; m = 1, \ldots, F, \ldots, M \qquad (1)$$

where

d_{fm} = marginal input coefficient;

v_m = change in production of sector m;

i_{fm} = change in investment requirements by sector m from sector f;

x_f = change in balance of imports and exports of sector f;

q_f = change in consumption of product f (the secondary effects of the investment programme[2]), given, function of y, see below).

The change in investment requirements i_{fm} can be written as the difference between the corresponding present and past investment requirements, assuming no time lag between investment and increase in production. Thus

$$i_{fm} = c_{fm} v_m - \bar{\bar{i}}_{fm} , \qquad (2)$$

where c_{fm} = marginal sector-to-sector capital coefficient; $\bar{i}_{fm}$ = investments requirements by m from f one time unit before.

This identity is substituted in (1) where we write b_f for the difference between q_f, the change in consumption of f (q from quonsumption, of quourse) and

[2]) See Tinbergen [3], p. 180.

$\sum_m \bar{i}_{fm}$, output of investment good f one time unit earlier. We obtain

$$\sum_m d_{fm}v_m + \sum_m c_{fm}v_m - x_f + b_f = v_f . \tag{3}$$

Note that for sectors producing investment goods the new symbol b will almost certainly assume negative values.

Taking account of the characteristic property of a national sector which is precisely that exports and imports of its products are virtually impossible, its characteristic production equation becomes

$$\sum_m d_{nm}v_m + \sum_m c_{nm}v_m + b_n = v_n , \quad n = F + 1, \ldots, M ; M = F + N . \tag{4}$$

Further it is assumed that the rise in national income to be generated by the investment programme has been given as a target; the value added contributions by each of the sectors must, of course, add up to this amount:

$$\sum a_{0m}v_m = y , \tag{5}$$

where a_{0m} = marginal value added coefficient of sector m; y = rise in national income (target, given).

Finally, investment outlays are to be minimized:

$$\text{Minimize} \sum c_m v_m . \tag{6}$$

2.2. It will be noticed that the system has been reduced to a basic form which cannot readily be applied to practical problems. For the moment, however, this property entails no drawback; in as far as some practical complications may affect the selection procedure they are dealt with in sections 4 and 5. Indeed, the equations may be aggregated even further by taking together input coefficients relating to intermediate products and investment products ($d_{mm'}$ and $c_{mm'}$ respectively). The resulting new coefficients will be denoted by $a_{mm'}$. After bringing the constant terms to the right-hand side of the equality sign the full tableau becomes: (see page 178).

2.3. From (7) it can be derived that

$$\sum_m c_m v_m - \sum_f x_f = y - \sum_m b_m , \tag{9}$$

where the form on the right-hand side of the equality sign is a constant. Consequently, the difference between total investment outlays and the change in the deficit on the balance of payments is a fixed amount. Therefore, minimization of the objective function (8) implies simultaneously minimiza-

$$
\begin{array}{lllll}
(1 - a_{11})\, v_1 - \dots\dots\dots\dots & - a_{1M} v_M & + x_1 & & = b_1 \\
\dots\dots\dots\dots\dots\dots & & & & \dots \\
- a_{F1} v_1 - \dots + (1 - a_{FF})\, v_F - \dots\dots & - a_{FM} v_M & & + x_F & = b_F \\
- a_{(F+1)1} v_1 - \dots\dots + (1 - a_{(F+1)(F+1)})\, v_{F+1} - \dots\dots & - a_{(F+1)M} v_M & & & = b_{F+1} \\
\dots\dots\dots\dots\dots\dots & & & & \dots \\
- a_{M1} v_1 - \dots\dots\dots\dots & + (1 - a_{MM})\, v_M & & & = b_M \\
a_{01} v_1 + \dots\dots\dots\dots & + a_{0M} v_M & & & = y \\
c_1 v_1 + \dots\dots\dots\dots & + c_M v_M & & & - z = 0\,(\mathrm{Min.}z)
\end{array}
$$

(7)

(8)

where $v_1 \geqslant 0, \dots, v_M \geqslant 0$.

tion of the increase of the external deficit.[3] This is obvious because minimization of the increment of investments with given marginal domestic savings will lead to the lowest possible increase of the deficit or largest possible increase of the surplus on the current account. It has been assumed that, should the deficit increase, there will be no difficulties in financing it.

2.4. Applying the system described by (7) and (8) to an actual problem the simplex method can be employed in order to find a feasible and, ultimately, optimal basis. Here we shall follow the same line in general terms. First we have to find a feasible basis.

As there are $M+1$ constraints, we have to select $M+1$ activities satisfying the feasibility condition. There is, indeed, a number of variables readily available to serve that purpose such as the production activities of the national sectors $(v_{F+1}, \ldots, v_M)$ because demand for the corresponding products can only be satisfied by domestic production. The absence of choice forces these variables into the basis. Products of international sectors, however, can be obtained from abroad, if necessary. But not all international goods can be procured by imports because this would imply that all x_f $(f=1, \ldots, F)$ are positive. Although such a solution is not entirely impossible, it is a highly unrealistic proposition that would materialize only if an extremely large increase in the external deficit should be permitted. Without demonstrating explicitly how unrealistic the above outcome would be, we shall assume that in the present case the ratio of $\sum b_m$ to y, and, therefore, also the increase of the deficit, remains within reasonable limits. Although this condition is formulated in rather vague terms we may still safely conclude that it requires export earnings to finance at least part of the imports. Hence, next to the import activities which are positive, at least one activity among the x_f must be negative.[4] This means, in turn, that the production activity of the corresponding international sector must be positive and, therefore, be in the basis, since exports have to be generated by domestic production. This sector can be chosen arbitrarily from the set of international sectors; let us call it h.

2.5. Before passing to the algebra, a few remarks must be made on the notation employed. In what follows, small Latin letters are reserved for

[3] Pronk and Schreuel describe a similar conclusion in the semi-input–output terminology.
[4] Activities x_f, being defined as the change in the difference between imports and exports, are unrestricted in sign.

scalars, e.g. the parameters $a_{mm'}$, b_m, and the variables v_m, x_f. Small Greek letters denote vectors, where row vectors are indicated by a transposition sign. Finally, capital Latin letters denote matrices.

Counting now the number of variables in the basis we have N production activities of the national sectors, F international trade activities (composed of $F-1$ import activities and one export activity of product h) and one production activity of international sector h, together $N+F+1=M+1$ basic variables. This number equals the number of constraints and, though the proof has not been given here, it can be shown that the basis formed by the above activities will indeed in all probability be feasible.

It will prove to be convenient to distinguish between these three types of basic variables and to separate rows referring to international sectors, to national sectors and to the composition of value added. In matrix notation the partitioned basis obtains the following shape:

$$A(h) = \begin{bmatrix} \varepsilon_h - \alpha_{Fh} & -A_{FN} & I_{FF} \\ -\alpha_{Nh} & I_{NN} - A_{NN} & 0 \\ a_{0h} & \alpha'_{0N} & 0 \end{bmatrix}, \tag{10}$$

where

ε_h = the unit vector of $F-1$ zeros and unit in the hth row;

α_{Fh} = the column vector of input coefficients from the international sectors to h;

A_{FN} = the matrix of input coefficients from the international sectors to the national sectors;

α_{Nh} = the column vector of input coefficients from the national sectors to h;

A_{NN} = the matrix of input coefficients among national sectors;

α'_{0N} = the row vector of value added coefficients of the national sectors;

I_{FF} = the identity matrix of order $F \times F$;

I_{NN} = the identity matrix of order $N \times N$.

In this linear programming approach we shall need of course the inverse of this matrix. It reads: (see page 181).

2.6. With the help of $T(h)$ the dual solution corresponding to the present basis can easily be determined by premultiplying it by the row vector of cost coefficients of the basic activities. The values thus obtained can be interpreted as the prices of the constraints expressed in terms of the minimand, i.e. in terms of investment costs. In our evaluation problem we are, of course,

$$T(h) = \left[\begin{array}{c:c:c} 0 & \dfrac{-\alpha'_{0N}(I - A_{NN})^{-1}}{a_{0h} + \alpha'_{0N}(I - A_{NN})^{-1}\alpha_{Nh}} & \dfrac{1}{a_{0h} + \alpha'_{0N}(I - A_{NN})^{-1}\alpha_{Nh}} \\ \hdashline 0 & \begin{array}{l}(I - A_{NN})^{-1} + \\ -\dfrac{(I - A_{NN})^{-1}\alpha_{Nh}\alpha'_{0N}(I - A_{NN})^{-1}}{a_{0h} + \alpha'_{0N}(I - A_{NN})^{-1}\alpha_{Nh}}\end{array} & \dfrac{(I - A_{NN})^{-1}\alpha_{Nh}}{a_{0h} + \alpha'_{0N}(I - A_{NN})^{-1}\alpha_{Nh}} \\ \hdashline I_{FF} & \begin{array}{l}\dfrac{(\varepsilon_h - \alpha_{Fh})\alpha'_{0N}(I - A_{NN})^{-1}}{a_{0h} + \alpha'_{0N}(I - A_{NN})^{-1}\alpha_{Nh}} + \\ + A_{FN}(I - A_{NN})^{-1} + \\ -\dfrac{A_{FN}(I - A_{NN})^{-1}\alpha_{Nh}\alpha'_{0N}(I - A_{NN})^{-1}}{a_{0h} + \alpha'_{0N}(I - A_{NN})^{-1}\alpha_{Nh}}\end{array} & \dfrac{-(\varepsilon_h - \alpha_{Fh}) + A_{FN}(I - A_{NN})^{-1}\alpha_{Nh}}{a_{0h} + \alpha'_{0N}(I - A_{NN})^{-1}\alpha_{Nh}} \end{array}\right] = A^{-1}(h) \tag{11}$$

particularly interested in the dual price of value added because it relates costs (investments) to the benefit (or the target, namely value added).

The dual solution corresponding to the value added constraint – the latter being defined in the last row of $A(h)$ – is represented by the inner product of the row of basic cost coefficients and the last column of $T(h)$:

$$c_h \times \frac{1}{a_{0h} + \alpha'_{0N}(I - A_{NN})^{-1}\alpha_{Nh}} + \gamma'_N \times \frac{(I - A_{NN})^{-1}\alpha_{Nh}}{a_{0h} + \alpha'_{0N}(I - A_{NN})^{-1}\alpha_{Nh}} + 0,$$

where γ'_N = the row vector of cost coefficients of production activities of national sectors.

Bringing these terms together, we have

$$\frac{c_h + \gamma'_N(I - A_{NN})^{-1}\alpha_{Nh}}{a_{0h} + \alpha'_{0N}(I - A_{NN})^{-1}\alpha_{Nh}}. \tag{12}$$

In the numerator of this ratio we find the sum of the investment costs directly required by sector h and the accumulated investments of the national sectors required in order to generate sufficient intermediated deliveries from the national sectors to sector h, everything in proportion to the volume of production of h. In Tinbergen's semi-input–output terminology this term coincides with the investment costs of the 'bunch with sector h'. Similarly, the denominator indicates the sum of direct and accumulated indirect (often summarized as 'primary', see Tinbergen [3]) value added generated per unit of production of sector h, or briefly, value added created by the 'bunch with sector h'. In other words, (12) represents the cost–benefit ratio of the bunch which is precisely the criterion applied in the semi-input–output analysis for selection of the optimal sector.

The importance of this conclusion for the present purpose will be evident: in (12) we have found a method that allows a direct comparison between a linear programming approach to selecting the optimal sector and the semi-input–output method. The next section will make extensive use of this result; it will, therefore, be convenient to employ a shorthand notation for forms comprising the accumulated effects of the bunch. Below, such forms will be indicated by a hat ($\wedge$). Thus, for (12) we write

$$\hat{r}_h = \frac{\hat{c}_h}{\hat{a}_{0h}} = \frac{c_h + \gamma'_N(I - A_{NN})^{-1}\alpha_{Nh}}{a_{0h} + \alpha'_{0N}(I - A_{NN})^{-1}\alpha_{Nh}}, \tag{13}$$

where $\hat{r}_h$ = the cost–benefit ratio of the bunch with sector h.

3. The Semi-Input–Output Method as a Programming Problem

3.1. In a linear programming problem the optimal solution has been attained if no non-basic activities can be found which, upon introduction into the basis, produce a better result. On the other hand, the semi-input–output method seeks to find the bunch with the lowest cost–benefit ratio. In this section we shall examine and compare the optimisation processes of the two approaches.

According to the simplex method the solution to our programming problem is optimal if the relative cost coefficients of non-basic activities are all found to be non-negative. Here we want to find out in general terms which condition has to be fulfilled in order that such a result be obtained, so we shall take a closer look at the row of relative cost coefficients.

3.2. For each activity j this coefficient is defined as

$$\mathring{c}_j(h) = c_j - \pi'(h)\alpha_j, \tag{14}$$

where

$\mathring{c}_j(h)$ = the relative cost coefficient of activity j with the production activity of sector h in the basic set;

$\pi'(h)$ = the row of simplex multipliers with h in the basis;

α_j = the column vector corresponding with the jth activity.

Further, the simplex multipliers are defined as

$$\pi'(h) = \gamma'(h)\, T(h), \tag{15}$$

where $\gamma'(h)$ = the row of cost coefficients corresponding to the basic activities with h in the basis, or, in full,

$$\pi'(h) = [c_h \vdots c_{F+1} \ldots\ldots c_M \vdots 0 \ldots\ldots 0]\,[T(h)]$$

$$= \left[\begin{array}{c:c:c} 0\ldots0 & \begin{array}{l} c_h \times \dfrac{-\alpha'_{ON}(I-A_{NN})^{-1}}{\hat{a}_{Oh}} + \\ + \gamma'_N\{\hat{a}_{Oh} - (I-A_{NN})^{-1}\alpha_{Nh}\alpha'_{ON}\}\dfrac{(I-A_{NN})^{-1}}{\hat{a}_{Oh}} \end{array} & \begin{array}{l} c_h \times \dfrac{1}{\hat{a}_{Oh}} + \\ + \gamma'_N \dfrac{(I-A_{NN})^{-1}\alpha_{Nh}}{\hat{a}_{Oh}} \end{array} \end{array}\right]$$

Recalling that the last term in this vector was called $\hat{r}_h$, $\pi'(h)$ becomes:

$$\pi'(h) = \left[0 \ldots 0 \;\Big|\; \frac{-c_h \hat{\alpha}'_{0N}}{\hat{a}_{0h}} + \gamma'_N (\hat{a}_{0h} - \hat{\alpha}_{Nh} \alpha'_{0N}) \frac{(I - A_{NN})^{-1}}{\hat{a}_{0h}} \;\Big|\; \hat{r}_h \right], \tag{16}$$

where $\hat{\alpha}'_{0N} = \alpha'_{0N}(I - A_{NN})^{-1}$; $\hat{\alpha}_{Nh} = (I - A_{NN})^{-1}\, \alpha_{Nh}$.

3.3. The non-basic activities are the production activities of the international sectors with the exception of sector h. If j refers to non-basic activities, α_j can thus be partitioned conveniently into a part including the input coefficients of international sectors to $j\,(\varepsilon_j - \alpha_{Fj})$, a part with the input coefficients of national sectors to $j\,(-\alpha_{Nj})$ and, finally, the value added coefficient of $j\,(a_{0j})$. Therefore, after substitution of (16) in (14), $\mathring{c}_j(h)$ can be rewritten as

$$\mathring{c}_j(h) = c_j + \left\{ \left(\frac{-c_h \alpha'_{0N}}{\hat{a}_{0h}} - \frac{\gamma'_N \hat{\alpha}_{Nh} \alpha'_{0N}}{\hat{a}_{0h}} + \gamma'_N \right) (I - A_{NN})^{-1} \right\} \alpha_{Nj} - \hat{r}_h a_{0j} \tag{17}$$

or

$$\begin{aligned}
\mathring{c}_j(h) &= c_j + \left\{ \gamma'_N - \frac{c_h + \gamma'_N \hat{\alpha}_{Nh}}{\hat{a}_{0h}} \alpha'_{0N} \right\} \hat{\alpha}_{Nj} - \hat{r}_h a_{0j} \\
&= c_j + \gamma'_N \hat{\alpha}_{Nj} - \left\{ \frac{\hat{c}_h}{\hat{a}_{0h}} \alpha'_{0N} \right\} \hat{\alpha}_{Nj} - \hat{r}_h a_{0j} \\
&= \hat{c}_j - \hat{r}_h (a_{0j} + \alpha'_{0N} \hat{\alpha}_{Nj}) \\
&= \hat{c}_j - \hat{r}_h \hat{a}_{0j}\,.
\end{aligned}$$

It appears that in our linear programming problem we have hit on the optimal solution as soon as the following condition is fulfilled for all non-basic activities j and with h in the basic set:

$$\hat{c}_j - \hat{r}_h \hat{a}_{0j} = (\hat{r}_j - \hat{r}_h)\, \hat{a}_{0j} \geqslant 0\,. \tag{18}$$

It can now easily be shown that the solution is at an optimum if the international sector with the lowest $\hat{r}$ is in the basis, because if $\hat{r}_k = \hat{r}_f$ (min.), $(f = 1, \ldots, F)$, the form $(\hat{r}_j - \hat{r}_k)$ and, therefore, also $(\hat{r}_j - \hat{r}_k)\, \hat{a}_{0j}$ will be non-negative for all non-basic activities j.

We may conclude that implicit in the optimisation process of our programming problem is the selection of the international sector the bunch of which possesses the lowest cost–benefit ratio, or in other words a linear programming formulation of a simple sector-selecting problem such as the present one leads to the same result as the semi-input–output method and vice versa. Both approaches end up with exactly the same sector to be selected for an optimal investment programme, but it must be added that the semi-input–output method has the advantage of requiring fewer calculations.

3.4. In section 3.3 it has been shown that according to both methods the optimal sector k is found at the top of the priority list. It still remains to be seen if both methods attach the same rank to the other sectors. In the semi-input–output method ranking is based on the cost–benefit ratios of the bunches, whereas in linear programming a sector's rank depends on the value of the objective function with the production activity of that sector in the basis. At first sight there is, perhaps, no obvious connection between these criteria. This matter will be examined somewhat more closely in this section.

Let $z(h)$ be the value of the objective function corresponding to the basis including the production activity of sector h. If $\varphi(h)$ denotes the column vector of basic variables $(v_h, v_{F+1}, \ldots, v_N, x_1, \ldots, x_F)$, $z(h)$ becomes

$$z(h) = \gamma'(h)\,\varphi(h),$$

or

$$z(h) = \gamma'(h)\,T(h)\,\beta = \pi'(h)\,\beta, \tag{19}$$

where β = the column vector of constraint constants in the initial tableau $(b_1, \ldots, b_F, b_{F+1}, \ldots, b_M, y)$. Partitioning in the traditional way and substituting (16) for $\pi'(h)$, we obtain:

$$\begin{aligned} z(h) &= \left\{-\frac{c_h\alpha'_{0N}}{\hat{a}_{0h}} + \gamma'_N - \frac{\gamma'_N\hat{\alpha}_{Nh}\alpha'_{0N}}{\hat{a}_{0h}}\right\}(I - A_{NN})^{-1}\beta_N + \hat{r}_h y \\ &= \left\{-\frac{c_h + \gamma'_N\hat{\alpha}_{Nh}}{\hat{a}_{0h}}\alpha'_{0N} + \gamma'_N\right\}\hat{\beta}_N + \hat{r}_h y \\ &= \{-\hat{r}_h\alpha'_{0N} + \gamma'_N\}\,\hat{\beta}_N + \hat{r}_h y \\ &= \hat{r}_h(y - \alpha'_{0N}\hat{\beta}_N) + \gamma'_N\hat{\beta}_N\,. \end{aligned} \tag{20}$$

This result becomes a tautology after writing it in a slightly different form. Solving for v_h we find that:

$$v_h = \frac{1}{\hat{a}_{0h}}(-\alpha'_{0N}\hat{\beta}_N + y), \tag{21}$$

so that (20) can be interpreted as

$$z(h) = \hat{r}_h \hat{a}_{0h} v_h + \gamma'_N \hat{\beta}_N ,$$

or

$$z(h) = \hat{c}_h v_h + \gamma'_N \hat{\beta}_N , \tag{22}$$

which says that the investment costs of a programme are equal to the sum of investment requirements of the domestically producing sectors[5]): the first term accounts for the accumulated investments (direct + indirect) required for the international sector and the second term for the additional investments needed by the national sectors in order to satisfy final demand for national products.

Whatever the interpretation of (20) may be, it shows unequivocally that also in the linear programming formulation the ranking of non-optimal sectors depends directly on the cost–benefit ratios of the bunches: for all international sectors f ($f = 1, ..., F$) the corresponding values of the objective function ($z(f)$) consist of a term $\gamma'_N \hat{\beta}_N$ which is the same for all f and another term that varies only with $\hat{r}_f$.[6]) Again, semi-input–output and linear programming produce the same result.

4. Upper Bounds on the Production of International Sectors

4.1. In this section the impact of the existence of bounds on the domestic production of international commodities will be investigated. Such a bound will be introduced for the sector which in the preceding sections was found to be the optimal one, i.e. the sector which shows the lowest cost–benefit ratio for its bunch as a whole. Algebraically the newly added constraint takes the following very simple form:

$$v_k \leqslant \bar{v}_k . \tag{23}$$

4.2. With the introduction of the upper bound, the number of restrictions increases from $M+1$ to $M+2$. Consequently, the number of basic variables also increases by one. In the first instance we form a new basis by adding one of the international sectors to the old basis (10), so that the new set of

[5]) 'Domestically producing sectors' is employed here as a shorthand notation for 'sectors increasing domestic production'. This convention will be followed throughout this paper.
[6]) On an earlier occasion Zandee [5] has shown that final demand for national products does not affect the rank of sectors in semi-input-output either.

basic variables becomes

$$v_h, v_k, v_{F+1}, v_{F+2}, \ldots, v_M, x_1, x_2, \ldots, x_F. \tag{24}$$

The new basis then becomes:

$$A(h, k, \bar{v}_k) = \begin{bmatrix} \varepsilon_h - \alpha_{Fh} & \varepsilon_k - \alpha_{Fk} & -A_{FN} & I \\ -\alpha_{Nh} & -\alpha_{Nk} & I - A_{NN} & 0 \\ a_{0h} & a_{0k} & \alpha'_{0N} & 0 \\ 0 & 1 & 0 & 0 \end{bmatrix} \tag{25}$$

And its inverse may be written as:

$$A^{-1}(h, k) = \begin{bmatrix} \lambda'_1 & \lambda'_2 & l_1 & l_2 \\ \lambda'_3 & \lambda'_4 & l_3 & l_4 \\ L_1 & L_2 & \lambda_5 & \lambda_6 \\ L_3 & L_4 & \lambda_7 & \lambda_8 \end{bmatrix}, \tag{26}$$

where by partitioned inversion it is found that

$$\begin{aligned} \lambda'_1 &= 0; \\ \lambda'_2 &= -\frac{1}{\hat{a}_{0h}} \hat{\alpha}'_{0N}; \\ l_1 &= \frac{1}{\hat{a}_{0h}}; \\ l_2 &= -\frac{\hat{a}_{0k}}{\hat{a}_{0h}}; \\ \lambda'_3 &= 0; \\ \lambda'_4 &= 0; \\ l_3 &= 0; \\ l_4 &= 1; \\ L_1 &= 0; \\ L_2 &= (I - A_{NN})^{-1} \left[I - \frac{1}{\hat{a}_{0h}} \alpha_{Nh} \hat{\alpha}'_{0N} \right]; \\ \lambda_5 &= \frac{1}{\hat{a}_{0h}} \hat{\alpha}_{Nh}; \end{aligned} \tag{27}$$

$$\lambda_6 = \hat{a}_{Nk} - \frac{\hat{a}_{0k}}{\hat{a}_{0h}} \hat{a}_{Nh} ;$$

$$L_3 = I ;$$

$$L_4 = \frac{1}{\hat{a}_{0h}} (\varepsilon_h - \alpha_{Fh}) \hat{\alpha}'_{0N} + A_{FN}(I - A_{NN})^{-1} \left[I - \frac{1}{\hat{a}_{0h}} \alpha_{Nh}\hat{\alpha}'_{0N} \right] ;$$

$$\lambda_7 = \frac{1}{\hat{a}_{0h}} [-(\varepsilon_h - \alpha_{Fh}) + A_{FN}\hat{\alpha}_{Nh}] ;$$

$$\lambda_8 = -(\varepsilon_k - \alpha_{Fk}) + A_{FN}\hat{\alpha}_{Nk} - \frac{\hat{a}_{0k}}{\hat{a}_{0h}} [(\varepsilon_h - \alpha_{Fh}) - A_{FN}\hat{\alpha}_{Nh}] .$$

The vector of simplex multipliers can be determined from

$$\pi'(h, k) = \gamma'(h, k) A^{-1}(h, k), \tag{28}$$

where

$$\pi'(h, k) = (p_1 p_2 \ldots\ldots\ldots\ldots p_{M+2})$$

and

$$\gamma'(h, k) = (c_h c_k \vdots \gamma'_N \vdots 0) .$$

Written as a column the vector $\pi(h, k)$ becomes

$$\pi(h, k) = \begin{bmatrix} 0 \\ \dfrac{-c_h}{\hat{a}_{0h}} \alpha'_{0N} + \gamma'_N (I - A_{NN})^{-1} \left[I - \dfrac{1}{\hat{a}_{0h}} \alpha_{Nh}\alpha'_{0N} \right] \\ \hat{r}_h \\ -c_h \dfrac{\hat{a}_{0k}}{\hat{a}_{0h}} + c_k + \gamma'_N \left(\hat{\alpha}_{Nk} - \dfrac{\hat{a}_{0k}}{\hat{a}_{0h}} \hat{\alpha}_{Nh} \right) \end{bmatrix} \tag{29}$$

and the dual price of value added appears to be equal to $\hat{r}_h$, i.e. the cost–benefit ratio of the bunch corresponding to the newly added international sector.

4.3. Along exactly the same simple lines as in section 3, it can be shown that for any non-basic sector j the simplex criterion reads

$$\mathring{c}_j(h, k, \bar{v}_k) = \hat{c}_j - \hat{r}_h \hat{a}_{0j} . \tag{30}$$

It may be concluded again that the best sector to be included in the augmented basis is the one showing the lowest cost–benefit ratio for the bunch. The sector which satisfies this criterion apparently is the one which was second best in the absence of bounds.

4.4. We may now compare the position after the bound on production is introduced with the situation as it was in the absence of bounds. As the semi-input–output method runs in terms of changes in variables, this type of comparison of two alternative outcomes uses the concept of changes in changes, such as decreases in increases or increases in decreases. The interpretation of the result obtained in 4.3 may, therefore, seem slightly more complicated than it actually is.

The upper bound clearly limits the production expansion of sector k. The effect of this loss of production possibilities on the increase in net exports of sector k will always be unfavourable. Thus, sector k will also increase its exports less than it would do without its production bound (if the production limit is set at a sufficiently low level, it may even be necessary to increase imports of product k rather than its exports as used to be the case). In order to compensate for the loss of foreign exchange earnings another international sector, say h, will have to substitute domestic production for imports. Sector h may even start to export. On the other hand, the bound on v_k does not introduce an impediment to the expansion of sectors requiring intermediate deliveries from sector k because, if necessary, these deliveries can be obtained out of the balance of imports and exports of sector k.

4.5. In conclusion it may be said that the introduction of a bound on the production increase of the optimal sector does not affect the semi-input–output method. The number of producing international sectors increases, where the first sector to be newly included in the solution is the one which was second in rank in the absence of bounds. If no bound exists for this sector, its production may be expanded to such a level that all conditions of the model are satisfied. If the second best sector would in its turn also be subject to a bound on production, the thirdly ranking sector is to be introduced as soon as the bound becomes active, etc.

5. Upper Bounds on Exports

5.1. This section analyses the consequences of the introduction into the model of upper bounds on exports. To start with, the impact will be examined of an upper bound on the exports of the sector with the lowest cost–benefit ratio for the bunch. The algebraic form of the constraint is:

$$x_k \geqslant \bar{x}_k. \tag{31}$$

The value of $\bar{x}_k$ (a negative quantity because x_k stands for the change in import surplus) is, of course, chosen in such a way that the constraint (31) is binding.

5.2. Analogous to the method followed in the preceding section, a new basis is formed by introducing one more variable, say v_h, into the basis. The new basis, which may again be assumed to be feasible, then reads:

$$A(h, k, \bar{x}_k) = \left[\begin{array}{c:c:c:c} \varepsilon_h - \alpha_{Fh} & \varepsilon_k - \alpha_{Fk} & -A_{FN} & I \\ \hdashline -\alpha_{Nh} & -\alpha_{Nk} & I - A_{NN} & 0 \\ \hdashline a_{0h} & a_{0k} & \alpha'_{0N} & 0 \\ \hdashline 0 & 0 & 0 & \varepsilon'_k \end{array}\right] \tag{32}$$

For the present purposes it will emerge as useful to partition the basis in a slightly different way. Introducing some new symbols, we will now write:

$$A(h, k, \bar{x}_k) = \left[\begin{array}{c:c:c:c} \varepsilon_h - \alpha_{Bh} & -A_{BD} & I & 0 \\ \hdashline -\alpha_{Dh} & 1 - A_{DD} & 0 & \varepsilon_1 \\ \hdashline a_{0h} & \alpha'_{0D} & 0 & 0 \\ \hdashline 0 & 0 & 0 & 1 \end{array}\right] \tag{33}$$

In comparison to (32) the partitioning has changed in the following respects: (i) after rearrangement of the rows such that the row corresponding to sector k becomes the last of the upper part of (32), this row is included in the second row of blocks; (ii) the column which corresponds to sector k is included in the second column of blocks; (iii) the last column of the matrix is now written separately.

The order of the submatrices is different from that in (32):

$\varepsilon_h - \alpha_{Bh}$: a column vector of $F-1$ elements;
$-A_{BD}$: a matrix of order $(F-1)\times(N+1)$;
I : a unit matrix of order $F-1$;
$-\alpha_{Dh}$: a column vector of $N+1$ elements;
$I-A_{DD}$: a matrix of order $(N+1)\times(N+1)$;
ε_1 : a unit vector of $N+1$ elements;
a_{oh} : a scalar;
α'_{0D} : a row vector of $N+1$ elements.

The order of the 0's is self-explanatory; the unit in the lower right-hand corner is a scalar.

5.3. The economic meaning of the rearrangement of the matrix and of the interpretation of the new submatrices deserves some special attention. As the number of basic variables is $M+2$ we may now start from a position where already $M+1$ variables have been chosen and the $M+2$nd (here h) has to be decided upon. Among the first $M+1$ activities is the production of one international sector, which for the time being we assume to be v_k, the production of the sector that was optimal in the absence of bounds. The submatrix $I-A_{DD}$ of $A(h, k, \bar{x}_k)$ is the Leontief matrix for the sectors which have been chosen to produce domestically viz. the national sectors + sector k. All international sectors other than k form a set indicated by the subindex B. From this set one sector will be chosen which is to accompany k in increasing production.

5.4. The concept of the 'bunch' has also changed. The bunch of sector h now consists of the production of sector h itself and the corresponding production of all domestically producing sectors.[7]) Coefficients which describe the accumulated effect of the new type of bunch will now be indicated by a tilde, e.g.

$$\tilde{a}_{0h} = a_{0h} + \alpha'_{0D}(I - A_{DD})^{-1}\alpha_{Dh} \tag{34}$$

$$\tilde{c}_h = c_h + \gamma'_D(I - A_{DD})^{-1}\alpha_{Dh}\,. \tag{35}$$

Now $\tilde{a}_{oh}$ stands for the sum of value added directly generated by sector h and value added generated by the direct and indirect intermediate deliveries of all other domestically producing sectors. Analogously, $\tilde{c}_h$ represents the total direct and indirect investment per unit of production increase of sector h.

5.5. We may now partition the inverse of the basis as follows:

$$A^{-1}(h, k, \bar{x}_k) = G = \left[\begin{array}{cc|c|c} \psi'_1 & \psi'_2 & g_1 & g_2 \\ \hline G_1 & G_2 & \psi_3 & \psi_4 \\ \hline G_3 & G_4 & \psi_5 & \psi_6 \\ \hline \psi'_7 & \psi'_8 & g_3 & g_4 \end{array}\right] \tag{36}$$

[7]) We prefer to use 'domestically producing sector', as in the semi-input-output model 'national' is a characteristic of the commodity relating to its transportability, which does not change when a bound is introduced.

In section 2.6 we have concentrated on the last column of $T(h)$; here we are mainly interested in the penultimate column. The elements of this column are easily found to be

$$g_1 = \frac{1}{\tilde{a}_{0h}} \tag{37}$$

$$\psi_3 = \frac{1}{\tilde{a}_{0h}} (I - A_{DD})^{-1} \alpha_{Dh} \tag{38}$$

$$\psi_5 = -\frac{1}{\tilde{a}_{0h}} (\varepsilon_h - \alpha_{Bh}) + \frac{1}{\tilde{a}_{0h}} A_{BD} (I - A_{DD})^{-1} \alpha_{Dh} \tag{39}$$

$$g_3 = 0\,. \tag{40}$$

The dual price of value added is found by premultiplying this column of G by $\gamma'(h, k) = (c_h \vdots \gamma'_D \vdots 0)$. As the penultimate column of G is very like the last column of $T(h)$, it will not be surprising that the result of this multiplication is similar to what was found in section 2.6:

$$\gamma'(h, k) \times \begin{bmatrix} g_1 \\ \psi_3 \\ \psi_5 \\ g_3 \end{bmatrix} = \frac{\tilde{c}_h}{\tilde{a}_{0h}} = \tilde{r}_h(k)\,. \tag{41}$$

The dual price of value added now appears to be the semi-input–output type of cost–benefit ratio for the bunch corresponding to an extension of sector h. By 'bunch' is here understood the concept as described in section 5.4, i.e. the production activity of the international sector itself and the corresponding production activities of all domestically producing sectors. We write $\tilde{r}_h(k)$ in order to indicate that k is the international one among the domestically producing sectors.

5.6. Using the same type of algebra as in section 3 it can easily be shown that the simplex criterion now reads

$$\mathring{c}_j(h, k, \bar{x}_k) = \tilde{c}_j - \boldsymbol{r}_h(k)\, \tilde{a}_{0j}\,. \tag{42}$$

The lowest $\tilde{r}_f(k)$ $(f = 1, 2, \ldots, k-1, k+1, \ldots, F)$ would give us the optimum sector if we could be sure that sector k is necessarily in the basis. Further attention has to be given to the question whether sector k (the best sector in the absence of bounds) remains in the basis. This will be done in the following sections.

5.7. First we have to do some more partitioning. In the formulae we derived from the partitioned matrix (33) a crucial role is played by the inverse of one of the submatrices of $A(h, k, \bar{x}_k)$, viz. $(I - A_{DD})^{-1}$. It will emerge as useful to partition the matrix $(I - A_{DD})$ further as:

$$(I - A_{DD}) = \left[\begin{array}{c|c} 1 - a_{kk} & -\alpha'_{kN} \\ \hline -\alpha_{kN} & I - A_{NN} \end{array}\right] \tag{43}$$

Once more the method of partitioned inversion may be applied and the following result will be obtained:

$$(I - A_{DD})^{-1} =$$
$$= \left[\begin{array}{c|c} \dfrac{1}{1 - a_{kk} - \alpha'_{kN}\hat{\alpha}_{Nk}} & \dfrac{\alpha'_{kN}(I - A_{NN})^{-1}}{1 - a_{kk} - \alpha'_{kN}\hat{\alpha}_{Nk}} \\ \hline \dfrac{\hat{\alpha}_{Nk}}{1 - a_{kk} - \alpha'_{kN}\hat{\alpha}_{Nk}} & (I - A_{NN})^{-1}\left[I + \dfrac{\alpha_{nk}\alpha'_{kN}(I - A_{NN})^{-1}}{1 - a_{kk} - \alpha'_{kN}\hat{\alpha}_{Nk}}\right] \end{array}\right] \tag{44}$$

The notation applied has been explained above, under formula (16).

5.8. The partitioned inverse of $(I - A_{DD})$ may now be used to express parameters which carry a tilde in coefficients that wear a hat. Writing for instance

$$\tilde{a}_{0h} = a_{0h} + (a_{0k} \vdots \alpha'_{0N})(I - A_{DD})^{-1} \begin{bmatrix} a_{kh} \\ \alpha_{Nh} \end{bmatrix} \tag{45}$$

one finds, after some shuffling and reshuffling, the following expression:

$$\tilde{a}_{0h} = \hat{a}_{0h} + \frac{a_{kh} + \alpha'_{kN}\hat{\alpha}_{Nh}}{1 - a_{kk} - \alpha'_{kN}\hat{\alpha}_{Nk}}\,\hat{a}_{0k}\,. \tag{46}$$

This formula can even be further simplified if we introduce the symbols

$$\hat{a}_{kh} = a_{kh} + \alpha'_{kN}\hat{\alpha}_{Nh} \tag{47}$$

$$1 - \hat{a}_{kk} = 1 - a_{kk} - \hat{\alpha}'_{kN}\hat{\alpha}_{Nk}\,. \tag{48}$$

The coefficient $\hat{a}_{kh}$ represents the total direct and indirect (via the bunch in terms of national sectors) inputs by sector h of commodity k. The interpretation of $1-\hat{a}_{kk}$ is analogous.

Now we can rewrite (46) once again and find

$$\tilde{a}_{0h} = \hat{a}_{0h} + \frac{\hat{a}_{kh}}{1 - \hat{a}_{kk}} \hat{a}_{0k} . \tag{49}$$

A similar expression can, of course, be found for the accumulated cost coefficient

$$\tilde{c}_h = \hat{c}_h + \frac{\hat{a}_{kh}}{1 - \hat{a}_{kk}} \hat{c}_k . \tag{50}$$

5.9. The above results may now be applied to write $\tilde{r}$ in terms of $\hat{r}$. Some algebra leads to the following

$$\begin{aligned} \tilde{r}_h(k) &= \frac{\tilde{c}_h}{\tilde{a}_{0h}} \qquad (51) \\ &= \hat{r}_h + \left(\frac{\hat{a}_{kh}}{1 - \hat{a}_{kk}} \hat{c}_k - \frac{\hat{c}_h}{\hat{a}_{0h}} \frac{\hat{a}_{kh}}{1 - \hat{a}_{kk}} \hat{a}_{0k} \right) \frac{1}{\hat{a}_{0k} + \dfrac{\hat{a}_{kh}}{1 - \hat{a}_{kk}} \hat{a}_{0k}} \\ &= \hat{r}_h + (\hat{r}_k - \hat{r}_h) \frac{\hat{a}_{kh}\hat{a}_{0k}}{\hat{a}_{0h}(1 - \hat{a}_{kk}) + \hat{a}_{kh}\hat{a}_{0k}} . \end{aligned}$$

It should be noticed that $\tilde{r}$ is independent of the level at which the upper bound is fixed in the same way as $\hat{r}$ was independent of the final demand for national goods.

On the other hand (51) may also be rewritten as

$$\tilde{r}_h(k) = \hat{r}_k + (\hat{r}_h - \hat{r}_k) \frac{\hat{a}_{0h}(1 - \hat{a}_{kk})}{\hat{a}_{0h}(1 - \hat{a}_{kk}) + \hat{a}_{kh}\hat{a}_{0k}} \tag{52}$$

and it is easily seen that this result implies

$$\tilde{r}_h(k) > \hat{r}_k . \tag{53}$$

We can now summarize (51) and (53) into

$$\hat{r}_k < \tilde{r}_h(k) < \hat{r}_h . \tag{54}$$

Let us now indicate the second-best sector in the absence of bounds by j. We can then write

$$\hat{r}_k < \hat{r}_j < \hat{r}_h \text{ [8]} \tag{55}$$

where h indicates any international sector that is not among the best two. Using (54) it can be derived that

$$\tilde{r}_j(k) < \tilde{r}_j(h) \tag{56}$$

$$\tilde{r}_j(k) < \tilde{r}_h(j) \tag{57}$$

$$\tilde{r}_j(k) < \tilde{r}_h(h') \quad h' = 1, \ldots, F\,; \quad h' \neq h\,; \quad h' \neq j\,; \quad h' \neq k\,. \tag{58}$$

Hence, no combination of sectors not containing k can be better than the combination j with k. Still, a combination of another international sector with k can conceivably be better than j with k. However, the best set will anyhow contain k.

5.10. The algebraic results obtained in 5.9 may now be translated again into the economic terminology of the semi-input–output method. A numerical example briefly illustrating the above findings is presented in the appendix.

Three main types of conclusions can be drawn:

(i) In formula (54) we have compared the cost–benefit ratio for a bunch which because of an export bound contains two international sectors with the cost–benefit ratios as they would have been for the bunches corresponding to each of the two international sectors. It has been shown that the first is in between the other two, i.e. the combination is worse than the best, but better than the worst of the two. It can be concluded, therefore, that if upper bounds on exports prohibit complete specialization in one sector, the resulting combination leads to a higher cost–benefit ratio. If the selection problem is looked at as a linear programming problem this result is self-evident. Introduction of an additional constraint will lead to a deterioration of the optimum or at best will leave the optimum unchanged.

(ii) The introduction of an upper bound on the exports of the most attractive international sector leads to a selection of two international sectors which are to produce domestically. We have proved in (56)–(58) that one of these two sectors will be the international sector ranking as number one in the absence of bounds. This sector, after reaching its bound, is to be accom-

[8]) The very special cases where $\hat{r}_j = \hat{r}_k$ or $\hat{r}_j = \hat{r}_h$ may for practical purposes be left out of consideration.

panied by another international sector, but it will not be replaced by any other sector.

(iii a) In this section we have applied two types of cost–benefit ratios. On the one hand there is the semi-input–output criterion, the cost-benefit ratio of the bunch consisting of the production increase of one international sector and the corresponding expansion of national sectors. On the other hand we have introduced the cost–benefit ratio of an extended type of bunch. In this bunch we include the production increase of one international sector and its indirect effects via what we have called domestically producing sectors. Domestically producing sectors are the national sectors and the most attractive international sector.

An algebraic relation has been established between these two cost–benefit ratios in formula (51). This relation shows that the two ratios are not proportional. From this we may conclude that there is no reason to expect that the ranking of sectors according to one type of ratio would coincide with the ordering according to the other ratio. This means that the second-best international sector is not necessarily the one which is to join the most attractive sector in producing domestically, i.e. the optimal solution of the semi-input–output method if the exports of the most attractive sector are upper bounded cannot be found by simply including the second-best sector in the solution. When the best sector reaches the upper bound on its exports, the ranking of international sectors has to be established anew. For this purpose the most attractive international and the national sectors must be taken together as the set of domestically producing sectors and new cost–benefit ratios have to be calculated.

(b) The effect of more upper bounds on exports can easily be imagined through an extension of the above reasoning. If also an active bound exists on the exports of the sector which is selected to accompany the most attractive one, this sector has to be included in the group of domestically producing sectors and again cost–benefit ratios have to be calculated. These two sectors, the best and the one which joined it, will in any case remain in the solution. Which of the remaining sectors is to accompany them is to be determined by the new cost–benefit ratios. The same reasoning holds, of course, for still more upper bounds on exports that may be introduced.

(c) In order to isolate the effect of an export bound we have given a simplified picture. Our analysis dealt with the question of what happens if an active bound is introduced while the solution of the problem without that bound has already been obtained. In practice, however, we would have to face the problem with a given number of bounds without knowing in advance which of the bounds will appear to be active. One approach is to solve the linear programming problem as a whole.[9]) Another way to solve the problem is to follow an approach similar to the one described in this paper. In this approach first the cost–benefit ratios for each of the international sectors have to be calculated as if there were no upper bounds. If a bound limits the export possibilities of the most attractive sector and it appears to be active, a new round of calculations has to be done in order to determine the cost–benefit ratio for each of the other international sectors where the most attractive sector is dealt with as domestically producing. Again it has to be examined whether the sector that will be selected according to this criterion is subject to an active upper bound. If this is the case, still new cost–benefit ratios have to be calculated with the two selected international sectors as domestically producing. This procedure has to be repeated until the last selected sector is either unbounded or subject to a bound which appears to be inactive.

The latter approach is an extension of the semi-input–output method as applied in the unbounded case. It implies, however, a rather cumbersome series of calculations which seems to deprive the semi-input–output method under export bounds of a considerable portion of its computational simplicity.

Appendix: Numerical Example

A small numerical example using three national and three international sectors may illustrate the findings of chapter 5 of this paper. The assumed values for the coefficients which describe the relevant interrelations among the sectors are given in table 1. It should be noted that the coefficients in this table are not just the current input coefficients. The output of sector 4 also consists of investment goods. Consequently, as described in section 2.2, the corresponding coefficients include this element.

The Leontief matrix for national sectors reads

$$(I - A_{NN}) = \begin{bmatrix} 0.80 & -1.75 & -0.65 \\ -0.02 & 0.95 & -0.01 \\ -0.06 & -0.08 & 0.88 \end{bmatrix}$$

[9]) This procedure may be simplified by first eliminating all national variables and then solving the remaining L.P. problem. Waardenburg's approach [4] is based on this idea.

and its inverse[10]

$$(I - A_{NN})^{-1} = \begin{bmatrix} 1.39 & 2.66 & 1.06 \\ 0.03 & 1.11 & 0.04 \\ 0.10 & 0.28 & 1.21 \end{bmatrix}$$

TABLE 1

Relevant interindustry relations, value added coefficients and capital coefficients*).

		Sector					
		1	2	3	4	5	6
International sectors	1	0.10	0.01	0.19	0.08	0.05	0.03
	2	...	...	...	...	...	...
	3	...	...	...	...	...	...
National sectors	4	0.75	0.85	1.00	0.20	1.75	0.65
	5	0.04	0.06	0.05	0.02	0.05	0.01
	6	0.03	0.01	0.05	0.06	0.08	0.12
Value added coefficients		0.55	0.48	0.50	0.60	0.70	0.33
Marginal capital coefficients		1.75	3.20	3.60	1.00	5.00	1.50

*) Coefficients which are irrelevant for the present purpose have been omitted.

For each of the international sectors the cost–benefit ratio of the bunch, in our symbols $\hat{r}$, may be calculated. As can be seen from table 2, the most at tractive international sector appears to be sector 1 with sector 2 as second best.

Now suppose a binding upper bound is introduced on the exports of sector 1. With the aid of the formulae we derived in section 5.9 the new type of cost–benefit ratio, $\tilde{r}$, may be calculated. The resulting values, as given in table 2, show that the most attractive combination of international sectors

TABLE 2

Cost–benefit ratios and rank of international sectors.

Sector	$\hat{r}_h$	Rank according to $\hat{r}_h$	$\tilde{r}_h(1)$	Rank according to $\tilde{r}_h(1)$
1	2.56	1		
2	3.71	2	3.56	2
3	3.75	3	3.44	1

10) While the results are given in two decimal places, the actual calculations have been carried out in six.

is 3 with 1 rather than 2 with 1. This result illustrates our conclusion (iiia) in section 5.10: the sector which is to accompany the most attractive one is not necessarily that which ranked second best in the case without bounds.

References

[1] P. A. Cornelisse and C. B. Tilanus, The Semi-Input–Output Method, with an application to Turkish data, *De Economist*, vol. 114, nr. 9/10, 1966 or no. 32 of the reprint series of the Division of Balanced International Growth of the Netherlands Economic Institute.

[2] J. Tinbergen, *Development Planning*, World University Library, London, 1967.

[3] J. Tinbergen, *Economic Policy: Principles and Design*, North-Holland Publishing Company, Amsterdam, 1956.

[4] J. G. Waardenburg, Note on the Comparison of the Simplex Method, the 'Elimination Method', and the Semi-Input–Output Method, unpublished discussion paper.

[5] D. W. Zandee, A Note on the Semi-Input–Output Method, unpublished discussion paper.

FACTOR INTENSITIES IN MEXICO WITH SPECIAL REFERENCE TO MANUFACTURING

GERARD K. BOON*)

1. Introduction

In this article I will assess the factor intensities by sector for the Mexican economy. Use will be made of an aggregated version of the Mexican input–output table of 1960.

In section 2 of this paper direct and cumulated primary input coefficients will be computed for flow and stock ratios per sector. Sectors will be ranked according to the magnitude of these coefficients. In section 3 the foreign trade pattern of Mexico will be explained by the ranking order of the sectors in terms of labour- and capital-intensiveness.

In section 4, I will investigate by means of international C.E.S. production functions for the manufacturing sector, whether the factor proportions in Mexico are in line with an international sample.

The results of the comparison will be analyzed.

2. Primary Input Coefficients by Sector

The 45 by 45 input–output table for 1960 is aggregated into a 16 by 16 input–output table. The primary input coefficients are wages and salaries and capital and mixed income over total gross output. These primary input ratios are on a flow–flow basis, as the annual income of the production factors is related to the annual gross output of a sector. The primary

*) The author is working as a manufacturing industry advisor, for the United Nations Industrial Development Organization, with the National Investment Bank (Nacional Financiera, S.A.) of Mexico. He gratefully acknowledges administrative and computational facilities granted to him by Nacional Financiera and Petróleos Mexicanos. He also appreciates the opportunity he had to discuss certain aspects of the paper with Messrs. Gerardo M. Bueno, and Luciano Barraza. Sole responsibility for this study rests, however, with the author.

TABLE 1
Aggregated input–output table (1960), in millions of pesos*).

Sector	1	2	3	4	5	6	7	8	9	10	11	
1 Agriculture, etc.	2028	14	1	8049	1091	521	550	1	2	28	3	
2 Mining and quarrying	1	1007	128	25	4	8	93	109	455	143	216	
3 Petroleum and coal	621	154	2944	445	185	97	126	218	275	173	124	
4 Foodstuffs, beverages and tobacco	1660	12	11	4697	54	33	130	5	21	26	41	
5 Textile and leather products	522	12	15	94	2565	38	94	12	25	81	38	
6 Wood and paper products	123	35	74	438	100	1038	246	92	43	182	613	
7 Chemical and rubber products	741	99	54	134	661	134	1018	49	34	430	191	
8 Manufactured non-metal mineral products	3	12	7	252	8	13	56	180	63	51	1428	
9 Basic metal industries	48	68	25	144	58	39	66	33	873	1249	1166	
10 Machinery and metal products	224	50	48	317	114	51	95	43	57	904	867	
11 Construction	140	24	26	45	38	16	20	25	22	11	60	
12 Electricity	73	106	3	165	122	62	75	75	62	63	49	
13 Commerce	1199	165	197	2632	1527	483	869	249	314	544	1660	
14 Transportation	1	9	12	57	32	21	30	8	7	46	20	
15 Services of structures	—	62	46	217	203	151	59	21	72	113	36	
16 Other services	159	90	181	464	134	90	288	57	167	194	312	
Total intermediate inputs	7543	1919	3772	18175	6896	2795	3815	1177	2492	4243	6824	
Imports	548	61	704	567	599	440	1664	156	366	1934	921	
Government	105	25	21	93	28	21	57	13	46	47	88	
Wages + salaries	5456	805	1489	3370	2652	948	1233	532	725	1947	3796	
Capital + mixed income	17667	1338	2121	5990	2488	1212	1756	476	824	2022	1980	
Indirect taxes	89	7	657	741	34	—	25	27	—	82	—	
Depreciation	758	156	822	519	260	187	231	147	237	227	329	
Total inputs	32166	4311	9586	29455	12957	5603	8781	2528	4690	10502	13938	2

*) Derived from the Mexican input–output table 1960, Bank of Mexico, Department of Economic Studies.

inputs do not reflect, however, purely the capital and labour inputs as the wage and salaries only reflect the labour income of the employee workers and not of the self-employed workers. The labour income of the self-employed workers is included in capital and mixed income as is entrepreneurial income [2]. I leave this problem untouched.

3	14	15	16	Intermediate outputs	Private consumption	Government consumption	Exports	Investments	Change in inventories	Total final demand	Total output
4	—	—	18	12310	14846	13	2953	943	1101	19856	32166
0	7	—	6	2217	2	1	2007	24	60	2094	4311
53	1022	—	94	6857	2133	116	256	2	222	2729	9586
56	28	5	104	6885	19604	42	2490	40	394	22570	29455
90	12	20	64	3687	7990	23	636	27	544	9270	12957
28	48	6	351	3830	1277	117	130	50	199	1773	5603
78	304	67	251	4256	3635	217	221	73	379	4525	8781
20	2	1	16	2113	99	117	72	26	101	415	2528
2	27	61	88	4090	—	24	92	222	262	600	4690
6	97	381	82	3588	3280	281	208	2529	616	6914	10502
3	72	328	39	992	—	28	—	12787	131	12946	13938
0	30	—	156	1371	540	179	—	115	—	834	2205
1	619	562	718	12182	35835	222	1461	3625	214	41357	53539
3	24	1	129	3352	4309	180	112	87	—	4688	8040
0	74	—	1359	3322	9629	50	—	—	—	9679	13001
0	169	23	439	3516	10951	247	1383	377	—	12958	16474
4	2535	1455	3914	74568	114130	1857	12071	20927	4223	153208	227776
9	482	429	173	9097	1318	231	55	3840	479	5923	15020
6	27	239	105	1038	—	1048	10	—	—	—	—
0	3233	375	6640	38649	—	7204	1651	195	—	—	—
5	761	8811	4857	89880	—	—	—	—	—	—	—
0	102	—	361	6334	—	—	—	—	—	—	—
5	900	1865	424	8210	—	—	—	—	—	—	—
9	8040	13001	16474	227776	—	8244	13787	24962	—	—	—

By multiplying the row vectors for capital and labour inputs by the inverted $(1-A)$ matrix, where A stands for the matrix of technical coefficients, the cumulated primary input coefficients are obtained. The cumulated coefficients indicate the direct plus the indirect requirements for capital and labour inputs per unit of final output [2].

TABLE 2

Flow–flow primary input ratios.

Sector	Labour income–output		Capital income–output	
	Direct	Cumulated	Direct	Cumulated
1 Agriculture, etc.	0.169620	0.227755	0.549245	0.685571
2 Mining and quarrying	0.186732	0.320076	0.310369	0.534553
3 Petroleum and coal	0.155331	0.260165	0.221260	0.372413
4 Foodstuffs, beverages and tobacco	0.114412	0.260802	0.203361	0.593086
5 Textile and leather products	0.204677	0.344840	0.192020	0.494566
6 Wood and paper products	0.169195	0.293980	0.216313	0.499321
7 Chemical and rubber products	0.140417	0.249668	0.199977	0.438987
8 Manufactured non-metal mineral products	0.210443	0.340606	0.188291	0.413205
9 Basic metal industries	0.154584	0.308946	0.175693	0.434407
10 Machinery and metal products	0.185393	0.298768	0.192535	0.383320
11 Construction	0.272349	0.407065	0.142058	0.350552
12 Electricity	0.348299	0.426730	0.014512	0.124809
13 Commerce	0.087413	0.043414	0.701265	0.047933
14 Transportation	0.402114	0.480384	0.094652	0.248964
15 Services of structures	0.028844	0.058323	0.677717	0.736524
16 Other services	0.403059	0.453225	0.294828	0.434477

TABLE 3

Cumulated stock–flow primary input ratios.

Sector	Stock–labour output		Stock–capital output	
	Direct	Cumulated	Direct	Cumulated
1 Agriculture, etc.	0.1910	0.214005	1.66	2.176944
2 Mining and quarrying	0.0171	0.033159	1.28	2.691694
3 Petroleum and coal	0.0071	0.016174	1.68	2.800727
4 Foodstuffs, beverages and tobacco	0.0121	0.091981	0.72	2.168060
5 Textile and leather products	0.0295	0.069892	0.64	1.918388
6 Wood and paper products	0.0268	0.066531	1.08	2.552297
7 Chemical and rubber products	0.0154	0.045493	1.01	2.089498
8 Manufactured non-metal mineral products	0.0329	0.050308	1.65	3.052083
9 Basic metals	0.0139	0.032551	1.81	3.541654
10 Machinery and metal products	0.0290	0.045457	1.09	2.307019
11 Construction	0.0293	0.050022	0.46	1.774903
12 Electricity	0.0188	0.027244	6.69	7.590191
13 Commerce	0.0200	0.025801	0.97	1.666937
14 Transportation	0.0468	0.056560	5.62	6.487438
15 Services of structures	0.0003	0.004723	11.21	11.433145
16 Other services	0.0733	0.081556	1.79	3.177428

TABLE 4

Ranking according to magnitude of the primary input ratios.

Sector	Flow–flow ratio				Stock–flow ratio			
	Labour		Capital		Labour		Capital	
	Direct	Cumulated	Direct	Cumulated	Direct	Cumulated	Direct	Cumulated
1 Agriculture, etc.	10	14	3	2	1	1	7	11
2 Mining and quarrying	8	7	4	4	11	11	9	8
3 Petroleum and coal	12	12	6	12	15	15	6	7
4 Foodstuffs, beverages and tobacco	15	11	8	3	14	2	15	12
5 Textile and leather prod.	7	5	11	6	5	4	14	14
6 Wood and paper products	11	10	7	5	8	5	11	9
7 Chemical and rubber prod.	14	13	9	8	12	9	12	13
8 Manufactured non-metal mineral products	6	6	12	10	4	7	8	6
9 Basic metal industries	13	8	13	9	13	12	4	5
10 Machinery and metal prod.	9	9	10	11	7	10	10	10
11 Construction	4	4	14	13	6	8	16	15
12 Electricity	3	3	16	15	10	13	2	2
13 Commerce	16	16	1	16	9	14	13	16
14 Transportation	2	1	15	14	3	6	3	3
15 Services of structures	5	15	2	1	16	16	1	1
16 Other services	1	2	5	7	2	3	5	4

In addition to the factor income–output ratio also stock–flow ratios, direct and cumulated, will be computed. By a stock–flow ratio is meant the stock of labour (measured in number of workers) and the stock of capital over the gross output.

Table 1 presents the aggregated input–output table for Mexico, table 2 presents the direct and the cumulated labour and capital income–output ratios; table 3 presents the direct and the cumulated capital and labour stock–output ratios; table 4 presents the ranking order of the results obtained in tables 2 and 3. The ranking number 1 is attached to the highest values and the highest ranking number is given to the lowest values.

From table 4 a preliminary conclusion may be deduced, namely, that the stock–flow ratios give a better insight into the labour- and capital-intensiveness of sectors than the flow–flow ratios. For example, a priori, it might be expected that the agricultural sector would be among the most labour-intensive. Nevertheless, according to the ranking by labour-intensity, based on the flow–flow ratios, agriculture is in the tenth place. According to that based on the stock–flow ratios the agricultural sector is the most labour-intensive. Another example is the electricity production sector. According to the labour income–output ratio electricity ranks third, although generally speaking electricity production is not a very labour-intensive process. According to the labour stock–output ratio electricity production ranks tenth.

The reason for these discrepancies in ranking order is the distortion by factor pricing.

The agricultural sector is without doubt extremely labour-intensive in Mexico, but as wages in the primitive part of the agricultural sector are very low and the number of self-employed workers large, wage income severely underestimates the labour-intensiveness of that sector.

The sector electricity production is very capital-intensive indeed, but from the total value added generated in that sector a disproportionately small part is allocated to capital, yielding a rate of return on capital of only a few percent annually, while probably the equilibrium price of capital is of the order of 15 per cent annually. Wage income in the electricity producing sector is high but as this sector is a publicly–owned utility, the observed factor income allocation is possible. According to the stock–flow output ratios for this sector, it ranks tenth in labour-intensity and second in capital-intensity.

From table 4 evidence can also be obtained that the cumulated coefficients give a better insight into the factor needs than the direct coefficients. This can be illustrated with sector 4 (foodstuffs, etc.). In terms of the direct labour stock–output ratio it ranks fourteenth; its comparable cumulated coefficient ranks it second. Increased consumption or exports of the products of sector 4 would undoubtedly favourably affect employment. The cumulated labour income–output coefficient ranks the sector eleventh.

Striking differences between both types of cumulated coefficients are also observed for the agricultural and transportation sectors. Hence absolutely misleading conclusions would be obtained by using the direct or cumulated factor income–output ratios as the basis for policy recommendations.

In the next section the usefulness of these various types of coefficients will be further tested by trying to explain with these coefficients Mexico's foreign trade pattern.

3. Factor Proportions and Foreign Trade

Usually the foreign trade pattern of a country is explained by its factor prices relative to the factor prices of its trading partners. The most important trading partner of Mexico is the USA. Without question the factor endowment of the USA differs significantly from the Mexican one. This is also true for Mexico's European trading partners and Japan; for Mexico's Latin American trading partners it is less obvious. Nevertheless I will try to explain Mexico's trade pattern exclusively from the Mexican side.

In Mexico there still is a significant imbalance between the main production factors, capital and labour. Unskilled and lowly-skilled labour is relatively abundant; capital and highly skilled labour is scarce. For that reason the hypothesis is that Mexico exports mainly products and services from these sectors, which are labour-intensive and imports goods from those sectors, which are relatively capital- and skill-intensive.

In table 5 sectors are grouped as net importers and net exporters according to information obtained from the aggregated Mexican input–output table of 1960. The sectors are in the first column, ranked according to the magnitude of the net balance of trade.

From the second part of the table it can be noticed, that the foreign exchange earners of Mexico in descending importance, are the following sectors: agriculture, mining, food, commerce, other services and textiles–leather. Of these sectors agriculture, foodstuffs, other services and textiles–leather rank as the four most labour-intensive sectors according to the stock–

TABLE 5

Assessment of Mexico's foreign trade pattern.

Net importers ranked according to balance		Sectors	Rank cumulated coefficient			
			Stock–flow ratio		Flow–flow ratio	
Rank	No. sector		Labour	Capital	Labour	Capital
1	10	Machinery and metal products	10	10	9	11
2	7	Chemical and rubber products	9	13	13	8
3	11	Construction	8	15	4	13
4	3	Petroleum and coal products	15	7	12	12
5	14	Transportation	6	3	1	14
6	6	Wood and paper products	5	9	10	5
7	9	Basic metal industries	12	5	8	9
8	8	Manufactured non-metal mineral prod.	7	6	6	10
9	15	Services of structures	16	1	15	1
10	12	Electricity	13	2	3	15
Net exporters ranked according to balance						
1	1	Agriculture, etc.	1	11	14	2
2	2	Mining and quarrying	11	8	7	4
3	4	Foodstuffs, beverages and tobacco	2	12	11	3
4	13	Commerce	14	16	16	16
5	16	Other services	3	4	2	7
6	5	Textile and leather products	4	14	5	6

flow cumulated coefficient. Commerce is the least capital-intensive sector. Mining's export position is obviously based on Mexico's natural resource endowment.

Analyzing the first half of table 5, it can be seen that the net importers are all the sectors belonging to the manufacturing industry plus the domestic industries like construction, electricity and, to a certain extent, transport. For these latter industries it is generally speaking impossible to export, but imports are nevertheless required in the form of capital and intermediate goods. Except for construction these domestic industries are very capital-intensive. Manufacturing industry has, in general, inputs of labour and capital in the medium range, neither very labour-intensive nor very capital-intensive.

By analyzing the ranking numbers for the cumulated primary input coefficients it is clear that again the labour and capital stock–output ratios give a much better explanation of the true factor proportions of a sector than the labour and capital income–output ratios.

Summarizing the results from table 5: in 1960 Mexico's net exporting sectors were those most labour-intensive sectors or least capital-intensive with the addition of mining while the net importing sectors were the most capital-intensive sectors plus the manufacturing industry, which occupied an intermediate position. The production factor stock–output ratios are superior for an economy like the Mexican in indicating the factor-intensities of the sectors.

4. Assessment of Mexico's Manufacturing Industry

Although Mexico in 1960 was at a rather early stage of industrialization, and for that reason it could be considered normal that the manufacturing-industry sectors were net importers, it is of interest nevertheless to investigate somewhat further the factor proportions of the manufacturing-industry sectors.

As was noticed already some factor-price distortion is evident in Mexico. Labour incomes including social security allowances in the modern part

TABLE 6

Exchange rates for 1958 (U.S. cents per unit of domestic currency).

Country	Exchange rate Official (A)	Exchange rate Adjusted (B)	Change
1 U.S.A.	100.00	100.00	1
2 Canada	103.63	103.05	0.9944
3 U.K.	280.19	375.64	1.3407
4 Netherlands	26.49	34.80	1.3137
5 Finland	0.31	0.25	0.8065
6 Japan	0.28	0.33	1.1786
7 Brazil	0.72	0.78	1.0833
8 Mexico	8.00	8.94	1.1175
9 Peru	4.08	4.36	1.0686
10 Pakistan	21.00	21.16	1.0076

Source: The Growth of World Industry. International Analyses, tables 1938–1961, United Nations, New York, p. 310.

TABLE 7

International cross-section production functions by aggregated sector breakdown.

Input–output table 16/16	Input–output table 45/45	ISIC	Industries	Regression equation a	Regression equation b	Coefficient of Corre-lation	Coefficient of Deter-mina-tion	Standard error	T test	Degrees of free-dom	$b \neq 1$	Type of data
		20	Food, beverages, tobacco	2.782	0.755	0.972	0.945	0.181	11.653	9	0.005	A
4	8, 9, 10	21										
	11, 12	22		2.794	0.755	0.978	0.956	0.157	13.235	9	0.001	B
	13, 14	23	Textiles, clothing,	2.121	0.784	0.987	0.974	0.118	17.292	9	0.001	A
5		24	leather									
	15, 19	29		2.146	0.783	0.988	0.976	0.113	17.876	9	0.001	B
		25, 26	Wood, paper,	1.485	0.900	0.984	0.968	0.149	15.481	9	0.050	A
6	16, 17, 18	27, 28	printing	1.578	0.888	0.985	0.970	0.141	15.961	9	0.050	B
	20, 21, 22	31, 32	Chemicals, petroleum,	2.168	0.857	0.968	0.937	0.210	10.881	9	0.050	A
7	23, 24, 25		rubber									
	26, 27	30		2.337	0.834	0.964	0.929	0.215	10.302	9	0.025	B
8	28	33	Non-metallic mineral	1.782	0.860	0.979	0.958	0.182	13.474	9	0.025	A
			products									
				1.811	0.857	0.978	0.956	0.180	13.406	9	0.025	B
9	29	34	Basic metal industries	2.885	0.737	0.900	0.810	0.364	5.840	9	0.050	A
				2.851	0.745	0.899	0.808	0.370	5.790	9	0.050	B
10	30, 31, 32	35, 36	Metal products	2.011	0.814	0.972	0.945	0.204	11.628	9	0.010	A
	33, 34, 35	37, 38	industries									
		39		1.979	0.822	0.973	0.947	0.200	11.918	9	0.025	B

Source: the author.

of the economy seem to be somewhat high and interest rates in some sectors too low. In addition importation of capital goods is tax-free or subsidized. Importation of consumer goods is forbidden or hampered by high import taxes.

Moreover, her highly affluent neighbour to the north may, willy-nilly, set an example of high capital-intensity and technological sophistication in production.

All these factors may contribute to a choice of capital-intensity not in line with Mexican factor endowment, which may affect the international competitiveness of Mexican industry and the size of its internal market.

In the assessment of Mexico's factor proportions in the manufacturing sector use is made of an international 'Constant Elasticity of Substitution' production function. It is assumed that for a given sector all countries in the sample are on the same production function. The data for the C.E.S. production function refer to 1958. The composition of the international sample is presented in table 6. Two exchange rates are used indicated by A and B, respectively.

Table 7 summarizes the statistical results of the production functions. As the exchange rate B gives somewhat better statistical results, the production function based on this exchange rate will be used in the analysis. As will be recalled the C.E.S. function has the following general properties [1], [3]:

$$\ln(V/L) = a + b \ln w \tag{1}$$

where V/L = value added per worker per year; a = constant in logarithmic terms; b = elasticity of substitution between labour and capital; w = annual wage income per worker; ln = natural logarithm.

From the Mexican aggregated input–output table and data of numbers of workers engaged per aggregated sector, the value added per worker and the wage bill per worker are derived.

By using the function (1), the projected wage rate $(w)_p$ is computed for the observed labour-productivity $(V/L)_o$, also the projected labour productivity $(V/L)_p$, is computed for the observed wage rate $(w)_o$. The results obtained are indicated in table 8.

The results indicate that for the observed wage rate the labour productivity $(V/L)_p$, should be higher than the one actually observed, or for the observed

TABLE 8

Manufacturing-industry sectors	Labour productivity (U.S.$)		Wage rates (U.S.$)	
	Observed $(V/L)_o$	Projected $(V/L)_p$	Observed $(w)_o$	Projected $(w)_p$
4 Food, beverages, tobacco	2376	2433	754	734
5 Textiles and leather prod.	1135	1203	554	514
6 Wood, paper products	1249	1216	504	519
7 Chemical, petroleum rubber products	1919	2526	729	524
8 Manufactured non-metal mineral products	1138	1283	512	445
9 Basic metal industries	2186	2719	887	662
10 Machinery and metal prod.	1124	1220	512	450

labour productivity the corresponding wage rate $(w)_p$, should be lower than the observed wage rate. In other words the international function indicates that either Mexican wage rates are too high or the labour productivity is too low.

It seems that the production function does not apply to Mexico. If I try to understand this result, there seem to be several possible explanations.
(1) Total value added is underestimated for whatever reason. The number of workers engaged excludes, except for a few months, unemployment.
(2) Capital may be overestimated. Capital figures are not corrected for under-utilization; as the number of engaged indicates only those employed the capital–labour ratio may be overestimated. The capital–labour ratio corrected for underutilization of capital may be in line with the observed labour productivity.
(3) The level of the wage rate may not correspond to the level of the labour productivity due to institutional rigidities, such as minimum wage regulations and restrictions on the lay-off of labour; moreover, numerous fringe benefits hike up the cost of labour.

If the results are accepted as they are, there seems to me to be two major possibilities.
(a) to increase the labour productivity in order to bring it into line with the wage rates and implicitly with the capital intensity;
(b) to reduce the wage rates, for example, by means of subsidies.

Analyzing the first possibility, the target would be to move up the labour productivity to the projected magnitude leaving the wage rate and the capital–labour ratio unchanged until the target is reached. Without doubt there exist numerous possibilities of improving the labour productivity in Mexican manufacturing industry, on the individual firm level, as well as, presumably, on the sector level and on the intersectorial level, without increasing the capital intensity.

Hence, an output expansion is possible with given quantities of labour and capital, leading to improved labour productivity, initially at frozen wage rates.

Such an output expansion would favor the capital share of value added as the labour share initially remains constant. Under the conditions stipulated the labour–output ratio as well as the capital–output ratio would decline. This should, if the entrepreneurs operate under competitive conditions, increase the internal market and possibly also the external market. In the longer run both factors of production could benefit from the new equilibrium situation.

In order to show in which sectors the efficiency drive seems most needed, a comparison is made of the relative efficiency of Mexican manufacturing

TABLE 9

Sector	Labour–output ratio			Capital–output ratio		
	USA	UK	Mexico	USA	UK	Mexico
4	0.2	0.8	1	1.7	1.3	1
5	0.2	0.6	1	3.8	2.7	1
6	0.2	0.5	1	1.4	1.3	1
7	0.1	0.5	1	1.9	1.6	1
8	0.1	0.4	1	0.9	0.8	1
9	0.2	0.6	1	0.9	0.6	1
10	0.1	0.4	1	1.1	1.0	1

industry compared to the USA and the UK. The presented indices refer for the latter two countries to 1958, for Mexico to 1960. Mexican values are set at unity; US and UK values are deviations from unity (table 9).

The information, which refers to primary input–output ratios only, on which this table is based is independent from the production functions as presented in table 7.

From this information it may be deduced that Mexico is relatively speaking an inefficient producer in sectors 8, 9, and 10, as it uses more labour and more or equal capital per unit of output.

Analyzing the second possibility it should first be stressed that reductions of wage rates are nowhere a popular measure and although Mexican wage rates for some types of skill might be relatively high in absolute terms, wage income is low, according to the standards of the richer nations. The distribution of income between labour and capital is inequitable, socially speaking, and the present tax system aggravates this situation. In the following analysis it should be kept in mind that income can be distributed, by means of e.g. taxes, in whatever way desired, and that I in no way suggest that, in the final settlement capital income should be increased at the expense of labour income.

Starting with the projected wage rate, corresponding to the observed labour productivity, which is lower than the observed wage rate, it seems logical to scale down the observed capital intensity in order that labour productivity, wage rates and capital intensity are in line with each other. By assuming the rate of return on capital to remain the same the projected capital intensity is derived by using the following formula:

$$\ln (K/L)_p = b \ln (w_p/w_o) + \ln (K/L)_o . \qquad (2)$$

This yields the following results in U.S. dollars (table 10).

TABLE 10

Sector	$(K/L)_o$ (observed)	$(K/L)_p$ (projected)	$(K/L)_p - (K/L)_o$ (incremental)
4	4590	4370	− 220
5	1600	1530	− 70
6	3360	3020	− 340
7	3950	3670	− 280
8	3550	3110	− 440
9	8360	7260	− 1100
10	2700	2620	− 80

Especially in the basic metal-industry sector (sector 9) substantial reductions in capital-intensity are suggested by this procedure.

By multiplying the projected capital–labour ratio $(K/L)_p$ by the observed labour stock, the projected capital stock K_p can be obtained. In symbols:

$$L_o(K/L)_p = K_p \tag{3.1}$$

As the projected capital–labour ratio is smaller than the observed capital–labour ratio, the projected capital stock is smaller than the observed capital stock K_o, which corresponds to the observed wage rate. Hence

$$K_p < K_o \tag{3.2}$$

$$K_o - K_p = \text{excess capital.}$$

Assuming that capital can be reallocated and that the projected wage rate can be made effective to the entrepreneurs, then the new capital–labour ratio will come close to the one projected.

Consequently the potential employment capacity can be computed, by dividing the observed capital stock by the projected capital–labour ratio.

The incremental employment is the difference between the projected and the observed labour force (4.1).

In symbols:

$$K_o(L/K)_p = L_p \tag{4}$$

$$L = L_p - L_o \tag{4.1}$$

The numerical results from the application of formulas 4 and 4.1 are as in table 11.

TABLE 11

Sector	Employment-capacity (× 1000 workers)		
	Potential $(L)_p$	Observed $(L)_o$	Incremental (L)
4	369	358	11
5	416	383	33
6	144	150	−6
7	179	135	44
8	94	83	11
9	81	65	16
10	340	304	36
	1 623	1 478	145

The figures suggest that a substantial increase in employment seems possible.

Factor shares are approximated in the following way (as only two factors of production, labour and capital, are distinguished in the analysis, only the shares for labour and capital can be derived):

$$(V/L)_o \cdot L_p = V_p \tag{5}$$

$$(w)_p \cdot L_p = W_p \tag{6}$$

$$V_p - W_p = R_p \tag{7}$$

$$R_p/K_o = r_p \tag{8}$$

By multiplying the observed labour productivity by the potential employment, the potential value added (V_p) can be derived (5). By multiplying the potential employment by the projected wage rate, the total projected labour income is approximated (6); by deducing the latter from the potential value added, the projected capital income is derived (7).

By expressing the potential capital income as a percentage of the capital stock the potential rate of return (8) is obtained.

By working out the numerical results, the figures for the manufacturing sector as a whole are as indicated under 1 and 2 in table 12.

TABLE 12

Factor shares, Mexican manufacturing industry, 1960 (× 1000 pesos).

	W	R	$W+R$	r
	(millions of pesos)			
1 Existing situation	11407	14768	26175	0.24
2 New situation, projected wage rates, no subsidy	11271	20460	31731	0.30
3 New situation, obs. wage rates, with labour subsidy	12573	19158	31731	0.28

5. Summary and Concluding Remarks

The results indicated in table 12 contradict one popular contention which runs as follows: using more labour-intensive technologies will increase the total wage bill and total consumption; the capacity to save will be reduced as capital receives a smaller portion of the value added. Consequently the investible surplus is reduced and future economic growth is adversely affected.

The analysis presented here is not an overall analysis but a sectoral one.

According to the analysis presented it seems possible to employ more workers, with the observed capital stock. As each worker has a labour productivity equal to that observed and as the entrepreneurs experience lower labour costs it is quite obvious that the share of capital increases. By no means is it implied that the projected wage rate should be the guideline for the actual remuneration of labour.

The government has various means at its disposal to grant open or hidden subsidies, in order to reduce the observed labour cost. The cost of this operation may be recovered by the government by the increased revenues accruing, even at the existing tax rate, from the increased capital income. Also income-tax receipts would increase from the labour income of the increase in the number employed. Consequently by keeping the observed wage rates, but by making labour cheaper through subsidies, more or less to the extent of the difference between observed and projected wage rate, an income distribution could be obtained as indicated under 3 in the last table; (see Tinbergen's concept of accounting prices [4]). More social justice could be achieved by further sharing of the increment in income, leaving a rate of return of, for example, 25%.

Summarizing the last part of the analysis the following stands out. The observation that according to an international production function the observed labour productivity in the Mexican manufacturing sectors is too low or the observed wage rate too high, disregarding possible imperfections in the data, leads to two possible solutions:

(1) improve the labour productivity in order to bring it into line with the observed wage rate and consequently also with the observed capital–labour ratio. This would lead to an increase in national income and an increased share of capital in total value added. If entrepreneurs respond to competitive conditions, a new long-run equilibrium may evolve leading also to more employment.
(2) decrease the wage costs to the entrepreneurs, for example, by governmental subsidies. Again if the entrepreneurs are responsive, a new equilibrium will evolve, which will lead to a higher value added, more employment and a larger share for capital.

As pointed out the distribution of the value added over the production factors labour and capital can be modified by taxation. Which of these two solutions is to be preferred depends on how one interprets the actual economic situation in Mexico. The real conditions in the economy deviate considerably from those of the general competitive equilibrium model. The first solution is of immediate benefit for the entrepreneurs, but it requires an initiative from their side. However, due to market imperfections, the entrepreneurs make already such a high rate of return on capital (the Mexican rate of return on capital in manufacturing industry is possibly among the highest in the world), that they may lack the incentive to improve labour productivity with all the effort this would call for, even if it implies a still higher rate of return on capital.

As regards the second solution, the government could take the initiative. The government is supposed to promote the interests of all the participants in the economic society. The beneficial results of the second solution are important and more immediate: national income and employment could increase substantially. As no initiative from the entrepreneurs is required, merely an adjustment to a changed cost structure, it is more likely that the necessary response would be forthcoming. The manufacturing industry would move to a higher and more efficient equilibrium situation, which could also imply improved international competitiveness, in addition to all the benefits already mentioned.

References

[1] K. J. Arrow, H. B. Chenery, B. S. Minhas and R. M. Solow, 'Capital–Labour Substitution and Economic Efficiency'. *The Review of Economics and Statistics*, August 1961.

[2] G. K. Boon, *Economic Choice of Human and Physical Factors in Production*, Amsterdam, North-Holland Publishing Company, 1964. Fondo de Cultura Económica, México 1968.

[3] B. S. Minhas, *An International Comparison of Factor Costs and Factor Use*. Amsterdam, North-Holland Publishing Company, 1965.

[4] J. Tinbergen, *The Design of Development*, The Johns Hopkins Press, Baltimore 1958.

EXPORT POLICY IN PAKISTAN

NURUL ISLAM

1. Introduction

During the 1950's Pakistan maintained balance in her international payments, in the face of an excess of demand over the supply of foreign exchange at the prevailing rate of exchange, by the imposition of rigid quantitative restrictions on imports. The state of excess demand was subsequently aggravated by the inflationary forces in the domestic economy in the late fifties, which further contributed to the relative overvaluation of her exchange rate. Moreover, the Second Five-Year Plan starting in 1959–60 added considerably to the demand for the imported equipment and raw materials necessary for an acceleration of the rate of investment. The maintenance of a rigid system of import restriction during the 1950's had an important consequence for Pakistan's exports and export policy in that the effective import rate which resulted from the quantitative restrictions and tariffs was considerably higher than the effective export rate. A measure of the effective import rate prevailing in Pakistan can be gauged by the fact that the domestic prices of imported goods exceeded the corresponding c.i.f. prices by 81 per cent to 97 per cent in 1959–60 [9, ch. 4, table 4]. At the same time the effective export rate for the major export commodities like cotton and jute was below the official rate consequent on the imposition of export duties and for the rest of the agricultural commodities the export rate was equal to the official rate of exchange. Thus from the point of view of the allocation of domestic resources between import substitution, on the one hand and export expansion, on the other, the former was more attractive and profitable than the latter. A unit of domestic resources engaged in substituting for a dollar's worth of imports earned about Rs. 9 to 10 in the domestic markets, whereas the same amount of resources if devoted to the production for sales in the export markets did not earn more than Rs. 4.76. In addition, the manufactured exports of Pakistan, which were the products of her nascent manufacturing industries, suffered from high costs and prices in relation to the costs and prices of the competing products in world markets.

It was in the context of those circumstances that Pakistan, confronted in the early sixties with the urgent need to increase substantially her export earnings, especially earnings from manufactured exports, introduced a series of export promotion measures beginning in 1959. The main export promotion measures which covered some minor primary exports and all or many manufactured exports were:

(1) the export bonus scheme,

(2) the exemption from the indirect taxes on the imported inputs which go into the production of exports,

(3) the exemption from income tax on the earnings from exports, and

(4) the export performance licensing.

The most important component of the export promotion measures was the export bonus scheme which was introduced in 1959. The next most important measure was the export performance licensing which applied to a selected number of manufacturing industries starting in 1962. Whereas the exemption from indirect taxes on imported inputs had been in operation since 1956, its administration was considerably improved during the 1960's. The rebate on income tax on export earnings was introduced only in 1963. All of these measures combined to establish for various exports a number of different export rates of exchange. This paper is devoted to the discussion of the implications of various export policies in terms of the effective subsidies which they provide to the different exports in Pakistan, their effects on the growth of exports as well as on the efficiency of allocation of resources in the Pakistan economy.

2. Export Bonus Scheme and Export Performance Licensing

These two measures link the incentive or assistance to the exporters with entitlements to imports. The element of subsidy under these measures originates basically from the fact that the imports are rigidly controlled, and, therefore, earn high scarcity premiums in the domestic market. Under the export bonus scheme, the exporters receive a fixed percentage of their exports in terms of the entitlements to imports, which are transferable and can be freely bought and sold for the imports of a specified list of commodities. The scheme, therefore, provides a mechanism by which the high profits earned by the importers, in view of a great excess demand for scarce imports, are transferred to the exporters. The export bonus scheme, which was introduced in 1959, excluded from its purview the major commodities such as jute, cotton, tea, hides and skins, and wool which constituted in the early sixties about 80 per cent of Pakistan's total export earnings, and indeed many of them were subject to export taxes. The rest of the primary commodities which at the time of the inception of the scheme in 1959 did not constitute more than 6 per cent of the total exports, and all the manufactured exports were entitled to receive the import entitlements to the extent of 20 per cent and 40 per cent, respectively, of their export proceeds, with the exception of the jute manufacturing industries which were eligible for the same rate of import entitlement as the minor primary commodities, i.e., 20 per cent. In addition, some invisible items such as the earnings from shipping, ship and aircraft repairs, and salvage operations were entitled to a bonus at the rate of 20 per cent. The hotel industry and private remittances from abroad were subsequently included in the scheme, both of these items being entitled to a 20 per cent bonus rate.

The discrimination against agricultural exports which resulted from their exclusion from the bonus scheme and, in some cases, from the levy of export taxes, was based on the assumption that the foreign demand for them is inelastic – an assumption which, at least in the case of cotton and tea, with Pakistan's very small share of the world market in these commodities, was not realistic. There was the further assumption that the supply response of the agricultural exports was low, partly because of institutional rigidities in agriculture and partly because of the conservativeness of the farmers. But experience and empirical analysis in the late 1950's already demonstrated that the agriculturists responded strongly to changes in relative prices in terms of allocation of resources and land between alternative crops. Moreover, at the same time the possibility that a favorable shift in the relative prices of cotton and jute as against those of the competing crops, which included rice in the case of jute and a number of minor food crops in the case of cotton, might divert resources away from the competing crops and thus raise the cost of food, and, therefore, the cost of living was a restraining factor in an attempt to abolish or reduce the export taxes. Again, it was also felt that the export taxes, insofar as they kept down the domestic prices of cotton and jute, provided an indirect and necessary subsidy to the jute and cotton manufacturing industries, the most important export industries in the country. During the 1950's an important obstacle to the removal of export duties was the relative importance of these duties as a source of government revenue, specially as they provided the most convenient divisible pool of fiscal resources, to be shared between the central government and the provinces. By 1960 the relative importance of the export taxes as a source of revenue declined. This, combined with an increasing realization that the export duties were acting as a continual drag on the exports, led to their reduction in successive stages. In the case of tea, for example, a large increase in domestic consumption coupled with a stagnation in production left no or negligible exportable surplus and the export duty on tea was reduced gradually over the years until it was abolished in 1963. Similarly, there was a steady reduction in the export duty on cotton during the 1960's but there was no such decline in the export duty on jute, since the assumption of the inelasticity of foreign demand for jute was still a relevant consideration. Moreover, faced with the need of increasing the rate of agricultural growth, the government sought to offset or correct the disincentive effect of export taxes on the supply of export crops by systematic subsidization during the Second Five-Year Plan of the cost of agricultural inputs such as fertilizer, water and seeds, etc.; this policy was successful as the response of the supply of agricultural output to the availability of the cheap subsidized inputs turned out to be strongly positive. But the adverse impact of the export taxes on foreign demand for the major agricultural exports continued to be felt, especially in view of the fact that in the long run demand was more elastic than in the short run. It is highly likely, for instance, that one of the consequences of Pakistan's maintaining a high export price for raw jute via the imposition of export tax was the entry into the world market of the marginal producers like Brazil and Thailand with low-quality jute and high costs of production. Undoubtedly, while there were other factors which would have in any event contributed to the increasing competition from the synthetic substitutes, the continued maintenance of high export prices of raw jute might have speeded up the process.

The magnitude of the subsidy which is provided by the most important of the export promotion schemes, i.e., the export bonus scheme, is a function of the rate of bonus allowed on exports and of the price or the premium on the bonus vouchers. The list of eligible imports which may be purchased with the use of bonus vouchers has been changed frequently by the government, often from one six-month period to another. A large number of inessential consumer goods, including consumer durables, and raw materials for consumer goods was initially put on the eligible import list, which has gradually been expanded to include other intermediate products as well as capital goods. The demand for bonus vouchers is a function of

(a) the total demand for the eligible imports,

(b) the amount of such eligible imports which are allowed to be imported at the official rate of exchange under the system of import licensing, and

(c) the rates of import duty on bonus items. The authorities not only have changed from time to time the list of eligible imports, but also manipulated the factors (b) and (c) above.

A multiplicity of considerations has guided the changes over the years in the eligible list of imports under the bonus scheme. Firstly, those items which fetch a high scarcity premium in the domestic market are considered specially eligible, since they strengthen the demand for the bonus vouchers and hence keep up the level of premium on the bonus vouchers and consequently the magnitude of subsidy to the exports. The fewer the items allowed to be imported under the bonus scheme, the greater is the need for placing the items of imports with high profit margins on the bonus list, with a view to providing an adequate subsidy to the exports. Secondly, considerations such as the need to relieve the domestic shortage of those imported goods, the demand for which is not adequately met under the licensing system at the official rate, also influence the composition of the bonus list, especially if the resulting rise in the price of such items consequent on their transfer to the bonus list is not to affect substantially the low-income groups. It is felt that an effective restraint on the consumption of the high-income groups is often better enforced by raising, via the bonus market, the price they pay rather than by a complete ban on imports or by the imposition of high import taxes; both of these could be evaded and they put a great burden on the efficiency and the honesty of administration. Protection of the domestic manufacturing industry has also been a factor behind the manipulation of the bonus list in cases where the imports of the competing items exclusively on the bonus list raised the effective import rate, i.e., the degree of nominal protection enjoyed by the competing domestic industries.

The considerable fluctuations in the prices of the bonus vouchers in the early years were due mainly to the frequent changes in the permissible list of imports and in the rates of bonus allowed on the different export commodities. However, by the mid-sixties the desire to impart stability to the level of the premium on the bonus vouchers, with a view to stabilizing the rate of the effective subsidy accruing to the various exports, became an important factor behind the manipulation of the bonus import list. It is felt that with a stabilized premium it is easier to fix the rate of bonus with a view to adjusting the level of subsidy to the requirement of each exported product. While the adverse effects of fluctuations in the premium on the bonus vouchers on the long-term calculations of the traders and investors tend to inhibit the rational planning for investment in the development of exports, the magnitude of such fluctuations which arise only from the changes in the supply and demand for bonus vouchers and their adverse effects seems to have been exaggerated. In fact, a much greater degree of instability and uncertainty has originated from the frequent changes in the list of permissible imports and the rates of bonus allowed to the different exports. While the hedging operations in the bonus market develop as an offset against the fluctuations in the bonus premium, they can not possibly deal effectively with the speculations regarding the frequent changes in government policy about the effective rates of subsidy. In fact, however, a widening of the bonus market over the years has had the effect of reducing the degree of fluctuations in the premium. The first three years, i.e., 1959–60 to 1961–62, saw considerable fluctuations in the bonus premium. In fact the premium fluctuated between 81 per cent and 190 per cent during these years. The range of fluctuations decreased considerably by 1965–66 with the minimum and the maximum rates being 136 per cent and 158 per cent, respectively.

The percentage rates of bonus on exports started with only two rates, i.e., 20 per cent and 40 per cent; but, by 1964, they increased to five different rates, that is, 10 per cent, 20 per cent, 30 per cent, 35 per cent and 40 per cent [4, pp. 11–27]. More importantly, during these years, there were frequent changes in the percentage of import entitlements of the individual export commodities which were often very narrowly defined. For example, at one stage the textile exports received three different rates of bonus, depending upon the specific kind of product. The effective export subsidy for various commodities as a result of the export bonus scheme ranged between 30 per cent and 50 per cent of the f.o.b. value of exports during the period 1963–64. During the subsequent period while the rates of bonus were reduced on a large number of commodities, the level of the premium went up to compensate the decline in the rate of bonus. The differentiation between the individual commodities in terms of the percentage of bonus entitlement as well as changes therein over the years has been made hopefully in accordance with (a) the differences in the supply and demand elasticities of the different exports, and (b) the differences in the cost disadvantages of individual manufacturing industries. The amount of detailed information on costs as well as the demand and supply elasticities of the individual commodities which are available at the disposal of authorities for a successful and a rational differentiation between commodities is indeed very inadequate, with the result that often the highest rates are obtained by the commodities which face the stiffest competition in the export market or which have the highest cost disadvantage. The rates are differentiated or often changed in response to the pressure of special interests for exceptional treatment of individual commodities in view of the difficulties faced in selling abroad. Moreover, changes in the rates have also been made in a few cases in an attempt to restrain a considerable diversion of a relatively short domestic supply to the export markets with a view to reducing the hardship of the special groups of consumers or hardship of the individual domestic industries in case the export commodity is an intermediate input. The frequent variations of the bonus rates on cotton yarn which in fact went on and off and back again on the bonus list illustrate the case in point. By 1964, the multiplication and the proliferation of the bonus rates on the different export commodities became quite irrational with the result that a simplification of the rate structure was undertaken and the rates were brought down to two rates of 20 per cent and 30 per cent. However, the pressure for a multiplication of rates continued to build up from time to time in the following years with some success.

By 1962–63, an additional measure of export promotion was introduced in the form of export performance licensing, under which different exports, as under the export bonus scheme, are entitled to receive import entitlements at varying percentages of their exports, but unlike in the bonus scheme they are not freely transferable but can only be used for the imports of raw materials, spare parts, and machinery required by the industry concerned. The subsidy element in the export performance licensing arises from the fact that there is an excess demand and a consequent scarcity for most of the imported raw materials in the domestic market, specially in view of the widespread prevalence of excess capacity in the manufacturing industries.

In the presence of a continuing pressure of a strong pull of domestic demand, exports involve a surrender of sales in the highly profitable domestic market, which are sought to be compensated under this scheme by granting to the exporters additional import licenses or permits to import raw materials and spare parts. The latter may be used either for a larger domestic production destined for the domestic market or for outright sales at high profits to others similarly situated and suffering from excess capacity. Moreover, a greater utilization of capacity reduces unit costs and thus increases profits per unit of sale.

The additional import entitlement or export performance licence received by the export industries in the initial years was substantially in excess of the import component of exports, specially since the import entitlements were at 100 per cent of the f.o.b. value of exports. Until 1964 only 43 industries were eligible for the additional import entitlement, and the import entitlements were at a uniform rate of exports. While in the subsequent years the number of industries receiving additional licensing has been considerably expanded to about 250 industries in 1965–66, the percentage of import entitlements has also been reduced [3, 8]. Moreover, the import entitlements of each industry are to be fixed separately in the light of its own import component, but in no case is it to exceed 50 per cent of the f.o.b. value of exports. Thus, the degree of differentiation between commodities has considerably increased and so also the rates of subsidy accruing to the different industries widely differ. In 1965–66, the import entitlements as a percentage of the f.o.b. value of exports ranged from 10 per cent in the case of 16 industries to 50 per cent in the case of 54 industries [4, pp. 47–48; 9, ch. 4, table 5]. The jute and cotton textile industries have always been kept outside the purview of the scheme. The magnitude of the effective subsidy originating from this scheme varies between the different industries depending on the shortage at a given time of the specific raw materials which constitute the import component of a particular industry. Assuming a 40 per cent premium on the domestic sales of the scarce imported materials, the export performance licensing provides a subsidy at the rate of 4 per cent of the f.o.b. value of exports in the case of those exports which have 10 per cent import entitlement and at the rate of 20 per cent for those exports which receive 50 per cent import entitlement. The maximum percentage of export performance licensing has been reduced from 50 per cent to 30 per cent during 1966–67. The scheme places a considerable degree of strain and burden on the licensing authorities as it requires them to determine the import coefficients of the specific exports, especially since the exporters have all the incentive for overestimating their import requirements in order to increase their import entitlements.

3. Fiscal Incentives

In addition to the favorable multiple export rates which are provided under the export bonus and the export performance licensing, a number of additional fiscal measures is undertaken to promote exports. For example, exports are exempted from the indirect taxes such as the sales and excise duties which are imposed on their domestic sales. To the extent that the incidence of such taxes is partly on the domestic producer, exemption of the exports from such taxes increases the rate of return from the export sales vis-a-vis the sales in the domestic market. Moreover, to the extent that the export tax contributes to the high domestic price, exemption from it enables the exporters to reduce the export price abroad, thus stimulating demand. Under this incentive scheme, differences in the incidence of implicit subsidy as between different industries is related to (a) the differential rates of indirect taxes, on the one hand, and (b) the differential incidence of indirect taxes on the domestic producers, which depend upon the supply and demand elasticities of individual commodities, on the other. None of these factors are related to the relative costs and efficiency of the domestic industries. The exports of commodities with higher rates of taxes, facing a highly elastic domestic demand, receive a higher subsidy. This may help divert to export markets commodities whose domestic consumption is restrained by high taxes. Luxury goods may conceivably fall in this category. Another measure of relatively minor importance is the grant of the concessional freight rates on the transportation of exports to the point of shipping. However, it is difficult to quantify the total impact of such minor export promotion measures in terms of an effective rate of subsidy.

The most important fiscal measures which have been adopted in the 1960's are:

(a) the exemption of the import component of exports from the indirect taxes (import duties and sales tax), and

(b) the rebate of income tax on the earnings from exports.

The rates of indirect taxes on the imported raw materials have increased over the years between 1959–60 and 1965–66, considerably so in a number of cases so that in 1965–66 the rates of duties ranged from 40 per cent on the unprocessed raw materials to 81 per cent on the processed raw materials [10]. According to one estimate, in 1963–64, 21 per cent of the manufacturing industries have an average import component at 15 per cent of gross output and hence receive a subsidy varying between 6 per cent to 13 per cent of the f.o.b. value of exports. There is another 32 per cent of the industries with an import component of 22.5 per cent, which thus receive a rate of subsidy varying somewhere from 9 per cent to 21 per cent of the f.o.b. value of exports [4, pp. 5–8; 12].

The rate of rebate of income tax on the earnings from exports varies directly with the proportion of exports to total output but is applied without discrimination to all the industries, excepting the jute manufacturing industry and major raw materials such as jute and cotton. During the years 1963–67, exports which have constituted less than 10 per cent of their corresponding gross domestic output have received no rebate. The lowest rebate of 10 per cent has been allowed to those exports which constitute between 10 per cent and 20 per cent of the corresponding domestic outputs while the maximum rebate of 20 per cent is allowed to exports if the latter constitute more than 30 per cent of the output. The minimum and the maximum rates of rebates have been raised to 15 per cent and 25 per cent in 1967. On the basis of 30 per cent tax on corporate profits or income the implicit rate of subsidy therefore, has varied between the minimum of 0.2 per cent and a maximum of 1.2 per cent of the f.o.b. value of exports during the years 1963–67. The corresponding rates by 1967–68 are 0.8 per cent and 1.5 per cent. In view of the fact that the majority of industries exports less than 20 per cent of their output the change in the rate of rebates introduced during 1967–68 extends the benefit of the scheme to a larger number of industries. While under the other incentive schemes the rates of subsidy relate to the absolute value of exports, the system of the rebate of income tax on the earnings from exports relates the rate of rebate directly to the proportion of output exported. The larger the volume of sales and, consequently, the level of income or profits the larger, under the present system of rebates of income tax, is the saving on tax payments not only because the total tax obligations of the manufacturer are greater but also because he receives a higher rate of rebate. Thus, with a growth in the level of industrial output, there is a built-in incentive to sell a larger proportion of output in the exports markets.

4. An Evaluation of Export Policies

An attempt to evaluate or appraise the efficiency and achievements of the exports policies in Pakistan raises two separate but interrelated sets of questions. Firstly, what have been the effects of the various export policies in terms of the rate of growth of Pakistan's exports? Secondly, how efficient have these policies been? Have the exports which have developed and expanded under the impact of the export policies been in line with the long-run competitive advantage of the country? Do they encourage an economy in, or minimize, the use of scarce inputs per unit of export?

Insofar as the growth of exports is concerned, the various export promotion measures have been associated with a considerable expansion of the export earnings of Pakistan. Their impact on the growth of exports can be seen from the fact that the exports covered by these measures increased at an annual rate of 25 per cent between the years 1959–60 and 1965–66, whereas the rest of the exports grew at an average annual rate of 1.4 per cent[1]) [5, 6].

During the same period the relative importance of these exports as a proportion of total foreign exchange earnings increased from 22 per cent to 55 per cent. The manufactured exports have gained considerably in their relative importance, having increased from about 15 per cent of the total exports during 1955/56–1958/59 to about 43 per cent by 1965–66. The rate of growth of the various components of exports can be seen from table 1. The primary commodities covered by the export promotion measures recorded a considerable increase; for example, fish and rice which were relatively very unimportant items in the late 50's recorded a three- to four-fold increase, whereas the miscellaneous primary exports in 1965–66 almost doubled their average annual value during the period 1955/56–1958/59, with the result that these non-traditional primary exports which were covered by the export promotion measures constituted an increasing proportion of the total primary exports, that is, they increased from 8 per cent of the total primary exports to about 20 per cent by 1965. Among the manufactured exports cotton and jute textiles continued to dominate but there was a

[1]) The base year figure used for computing these rates of growth is the annual average value of exports during 1956, 1957 and 1958–59, i.e., the period during which the promotion measures were not in effect.

TABLE 1

Indices of annual average values of exports*).

	Agricultural Exports			Manufactured Exports					
	Total (1)	Fish and rice (2)	Other minor items (3)	Total (4)	Jute (5)	Cotton (6)	Leather and leather mft. (7)	Other mft. (8)	Grand total exports (9)
1955/56–1958/59	100	100	100	100	100	100	100	100	100
		(3)	(5)				(2)	(24)	
1959/60–1961/62	106	257	228	239	230	301	374	133	125
		(9)	(11)				(4)	(13)	
1962/63–1964/65	130	471	228	329	248	427	968	302	158
		(15)	(9)				(7)	(22)	
1965/66	123	367	195	556	447	589	2310	492	185
		(11)	(8)				(10)	(21)	
1966/67	–	483	–	–	506	657	3190	–	205

*) The minor items in column (3) exclude raw jute, raw cotton, tea, hides and skins, and wool. The figures in brackets indicate, in columns (2) and (3) percentage of respective items in total agricultural exports and in columns (7) and (8) proportion of respective items in total manufactured goods.

growing importance of the miscellaneous manufactured exports. During the 1950's, that is, between the two three-year periods, 1952/53–1954/55 and 1955/56–1958/59, the jute and cotton textile exports starting from a very negligible amount recorded a phenomenal increase, that is, about ten- or eleven-fold increase over a period of 8 or 10 years. During the same period the miscellaneous exports, also starting from a negligible base, increased about twofold. During the subsequent periods when the export promotion measures were introduced, there was a decline in the rate of growth of jute and cotton textile exports from the very high early rates of growth even though the absolute rates of growth were still very substantial during the 1960's.

What is, however, significant is that after the initial time lag following the introduction of the export promotion measures the miscellaneous manufactured exports picked up and recorded a considerable rate of increase starting in 1962–63. The average annual value of exports during 1962/63–1964/65 was three times the average annual value during 1955/56–1958/59.

There was a wide variety of manufactured exports which entered the export market during this period. About 54 per cent of the miscellaneous exports in 1965–66, excluding jute and cotton textiles, consisted of the manufactured products based on agricultural raw materials, whereas the manufactures based on non-agricultural domestic materials and traditional or special skills constituted about 23 per cent and the rest were manufactures based primarily on imported materials. The most important items in the first category were tanned leather, ready-made garments, carpets and rugs, woollen manufactures, molasses, confectionery and biscuits in that order of importance. The important items in the second category were sports goods, footwear and leather goods, toilet requisites and cosmetics, paints and varnishes, handicrafts, musical instruments, cutlery, plastic goods, etc. The leading items in the third category were drugs, chemicals and pharmaceuticals, surgical goods, electrical goods, hardware and sanitary fittings, tyres and tubes, diesel engines and pumps, and utensils and aluminum wares [7].

One may legitimately ask whether, in view of the fact that the major manufactured exports continue to consist of those commodities which represent a conversion into the manufactured form of the primary exports, there has been a substantial net gain in foreign exchange earnings. This question can be examined in two different ways. Firstly, from the point of view of the combined earnings in both raw and manufactured forms, of such major export commodities as jute, cotton, and hides and skins, it is clearly seen that aggregate export earnings have increased over the years. The annual average exports of jute, both raw and manufactured, were 30 per cent higher during the three-year period, i.e., 1962/63–1964/65 compared to their annual average value during the earlier three-year period, i.e., 1955/56–1958/59. The corresponding increase during the same period for cotton, raw and manufactured, was 67 per cent and for hides and skins, raw and manufactured in the form of leather manufactures, was 80 per cent. Moreover, the increase in the manufactured exports has not necessarily taken place at the expense of a decline in the raw material exports. In fact, the exports of raw jute and raw cotton have increased over the years, thanks to the accelerated progress in the field of agricultural production, excepting for cotton during the period 1959/60–1961/62. However, the exports of raw hides and skins have declined but have been more than compensated by the increase in the exports of the leather manufactures. This is due, to a considerable extent, to a relative sluggishness in the domestic production of raw hides and skins.

An additional question relating to the evaluation of the increase in the manufactured exports is whether these commodities make a net addition to foreign exchange earnings when they are exported in the manufactured form rather than as raw materials, especially in view of the fact that (a) they require additional inputs of imported raw materials and spare parts, and (b) they have to lower their export prices in order to compete abroad.

Evidence suggests, however, that there has been a positive net gain in foreign exchange earnings in each of these cases consequent on the substitution of the manufactured exports for the exports of their raw material contents in spite of the price reducing effects of the export subsidies implied in the various export promotion measures [1]. Admittedly, the magnitude of net gain in such items as cotton yarn or tanned leather in which the proportion of domestic value added is negligible is very small, but over the years the proportions of the manufactured exports at the higher stages of fabrication based on cotton, hides and skins and jute are increasing.

It is noteworthy that during this period the unit value of Pakistan's manufactured exports, though on the average, is lower than its level during the period prior to the introduction of the export promotion measures, has not recorded any declining trend. The average index of the unit values of manufactured goods, mainly consisting of jute goods, cotton textiles, and leather products and woollen textiles was 118.2 during the years 1955/56–1957/58, whereas the same average index was about 112.6 during the two subsequent three periods, i.e., 1959/60–1961/62 and 1962/63–1964/65. In fact, in the years starting 1963–64 there is a continuous improvement in this index. It rose from 112.14 to 144.17 between the years 1963–64 and 1965–66. The available index of the unit value of the miscellaneous manufactured exports is not very representative being dominated by sports goods and footwear, and has fluctuated over the years. The average index of unit value increased to 133.3 during the three-year period 1959/60–1961/62 from 127.6 during the three-year period 1955/56–1957/58; in the subsequent three-year period there was a decline to 120.8 [2][2]).

The question was raised earlier as to how efficient the export promotion

[2]) For figures subsequent to 1963–64 the source is Central Statistical Office. The base year for the computation of all these indices is 1953–54.

schemes have been. For one thing, because of the multiplicity of the effective export rates and because of the complicated nature of some of the incentive schemes, it is not very easy to calculate the total impact in terms of an effective subsidy accruing to the individual export commodities. Excepting in the case of the export bonus scheme which is simple and clear, the subsidy element in other schemes, in the absence of accounting practices which reflect their impact in terms of savings in costs or increase in revenue, does not appear in a simple and a clear-cut fashion to the exporters. Uncertainty about the magnitude of subsidy or lack of definite knowledge about the quantum of subsidy may affect the degree of response of exports to the export incentive schemes. The complaints about delays and red-tapism involved in the administration of the various schemes of tax exemption on outputs, income and imported inputs has frequently been made by the exporters.

The present system of the implicit import rates under the bonus scheme creates a wide range of rates, ranging from the official rate of 4.76 Rs. per dollar to about 21 Rs. per dollar. Such an extreme divergence between the import rates is not related to the differences in the competitive cost disadvantages or to the relative degrees of infancy of the various manufacturing industries to which these rates apply. The excessively high effective import rates for the bonus imports encourage import substitution – often excessive – in the areas which suffer from very high costs. Frequently the high effective rates apply to the luxury consumer goods or consumer durables, the very field in which import substitution often is not in consonance with the priorities set by the Government. It is true that in spite of the tendency towards an excessive investment in these areas, the domestic investment can be and has been regulated by direct controls, but in view of the movement towards the relaxation of direct controls on the domestic investment, the adverse effects of the very high effective import rates can only be countered by the high domestic taxes on consumption or on income.

The effective export rates which result from the various export promotion schemes can roughly be outlined as in table 2.

Though the effective rates for exports have increased over the years, they still continue to be lower than the effective rate for imports. Though the differential between the two has narrowed insofar as the import rates relating to the non-bonus imports are concerned, the effective rates for import in 1966–67 under the bonus scheme have ranged between Rs. 12 per dollar

TABLE 2

Effective export rates in 1966–67.

Commodity groups		Effective export rate (Rs. per dollar)	Percentage of foreign exchange earnings
(A) Raw jute		4.56	35–38
Raw cotton		4.63	
(B) Hides and skins, rice, certain invisibles and wool		4.76	20–25
(C) Jute manufactures		6.14	15–19
		6.67	
(D) Cotton manufactures (with 20 per cent bonus)		6.24	2–3
(E) Cotton manufactures (with 30–40 per cent bonus) and invisibles (30 per cent bonus)		7.00–7.71 [1]	11–14
(F) Other manufactures	(a)	7.00–7.71 [2] (including only effect of bonus)	6–8
		7.48–8.19 [3]	
	(b)	(a) + effect of tax exemption on import components	
		7.48–8.25 [4]	
	(c)	(b) + effect of income tax rebate	
		8.27–8.99 [5]	
	(d)	(c) + effect of export performance licensing	

[1]) Some cotton manufactures receive 40 per cent bonus.

[2]) Other manufactures receive 30 per cent bonus in some and 40 per cent bonus in other cases.

[3]) On the assumption of a weighted average import component of 14 per cent and a simple average rate of indirect tax on imports at the rate of 63 per cent.

[4]) Including minimum and maximum income tax rebate.

[5]) On the assumption that weighted average rate of import entitlement is about 38 per cent of the f.o.b. value of exports and the average premium on import entitlement at about 40 per cent.

and about Rs. 21 per dollar while the maximum effective rate for export for a small fragment of the miscellaneous exports has not exceeded twice the official rate. Thus, import substitution continues to be more attractive than export expansion, with all its attendant disadvantages.

At the same time, the import rates applicable to the purchases of import requirements by the export industries continue to be lower than the effective rates earned on their exports. This is not only because most of the import requirements of the export industries are generally very liberally licensed under the normal licensing scheme and are given the additional export performance licensing, both at the official rate, but also because they are exempted from the indirect taxes on their import components. The result is that the imported inputs are cheaper than their domestic substitutes which encourages a greater use of imports in the production process as well as discourages the progress of import substitution in domestic intermediate goods industries. In addition, as between the different export industries, the provision of cheap imported inputs have the effect of encouraging the more import-intensive technology and industries. In the extreme case, it creates the possibility of a foreign exchange loss insofar as the substantial subsidy received on the sale of the bonus vouchers and the surplus import entitlements under the export performance licensing, induces a fall in the export price below the value of the import components. In view of the bias of the export promotion schemes in favor of a more liberal use of imported inputs, it has been suggested that the bonus should be related to net foreign exchange earnings. A uniform percentage of bonus which is related to the net foreign exchange earnings, i.e., foreign exchange earnings net of foreign exchange costs in terms of imported inputs, will encourage those with the least import requirements per unit of output. Even though in the short run this modification of the bonus scheme would tend to increase the net foreign exchange earnings per unit of exports, there would appear to be no correlation between the relative import intensities and the long-run competitive advantage of different industries. Moreover, industry with a low import-intensity in terms of the current requirements could be very heavily import-intensive in terms of the imported capital requirements. Thus, a simpler method is to replace the existing exemption on the imported inputs as well as the present system of the export performance licensing by a larger straight-forward bonus or a higher income tax rebate.

5. Future Export Policy

The existing discrimination between the agricultural and manufactured goods appears to be excessive. Even though the abolition of export duties in late 1967 has reduced the degree of discrimination against the agricultural exports, it has not eliminated it altogether. The inclusion of the major agricultural exports in the bonus scheme is likely not only to stimulate their production and increase supply but also to increase the profitability of export sales and consequently, expand exports. A lower rate of bonus may, therefore, be introduced for agricultural exports, let us say at 10 per cent of f.o.b. value of exports, in gradual steps as an experimental measure to test the degree of response of supply and demand to the variations in effective export rates. An increase in the cost of raw materials for the domestic jute and cotton manufacturing industries can be offset by increasing the rate of bonus to these industries.

The differential subsidies or export rates for different manufacturing exports are the combined result of:

(a) Export performance licensing which is related to the differential import components.

(b) The differential bonus rates.

There has been a tendency for the more import-intensive industries or the industries with higher costs of production, or confronted with a stiffer competition in sales promotion abroad, to be given the higher rates of bonus. A highly differentiated export rate structure has the effect of focusing attention on the short-run difficulties and on attempts to improve the poor performance of some exports by additional bonus rather than of other exports which may be doing well but could perform even better if given an additional bonus. The original distinction between the jute and the cotton industries, on the one hand, and the rest of the manufacturers, on the other, was justified on the grounds that:

(a) export taxes on jute and cotton provided an additional indirect subsidy to these industries,

(b) that these industries because of their longer experience suffered from lower cost-disadvantage than the newer infants, and

(c) the newer manufacturers had extra selling costs for making an initial entry in markets.

The inclusion of raw jute and cotton in the bonus scheme as suggested earlier would remove one of the reasons for granting lower rates of bonus for jute and cotton manufacturing industries. As for the difficulties in breaking into export markets, jute and cotton textiles also face the difficulties of diversifying into new markets, since old markets are getting saturated sometimes because of domestic industrialization in the importing countries. In addition they face the need to overcome (a) the trade restrictions on the textile imports in the major markets of the advanced countries, and (b) the threat of increasing competition from the emergence of new producers and of synthetic substitutes. It is obvious that export promotion in an imperfect international market is not merely a matter of price differential but also of trade names, consumers' preference and sales promotion including trade displays and fairs, establishment of contacts and offices abroad, all of which involve additional costs. This is specially true for the new manufactures. All these suggest that the export subsidies need to be higher than what is necessary to compensate only for the cost disadvantages of the infant industries, though they do not provide any rationale for discrimination among individual commodities, especially since a detailed knowledge of their supply and demand conditions in different markets is not at the disposal of the authorities. Specially higher rates may only be justified in cases where the infant industries with high present costs but prospects of a considerable improvement in efficiency over time can be clearly identified. Moreover, in such cases, especially high bonus rates should have a definite time horizon and should be provided only at a declining rate, disappearing within a period of a fixed number of years. The multiplication of rates should be kept to the minimum because past experience shows that once an exception is made the case for additional exceptions is built up quite fast and the pressure often becomes irresistible on the administrative authorities.

The future of export policy in Pakistan relates to the future of its most important instrument of export promotion, that is, the export bonus scheme. The export bonus scheme was conceived as a temporary measure, originally introduced for one year, subsequently extended from time to time, until the end of the Second Five-Year Plan in the first instance and then eventually until the end of the Third Five-Year Plan ending in 1970. The uncertainty regarding the continuance of this scheme in the past years combined with the uncertainty regarding frequent changes, mentioned earlier, in the coverage as well as in the rates of the bonus detracted from its effectiveness. Export expansion requires long-term commitments of resources in the development of export markets as well as in investment for the production of exportables. This is inhibited by a continued uncertainty regarding the future of the bonus scheme as it aggravates the uncertainty of future returns from present investment.

The principal consequence of the export bonus scheme as it was introduced in 1959 was to compensate for the relative overvaluation of the rate of exchange in Pakistan. The state of overvaluation was due not only to a level and a structure of domestic costs and prices in Pakistan which had grown out of line with the level of international costs and prices during the 1950's partly as a result of domestic inflationary financing, but also was due to the high costs of the infant industries as well as to difficulties of new exports breaking into world markets or markets which were hitherto unexplored. The expansion of exports of new manufactures has also to encounter a considerable degree of non-price competition in an imperfect world market in which the consumers' preference and the dominance of established trade names play an important part. It is interesting to observe that in the initial years there was considerable resistance to the idea in official as well as in business circles that the export bonus scheme did represent a partial devaluation, in fact, a floating exchange market for a portion of foreign exchange transactions. This possible illusion in the public mind might have had a positive beneficial effect insofar as a public reaction to a straightforward and open devaluation leads to speculative reactions or movements, sometimes in anticipation of further devaluations, as well as inflationary tendencies in the domestic economy. It is remarkable that during the 1960's Pakistan has had considerable monetary stability and a very modest rise in the cost of living and in wholesale prices.

Pakistan can grow eventually into the present official rate of exchange only if domestic costs and prices come tumbling down – an unlikely possibility in the foreseeable future. It is especially unlikely for the prices and costs of manufactured exports in the case of which the effective export rate, as the result of the various incentive schemes, now ranges between 60 to 100 per cent higher than the official rate. Pakistan is fast approaching the state where the growth of her traditional industries, that is, textiles and leather industries, will slow down in the domestic as well as in the export markets. The new manufacturing industries which would increasingly be in the field of intermediate and capital goods industries with a substantially higher level of costs but which are expected to provide an increasingly larger share of her foreign exchange earnings will continue to need an especially favorable rate of exchange for exports, for quite some time to come in the future. Moreover, the long-run equilibrium rate of exchange for Pakistan would be closely related to (a) the rate of economic growth she seeks to achieve during her successive Five-Year Plans which in turn would require a rising import bill of materials and equipment, (b) the amount of expected inflow of foreign economic assistance, i.e., aid and direct investment, and (c) the optimum degree of quantitative restrictions on trade which she intends to maintain in order to keep the equilibrium in her balance of payments. The rate of exchange is among the many instruments of economic policy, including fiscal and monetary policy. Pakistan has persevered in the past in trying to follow, with occasional lapses, a conservative fiscal and monetary policy with a view to keeping a balance between the pressure on aggregate monetary demand on the one hand, and an increasing mobilization of domestic resources for development, on the other. Given that this tendency continues and given an increasing recognition of the inefficiencies of the system of quantitative restrictions, the future policy should be to widen gradually the area of the bonus market and also to allow the bonus market to reflect the changes in relative costs as well as supply and demand situations of her exports and imports.

A floating exchange market which is provided at present by the bonus scheme is a very limited and a narrow one; moreover, its operation is subject to constant interference and manipulation by the government authorities out of a mutiplicity of considerations which have been mentioned earlier. The forces of demand and supply for imports and exports are allowed to impinge on this narrow market only to the extent and in the way the government from time to time desires them to do so.

With a given list of items to be imported at the official rate under the system of import licensing and with no restrictions in terms either of amounts or of items of imports under the bonus scheme, irrespective of whether these items are allowed under official licensing or not, the bonus market will respond to the forces of supply and demand for foreign exchange. The widening of the bonus market would, however, require that a smaller proportion of foreign exchange earnings is disposed of under the licensing system and that exporters are able to sell in the free market a larger proportion of their earnings. It will also require that a larger proportion of imports is shifted onto the bonus market. At present, out of Pakistan's foreign exchange resources, exclusive of foreign aid, which are disbursed under the licensing system, about 36 per cent is used for the imports of intermediate goods, 14 per cent is used for debt service payments abroad, 28 per cent is used for imports on the government account, with the private invisibles and food imports utilizing 11 per cent each [11]. It may be desirable, however, to continue to meet the debt service payments and food imports at the official rate of exchange; as far as the first item is concerned any adjustment of the rate of exchange for debt service payments on past loans and debts fixed in terms of foreign currency will involve capital losses on the part of those holding foreign currency debts, both in the private and public sectors and may thus hamper enterprise and investment, including investment in the export sector. As for the application of the official rate of exchange to the import of food, the consideration is mainly one of equity, i.e., the prevention of a rise in the cost of living of the masses, the need for which will decline as the growth in the domestic agricultural production is accelerated. Further, whether the government receipts as well as payments should not also be made at a higher price of foreign exchange is a moot question and it involves a readjustment of the whole structure of tax and expenditure system of the government.

The most significant direction in which the next step in widening the bonus market needs to be taken is to divert a larger proportion of intermediate goods away from the system of licensing to that of the bonus market. There has been a gradual expansion of the bonus list in terms of the imports of consumer goods over the past few years. Recently even in the field of intermediate goods, domestic industries had been allowed to import their requirements, in excess of what they had been allowed under the licensing system, in the bonus market, without restrictions as to the items of imports or their amounts. The movement in the direction of widening the bonus market in the past years or so has been partly caused by a shortfall in the inflow of foreign aid, aggravated by an increase in foreign exchange expenditure on account of the expanded defense requirements and by a short-run increase in food imports. While moving in the direction of widening the bonus market, it has been necessary to keep the apparatus of quantitative controls intact so that the latter can be called into action in the case of a sudden unfavorable change in the shortrun. Since a sudden widening of the bonus list may raise considerably the import costs all along the line, especially in view of the shortrun inelasticity of demand and supply, the process of adjustment of the domestic economy to widening of the bonus market needs to be a slow and a gradual one. It suggests a gradual approach; the gradual expansion of the bonus market may be adjusted to the availability of aid, both long-term and short-term, as well as to the rate of expansion of export earnings.

It may be legitimately asked whether a fluctuating bonus market combined with a licensing system for a portion of the imports is preferable to devaluation coupled with taxes and subsidies or the continuation of the present rate of exchange coupled with an adjustment of taxes and subsidies at a higher level. It seems clear that if the present official rate has to be maintained by means entirely of taxes and subsidies, without recourse to the quantitative restrictions, this will place a very heavy burden on the administration of taxes and subsidies – not a very welcome situation – not only in view of the limited administrative capacity but also because the rates of taxes and subsidies which are necessary under the circumstances to keep the balance of payments in equilibrium would be considerably high. If the entire burden of adjustment is to fall on only one instrument instead of all three as at present, i.e., quantitative restrictions, tariffs and various export promotion schemes, it is expected to strain the competence and the honesty of administration. The likelihood of corruption increases with the profitability of engaging in it and the higher the rates of taxes and subsidies, the higher will be the profitability of taking the risks of evasion or manipulation of the rates of taxes and subsidies in favor of particular groups. Moreover, a devaluation coupled with a system of taxes and subsidies does not appear to be a superior alternative to a partial floating exchange market because the frequent changes in the rates of taxes and subsidies in response to the changing supply, demand and cost conditions involve not only a considerable amount of administrative discretion but also a great deal of knowledge and expertise regarding the supply and demand conditions of individual commodities. The bonus market provides a more flexible and automatic mechanism for accommodating such changes in costs and demand. Moreover, a system of tax and subsidies usually has a greater tendency to multiply than a freely floating bonus market, even though this particular characteristic has been equally shared by the bonus rates in Pakistan, because of frequent discretionary changes made by the government in the rates of bonus and in the import lists. The bonus market which will be gradually widened will also be able to deal with invisibles and capital inflows which a system of taxes and subsidies usually neglects. A wider bonus market would also narrow the range of fluctuations by spreading the dealings in the bonus market over a larger number of items.

In conclusion it needs to be pointed out, however, that an expansion of the bonus market and a consequent relaxation of the quantitative controls are hindered by two factors in Pakistan's foreign exchange situation. One is the presence of tied aid and the other, which as yet is not very significant but is of growing importance, is the trade through the barter agreements which have the effect of tying the imports with the exports to the specific countries. In 1966–67 only about 8 per cent of all intermediate goods and a much smaller proportion of capital goods imports, that is about 3 per cent or so, have been obtained under barter agreements. So long as aid is tied to individual countries and to particular commodities and projects within the aid-giving countries, multiple rates, relating to the foreign exchange resources available from each of these sources of aid, would persist, since it would not be possible to merge in one market the tied aid funds received from various sources and the untied foreign exchange earnings of the country concerned. This is because of a significant price differential between the various sources of supply. While it is true that the quantitative restrictions on the administration of aid funds can be replaced either by a separate auctioning of the aid funds from each of the sources or by an issuance of separate country and commodity-tied bonus vouchers, each of these latter alternatives involve in practice the maintenance of multiple rates of exchange.

References

[1] Q. K. AHMED, 'The Operation of the Export Bonus Scheme in Pakistan's Jute and Cotton Industries', *The Pakistan Development Review*, spring 1966.

[2] Government of Pakistan, Central Statistical Office, *Index Numbers of Terms of Trade*, Unit Values and Quantum of Exports and Imports of Pakistan, unpublished monograph, 1964.

[3] Government of Pakistan, Chief Controller of Exports and Imports, *Gazette of Pakistan, Extraordinary, for various shipping periods*, 1963–64, 1964–65, 1965–66 and 1966–67.

[4] Government of Pakistan, Export Promotion Bureau, *Fiscal Incentives for Exports*, Karachi, 1966.

[5] Government of Pakistan, Export Promotion Bureau, *Foreign Trade of Pakistan*, Karachi, 1964–65, 1965–66.

[6] Government of Pakistan, Ministry of Finance, *Economic Survey of Pakistan*, Rawalpindi, 1965–66, 1966–67.
[7] Government of Pakistan, Planning Commission, *Current Economic Situation and Prospects*, 1966–67, Karachi, Jan. 1967, pp. 30–31.
[8] W. E. HECOX, 'The Use of Import Privileges as Incentives to Exporters in Pakistan'. *Research Report* no. 30, Pakistan Institute of Development Economics, Karachi.
[9] S. R. LEWIS, *Economic Policy and Industrial Growth in Pakistan*, unpublished manuscript, 1966.
[10] P. THOMAS, 'Import Licensing and Import Liberalization in Pakistan,' *Pakistan Development Review*, winter 1966, p. 532.
[11] W. TIMS, *Import Policy 1967/68; Some Suggestions*, unpublished manuscript, Planning Commission, Rawalpindi, June 1967.
[12] W. TIMS and J. STERN, *Input–Output Table for Pakistan 1963–1964*, a mimeographed, unpublished document, Planning Commission, Government of Pakistan, 1965.

INTERINDUSTRY RELATIONS; AN ATTRACTION MODEL

A PROGRESS REPORT

L. H. KLAASSEN and A. C. VAN WICKEREN

1. General

1.1. *Introduction*

In regional economic studies it is usual to distinguish between basic and non-basic activities. A non-basic activity is defined as an activity that, for economic reasons, *necessarily* has to be performed within the area considered, while, consequently, a basic activity is one that, although performed within the boundaries of the area, need *not* be located there. It follows from this definition that non-basic activities are not exported to other areas. Since this holds for the other areas as well, there are also no imports of those activities: by definition therefore, there is no interregional trade of services and goods produced by non-basic industries.

On the other hand, a basic industry is not necessarily an exporting industry. It *might* export just as the area *might* import its products. The contribution of the basic industry to the balance of payments therefore will be that either it reduces imports or it contributes to exports (or both). In both cases the influence of a basic industry on the balance of payments of the area is similar: it saves 'foreign' currency.

Thus it is basic industry that generates initial income in the area. This income will be spent partly in the area, partly somewhere else. If the non-basic industries are defined well, *their* products and services will be bought exclusively within the area. From this (repeated) spending of income on non-basic products and services, a multiplier effect results. Estimates of this multiplier for Dutch cities up to 100,000 inhabitants yield figures around 2. Each money unit created in basic industries creates one additional money unit in non-basic industries. We will call this multiplier the *average regional demand multiplier*.

1.2. *Size of the area*

In the analysis above a considerable number of assumptions are made that require further study. First, what role is played by the size of the areas considered? If we are concerned with the whole world, all industries would be non-basic. But if we would consider a small neighbourhood, practically all activities would be basic. It is therefore useful to take the size of the area into consideration and realize that the concepts of basic and non-basic industries will differ for areas of different sizes. In a large region many activities will be classified as non-basic, while for a smaller region the same activities would be basic. The larger the region the less important (at least relatively speaking) will be the so-called basic component of all economic activities.

Although the comparison is not fully justified, the same tendency is found in the relative share of international trade in large and small countries. The larger the country, the smaller its 'dependence' on the outside world.

Leontief introduced the concepts of local, regional, and national industries [3]. Walter Isard implemented these concepts. 'National commodities are those commodities which production and consumption balance only within the nation as a whole. Regional commodities of the first order are those whose production and consumption balance within the nation as well as within each first-order region. Regional commodities of the second order, whose markets are smaller than those of the first order, are those whose production and consumption balance not only within the nation and each region of the first order but also within each region of the second order. Finally, local commodities (regional commodities of the nth order) are those whose production and consumption balance not only within the nation, each region of the first order, each region of the second order, ..., and each region of the $(n-1)$th order, but also within each local area (region of the nth order)' [1].

Although neither Leontief nor Isard make very clear what is meant by a nation (Monaco or Russia or both) it is evident that the size of the area concerned determines the order of the activity they have in mind. Tinbergen adopted this approach [1]) and based on it his theory of the hierarchy of nuclei.

It is clear that there is not only a positive relationship between the number

---

[1]) See e.g. [5].

of activities to be called non-basic and the size of the region but also between the size of the average demand multiplier and this size. Since in larger regions more activities are non-basic, more of the secondary effects of an increase in the level of basic activities will take place within the area itself. On the other hand fewer activities will be called basic. Thus, the size of the area is of considerable importance in defining basic and non-basic components of an area's economy.

1.3. *A reconsideration of the concept of a non-basic activity*

In considering types of activities further it seems justified to speculate whether non-basic means those activities that result from the spending of consumers' income earned in basic activities or also spending by the basic industries themselves. If basic industries purchase transportation services, part of these services might have to be performed within the area but certainly are not non-basic in the sense used so far. These services are rendered (or, in the case of goods, these goods are produced), only because the basic industry is located in and producing within the area. It is induced or secondary production.

Once these secondary activities are taken into account, the distinction between basic and non-basic becomes more vague. The only thing that is clear is that secondary effects should be called non-basic in so far as they necessarily have to be produced within the area and basic in so far as they do not. To what extent this will be the case depends on the nature of the basic industry. One industry might require considerably more non-basic services than another.

Thus, the concept of the regional multiplier becomes less clear. If the extent to which secondary activities demanded in the area depend on the nature of the basic industry present in the area, the size of the regional multiplier also will differ among industries. Some will create more, others less secondary activities. The picture thus becomes somewhat more obscure and it will be well to distinguish between multipliers for different industries. We will call these multipliers *regional demand multipliers*.

1.4. *Supply factors*

Sofar we have considered only the effects on *demand* resulting from the location of the basic industry within the area. Although we have distinguished between final demand and industrial demand, we have limited ourselves to demand and have ignored the supply side. Supply considerations are relevant for the location of a given industry in a given area and will induce other industries to locate in the neighbourhood [2]) of the first one. This is true not because the first industry demands given products or services but because it *supplies* other industries which are users of those products in their own industry. The petro-chemical industry is a clear-cut example. The products of refineries give rise to secondary production in related products close to the refineries because these refineries are favourable supply-points for the products that serve as inputs to other industries.

When speaking of secondary effects, therefore, it seems indispensable to consider the demand effects but also the supply effects plus the demand effects again resulting from these supply effects. Consequently, our concept of the regional multiplier must be modified again. One industry might create considerably more supply effects than another and thus have a considerably higher regional multiplier. The higher both supply and demand effects of a given industry are, the higher will be its *total regional multiplier*.

Those industries which have the highest total regional multiplier will be called propulsive or strategic industries. Clearly, they are essential to industrialization policy.

1.5. *Size of the area again*

In introducing the assumption that the supply of given products in an area will generate demand for secondary activities 'in the neighbourhood' of the first industry we were not very clear what was meant by 'neighbourhood'. The word suggests that size of area determines the extent to which secondary activities are created in the same area as the primary activities. This is true, since the likelihood that secondary activities will be located in the area increases with the size of the area. Again we find that for these secondary activities (analogous to the non-basic activities) the size of the area is also extremely relevant.

Reviewing what we did for the basic and non-basic activities suggests a procedure for determining which activities are non-basic for each specific basic industry by comparing which activities are present in areas where these basic industries are represented with those where they are not or represented to a lesser extent. The procedure, however, leads to difficulties

---

[2]) To be defined later.

since the secondary activities might not only be demanded by the industry studied but also by others not studied. The procedure is therefore not foolproof as soon as we consider different basic industries and different secondary activities. It only works in the basic–non-basic dichotomy.

The difficulties become even greater when we consider the supply effects. How should we determine whether the presence of a basic industry is the result of the presence of another one or not? It might result from the presence of third industries or even of the presence of the first industry in a 'neighbouring' area. Given the size of the region, it is therefore difficult to determine which is the cause of which if we do not incorporate all the relationships considered into one *system* of relationships or a complete model of interindustry relations.

1.6. *The usefulness of the input–output table*

The approach suggested here is to make use of input–output tables which specify the network of relationships among industries through the money flows from one industry to another. Such an approach suggests that the larger the money flow from one industry to another, the more intensely these industries will be connected with each other and *thus* the stronger the tendency for the two to be located in close proximity.

Still, the generalization must be considered cautiously. A processing industry buying a very cheap mineral from a mine might tend to locate very close to the mine to minimize transportation costs which the mineral otherwise could not stand. The money flow from the processing industry to the mine in this case might be very small although the *attraction* is very large. Or, in other words, the attraction results from the very fact that a large money flow would render the whole situation unprofitable.

Attraction also might be very large even if longer distances would not have a very large influence on the money flow between industries. Manufacturing industries and repair shops, engineering bureaus, business services, banking and insurance institutions are examples. In these cases the tendency to locate in close proximity to each other is very strong although the money flow between those activities might appear small in the input–output table.

This second point, which actually stresses the importance of *communication* rather than *transportation*, becomes of major importance in a world where industries more and more tend to become independent of transportation and thus can choose locations more freely. Today only the location of the heaviest industries, as well as some agricultural processing industries seems to be dictated by transport cost considerations.

This and the foregoing argument imply that, although we might take the size of the money flows in the input–output table as a first approximation of the degree of attraction two industries exert upon each other, they are by no means definitive. Furthermore, since it might be difficult to measure the real costs of communication, the problem of measuring the degree of attraction that industries exert upon each other has to be solved indirectly. The indirect method is simple. If two or more industries mutually attract each other, they frequently will be located in each other's 'neighbourhood'. The more frequent this is the case, the more attraction they exert.

1.7. *The basic elements in the model*

The model to be used[3]) is thus built up by determining to what extent the size of a given industry in a given area is determined by (a) final demand, (b) interindustry demand, (c) supply by other industries.

In equations specifying the relationships, items (a) and (b) could be summed to represent total demand.

Industries supplying a certain minimum percentage of gross output of the industry studied are selected as supplying industries. The influence of demand and of the supplies can be determined by regression analysis.

If the supply-coefficients are not significantly different from zero then the industry is completely demand-oriented.

This concept is related closely to that of a non-basic industry. In the location literature, however, non-basic usually refers to only final demand, while our notion of demand-orientation includes interindustry demand. If all coefficients are zero except for the jth supplying industry then the industry is said to be j-supply-oriented. In all other cases the industry is oriented to demand as well as to supply.

For small regions the fit is probably poor although the coefficients might be highly significant – that is, have small standard errors. The fit can then be improved by building larger regions out of sets of neighbouring regions. This process is to be continued until a good fit is obtained. The size of the region is defined as the *relevant region* for the industry studied. If the industry is demand-oriented the relevant region is the area delimited by borders

[3]) For a more elaborate exposition, see [2].

over which no products of this industry are exported or imported. The larger the relevant region the higher the order of the industry in the Leontief–Isard sense. If the industry is jth supply-oriented the relevant region has borders over which no j-supplies are exported or imported. For an industry which is partly supply-oriented and partly demand-oriented, interregional trade in both products will take place to an extent inverse to the size of the relevant coefficients of attraction and proportional to local demand and production of supplies.

It should be remarked that one and the same industry might appear twice in the equation, viz. as a purchaser of the products of the industry studied (demand side) as well as a seller of supplies to this industry (supply side). In the final equation both coefficients might be added together to form one coefficient of attraction.

1.8. *The mathematical model*

Write

$$x_{kj} = g_{kj} - d_{kj} \tag{1}$$

in which

x_{kj} = exports of product k from region j

g_{kj} = production of products k in region j

d_{kj} = demand for products k in region j.

Write further

$$m_{klj} = \beta_{kl} g_{kj} - \alpha_{lk} g_{lj} \tag{2}$$

in which

m_{klj} = imports of products of industry l by industry k in region j

β_{kl} = the fraction of gross production of industry k required from industry l.

α_{lk} = the fraction of gross production of industry l sold to industry k.

Now assume that transportation and communication costs (giving the highest weight to the latter) of one unit of sales of product k within the region equal zero and of one unit sold outside the region equal t_d. Also assume that these costs for one unit of requirements l bought within the region equal zero and equal t_l if the requirement is imported.

Then total transportation plus communication costs for industry k in region

j are by definition

$$t_{kj} = t_d x_{kj} + \sum t_l m_{klj}, \tag{3}$$

which can be rewritten as

$$t_{kj} = (t_d + \sum t_l \beta_{kl})\, g_{kj} - t_d d_{kj} - \sum t_l \alpha_{lk} g_{lj},$$

from which follows

$$g_{kj} = \frac{t_d}{t_d + \sum t_l \beta_{kl}}\, d_{kj} + \sum \frac{t_l \beta_{kl}}{t_d + \sum t_l \beta_{kl}} \cdot \frac{\alpha_{lk}}{\beta_{kl}}\, g_{lj}. \tag{4}$$

Write

$$\lambda_d = \frac{t_d}{t_d + \sum t_l \beta_{kl}} \quad \text{and} \quad \lambda_l = \frac{t_l \beta_{kl}}{t_d + \sum t_l \beta_{kl}}$$

then (4) becomes

$$g_{kj} = \lambda_d d_{kj} + \sum \lambda_l \frac{\alpha_{lk}}{\beta_{kl}}\, g_{lj} \tag{5}$$

in which

$$\lambda_d + \sum \lambda_l = 1. \tag{6}$$

The λ's will be called attraction coefficients. λ_d represents the demand-attraction and λ_l represents the l-supply attraction. If $\lambda_d = 1$, all other λ's are zero and the industry is completely demand- or market-oriented. If $\lambda_l = 1$, all other λ's are zero and the industry is completely l-supply oriented. The industry is footloose if all t's are zero.

Since the λ's are unknown they must be empirically estimated. The estimation procedure is the following. Take the relevant data for the smallest regions for which data are available. Determine by regression analysis the values for all λ's as well as the coefficient of correlation. Select the industries for which significant λ's are obtained and repeat the analysis. If the regression coefficients are now significant but the coefficient of correlation is not, proceed by combining regions into larger regions. This combination should be based on two criteria. First, the combined regions should have a common border. Second, a combination of regions should show a smaller volume of net exports (or imports) than the original regions. Proceed with the combination until a result is found with significant coefficient of regression and an acceptable value for the coefficient of correlation. The size of the regions found is then the relevant region.

Since for only very few countries data (e.g. regional input–output tables) are available for all regions of different sizes, the determination of the relevant region is usually not possible in the way indicated. The first part of the procedure, the estimation of the λ's, however, remains possible for the regional sizes for which input–output tables are available. Holland provides an illustration.

2. The Testing of the Model for Dutch Provinces

2.1. *The statistical material*

The selection of the statistics was not a serious problem since the 'Centraal Bureau voor de Statistiek' (C.B.S.) recently published the first regional data [4]) needed for the analysis. The material relates to 1960, the year of the last census.

From this publication the 'observations' for the regression analysis were collected. Table 1 summarizes the data gathered from the provincial input–output tables.

A few remarks concerning the data are in order. First, the C.B.S. did not only collect figures for each of the eleven Dutch provinces but also the two main provinces, 'Noord-Holland' and 'Zuid-Holland', were divided into seven sub-regions. These districts are:
'Nieuwe Waterweg'-district
The Hague-district
The rest of Zuid-Holland
Amsterdam-district
The Zaanstreek
The part of Noord-Holland south of the North Sea Canal
The rest of Noord-Holland.

In spite of the fact that additional material usually provides additional information, it was decided not to extend the analysis below the provincial level because it was felt that the use of districts so different in size would violate the assumptions underlying the theory.

The second remark relates to the extra-territorial sector that has been

4) Cf. [4].

TABLE 1

Provincial production and demand in millions of guilders in 1960.

		Groningen		Friesland	
		p*)	d*)**)	p	d
I	1 Agriculture, forestry, fishing	395.3	–	538.6	–
	2 Coalmines	–	–	–	–
	3 Winning of oil and salt, peat cutting, sanddigging	10.8	–	1.6	–
	18 Building	255.2	–	240.6	–
II	4 Foodstuffs (working up animal products)	161.1	98.2	497.1	104.3
	5 Foodstuffs (working up other products)	363.1	217.5	324.4	273.5
	6 Production of drinks and tobaccos	94.4	46.6	71.0	35.0
	7 Textiles	22.8	59.2	26.9	41.1
	8 Footwear and clothing	92.6	55.4	24.3	59.3
	9 Wood and furniture	51.7	38.2	64.7	39.8
	10 Papermills	186.3	68.8	18.8	23.8
	11 Printers and publishers	56.1	58.6	31.5	45.2
	12 Leather- and rubberindustry	10.7	13.9	15.4	13.6
	13 Chemicals incl. oil refineries	186.0	112.3	16.9	86.8
	14 Production of potting, glas, stones, etc.	28.2	33.2	18.4	29.7
	15 Metalproduction and machine-building	97.8	97.8	103.2	106.4
	16 Transport-articles (construction of cars, shipbuilding)	92.7	53.9	82.8	50.6
	17 Other metalindustry and diamond cutting	97.6	92.4	98.3	80.1
	19 Public utilities	73.4	57.4	45.8	49.3
III	20 Wholesale and retail (marges)	–	–	–	–
	21 Banking and clearing	–	–	–	–
	22 Insurance companies	–	–	–	–
	23 Exploitation of dwellings	–	–	–	–
	24 Shipping and air-transport	–	–	–	–
	25 Other transports	–	–	–	–
	26 Communication	–	–	–	–
	27 Medical and health services	–	–	–	–
	28 Free professions	–	–	–	–
	29 Entertainment	–	–	–	–
	30 Hotels, restaurants	–	–	–	–
	31 Other personal services	–	–	–	–
	Total (III)	809.0	676.7	657.6	610.5

*) p = production; d = total demand, except exports to abroad.

**) See this footnote on p. 257.

Table 1 *(continued)*

	Drente		Overijssel		Gelderland	
	p*)	d*)**)	p	d	p	d
I 1	388.2	—	733.6	—	1,126.0	—
2	—	—	—	—	—	—
3	77.8	—	59.1	—	9.2	—
18	173.0	—	415.0	—	716.8	—
II 4	267.8	95.7	543.3	226.6	602.8	335.2
5	96.2	158.7	305.4	421.9	655.3	799.0
6	5.4	19.1	46.4	74.6	131.9	124.8
7	17.9	30.3	1,181.8	423.5	203.1	180.5
8	29.0	43.2	181.6	102.6	193.0	170.8
9	11.8	19.7	50.1	54.6	177.2	102.4
10	7.4	16.3	14.2	59.6	423.1	143.0
11	24.4	30.9	105.6	93.7	100.9	124.2
12	6.9	9.8	78.4	23.9	105.1	53.5
13	183.0	104.8	106.5	180.8	344.7	308.5
14	20.1	21.6	48.6	54.3	174.9	92.7
15	92.0	58.4	416.1	177.9	425.3	246.8
16	30.0	31.9	53.6	75.8	182.6	117.4
17	23.4	63.5	245.0	195.3	416.2	248.5
19	13.1	29.6	115.7	105.2	153.2	143.7
III 20	—	—	—	—	—	—
21	—	—	—	—	—	—
22	—	—	—	—	—	—
23	—	—	—	—	—	—
24	—	—	—	—	—	—
25	—	—	—	—	—	—
26	—	—	—	—	—	—
27	—	—	—	—	—	—
28	—	—	—	—	—	—
29	—	—	—	—	—	—
30	—	—	—	—	—	—
31	—	—	—	—	—	—
Total III	359.8	375.7	1,012.3	1,057.6	1,801.4	1,723.2

*) p = production; d = total demand, except exports to abroad.
**) See this footnote on p. 257.

Table 1 *(continued)*

	Utrecht		Noord-Holland		Zuid-Holland	
	p*)	d*)**)	p	d	p	d
I 1	302.5	—	697.7	—	1,088.2	—
2	—	—	—	—	1.6	—
3	4.6	—	12.0	—	77.9	—
18	367.9	—	1,126.9	—	1,638.3	—
II 4	179.9	152.1	424.1	460.1	716.3	602.8
5	352.7	320.8	1,638.5	833.3	1,748.6	1,251.5
6	55.5	87.4	307.4	303.9	455.5	375.7
7	114.5	92.0	240.8	329.2	181.8	319.7
8	58.7	101.9	472.6	351.7	215.3	434.2
9	41.8	48.8	187.5	169.8	255.8	253.8
10	29.9	46.9	273.0	235.6	119.6	212.3
11	137.9	107.2	633.2	441.2	446.7	431.4
12	25.6	20.8	62.7	68.5	58.2	85.3
13	152.0	134.1	682.5	491.8	3,436.9	761.2
14	46.9	48.2	81.0	142.4	215.8	224.9
15	356.9	178.1	655.7	502.0	999.9	829.0
16	77.3	72.1	644.8	232.8	1,335.9	329.9
17	321.7	201.5	2,747.2	1,643.8	941.1	861.7
19	101.2	87.1	339.0	316.4	402.5	386.2
III 20	—	—	—	—	—	—
21	—	—	—	—	—	—
22	—	—	—	—	—	—
23	—	—	—	—	—	—
24	—	—	—	—	—	—
25	—	—	—	—	—	—
26	—	—	—	—	—	—
27	—	—	—	—	—	—
28	—	—	—	—	—	—
29	—	—	—	—	—	—
30	—	—	—	—	—	—
31	—	—	—	—	—	—
Total III	1,269.0	1,083.5	5,258.4	3,694.0	6,544.2	4,588.2

*) p = production; d = total demand, except exports to abroad.

**) See this footnote on p. 257.

Table 1 *(continued)*

		Zeeland		Noord-Brabant		Limburg	
		p*)	d*)**)	p	d	p	d
I	1	366.7	—	990.1	—	514.1	—
	2	—	—	—	—	763.4	—
	3	4.6	—	7.5	—	36.9	—
	18	171.3	—	788.0	—	450.0	—
II	4	34.3	68.2	779.8	446.9	171.0	216.8
	5	130.6	111.1	1,032.4	791.8	206.8	406.4
	6	3.2	25.0	315.5	157.6	32.8	90.3
	7	36.5	31.9	926.5	483.4	67.4	117.6
	8	15.2	34.8	454.7	184.7	126.0	134.0
	9	11.3	19.6	143.2	124.3	41.9	55.0
	10	—	9.4	50.1	107.7	172.6	68.5
	11	20.1	29.8	133.6	105.8	51.0	88.0
	12	1.3	6.4	268.9	137.3	36.8	29.8
	13	161.7	67.5	174.4	315.6	646.4	206.1
	14	26.9	24.3	59.5	109.5	228.7	62.2
	15	15.5	57.9	497.8	321.8	177.8	162.9
	16	129.3	34.6	331.1	221.5	50.9	79.2
	17	28.6	46.0	2,172.9	899.9	265.0	172.2
	19	33.1	33.4	161.4	167.6	94.6	131.1
III	20	—	—	—	—	—	—
	21	—	—	—	—	—	—
	22	—	—	—	—	—	—
	23	—	—	—	—	—	—
	24	—	—	—	—	—	—
	25	—	—	—	—	—	—
	26	—	—	—	—	—	—
	27	—	—	—	—	—	—
	28	—	—	—	—	—	—
	29	—	—	—	—	—	—
	30	—	—	—	—	—	—
	31	—	—	—	—	—	—
Total III		422.9	379.3	1,846.7	1,986.7	1,155.8	1,132.6

*) p = production; d = total demand, except exports to abroad.

**) The figures used in the analysis are the ones given in the columns 'd', increased with the exports abroad. While preparing this article the full regional accounts (Regionale Rekeningen [4]), were not available, but only the summaries. Therefore, we had no insight in the regional exports abroad, but only in the total sectoral exports. If, for example, total exports of a given sector were 20 percent of its total production, it has been assumed that regional exports abroad of this sector were also 20 per cent of its regional production.

defined by the C.B.S. The production of Schiphol-Airport, for example, and of the two big harbours of Rotterdam and Amsterdam were excluded from the total production of their respective provinces (Noord- and Zuid-Holland). This implies that the sum of the provincial products is not equal to the country's total.

Third, some small corrections in sectoral provincial demands were made because of extraordinarily large changes in stocks. The 'weights' of the productions – α_{lk}/β_{kl} – are obtained from the 1960 input –output table for the nation, except in a case that will be considered in the next section.

2.2. *Some special problems*

Before applying the attraction model to the Netherlands provinces – given the statistical data – it was necessary to elaborate it on three points. These elaborations concern:

(a) exports and imports,
(b) the intra-industry deliveries,
(c) the influence of highly developed areas.

Sub a In the original model exports and imports were supposed to be zero for the country as a whole. When applying the theory to some industries in the United States this hypothesis could be maintained. But the Netherlands, however, is a country where international trade is extraordinarily important. Therefore the influence of export and import flows had to be considered.

First, total sectoral provincial demands, consisting of the demand for intermediate products and final demand, should be increased (see note on p. 257) with exports.

A second problem concerns the weighting coefficients for the supplying industries. In writing r_{kl} for the requirements of industry l from industry k and s_{lk} for the sales of industry l to industry k, two relations hold, namely

$$s_{lk} = \alpha_{lk} g_l \tag{7}$$

and

$$r_{kl} = \beta_{kl} g_k . \tag{8}$$

It follows that the weights of the λ's in equation (5) can be written as:

$$\frac{\alpha_{lk}}{\beta_{kl}} = \frac{s_{lk}}{r_{kl}} \cdot \frac{g_k}{g_l} . \tag{9}$$

The figures at the right hand of (9) now can be defined in two ways, that is including imports and excluding imports. In the first case s_{lk}, r_{kl} and g_l are all taken as including imports and g_k represents total production of k. In the second case s_{lk}, r_{kl} and g_l only relate to domestic production and g_k to the production of k possible with domestically produced requirements.

Both methods give the same results if and only if the imported inter-industry deliveries are distributed over the receiving industries in the same proportion as those domestically produced. In the analysis the first definition is chosen, as a first attempt.

Sub b Actually the division of all industrial production in only fifteen (see table 1, group II) industries is very rough. But as a consequence of the more detailed classification that was originally intended by the C.B.S. statisticians, the regional production of some sectors appeared to be produced by only one or two firms. This was due to disclosure rules which necessitated aggregation of these sectors with others. As an important consequence deliveries between sub-sectors in the consolidated table appear as deliveries within the same sector.

An example relating to the textiles industry will make this clear. Suppose the textile sector can be divided into three sub-sectors: spinning, weaving, and finishing. The relations between these sub-sectors can be shown as follows.

	finishing	weaving	spinning
finishing			
weaving	S_{wf}		
spinning	S_{sf}	S_{sw}	

S_{wf}: deliveries from weaving to finishing

S_{sf} deliveries from spinning to finishing

S_{sw}: deliveries from spinning to weaving

The supply of yarn by the spinning mills might induce the weaving mills and finishing firms to locate in the neighbourhood of the spinning mills. The supply of cloth by the weaving mills might induce the finishing firms to locate in the neighbourhood of the weaving mills. On the other side, the demand for cloth by the finishing firms might attract weaving mills and the demand for yarn by the weaving mills and the finishing firms might attract spinning mills.

Clearly, according to the theory presented earlier, all intra-sectoral deliveries might attract supplying and demanding firms within the same sector. To consider intra-sectoral activities only as a demand factor and to include them (only) in total demand would be a denial of their supply influence. Consequently for industry k, industry k should be regarded as a demanding as well as supplying industry. Equation (5) then becomes

$$g_{kj} = \lambda_{dk}(\sum_l d_{kl} + d_F) + \sum_l \lambda_{kl} \frac{\alpha_{lk}}{\beta_{kl}} g_{lj} \quad (l = 1, 2, \ldots, k, n) \tag{10}$$

Placing g_{kj} left and right from the $=$ sign introduces a technical problem. The question is how to weight the supplying industry k_{kj}. The correct coefficient, according to the present theory, cannot be calculated because we do not know the separate deliveries and productions from the sub-industries. Using α_{kk}/β_{kk} would make the weighting coefficient equal to unity and g_{kj} to both dependent and independent variable. Of course λ_{kk} would become 1 and all other attraction coefficients zero. There are yet two other possibilities for defining the weighting coefficient of g_{kj}.

These are

$$\frac{\alpha_{kk_j}}{\beta_{kk}} \quad \text{and} \quad \frac{\alpha_{kk}}{\beta_{kk_j}}.$$

So eleven different α_{kk_j} and β_{kk_j} are introduced, one for every province j. Because α can be considered as an allocation coefficient and β as a technical coefficient we have preferred to use β_{kk_j}.

As a consequence the influence of supplied intermediate goods was not incorporated into the numerator of the weighting coefficient but reserved for the attraction coefficient.

The differences in the denominators (β_{kk_j}) are in the first instance caused by differences in the technical processes.

Sub c Since not only the supply of goods from different individual industries will be important for the location of a firm but also highly industrialized and densely populated areas offering all kind of services like transport, medical services, theatre, education, and skilled labourers might be an attraction as well, the whole service sector (see table 1, group III) was included as an 'attracting' sector in the analysis.

2.3. *The results of the regression analyses*

The results of the multiple regression analyses are shown in table 2. The numbers of the industries correspond to the numbers given in table 1.[5]) The sum of the attraction coefficients (λ's) in every equation is unity. This was reached by introducing this constraint into the regression analysis, which consequently was also made without constant term.

TABLE 2

Final variables, regression, and correlation coefficients of the analyses*).

$g_{4j} = 0.408\, d_{4j} + 0.592\, g_{15j}{}^{\mathrm{I}}$	$R = 0.594$
$g_{5j} = 0.1956\, \mathrm{d}_{5j} + 0.2472\, g_{5j}{}^{\mathrm{I}} + 0.5572\, g_{20j}{}^{\mathrm{I}}$	$R = 0.986$
$g_{6j} = 1.000\, g_{5j}{}^{\mathrm{II}}$	$R = 0.981$
$g_{7j} = 0.419\, d_{7j} + 0.581\, g_{7j}{}^{\mathrm{I}}$	$R = 0.938$
$g_{8j} = 0.539\, d_{8j} + 0.461\, g_{12j}{}^{\mathrm{I}}$	$R = 0.777$
$g_{9j} = 0.904\, d_{9j} + 0.096\, g_{9j}{}^{\mathrm{I}}$	$R = 0.799$
$g_{10j} = 0.541\, d_{10j} + 0.459\, g_{10j}{}^{\mathrm{I}}$	$R = 0.986$
$g_{11j} = 1.000\, g_{11j}{}^{\mathrm{I}}$	$R = 0.991$
$g_{12j} = 0.591\, d_{12j} + 0.409\, g_{12j}{}^{\mathrm{II}}$	$R = 0.879$
$g_{13j} = 0.886\, d_{13j} + 0.114\, g_{13j}{}^{\mathrm{I}}$	$R = 0.996$
$g_{14j} = 0.5574\, d_{14j} + 0.2064\, g_{3j}{}^{\mathrm{I}} + 0.2362\, g_{14j}{}^{\mathrm{I}}$	$R = 0.977$
$g_{15j} = 0.7569\, d_{15j} + 0.2431\, g_{15j}{}^{\mathrm{II}}$	$R = 0.922$
$g_{16j} = 0.8632\, d_{16j} + 0.1368\, g_{16j}{}^{\mathrm{I}}$	$R = 0.982$
$g_{17j} = 0.4834\, d_{17j} + 0.5166\, g_{17j}{}^{\mathrm{I}}$	$R = 0.842$
$g_{19j} = 0.1000\, d_{19j}$	$R = 0.996$
$g_{20j} = 0.8769\, d_{20j} + 0.1231\, g_{20j}{}^{\mathrm{II}}$	$R = 0.995$

All regression coefficients have standard errors less than half the regression coefficients.

*) $g_{i,j}{}^{\mathrm{I}}$ and $g_{i,j}{}^{\mathrm{II}}$ mean the weighted production of sector i in region $j(g_{i,j})$. If $g_{i,j}$ occurs twice in this table, the first time is written $g_{i,j}{}^{\mathrm{I}}$ and the second time $g_{i,j}{}^{\mathrm{II}}$. Different indices are used in order to make visible that in both cases $g_{i,j}$ has not the same weighting coefficient.

3. General Application to Regional Industrialization Policy

The foregoing results enable us to rank the industries by demand-orientation or supply-orientation and to determine how the growth of one industry in a particular region influences the growth of other industries in a direct way. It may be stressed once more that the attraction coefficients in table 2 are not comparable to the technical coefficients in a normal input–output table. They represent the influence of the growth of a given industry in a given

[5]) If the deliveries of a supplying industry k to a demanding industry l are so small that $\beta_{kk} < 0.02$, this industry k is omitted from the analysis.

region upon the growth of other industries *in the same* region through stimulation of both *demand and supply.* These two differences are basic elements in the analysis and form an essential difference with the usual regional input–output analysis where it is assumed that changes only take place through increased demand and that this increased demand is met within the region in the same proportion as was the case in the regional input–output table itself, in other words, as has been the case in the past. It seems that these two properties will enable us to analyse more realistically the consequences of the introduction of new industries in a given region than is possible on the basis of the regular input–output models.

In order to demonstrate the procedure that has been followed the following notation has been adopted.

In equation (5) the λ_d's were the demand-attraction coefficients and λ_l were the supply-attraction coefficients. Since the same industry might demand from as well as supply to industry k, this industry might appear twice in the equation. The attraction coefficient for this industry then consists of the correctly weighted sum of the demand- and supply coefficient.

Now let g be the vector of sectoral productions. Furthermore, let A be the matrix of weighting coefficients of the supplying industries, each coefficient multiplied by the relevant supply-attraction coefficient. This matrix thus consists of the elements

$$\lambda_{lk} \frac{\alpha_{lk}}{\beta_{kl}}.$$

Finally, write

$\hat{l}$ for the diagonal matrix of demand coefficients,

e for the vector of final demand for products of different industries, and

B for the matrix of technical coefficients β_{lk}.

Although the regional production of only sixteen industries (see table 1, group II) is considered, the order of the matrices used is 20. This results from the fact that the distribution of agriculture, mining, quarrying and building production is not analyzed. Instead, these activities are included as 'explaining' variables.

Recalling that equation (5) is used in the analysis, and considering that this equation also can be written as

$$g_k = \lambda_{dk} \sum \beta_{lk} g_l + \sum \lambda_{lk} \frac{\alpha_{lk}}{\beta_{kl}} g_l + \lambda_{dk} e_k \tag{11}$$

the solution for g_k from the whole system of equations can be found as follows:

$$g = [\hat{l}B + A]\, g + \hat{l}e\,. \tag{12}$$

This can be written as

$$g = (I - [\hat{l}B + A])^{-1}\, \hat{l}e\,. \tag{13}$$

If $\hat{w}$ is the diagonal matrix of value-added fractions in gross production and v is written for the vector $\hat{l}e$, the vector of cumulated values added, for which we write t, and where F is defined as $\hat{l}B + A$, becomes

$$t = \hat{w}([I - F]^{-1})'\, v\,.$$

If the elements of v are chosen in such a way that the elements on the leading diagonal of $\hat{w}([I - F]^{-1})'$, multiplied by the corresponding elements of v, are one, then t consists of the value-added multipliers.

This special t-vector is shown in table 3. If the demand coefficient is say 1/2, the corresponding $\hat{v}$ element becomes half the increase in final demand. It is clear that the location effect is a value-added effect.

Similarly, employment effects can be calculated by using labour-intensity coefficients instead of value-added fractions. The corresponding multipliers are employment multipliers. It should be stressed that the multipliers calculated according to our method are *not total* regional multipliers but indicate the multiplicative effect only for those sectors that have been included in the analysis.

The industries shown in table 3 have been grouped in a way which requires further explanation. Since an industry will be more non-basic the fuller its column and the emptier its row, two industries, services and public utilities, obviously appear as completely non-basic. These industries both have low regional multipliers. But this conclusion holds only at the provincial level. If smaller regions were considered, many activities in both sectors would become basic at that level. The remaining industries[6]) have been grouped

[6]) Results from the chemical industry are not presented in the table since they in many ways seem to be inconclusive. This probably results from the fact that non-basic activities in this sector (pharmacies) are included with the typical basic activities (refineries). Further studies of this industry are in progress.

TABLE 3

Vectors of partial regional multipliers for 15 industries*).

		20	19	14	9	4	5	6	10	8	7	12	11	17	16	15	t
Services	20	1.00	+ 0.02	+			+ 0.07	+ 0.07									1.16
Public utilities	19	0.05	+ 1.00														1.05
Pottery, glass and stone	14	0.12	+ 0.05	+ 1.00													1.17
Wood and furniture	9	0.15	+ 0.02	+	1.00	+										+ 0.03	1.20
Foodstuffs (animal pr.)	4	0.23	+ 0.03	+		1.00	+ 0.02	+ 0.02	+							+ 0.09	1.39
Foodstuffs (other pr.)	5	0.23	+ 0.04	+	0.02	+	1.00	+ 1.03	+ 0.02								2.34
Drinks and tobaccos	6	0.04	+					+ 1.00									1.04
Papermills	10	0.40	+ 0.06	+			+ 0.03	+ 0.03	+ 1.00							+ 0.02	1.54
Footwear and clothing	8	0.16	+ 0.02	+						+ 1.00	+ 0.08	+ 0.03					1.29
Textiles	7	0.27	+ 0.08	+			0.02	+ 0.02	+ 0.02	+ 0.02	+ 1.00					+ 0.02	1.45
Leather and rubber	12	0.53	+ 0.09	+		+ 0.02	+ 0.04	+ 0.04	+ 0.02	+ 2.51	+ 0.16	+ 1.00	+	0.05	+	0.07	4.53
Printing and publishing	11	0.19	+ 0.02	+					+ 0.06	+			1.00				1.27
Other metal industry	17	0.27	+ 0.05	+		0.02	+ 0.02	+ 0.02	+					1.00	+	0.06	1.44
Means of transport ind.	16	0.15	+ 0.03	+	0.02	+ 0.04	+			0.04	+			0.06	+ 1.00	+ 0.15	1.49
Metal products and machinery	15	0.20	+ 0.04	+		0.24	+ 0.02	+ 0.02						0.10	+	1.00	1.62

*) Values of 0.01 or smaller omitted.

in three categories. The first consists of 'primary manufacturing' consisting of agricultural and forestry products and pottery, glass and stone. The production processes in this category are simple. With the exception of the relation between the drinks and tobacco industry and the food-stuff industry (non-animal products) the interrelations between the industries in this category are negligible. The industries are thus footloose and the entire category is footloose. The category represents the first stage of industrialization. Apart from services and public utilities no other industries are needed at the provincial level to make the industries in this category operate. An exception to this rule is the metal products industry which is needed by many other industries and itself creates activities in a number of other sectors. This industry thus is of a mixed basic–non-basic character. The regional multipliers in this category are considerably higher than those of the non-basic industries.

The second category contains 'secondary' manufacturing activities and consists of the tightly interrelated activities, footwear and clothing, textiles and leather and rubber. Production processes in this category are somewhat more complex than in primary manufacturing but are still related to agricultural production. Moreover, it appears that these industries create activities not only in the non-basic sectors but also in 'primary manufacturing'. Consequently, the regional multipliers again are higher than in the lower ranked groups.

The final category consists of the inorganic and more complicated processes associated with a higher degree of industrialization. Included are printing and publishing, metal products and machinery, means of transport, and other metal industry. These activities will be called 'tertiary manufacturing'. Multipliers in this category are high, and the creation of activities in other branches (especially primary manufacturing) are considerable.

The metal products and machinery industry, mentioned before, are somewhat 'outside' the categories. The double character of this industry implies, on the one hand, that its nature is non-basic since its activities are required by most other industries but, on the other hand, its production creates a great number of additional activities in other industries. The position of this industry in industrialization policy thus seems to be of utmost importance.

The sequence of the categories indicates the evolutionary process in industrialization. Many countries and regions are still in the first phase, that is, the processing of agriculture and forestry products. As industrialization proceeds, secondary manufacturing activities are introduced and an initial start in the metal products and machinery industry will be made. The final stage of industrialization consists of tertiary manufacturing with more complicated production processes in which metal industries play a dominant role.

4. Application at the Regional Level

The attraction model and its statistical testing have been considered in preceding sections. For the practical application of the results to a given region, two more steps are needed. These will be discussed in this section.

First, it is assumed that the location of a given industry is more attractive the higher its growth rate and the higher its regional multiplier. Because the leather and rubber industry as well as the metal industries appear to satisfy both criteria, both should be considered as 'strategic' or 'propulsive' industries.

An objection to this approach could be that the analysis results in identical advise to each province, that is, to promote the propulsive industries and no others. Indeed, this would be the case only if the rates of growth of industries were taken into account. However, (for more than one reason) there may be a discrepancy between the growth prospects of a given industry and of the region where this branch is located.

Although long-term prospects for a given industry are favourable, it is by no means certain that the original location is the most profitable. Technological change and rising wages are two reasons why other regions (or countries) become more attractive as potential sites. On the other hand, the higher the investment rate and proportion of foreign capital, the less an industry is bound to the original region or country of location, thus the more mobile an industry is.

Because rapid technological change, rising wages, high investment rates, and use of foreign capital all characterize growth industries, there seems to be a contradiction between high short-term growth prospects and more stable long-term economic development. In order to bound all these risks, and the more traditional risk of a declining growth rate of former propulsive industries (no matter where these plants are located) another notion, the rate of diversification, should be introduced. Usually, stability characterizes diversified industry structures. This holds because temporary unemployment in an industry which accounts for a relatively small share of total employment will have little influence on the region as a whole and can be compensated by growth of another industry.

It follows that mono-structured regions should not be advised to expand in the already overdeveloped sector. Thus, a city like Eindhoven should not develop the electronic industry and Leverkussen, Germany, should not further expand its already highly developed pharmaceutical industry.

The stronger an industry is represented in a given region, the more its economy will depend on this activity and the more urgent is the need for additional employment in other industries. This holds even if these industries have lower growth rates or smaller multipliers.

For these reasons additional employment in other industries, although maybe not as attractive from a general growth point of view, does seem appropriate in all cases where one-sidedness is a characteristic of the economy. This holds even at the national level. Textile and coal regions suffer as much from their one-sidedness as coffee or cotton countries.

Hence, the second step in the application of the attraction model to a given region is to determine in which respect the regional industrial structure is defective so far as stability is concerned; in other words, which industries could contribute most to its diversification. In comparing its structure with a 'stable' structure (e.g. the national structure or the structure of the countries of the EEC taken together) 'defective' industries can be traced. Then the industries to be promoted in the region are those which have

(1) the highest possible multipliers;
(2) the highest possible growth rates;
(3) the highest relative difference from the 'stable' structure.

It should be remarked that, in one respect, the foregoing procedure is not consistent. 'Industries' really means 'bunches'[7]) of industries. This is of particular importance for comparison with the 'stable' structure. The relevant industry (to complement the existing structure) is not the industry most defective but rather the bunch of industries that is most defective of all possible bunches, that should be chosen.

5. Further Research

In the foregoing a method was demonstrated that can be considered as a possible approach to problems of industrialization.

[7]) Term of J. Tinbergen.

It seems that possibilities for application could be improved on at least two points.
(1) It has been assumed implicitly in the model (transformation of eq. 3 to 4) that the transportation sector itself exerts no attraction on industries since this sector adjusts itself completely to the needs of the region. This hypothesis is worthy of statistical testing.
(2) The weighting coefficient α_{kk}/β_{kk_j} used to explain g_{kj} should be defined more precisely from information on the importance of the subsectors of k in the regions considered.

This paper has dealt with a possible approach to regional industrialization policy. It seems necessary to further improve the approach in the light of the two points noted above.

Moreover, the model should find application not only to regional industrialization problems but also to national industrialization policy, particularly in so far as underdeveloped countries are concerned. The lack of data might hamper the application to underdeveloped countries but a simplified approach, using employment data, seems possible.

References

[1] W. ISARD, *Methods of Regional Analysis: An Introduction to Regional Science*, Massachusetts, New York–London, 1960, pp. 345–346.

[2] L. H. KLAASSEN, *Methods of Selecting Industries for Depressed Areas*, OECD, Paris, 1967.

[3] W. LEONTIEF et al., *Studies in the Structure of the American Economy*, Oxford University Press, New York, 1953.

[4] Regionale Rekeningen 1960, C.B.S. 1968.

[5] J. TINBERGEN, *Shaping the World Economy*, The Twentieth Century Fund, New York, 1962.

THE OPTIMAL NUMBER OF FACTORIES IN A SPATIAL MARKET*

JAN SERCK-HANSSEN

1. Introduction

The optimal number of factories in spatial markets has been investigated in several studies under the assumption that average cost of production of a factory exceeds marginal cost of production. Bos [1, pp. 25–36] assumes that the cost of production of a factory is a linear function of its output and derives explicit expressions for the optimal size of factories under alternative assumptions about the spatial distribution of demand. In empirical studies, the optimal number of factories has been determined by Vietorisz and Manne [4] among others.

In this study we do not assume, *a priori*, that average cost of production exceeds marginal cost of production for all levels of output, but rather show that under relatively weak assumptions, average cost of production will exceed marginal cost of production when the number of factories is optimal, provided that the optimal number of factories is finite. This conclusion adds support to the doubt expressed by Koopmans [2, p. 154] concerning the possibility of sustaining an efficient locational distribution of economic activity through a pricing mechanism under the usual assumptions about behaviour by the market agents.

Consider the following problem: let a spatial market exist in which consumers are uniformly distributed. Assume that these consumers are to be supplied with a single commodity in the 'best possible way'. Assume further that we are free to choose (a) the number of factories producing the commodity; (b) the locations of the factories; and (c) the output of the commodity by each of the factories.

*) I am indebted to M. A. Grove for valuable comments on an earlier draft of this article.

In this paper, we shall restrict ourselves to only one aspect of this optimization problem, viz., the choice of the optimal number of factories. Let all factories be equally large, and let the geographical forms of the markets of all factories be the same.[1]) Under these assumptions we shall show that the condition for the optimal number of factories has the following implications:

1. If each factory charges an f.o.b.-price equal to its marginal cost of production, then it will normally operate at a deficit.
2. The deficit of a factory will have an upper limit equal to the difference between

(a) total rent of land received within the market of the factory in a competitive economy; and

(b) the rent of land that would have been received within the market of the factory if the rent at all points in the market had been equal to the rent at that point within the market which pays the lowest rent in a competitive economy.

In some important cases the deficit of a factory will equal the difference between (a) and (b) – and in other important cases the deficit will be almost as large as this difference.

For pedagogical reasons, we shall first prove equality in a very simple case in section 2. In section 3 we shall consider a more general case for which we shall prove the above statement. Finally, in section 4, we shall suggest a (probably rather impractical) market mechanism, including an entry mechanism.

2. A Simple Special Case

Consider a one-dimensional market, i.e., a line. Consumers are distributed along this line with uniform density.[2]) The demand for the commodity by a consumer is perfectly inelastic and the same for all consumers.

Since the quantity supplied at any point in the market is given, the optimization problem consists only of determining how these supplies can be provided with the least possible use of resources. In order to simplify matters, we shall assume that only one factor of production is needed to produce and distribute the commodity, and that this factor of production is freely mobile.

---

[1]) In terms of the symbols to be defined in section 3, the geographical forms of the markets of two factories will be said to be the same if the forms of the functions $G(\mu, \lambda)$ applied to each of the two factories are the same.

[2]) Although the formulae imply a continuum of consumers along the line, we shall occasionally discuss assumptions and results as if there were a discrete distribution of consumers in the market.

We shall distinguish two types of cost or use of resources in supplying consumers with the commodity: cost of production and cost of transportation. We shall assume that the cost of producing a quantity, X, in a factory is the same no matter where the factory is located. We shall assume, further, that the transport cost per delivery is proportional to the quantity delivered and an increasing function of the distance over which the delivery takes place.

In the present model, we shall assume that each factory is located at the centre of the market that it supplies.[3] The type of variation under which we shall study the variation of costs is thus: suppose a line which is 100 km long is to be supplied. This line can be supplied either by one factory supplying a market of 50 km on each side of it; or by two factories, each supplying a market of 25 km on each side of it; or by three factories, each supplying a market of $16\frac{2}{3}$ km on each side of it; and so on. In the computations, we shall assume the size of the market of a factory to be continuously variable, thus disregarding the condition that the number of factories should be an integer.

Let us now introduce the following definitions:

X = quantity produced by a factory;

$b[X]$ = cost of producing a quantity, X, in a factory, no matter where this factory is located;

$T[X]$ = cost of transporting the output of a factory producing a quantity, X, to the consumers;

D = constant density of demand for the commodity (for example, tons per km);

$t(\mu)$ = cost of transporting one unit of the commodity over μ units of distance;

L = length of the whole market to be supplied;

2λ = length of the market supplied by one factory. (The number of factories is thus $L|2\lambda$).

We shall always assume all functions to be sufficiently smooth. The above variables and functions satisfy the following conditions:

$$X = 2D\lambda\,, \tag{1}$$

$$T[X] = 2D\int_0^\lambda t(\mu)\,\mathrm{d}\mu\,. \tag{2}$$

[3]) Under our assumptions, this is the optimal location of a factory.

The total cost of supplying the whole market will be given by

$$C = \frac{L}{2\lambda}\left(b\left[2D\lambda\right] + T\left[2D\lambda\right]\right). \tag{3}$$

This expression is to be minimized with respect to λ. Let $\tilde{\lambda}$ be that value of λ which minimizes C. Provided that $\tilde{\lambda}>0$, the optimal production volume $\tilde{X}=2D\tilde{\lambda}$ must satisfy the condition that the derivative of C with respect to λ be zero for $\lambda=\tilde{\lambda}$. This requires that

$$b[\tilde{X}] - b'[\tilde{X}]\,\tilde{X} = T'[\tilde{X}]\,\tilde{X} - T[\tilde{X}], \tag{4}$$

i.e., the difference between average and marginal cost of production should equal the negative of the difference between average and marginal cost of transportation.

A value, $\tilde{X}$, of X satisfying (4) yields a local minimum of C if the second derivative of C with respect to λ is positive at this point. This requires that

$$b''[\tilde{X}] + T''[\tilde{X}] > 0, \tag{5}$$

i.e., that the sum of marginal costs of production and transportation should be increasing in an optimal point.

In what remains of this section, we shall discuss the interpretation of condition (4). The left-hand side of the equation equals the deficit of a factory which charges an f.o.b.-price equal to its marginal cost of production for its entire output. We now want to show that the right-hand side of eq. (4) can be interpreted as the sum over all points in the market of a factory of the rent of land at the point in excess of the rent of land at a point on the outer boundary of this market, if one assumes that each consumer pays a price for the commodity equal to the f.o.b.-price plus transport cost from the factory. Let us first note that since the demand density is constant at all points, the increase in transport cost induced by a small increase in the production volume of a factory equals the cost of transporting the additional production volume to the boundary of the market, i.e., $T'[2D\lambda]=t(\lambda)$. We can now rewrite the right-hand side of (4) in the following way:

$$2D\tilde{\lambda}t(\tilde{\lambda}) - 2D\int_0^{\tilde{\lambda}} t(\mu)\,\mathrm{d}\mu = 2D\int_0^{\tilde{\lambda}} \left[t(\tilde{\lambda}) - t(\mu)\right]\mathrm{d}\mu\,. \tag{6}$$

The expression within brackets in (6) will, under our assumptions, equal the difference between the price payed for the commodity by a consumer who is located at the boundary of the market and the price payed by another consumer who is located at a distance μ from the factory. This difference multiplied by the total consumption of a consumer equals the maximum sum a consumer at the boundary of the market would be willing to pay in order to be moved from the boundary to a point at a distance μ from the factory. If the same difference multiplied by the consumption of a consumer equals the difference between rent of land payed by each person living at a distance μ from the factory and the rent of land payed by each person living at the boundary of the market, then any person will be indifferent as to whether he lives at the boundary or at a distance μ from the factory. In a competitive economy, we would expect rent of land to be determined in this way.

Let us conclude our examination of this special case by commenting briefly on the conclusion that all factories in a spatial market of the above type will operate at a deficit if factories are of optimal size and if they charge an f.o.b.-price equal to marginal cost of production. Since the density of demand is given at any point, the objective must be to minimize the sum of the costs of production and transportation. Since the given density of demand is the same at all points, one should minimize the average cost of producing and transporting the quantity produced in each factory. The average cost of production and transportation will be at a minimum when it equals the marginal cost of production and transportation. Due to the assumptions we have made about the transport cost function, average cost of transportation for the production of any given factory will always be smaller than marginal cost of transportation. Consequently, average cost of production should be higher than marginal cost of production.

3. A General Case

Let us now attempt to generalize the result of the previous section. We shall show that the deficit of a factory of optimal size should at most equal the sum of money all consumers supplied by the factory would be willing to pay to avoid being moved to the most distant point supplied by that factory, i.e., to the point at which transport cost per unit of the commodity is highest.

Comparing the model of this section with that of the previous section, we may note that in the formulation of the model to be presented below, we shall assume explicitly:

(a) that the marginal utility of the commodity is a decreasing function of its consumption by one person;

(b) that two-dimensional as well as one-dimensional markets may exist;

(c) that the location of a factory within its market need not be optimal.

We shall assume that total population is uniformly distributed in the market, i.e., with the same number of persons per unit of length of the market (if the market is one-dimensional) or per unit of area of the market (if the market is two-dimensional) at all points in the market.

Let us introduce the following set of definitions:

λ = the distance from a factory to the most distant point supplied by that factory (λ in the previous section can also be interpreted in this way);

$G(\mu, \lambda)$ = a function the value of which for $\mu \leqq \lambda$ gives the density of area or of length of market of a factory which is located at a distance μ from the factory, when the most distant point supplied is at a distance λ from the factory.

We shall assume that the function $G(\mu, \lambda)$ applies to all factories in the market and that λ is the same for all factories.[4]

The variations in market patterns under which we shall examine the variation of total costs shall be generated by variations in λ. Let us consider some examples to illustrate what this implies.

Let us first consider the special simple case of the previous section. In that case, each factory would supply a market of length $\mathrm{d}\mu$ on either side of the factory at distances between μ and $\mu+\mathrm{d}\mu$ from the factory, provided that $\mathrm{d}\mu>0$ and $\mu+\mathrm{d}\mu \leqq \lambda$. Thus, in this case, $G(\mu, \lambda)=2$ for $\mu \leqq \lambda$.

As a second example, assume that a one-dimensional market is supplied by factories each of which is located at one end of the market it supplies. In this case $G(\mu, \lambda)=1$ for $\mu \leqq \lambda$.

---

[4] In principle, one may have different values of variables defined as λ and different forms of functions defined as $G(\mu, \lambda)$ for each factory. Since we always assume that the λ's and the G-functions of all factories are the same, we shall omit an index to the λ's and the G-functions indicating the factory to which these symbols apply. By stating that the geographical forms of the markets of all factories are the same, we mean that the G-functions of all factories are the same. When both the G-functions and the λ's of all factories are the same, the geographical forms of the markets of the factories and the size of the factories are the same.

As a third example, let us assume that the market of a factory is a circle, and that the factory is located at the centre of the circle.[5]) In this case $G(\mu, \lambda) = 2\pi\mu$ for $\mu \leqq \lambda$.

In each of these cases, $G(\mu, \lambda)$ is independent of λ for $\mu \leqq \lambda$, i.e., $(\partial/\partial\lambda)G(\mu, \lambda) = 0$ for $\mu \leqq \lambda$. This will, however, not always be the case – an important exception being the hexagonal market.[6]) Consider a factory supplying a hexagonal market, the factory being located at the centre of this market. If we increase the size of the market of this factory by increasing the greatest radius of the hexagon, λ, then we will increase the density of area to be supplied at all distances, μ, from the factory, $\frac{1}{2}\lambda\sqrt{3} < \mu \leqq \lambda$.

The total size of the market of a factory, the most distant point in which is λ units distant from the factory, is given by the expression

$$P(\lambda) = \int_0^\lambda G(\mu, \lambda)\,\mathrm{d}\mu\,. \tag{7}$$

When determining the optimal number of factories, we shall employ the traditional assumptions made in cost–benefit analysis. Let a world exist in which there are two commodities, the commodity we consider and money. All persons in the market have identical tastes in these two commodities, and we assume that the common indifference maps of all consumers can be represented by a utility function written as a sum of

(a) a degressively increasing function of the consumption of the commodity we consider;

(b) the amount of money the consumer receives in addition to what he uses to buy this commodity.

Our problem then is one of a planner who seeks to maximize the sum of the utilities of all inhabitants of the country, and who considers the marginal utility of money to be constant and the same for all persons in the market.

From these assumptions it follows that the planner may employ a function of the form

$$U\{D\} + r \tag{8}$$

[5]) A circle is not a possible form of the markets of factories supplying a two-dimensional market, as a two-dimensional space cannot be covered by non-overlapping circles.

[6]) A regular hexagon is the optimal form of the market to be supplied by a factory in a two-dimensional market with the same density of consumers at all points, cf. A. Lösch [3].

to express the density of utility at a point which receives a density of supply, D, of the commodity we consider and in addition a density of supply of money, r.

We shall assume that the integral of r over the whole market equals a constant minus the cost of producing and distributing the commodity we consider. Therefore, if we want to increase the supply of this commodity to one consumer, while keeping the supply to other consumers constant and the division of the total market between factories unchanged, we have to reduce the total supply of money to all consumers taken together. If we let a small region obtain an additional supply, ΔX, of the commodity we consider, this will induce an increase in utility within this region derived from consumption of this commodity equal, as a first approximation, to the quantity

$$U'\{D\}\,\Delta X\,, \tag{9}$$

if the density of supply to all points within the region is D.

The cost of providing this additional supply to the region depends upon the production volume in the factory supplying it, and upon the distance from this factory to the region. If the factory has a production volume, $X(\lambda)$, and if the distance from the factory to the region is μ, then the cost of providing the additional supply to the region equals, as a first approximation, the sum

$$(b'[X(\lambda)] + t(\mu))\,\Delta X\,. \tag{10}$$

It follows from our assumptions that this increase in cost of providing the market with the commodity we consider[7]) will cause an equally large decrease in the total sum of money available to the consumers. Thus, all consumers taken together will get a decrease in the part of their utility derived from use of money equal to the sum (10) (cf. (8)).

If, at an optimum, a point is supplied from a factory producing a quantity $X(\lambda)$ at a distance μ from the point, then the point should be supplied with a density D given by equating the expressions in (9) and (10). Thus, the demand density at such a point will be a function of $b'[X(\lambda)]+t(\mu)$, which we shall write as

$$D(b'[X(\lambda)] + t(\mu))\,, \tag{11}$$

[7]) Assuming the supply of the commodity to all points outside the region as well as the division of the total market between factories to be unchanged.

where the function D is the inverse of the function U', i.e.,

$$U'\{D(b'[X(\lambda)] + t(\mu))\} \equiv b'[X(\lambda)] + t(\mu). \tag{12}$$

We shall assume the cost functions and the utility function to be such that for any chosen value of λ and for any given function $G(\mu, \lambda)$, the following equation has a unique solution for $X(\lambda)$:

$$X(\lambda) = \int_0^\lambda G(\mu, \lambda)\, D(b'[X(\lambda)] + t(\mu))\, \mathrm{d}\mu. \tag{13}$$

This requires that for any given geographical form and size of the market of a factory, there is a unique production volume for the factory for which there is equality between production and demand within its market, when the demand density at all points in the market is given by the demand function (11). We further assume that the available supply of money is sufficient to produce and distribute the quantities given by (13).

We shall now maximize total utility in the whole market with respect to the size of the factories, which is represented by λ. Let P denote the length or area of the whole market to be supplied, and let R denote the amount of money available for the consumers if none of the commodity we consider is produced. Assuming all factories to be of equal size, total utility in the market will then be given by the sum

$$\begin{gathered}\frac{P}{P(\lambda)} \int_0^\lambda G(\mu, \lambda)\, U\{D(b'[X(\lambda)] + t(\mu))\}\, \mathrm{d}\mu \\ + \left\{R - \frac{P}{P(\lambda)} \int_0^\lambda G(\mu, \lambda)\, t(\mu)\, D(b'[X(\lambda)] + t(\mu))\, \mathrm{d}\mu - \frac{P}{P(\lambda)}\, b[X(\lambda)]\right\}.\end{gathered} \tag{14}$$

In this sum, the first component equals the utility obtained by the whole market from consumption of the commodity we consider. The remaining part of the sum equals the utility derived from money (see (8)), which equals the constant R minus total costs in the whole market of producing and distributing the commodity.

If the value, $\tilde{\lambda}$, of λ maximizing the sum (14) is positive, then the derivative of the sum (14) with respect to λ should be zero for $\lambda = \tilde{\lambda}$.

Before differentiating the sum (14), let us differentiate the definitional equation (13) with respect to λ for later use:

$$X'(\lambda) = G(\lambda, \lambda)\, D\big(b'[X(\lambda)] + t(\lambda)\big) + \int_0^{\lambda} G(\mu, \lambda) \frac{\partial D}{\partial \lambda}\, d\mu + \int_0^{\lambda} D\big(b'[X(\lambda)] + t(\mu)\big) \frac{\partial G}{\partial \lambda}\, d\mu, \qquad (15)$$

where

$$\frac{\partial D}{\partial \lambda} = \frac{\partial}{\partial \lambda} D\big(b'[X(\lambda)] + t(\mu)\big).$$
$$\frac{\partial G}{\partial \lambda} = \frac{\partial}{\partial \lambda} G(\mu, \lambda). \qquad (16)$$

We then equate the derivative of the sum (14) with respect to λ to zero, omitting the factor $P/P(\tilde{\lambda})^2$.
This yields, using (15),

$$P(\tilde{\lambda})(A_1 + A_2 + A_3) - P'(\tilde{\lambda})\, A_4 = 0, \qquad (17)$$

where,

$$A_1 = G(\tilde{\lambda}, \tilde{\lambda}) \{U\{D(b'[X(\tilde{\lambda})] + t(\tilde{\lambda}))\} - D(b'[X(\tilde{\lambda})] + t(\tilde{\lambda})) \times [t(\tilde{\lambda}) + b'[X(\tilde{\lambda})]]\},$$

$$A_2 = \int_0^{\tilde{\lambda}} G(\mu, \tilde{\lambda}) \frac{\partial D}{\partial \lambda} [U'\{D(b'[X(\tilde{\lambda})] + t(\mu))\} - t(\mu) - b'[X(\tilde{\lambda})]]\, d\mu, \qquad (18)$$

$$A_3 = \int_0^{\tilde{\lambda}} \frac{\partial G}{\partial \lambda} \{U\{D(b'[X(\tilde{\lambda})] + t(\mu))\} - D(b'[X(\tilde{\lambda})] + t(\mu)) \times [t(\mu) + b'[X(\tilde{\lambda})]]\}\, d\mu,$$

$$A_4 = \int_0^{\tilde{\lambda}} G(\mu, \tilde{\lambda})\, U\{D(b'[X(\tilde{\lambda})] + t(\mu))\}\, d\mu - \int_0^{\tilde{\lambda}} G(\mu, \tilde{\lambda})\, t(\mu) \times D(b'[X(\tilde{\lambda})] + t(\mu))\, d\mu - b[X(\tilde{\lambda})],$$

the derivatives defined in (16) being evaluated for the value, $\tilde{\lambda}$, of λ.

From (12) follows that $A_2 = 0$. Assuming $P'(\lambda) \neq 0$, we then solve (17) with respect to the deficit of a factory selling its entire production at an f.o.b.-price equal to marginal cost of production and obtain the condition

$$b[X(\tilde{\lambda})] - X(\tilde{\lambda})\, b'[X(\tilde{\lambda})] = A_4 + b[X(\tilde{\lambda})] - X(\tilde{\lambda})\, b'[X(\tilde{\lambda})] - \frac{P(\tilde{\lambda})}{P'(\tilde{\lambda})}(A_1 + A_3). \qquad (19)$$

The sum $A_4 + b[X(\tilde{\lambda})] - X(\tilde{\lambda})b'[X(\tilde{\lambda})]$ equals the sum of consumers' surplus for all persons in the market of a factory derived from the consumption of the commodity considered if each person obtains a quantity of this commodity as given by (11) and pays a price for it equal to the sum of marginal cost of production and transport cost from the factory. The sum $(1/P'(\tilde{\lambda}))\,(A_1 + A_3)$ equals the unweighted average of consumers' surplus for the new persons being supplied by the factory as λ is increased[8]), measured in utility per unit of length or area.

The result, (19), can be stated as follows: let the expression 'the average consumers' surplus at the boundary weighted by entry rates' be defined as $(1/P'(\tilde{\lambda}))\,(A_1 + A_3)$. Then (19) states that the deficit in a factory should equal the excess of (a) total consumers' surplus derived from the consumption of the commodity in the market of the factory, over (b) the consumers' surplus that this market would have obtained from this commodity if all persons in the market had a consumers' surplus equal to the average consumers' surplus at the boundary weighted by entry rates.

Now assume that the difference between rent of land at two points equals the difference between consumers' surplus obtained from consumption of the commodity considered at these two points. The condition (19) may then be stated as follows: the deficit in a factory should equal the excess of (a) rent of land in the market of this factory, over (b) the rent that would have been obtained if the rent of all land had been equal to the average rent at the boundary weighted by entry rates.[9])

There are some further conclusions obtainable from (19). Let us first assume that

$$\frac{\partial}{\partial \lambda} G(\mu, \lambda) = 0 \quad \text{for } \mu < \lambda . \qquad (20)$$

---

[8]) By differentiating (7), we find that the sum of the weights sum to one. In the interpretation of the formulae we shall assume $\partial G/\partial \lambda$ to be non-negative for all μ.

[9]) The rent at various points at the boundary should be weighted by the weights by which consumers' surplus at these points are weighted in the expression $(1/P'(\lambda))\,(A_1 + A_3)$.

If the condition (20) is satisfied, then the deficit of a factory should equal the rent of land in the market of this factory in excess of the rent that would have been obtained if the rent of all land had been equal to the rent of the least valuable land. As we have stated in the discussion of the function $G(\mu, \lambda)$ above, condition (20) will be satisfied in, e.g., the markets considered in section 2, but not satisfied for the optimal geographical form of two-dimensional markets, i.e., the hexagonal markets. However, earlier comparisons of hexagonal markets and circular markets (for which condition (20) is satisfied) indicate that these two geographical forms of markets are almost identical in such characteristics as transport cost per unit of area.[10]) It seems plausible, therefore, that in hexagonal markets the deficit of the factories should be almost as high as the rent of land, if the rent of the least valuable land is zero.

Note that the deficit $b[X(\tilde{\lambda})] - X(\tilde{\lambda})\, b'[X(\tilde{\lambda})]$ in (19) need not necessarily be positive. But it seems obvious that this deficit will be positive in all 'normal' cases. It will be positive if the average rent of land at the boundary of the market of a factory, weighted by entry rates, is smaller than the unweighted average of rent of land at all points in the market.

4. An Implementation Procedure

Suppose all consumers in the market are quantity adapters and that they regard prices at all locations to be constant. From the reasoning leading to (11), it then follows that a necessary condition for a solution in such a market to be Pareto-optimal is that the price faced by each consumer equals marginal cost of production plus transport cost for one unit of the product from the factory to this consumer. This conclusion and the result obtained in (19) imply that if the optimal number of factories is finite, if the factories are not to be subsidized, and if the factories receive their entire income from selling the commodity, then in all normal cases one cannot implement an optimal solution. This result obtains no matter what strategy one prescribes for producers.

An implementation procedure might be suggested on the basis of the above reasoning. All rent of land in excess of the rent of the least valuable land should be taxed one hundred per cent – or almost this much – and earmarked for subsidies to the factories. The strategy of the factories should

[10]) See H. C. Bos [1, pp. 31–33].

be a rather passive one: they should sell whatever is demanded by the consumers at an f.o.b.-price equal to marginal cost of production. We have shown that if the number of factories is optimal, then all factories will earn zero profit including subsidies by this remuneration system.

In the simple case discussed in section 2, it is not difficult to see that if the factories are too large, then the profit of the factories accruing from this mechanism will be positive. Let the value, $\tilde{X}$, be replaced by the variable, X, in the functions on both sides of eq. (4). Consider the function obtained by subtracting the left side of eq. (4) from the right side of this equation, both sides being considered as functions of X. This difference equals the profit of a factory which sells its entire output at an f.o.b.-price equal to its marginal cost of production and which receives a subsidy equal to the rent of land within its market, assuming the rent of the least valuable land to be zero. According to eq. (4), this profit is zero if the size of the factory is optimal. By differentiating the difference with respect to X and comparing with eq. (5), one obtains the conclusion that if the factory is too large (small), then the profit of the factory including the subsidy is positive (negative).

This result suggests an entry mechanism: if the existing factories earn a positive profit including rent of land, then new factories should be established; if the existing factories earn a negative profit, then some factories should leave the market.

A condition for the functioning of this mechanism is free mobility of all factories. If the factories are not mobile, we may have either

(a) a locational pattern with too few factories in which no improvement can be made by establishing new factories, no matter where they may be located, or

(b) a locational pattern with too many factories in which no improvement can be made by stopping the production in any of the existing factories.

References

[1] H. C. Bos, *Spatial Dispersion of Economic Activity*, Rotterdam, Rotterdam University Press, 1965.

[2] T. C. Koopmans, *Three Essays on the State of Economic Science*, New York, McGraw-Hill Book Company, Inc., 1957.

[3] A. Lösch, *The Economics of Location*, New Haven, Yale University Press, 1954.

[4] T. Vietorisz and A. S. Manne, 'Chemical Processes, Plant Location and Economies of Scale' in: A. S. Manne and H. M. Markowitz (eds.) *Studies in Process Analysis*, Cowles Foundation for Research in Economics at Yale University, Monograph 18, New York, John Wiley and Sons, 1963.

SOME REFLECTIONS ON THE EFFECTIVENESS OF PROJECT VERSUS PLAN AID*

J. P. PRONK and E. J. SCHREUEL

1. Introduction

1.1. Not only the volume, but also the type of aid is important with regard to its effectiveness. Several types of aid can be distinguished: capital aid and technical assistance, loans and grants, multilateral aid and bilateral aid, (procurement) tied aid and non-tied aid, plan, programme and project aid. Opinions differ rather widely about the degree of effectiveness of all these types of aid. For a considerable part this is due to different valuations of cost of or of revenues from the aid concerned. This is connected with the fact that in practice the aims of donors and recipients do not coincide, while moreover a donor usually does not supply all the means needed by the recipient (neither do all donors together). A more basic cause might be the fact that general statements about effectiveness are hardly possible because of the different circumstances in the various recipient countries, and the rather confusing way in which notions about aid are used.

This is especially true for the question as to whether aid should be given on the basis of plans, programmes or projects. In this article we will first summarize the different positions of the various authors with regard to this question and secondly give some numerical content to one of the issues involved, viz. the importance of the indirect effects of a project on investment requirements and the balance of payments. Because we have applied in these calculations the semi-input–output method a résumé of this method also has been included.

1.2. In evaluating the merits of the different kinds of aid considered it is

*) We would like to thank Professor H. C. Bos for his general comments on earlier drafts of this paper, without, of course, shifting to him the responsibility for what will be stated.

important to make it clear at the outset that we will consider as *the only relevant aim* of aid the development of the recipient country. 'Aid' given to further the commercial, political, and military interests of a donor cannot properly be considered as aid. (Cf. on these points Little and Clifford [5, chapter III].)

1.3. The arguments of the various participants in the discussion center mainly around the following questions:
(a) Is the development of the recipient the only aim of the assistance, or are there also other, perhaps conflicting, aims?
(b) Is the recipient or the donor considered to be the best judge of what is good for the attainment of the development aim?
(c) Are only the direct means needed and the direct returns taken into account, or also the indirect ones?

Before taking up these points in succession, we must define the different types of development assistance here considered.

1.4. Following the approach of Little and Clifford [5, p. 188], we define a project as 'any unit of expenditure, which, for reasons of administration, accounting or purpose, it is convenient to define as such'. *Project aid* may be defined as any such unit of expenditure (consisting of capital equipment, current inputs, skill, etc.) including the direct cost of the project only (i.e. disregarding the costs that arise in the sectors complementary to the project sector), allocated to further the development of the recipient. [1]) To be able to make a clearer distinction between the different types of aid, we introduce a new notion: *'bunch' aid*, which will be called aid tied to a bunch as introduced by Tinbergen in his semi-input–output method. A bunch may be defined for the moment as a project combined with its *necessary* complementary projects. The latter are the induced projects in those sectors of which the products cannot be imported. We will come back to this more fully in section 5. *Plan aid* will be defined as assistance to make possible a certain level of the total development expenditures, without reference to specific development projects. It seems useful to us to distinguish explicitly bunch aid from the other two types of aid. [2]) If aid for bunches is included in project

[1]) A more narrow concept, thus, than that of Little and Clifford.
[2]) We leave out from now on the concept of programme aid because of the confusing way in which it is used by different authors.

aid, too many different types of aid are brought under one heading. This does not contribute to clearness when one tries to judge these types of aid.

1.5. In order to appraise the merits and demerits of project, bunch, and plan aid we will choose project assistance, like most authors do, as our starting point. This seems rational because, as Carlin [2, p. 50] points out, project assistance can be considered plan aid – or in the same way bunch aid – with additional restrictions on its use. Indeed the most relevant question is that of the effectiveness of these restrictions.

2. Aims

Restrictions on the free disposal of aid funds by the recipient for other than developmental reasons will not be taken into consideration when appraising project or bunch aid as such, as was stated above. This means that all matters related to procurement tying can be neglected: 'there is no necessary connection between procurement- and project tying' [5, p. 289]. What remains is thus the question whether one of the three types of aid is more effective in furthering the development of the recipient than the others. This will be examined in the following sections.

3. Influence

3.1. It is generally agreed that the more ample availability of skills in and the greater experience of the donor countries give some weight to their view as to what constitutes development and what is good for the recipient. Moreover, the donor, though possibly agreeing with the recipient's views, may have no confidence in the recipient's ability either to formulate or to implement a development policy.

True, most countries formulate at least a short list of projects. This 'formulating' does not need to be the same as 'the technically sound preparation of a project', however. It is justifiable for the present argumentation to circumscribe it in a broad way, for instance as 'having the intention to implement a project'.

3.2. When the recipient does have this intention, a basic argument against the tying of aid to specific projects or bunches comes in: the well-known 'fungibility argument'. According to this argument, put forward very strongly by Singer [7, p. 539], 'the project actually financed by aid may be quite different from the one to which the aid is ostensibly tied'. Indeed, if the project (or bunch) to which the aid is tied, was already on the list formulated by the recipient, then the aid given enables the recipient to release resources set apart for this project and utilize them in order to add a new one (developmental or not). In this case the influence of the donor on the development policy of the recipient would be far less than it seems to be, depending on the amount set free (in the case of bunch aid it would even be nil). There appears to be no agreement among the various authors about the practical value of this argument. According to Little and Clifford [5, pp. 301–302]: 'This kind of re-direction of resources can occur only in countries whose governments include development among their objectives, and have a reasonably clear understanding of development priorities' and 'Such cases are much rarer than might appear at first sight'. Chenery [3, p. 15], on the other hand, states: 'There are many examples of well engineered projects in countries with poorly run economies in which their net contribution to development is very low', because of the re-direction of resources to which the fungibility argument refers. Be this as it may, it might be useful to trace two main lines of argumentation connected with the fungibility issue.

3.3. The first line of thought stresses that it would make more sense to tie the aid, if one wants to stick to aid given for projects[3]) to the marginal project made possible by the aid. This depends on the possibility of identifying the marginal project. Here too opinions diverge. Singer [7, p. 543] considers it to be 'inherently impossible except in rare circumstances'. In principle he is, in our opinion, right, because, as he points out, the identification would require two development plans of the recipient country: one without aid ('Plan I') and one with aid ('Plan II'). These plans will show a different composition of projects because of the interrelations of the various sectors. The greater amount of means available in Plan II together with existing capacities, indivisibilities, and market possibilities will lead to the inclusion in Plan II of projects which may or may not be identical with those in Plan I, but the first 'may well be carried out with a different technology, on a different scale and on a different time schedule'. To ascertain the composition of these plans a macro-model is needed. Many developing countries, however, do not have a sound macro-model. In these cases the

[3]) In the rest of section 3 one may read for project also bunch.

identification of marginal projects is not possible. The attempts of the I.D.A. to identify them in India, quoted by Carlin [2, p. 51] as an example of the actual identification of marginal projects, refers precisely to one of the rare cases a macro-model is available (assuming, moreover, that the attempts were theoretically sound).

Two remarks may be added. In the first place, if the donor wants to use his influence in an optimizing way, he has to appraise the total plan and to solve the macro-model of the economy of the recipient for two different amounts of foreign exchange available. In other words, when eventually the aid is given for the marginal project thus found it is no longer possible to speak of project aid: it has been combined with plan aid.

In the second place, many developing countries' governments, in the absence of a macro-model, will have only a faint notion of the priority of the various projects. Following Singer [8, p. 964] who states that 'Governments in their development plans clearly tend to identify development with new projects and new capacity rather than with increased output from existing capacity', it would seem probable that the choice of a donor, even when this choice is not made in an optimizing way based on a macro-model, but provided it is made to further development, will not coincide with the choice of the recipient. In this case there would be no fungibility issue at all.[4]) Here again the diverse experiences of Little and Clifford on the one hand and Chenery on the other come in. The fungibility issue can occur only in countries where a fairly sophisticated development policy exists. One's opinion about this will depend upon one's experiences.

3.4. The second line of thought stresses that, in spite of the fungibility issue, it is still useful to tie the assistance to specific projects because it will promote better implementation of these projects. Two main reasons are mentioned for this:

(i) the greater opportunity for the donor to exercise influence over the implementation of the projects nominally financed;

(ii) the greater opportunity for a better implementation of these projects by linking the transfer of know-how directly to the transfer of capital.

[4]) A conclusion contrary to the one of Singer [8, p. 164]: if the fungibility argument exists because donor governments (or private aid givers) make the same mistakes as the recipient governments, this cannot be used as an argument against project aid: it is an argument against the ways in which the aid is given.

The main differences between those involved in the discussion relate to the weights attached to these benefits.

3.4.1. With regard to the former argument two remarks can be made. First, the implementation of a project often has not been improved by the tying of aid to this project, but only retarded, because both the donor and the recipient must appraise, agree, and decide on the utilization of the funds. (Little [6, p. 57].)

The second remark is that project assistance implicitly means a choice between exercising influence on the project-level and on the macro-level in favour of the first. The tying of aid to specific projects may at best open opportunities for exercising influence on policies in sectors related to these projects. However, for a donor disagreeing with the recipient as to what contributes to development, or lacking confidence in the recipient's capacities to formulate or implement a development policy, it seems to be more rational to exert influence at the macro-level. In the framework of plan assistance the donors can look at total savings, total investments and its sectorial composition, taxation, employment, the balance of payments, and so on. A discussion of the basic issues of development policy, perhaps resulting in a better manipulation of these overall magnitudes, may in some cases contribute more to development than the more efficient carrying-out of individual projects. (Cf. Chenery [3, p. 21] and Little [6, p. 66].) Moreover, its contribution may well extend to individual projects, for the efficiency of each project depends on the soundness of the overall policy. Of course this emphasis on influence at the macro-level does not mean that individual projects should not be controlled at all; these controls, however, can be kept 'at the lower levels in the planning machinery and very often in the countries themselves' (Tinbergen [12, pp. 21 and 95]).

3.4.2. The latter argument is especially valid for countries in which lack of skills is the main bottleneck. Linking the transfer of know-how to the implementation of a project seems indeed a most appropriate way of giving this kind of aid. The importance of the transfer of know-how can also be exaggerated, however. De Vries [13], for instance, considers technical assistance of such an importance that he proposes that the nature of aid provided to a country be dependent on the range and extent of its technical assistance needs and that the aid be directed primarily to those sectors and projects where this need is greatest. This proposal suffers from the same shortcoming, namely one-sidedness, as that with which De Vries charges other authors. The nature of aid to a country must depend on the range and extent of its needs with regard to all means necessary for development. In some cases this will mean that special attention has to be given to the transfer of skills, while in other cases other means are the main impediments to an efficient implementation of the projects.

4. Indirect Effects

4.1. We come now to a most serious drawback of project aid as compared with bunch aid: the fact that in making the choice of a project donors and recipients often do not appraise all of the project's returns nor all of the cost it entails.

First considering the returns, frequently only direct effects are estimated. This should be understood in the general meaning of taking into account only the expected contribution to some partial target as well as in the more strict sense of disregarding the induced returns yielded by complementary sectors. Examples of the former are the contribution of a project in the health sector to a reduction in the death rate, of an agricultural project to the yield of certain crops or of an educational project to the increase of the stock of workers with a certain skill.

The only indirect effect which is generally mentioned is the demonstration function: a well-implemented directly aid-financed project will provide an incentive for developing a larger number of acceptable projects than otherwise would be the case. Carlin [2, p. 53] even proposes consideration of the proper functioning of this incentive as 'a meaningful measure of the recipient's performance and absorptive capacity', to be utilized by the donors as an objective guide in setting country aid levels. This built-in incentive would stand 'in marked contrast to programme aid (i.e. in our terminology plan aid), where the incentives normally work in the opposite direction, since the larger the balance of payments or budget deficit (the usual criteria, in absence of any objective criterion of performance), the larger the aid'. There are, however, other performance criteria available which can be used by donors giving plan aid, e.g. the increase in domestic savings, an induced change in the taxation policy or the progress made in land reform. In several cases these indicators will be of more importance for the development of the recipient than the demonstration function of a project.

Often, however, donors do not look at an indirect effect like the potential increase of domestic savings. To reckon with all effects, one should calculate the direct plus indirect contribution of the project to an overall target, preferably 'general welfare'. Because it is as yet impossible to measure this, a practical solution in the economic field could be the contribution to national income (possibly combined with employment and income distribution). This means that project aid proper, the choice of a project out of a list of 'priority' projects set up without reference to a macro-model, cannot be taken as contributing to maximizing development. The argument against project aid given here is of far greater importance than those connected with the fungibility issue. It points to the impossibility of looking at a project in isolation.

4.2. On the cost side the same neglect of the indirect effects prevails. Strangely enough less attention has been paid in the aid literature to this side than to the return side. Tinbergen [12, p. 20] states: 'The total import needs are not only caused by the direct foreign currency costs of the projects concerned but necessarily also by the indirect effects of the execution of these projects. There is nothing, given that the total plan of a country is sound, against financing these import needs even if not all of them are for investment but partly cover other types of expenditure.' The neglect of it, nevertheless, can be explained perhaps by a passage in Little and Clifford [5, p. 187]: 'In reality, in many economies, the degree to which projects and programmes are closely interrelated is limited. In any case one does not know exactly what the proper relation, or balance, is.' While we have strong reservations about the validity of the first statement, the second one is only too true. In section 6 we will give a numerical example based on an input–output table for India, which might give an impression of the order of magnitude of some of the indirect cost items as well as of the indirect contribution to national income. The amounts involved are such that it would pay for many developing countries first to turn their attention to the interrelations in their economy. In aid terms this means plan aid. Countries already disposing of a fairly good plan could get bunch aid too.

5. The Semi-Input–Output Method

5.1. In calculating the indirect effects of a project we will make use of the semi-input–output method. This method has been introduced by Tinbergen [9, pp. 92–99] and is meant primarily as a way to appraise sectors. A résumé of the method with its underlying assumptions will be given here, as far as it is necessary for our purpose.

The method rests on three basic assumptions:

(a) The development policy aims at a so-called 'ideal development process'. This is described in [11] as 'a process during which all existing capacities are being utilized, all qualified manpower needed is actually available and no shortages or surpluses occur'.

(b) A distinction can be made between domestic or national and international products of economic activity. The former cannot be imported or exported for technological, cultural or legal reasons.

(c) The normal assumptions about the production relationships of the input–output analysis are valid.

From assumptions (a) and (b) it follows that the productive capacity in the national sectors (the sectors which produce national products) is fully used to meet the demand for their products inside the country. An expansion of their capacities will be only required by the capacity expansion of one of the international sectors (or by a structural change in consumption; we will, however, take the consumption pattern as fixed). This means that it makes no sense to introduce a project in a national sector in isolation. An aid programme should always have as its core a project in an international sector. The combination of the international sector concerned with the complementary national sectors is called a bunch. A bunch thus comprises the repercussions of a project in an international sector on the production which *necessarily* has to be supplied by the domestic economy. The intermediate deliveries needed from other international sectors can always be imported and that is why they are taken as such in the semi-input–output method. This implies that, in calculating the indirect effects of a project with the semi-input–output method, one has to consider only the bunch of the project-sector. Having decided upon the level of production of the project-sector the induced production levels of the national sectors in the bunch can be calculated. Together these production levels determine the total need of investments and foreign exchange.

After this verbal treatment of the semi-input–output method we will set out its characteristics in the context of a simple model.

5.2. The following model (to be called 'Model I') describes an economy with H sectors of which H^* are international and $H-H^*$ are national. Prices are taken to be equal to unity. No time lag is supposed to exist between investment and the resulting capacity expansion. All Latin symbols refer to the differences between the values which the various magnitudes will take as a result of the capacity expansion of an international sector, implied by a project, and the values they would take without the project. Thus, these symbols do not refer to a change over time but to a difference in value during the same period. [5])

Variables:

v^h volume of production of sector h;
a^h volume of current inputs taking the form of product h;
c^h volume of consumption (private and public) of product h;
j^h volume of new investments (fixed investment goods as well as stock formation) taking the form of product h [6]);
e^h export minus import of product h;
y^h value added resulting from sector h;
s total saving.

Parameters:

$\alpha^{hh'}$ current input coefficient from sector h into sector h′;
γ^h propensity to consume product h;
$\iota^{hh'}$ partial incremental capital-output ratio from sector h into sector h';
σ marginal domestic savings ratio.

Model I:

For the international sectors:

$$v^h = a^h + c^h + j^h + e^h \quad (h = 1, \ldots, H^*) \tag{1}$$

For the national sectors:

$$v^h = a^h + c^h + j^h \qquad (h = H^* + 1, \ldots, H) \tag{2}$$

For all sectors:

$$a^h = \sum_{h'=1}^{H} \alpha^{hh'} v^{h'} \qquad (h = 1, \ldots, H) \tag{3}$$

---

[5]) The reader is warned that this way of defining the symbols differs from the one adopted in e.g. [9] or [10]. In these papers the symbols do refer to a change over time.
[6]) Deliveries to restore depreciated capital are of no relevance in our context.

$$j^h = \sum_{h'=1}^{H} \iota^{hh'} v^{h'} \qquad (h = 1, \ldots, H) \tag{4}$$

$$y^h = (1 - \sum_{h'=1}^{H} \alpha^{h'h})\, v^h \quad (h = 1, \ldots, H) \tag{5}$$

$$c^h = \gamma^h y \qquad (h = 1, \ldots, H) \tag{6}$$

$$s = \sigma y \tag{7}$$

$$y = \sum_{h=1}^{H} y^h \tag{8}$$

$$c = \sum_{h=1}^{H} c^h \tag{9}$$

$$j = \sum_{h=1}^{H} j^h \tag{10}$$

$$e = \sum_{h=1}^{H^*} e^h . \tag{11}$$

These equations will need no explanation except perhaps (4). Equation (4) is derived as follows:

Let the lower indices 1 and 0 stand for the present and immediately previous period, respectively; let a single bar indicate the absolute values which the variables would take without the project to be considered and a double bar indicate the absolute values of the variables including the project. Then we get:

$$\bar{\bar{j}}_1^h = \sum_{h'=1}^{H} \iota^{hh'} (\bar{\bar{v}}_1^{h'} - \bar{\bar{v}}_0^{h'}), \text{ in which } \bar{\bar{v}}_0^{h'} = \bar{v}_0^{h'} \text{ (no project at time 0)}$$

$$\bar{j}_1^h = \sum_{h'=1}^{H} \iota^{hh'} (\bar{v}_1^{h'} - \bar{v}_0^{h'})$$

$$- \overline{\qquad\qquad\qquad\qquad}$$

$$j^h = \sum_{h'=1}^{H} \iota^{hh'} (\bar{\bar{v}}_1^{h'} - \bar{v}_1^{h'})$$

$$= \sum_{h'=1}^{H} \iota^{hh'} v^{h'} .^{7)}$$

The semi-input–output method takes the v^h of the international sector to be appraised (say sector 1) equal to an arbitrary value (say x) and the v^{h}'s of

[7]) We are indebted to Professor H. C. Bos for pointing out to us the possibility of defining the symbols in this way.

all the other international sectors equal to zero. Characteristic of this method thus are the following equations:

$$v^1 = x \tag{12}$$

$$v^h = 0 \quad (h = 2, \ldots, H^*). \tag{13}$$

From the national accounts identity it follows as a side condition:

$$\sum_{h=1}^{H} \gamma^h + \sigma = 1 . \tag{14}$$

There are $5H + H^* + 5$ independent linear equations. The number of variables equals $H(v^h) + H(a^h) + H(c^h) + H(j^h) + H^*(e^h) + H(y^h) + 5(s, y, c, j,$ and $e)$ or $5H + H^* + 5$ too. Thus, the system gives a unique solution. This may be shown more clearly by reducing the system to equations containing only v^1 and the macro-variables ($y, c, j, e,$ and s). The reduced system (*Model I'*) will read:

$$v^1 = x \tag{12}$$

$$y = \varphi^1 v^1 \tag{15}$$

$$j = \psi^1 v^1 , \tag{16}$$

in which φ^1 and ψ^1 are combinations of the $\alpha^{hh'}$, γ^h and $\iota^{hh'}$,

$$s = \sigma y \tag{7}$$

while by definition

$$c \equiv y - s , \tag{17}$$

and as a residual will follow

$$e \equiv s - j . \tag{18}$$

It will be clear that there is no reason to suppose $e = 0$, i.e. balance of payments equilibrium. This will come about if $\psi = \sigma\varphi$. Such an equality would be merely a matter of chance. Adding the equation $s = j$ would either mean introduction of a redundant equation or make the model inconsistent. If one wants, nevertheless, to impose the condition of balance of payments equilibrium, one of the equations in Model I' has to be abandoned or a new variable has to be introduced. One is not, of course, free in choosing

this equation or variable. To keep the system consistent the changes have to be in either (16) or (7). Two possibilities are thus open:
Abandoning (16) leads to the following

Model II:

$$v^1 = x \tag{12}$$
$$y = \varphi^1 v^1 \tag{15}$$
$$s = \sigma y \tag{7}$$
$$c \equiv y - s \tag{17}$$
$$e \equiv s - j \tag{18}$$
$$s = j\,. \tag{19}$$

For Model I this change implies leaving out (10) and replacing (4) in either of two ways, by:

$$j^h = \iota^h j \text{ with the side condition } \sum \iota^h = 1\,, \tag{4a}$$

or

$$j^h = \sigma^h y \text{ with the side condition } \sum \sigma^h = \sigma\,. \tag{4b}$$

Both equations say that the composition of the investments is always the same independent of the bunch considered.
Abandoning (7) leads to

Model III:

$$v^1 = x \tag{12}$$
$$y = \varphi^1 v^1 \tag{15}$$
$$j = \psi^1 v^1 \tag{16}$$
$$c \equiv y - s \tag{17}$$
$$e \equiv s - j \tag{18}$$
$$s = j\,. \tag{19}$$

In fact this case means that σ becomes variable. To keep the consumption equations in Model I consistent, one could make the c^h's dependent on the available income, i.e. $y - s$. In Model I, thus, (7) should be left out and (6) and (14) replaced by:

$$c^h = \gamma^h (y - s)\,, \tag{6a}$$

and

$$\sum \gamma^h = 1\,. \tag{14a}$$

5.3. We may now compare the three models. All are based on assumptions (a), (b) and (c) from section 5.1. With respect to the implicit assumptions about the scarcity of capital and foreign exchange the three models differ, however.

In Model I the domestic savings ratio is fixed but the balance of payments follows as a residual. This could be interpreted to mean that possible foreign exchange needs can be taken for granted, i.e. the size of balance of payments effects is mainly of importance as a guide to short-term domestic policy and to the aid policy of donors. The criteria for appraisal would then take into account only the ratio between j and y (or another aim of economic policy, not, however, included in the model, such as employment or income distribution). It may be noted that this criterion will give the same ranking of the sectors as the ranking according to balance of payments effect *per unit of value added.* From (18) it follows:

$$s \equiv j + e,$$

and from (7)

$$\frac{s}{y} = \sigma,$$

which together give:

$$\sigma = \frac{j}{y} + \frac{e}{y}.$$

As long as σ is constant, investments per unit of value added and balance of payments effect per unit of value added must move in opposite directions. In general one is interested, however, in the absolute balance of payments effect, and this if used as a criterion for appraisal, would give another ranking.

Model II implies balance of payments equilibrium. Moreover a fixed ratio between j and y is implied, i.e. the criterion for selecting sectors has in all cases the same value ($=\sigma$). There is nothing to appraise. This seems a highly improbable picture of reality.

Model III implies, besides balance of payments equilibrium, that the σ which follows from (15) and (19), can be realized. The stress is on the scarcity of foreign exchange. This model is the opposite of Model I.

We think we can omit further consideration of Model II, because of its poor description of reality. With the other two models we have, in fact, come near the 'gap problem': which 'gap' is dominant? Model I considers domestic savings as the more important bottleneck, while in Model III the basic restrictions are assumed to be imposed by the foreign currency available.

6. Numerical Example of the Indirect Effects of a Project

6.1. After this digression into the characteristics of the method used for our calculations we will present their results.[8]) For each of the international sectors distinguished we have calculated the total as well as the direct effect of a capacity expansion of the international sector concerned with respect to the following magnitudes: value added, fixed investments and stock formation (both national and international), and the balance of payments. These subdivisions make it possible not only to point to the importance of indirect effects in general, but also to the quantitative consequences of tying aid solely to the import content or solely to the fixed capital needs of a project or a bunch. The latter subjects have not been dealt with so far, because they are not necessarily connected with project or bunch aid; nevertheless such a link is often made.

In [4] the Indian economy is aggregated into eleven sectors; these sectors are, with the numbers as indicated in the appendix:

1. Agriculture and plantation 2. Mining and metals 3. Equipment 4. Chemicals 5. Cement, glass, wooden products, etc. 6. Food, clothing and leather	International sectors
7. Electricity 8. Transport 9. Construction 10. Housing 11. Others and margin.	National sectors

In deciding which sectors will be considered as national and which as international we have based ourselves on the figures given in [4] for the

[8]) We are obliged to Messrs. R. S. Eckaus and K. S. Parikh who permitted us to use some of the tables compiled under their guidance and published in [4]. These tables are given in the appendix.

Fourth Plan Period (1966/67–1970/71). The first six sectors are clearly international, sectors 7–10 clearly national. Sector 11 – 'including other industries, other transport and commerce and services' – constitutes a difficulty. It comprises an important part of the national part of the economy (domestic commerce and services). Because of its heterogeneous character, however, projected exports amount to 13% of total exports. On the other hand its competitive imports are set at zero. In one of the two projections made in [4] for the Fourth Plan period, the same applies to the non-competitive imports. These features of the sector provide grounds for considering it as national – as we have done – when appraising bunches connected with the first six sectors.

Three sectors – 3, 9, and 11 – supply fixed investment goods. Deliveries for stock formation are made by all international sectors (and none by the national sectors).

The model used by us in calculations, is Model I described in section 5. A small refinement has been made by distinguishing explicitly between fixed investment and stock formation. This distinction will be indicated by:

${}^{1}\iota^{hh'}$ = partial incremental fixed capital–output ratio from sector h into sector h';

${}^{2}\iota^{hh'}$ = inventory-output coefficient from sector h into sector h'.

Equation (4) should now be read as:

$$j^h = \sum_{h'=1}^{H} \left({}^{1}\iota^{hh'} + {}^{2}\iota^{hh'}\right) v^{h'} . \tag{20}$$

6.2. The solution of the endogenous variables in the model is a very simple one. First the increases in the production levels of the national sectors (2) are expressed in terms of the given increase in the output of the international sectors to be appraised by using (3), (20), (5), and (6). All production volumes are now known. The investment needs are linearly dependent on these production volumes according to (20) and follow thus directly from (20) and (10).

To calculate the balance of payments effect the only thing one still needs to know is s, which can be derived easily from (5), (8), and (7). With the national accounts identity (18), given in Model I′, e is then determined.

Our results have been put together in table 1. For convenience we have set x in (12) equal to 1.

TABLE 1

	Bunch connected with sector					
	1	2	3	4	5	6
	Agriculture and plantation	Mining and metals	Equipment	Chemicals	Cement, glass, etc.	Food, clothing and leather
Capacity expansion of the international sector to be appraised						
1. Agriculture and plantation	1					
2. Mining and metals		1				
3. Equipment			1			
4. Chemicals				1		
5. Cement, glass, etc.					1	
6. Food, clothing and leather						1
Required expansion of gross output levels of the national sectors						
7. Electricity	0.006	0.028	0.015	0.020	0.026	0.016
8. Transport	0.125	0.273	0.141	0.175	0.143	0.091
9. Construction	2.594	2.392	1.200	1.362	1.306	0.646
10. Housing	0.104	0.096	0.059	0.064	0.063	0.034
11. Others and margin	1.185	1.313	0.850	0.816	0.839	0.480
12. Total value added	3.590	3.325	2.051	2.217	2.179	1.189
13. Direct value added	0.890	0.503	0.442	0.521	0.512	0.284
14. Total investments	4.028	5.207	2.749	3.173	2.635	1.786
of which international	1.367	2.568	1.443	1.695	1.234	1.066
15. All direct investments	1.902	2.713	1.339	1.583	1.098	0.917
of which international	0.601	1.482	0.876	1.025	0.619	0.710
16. All fixed investments	3.443	4.786	2.271	2.539	2.296	1.374
of which international	0.783	2.148	0.965	1.061	0.895	0.654
17. Fixed direct investments	1.509	2.477	0.955	1.055	0.862	0.557
of which international	0.208	1.246	0.492	0.497	0.383	0.350
18. Total balance of payments effect (minus)	2.861	4.126	2.082	2.453	1.926	1.399
19. Direct balance of payments effect (minus)	0.725	1.130	0.761	0.458	0.217	0.425

It might be useful to indicate in symbols the precise content of the different rows. The sector being appraised will be indicated by the index p (of project):

Rows	*Formula or symbol*
1–6	$v^p = x = 1;$
7–11	$v^h \quad (h = 7, \ldots, 11);$
12	$y;$
13	$y^p;$
14	$\sum_{h'=1}^{11} \sum_{h=1}^{11} ({}^1\iota^{hh'} + {}^2\iota^{hh'})\, v^{h'} = j,$ international: $h = 1, \ldots, 6;$
15	$\sum_{h=1}^{11} ({}^1\iota^{hp} + {}^2\iota^{hp})\, v^p,$ international: $h = 1, \ldots, 6;$
16	$\sum_{h'=1}^{11} \sum_{h=1}^{11} {}^1\iota^{hh'} v^{h'},$ international: $h = 3;$
17	$\sum_{h=1}^{11} {}^1\iota^{hp} v^p,$ international: $h = 3;$
18	$j - \sigma y = e;$
19	$v^p - \sum_{h=7}^{11} (\alpha^{ph} + {}^1\iota^{ph} + {}^2\iota^{ph})\, v^h - \sum_{h=1}^{6} (\alpha^{hp} + {}^1\iota^{3p} + {}^2\iota^{hp})\, v^p - \gamma^p y.$

To get a clearer picture of the consequences of tying aid to part only of the total investment needs of a project, table 2 has been set up.

Insofar as these findings for India can be generalized, we think they are

TABLE 2

	Bunch connected with sector					
	1	2	3	4	5	6
I Percentage of total investments neglected when considering only						
fixed direct investments	63	52	65	67	67	69
all direct investments	53	48	51	50	58	49
all fixed investments	15	8	17	20	13	23
II Percentage of the total need of international investment goods neglected when considering only						
fixed direct investments	85	51	66	71	69	67
all direct investments	56	42	39	40	50	33
all fixed investments	43	16	33	37	27	39
III Indirect balance of payments effect as a percentage of total balance of payments effect	75	73	63	81	89	70

a strong argument against project aid. When project aid, as is usually the case, takes into account *fixed direct* investments only, a heavy burden is put on the recipient country. This is the evidence of part I of table 2. The burden varies from an amount about equal to the aid given (sector 2) to an amount as high as double the aid (sectors 4, 5 and 6). When project aid includes also the stock formation part of direct investments, the recipient still has to finance investments to the amount of the aid. From the third line of I it appears that in most cases stock formation constitutes a considerable part of total investments. Thus, even when aid considers the indirect investment needs, it may not be justifiable to neglect stock formation.

In several recipient countries the semi-input–output assumption that international goods are imported, may be valid, especially as far as the investments are concerned. Part II of table 2 gives an impression of the foreign exchange burden left to such a recipient when aid is given to finance the import content of a project's *direct* investments or even of its total *fixed* investments only. Even neglecting current inputs of international goods for the moment, balance of payments problems are not solved by aid financing on such a limited basis. In many cases they will only be starting because the execution of the project depends on the availability of the international investment goods indirectly required or of the goods necessary for stock formation. All this applies also to sector 3, the only sector which supplies international fixed investment goods. Although in the case in which this sector is expanded these goods will not be imported, the negative effect on the balance of payments will remain, because less will be left for export.

Part III of table 2 shows the considerable mistake which is made, in a situation of scarce foreign exchange, when attention is directed solely to the *direct* balance of payments effect of a project, even when imported current inputs are also – as here – considered.

6.3. The figures given in table 1 may also be used to rank the international sectors on the basis of a criterion which measures the investment cost per unit of value added created. According to whether one takes into account the *total* investments, the *direct* investments only or *fixed* investments only, different ways of ranking can be distinguished. These are to be found in table 3. For comparison we have added the ranking which follows when using as a criterion the absolute balance of payments effect (total as well as direct). The numbers in table 3 refer to the rows in table 1.

TABLE 3

	Bunch connected with sector					
	1	2	3	4	5	6
Criterion of investments per unit of value added calculated as the quotient of						
(14) and (12)	1.12	1.57	1.34	1.43	1.21	1.50
(15) and (13)	2.14	5.39	3.03	3.04	2.14	3.23
(16) and (12)	0.96	1.44	1.11	1.15	1.05	1.16
(17) and (13)	1.70	4.92	2.16	2.02	1.68	1.96
Rank according to investment criteria						
(14):(12) } bunch approach	1	6	3	4	2	5
(16):(12) } bunch approach	1	6	3	4	2	5
(15):(13) } project approach	1/2	6	3	4	1/2	5
(17):(13) } project approach	2	6	5	4	1	3
Rank according to foreign exchange criteria						
(18)-bunch approach	5	6	3	4	2	1
(19)-project approach	4	6	5	3	1	2

Some interesting conclusions may be drawn from this table:
Firstly, neglecting stock formation does not seem to be of any importance in ranking the sectors according to the bunch approach.
Secondly, taking into account the direct investments only, also makes scarcely any difference.
Thirdly, restricting one's consideration to the fixed direct investments changes the ranking considerably.
Fourthly, using the foreign exchange criterion with the bunch approach appears only to interchange two sectors compared with the result given by the corresponding investment criteria.
Fifthly, considering only the direct balance of payments effect gives an important change in ranking in comparison with all other criteria.

The second and fourth conclusion are of special interest. The former might be thought to imply, given the possibility of generalizing our findings, that one does not need to consider the indirect effects when ranking the sectors. It may be added, however, that our ranking of the sectors is based on a very simple model indeed. It does not take into account the several 'bounds' that exist in reality, such as export restrictions imposed by outside governments, import restrictions by domestic governments, insufficient demand on the world markets, or the impossibility of carrying out a project below a certain minimum size (the so-called 'indivisibilities'). Introducing such bounds may well lead to a ranking order different, except in the case of the most preferable sector, to that found using the semi-input–output method and given by us. This is shown in the paper by P. A. Cornelisse and J. Versluis in this book, for the case of export restrictions.

The fourth conclusion might be interpreted as meaning that there is no good reason to include balance of payments effects in the appraisal (this is in accordance with the 'background' assumption of Model I as indicated in section 5.3). It should be pointed out, however, that the interchanging sectors are just at the extremes of the range. Besides, when investment goods as well as foreign exchange are scarce, the right procedure would necessarily be to consider both, using a weighted criterion. It remains to be seen what ranking would then result.

7. Conclusions

In the discussion, in the literature to which reference has been made, of what type of aid to give, many arguments for and against the several types have already been put forward. The reader is referred especially to the book by Little and Clifford [5]. We have merely tried to highlight some of the central issues by stripping the arguments of political overtones and ignoring all the various ways of built-in self-protection used by donors. As soon as this sort of considerations is taken into account one is faced with another subject: a critical study of the practices of aid giving. A lot could and should be said about this: in many cases these attendant considerations render it impossible to speak of aid proper. Of course, as Balogh [1] states, for the moment 'the alternative to (procurement) tying aid is cutting it; under these conditions I prefer tying'. One should not stop here, however. An intensive educational process will be needed to impress upon the governments (and general public) of the donor countries the notion that aid should be given in the most effective way, i.e. rendering a maximum contribution to the development of the recipient.

We have deliberately stressed in this paper the importance of the indirect effects of a project. Hitherto, inadequate attention has been devoted to this aspect; it has been dealt with largely 'in passing'. If our findings for India may be generalized they indicate clearly the inadequacy of looking at a project in isolation. The first thing needed by the recipient countries is a plan if insurmountable bottlenecks and consequent wasting of aid are to be avoided. For the donor countries this will mean giving plan aid and thus mutual cooperation – in multilateral organization or otherwise – because most donors are too small to be able to afford the machinery needed to assist recipient countries in preparing a plan. For the recipient countries it means accepting foreign influence at the macro-level. How far they are willing to do this is again a point of disagreement between Little and Chenery [6, pp. 56, 65, and 67]. One may argue that if both the donor and the recipient aim at development, less objection against foreign influence at the macro-level must exist on the part of the recipient.

Although we emphasize the importance of directing the development assistance efforts to plan aid, most developing countries for lack of technical know-how cannot dispense with technical assistance for specific projects. This kind of aid should be looked at, however, in the context of an appraisal of the general needs of the recipient and, therefore, need not be the major subject of international negotiations.

Appendix

TABLE 4

Coefficients of the current input–output matrix ($\alpha^{hh'}$).

Sector	1	2	3	4	5	6	7	8	9	10	11
1	0.079	0.000	0.010	0.048	0.134	0.502	0.000	0.000	0.035	0.000	0.035
2	0.000	0.235	0.263	0.027	0.048	0.004	0.131	0.037	0.118	0.005	0.001
3	0.000	0.018	0.033	0.014	0.003	0.003	0.000	0.000	0.013	0.000	0.000
4	0.010	0.023	0.030	0.198	0.082	0.029	0.028	0.202	0.006	0.000	0.003
5	0.000	0.013	0.005	0.011	0.026	0.003	0.000	0.000	0.180	0.015	0.000
6	0.008	0.002	0.002	0.034	0.015	0.056	0.000	0.000	0.000	0.000	0.001
7	0.001	0.023	0.012	0.016	0.022	0.014	0.000	0.004	0.000	0.000	0.001
8	0.007	0.150	0.071	0.099	0.068	0.050	0.118	0.043	0.018	0.007	0.021
9	0.000	0.000	0.000	0.000	0.000	0.000	0.000	0.000	0.000	0.000	0.000
10	0.000	0.000	0.000	0.000	0.000	0.000	0.000	0.000	0.000	0.000	0.000
11	0.005	0.033	0.132	0.032	0.090	0.055	0.068	0.018	0.090	0.045	0.000
y^h/v^h	0.890	0.503	0.442	0.521	0.512	0.284	0.655	0.696	0.540	0.928	0.938

Source: tables 3–5 in [4, Volume II].

TABLE 5

Sector shares of (public and private) consumption in value added (γ^h).

Sector	γ^h
1	0.242
2	0.000
3	0.024
4	0.022
5	0.004
6	0.099
7	0.001
8	0.011
9	0.010
10	0.029
11	0.233
$\Sigma\gamma^h$	0.675
σ	0.325

Source: tables 3–23 and 3–24 in [4, Volume II].

TABLE 6

Coefficients of the inventory-output ($^{2}\iota^{hh'}$) and fixed investments-output matrices ($^{1}\iota^{hh'}$).

	Sector	1	2	3	4	5	6	7	8	9	10	11
$^{2}\iota^{hh'}$	1	0.318	0.000	0.011	0.076	0.102	0.302	0.000	0.000	0.007	0.000	0.007
	2	0.001	0.190	0.295	0.042	0.037	0.003	0.106	0.003	0.023	0.000	0.000
	3	0.000	0.015	0.037	0.023	0.002	0.002	0.000	0.000	0.003	0.000	0.000
	4	0.041	0.019	0.033	0.315	0.063	0.017	0.023	0.016	0.001	0.000	0.001
	5	0.002	0.010	0.006	0.018	0.020	0.002	0.000	0.000	0.035	0.000	0.000
	6	0.031	0.002	0.002	0.054	0.012	0.034	0.000	0.000	0.000	0.000	0.000
ICOR *) for stock formation		0.393	0.236	0.384	0.528	0.236	0.360	0.129	0.019	0.069	0.000	0.008
	Sector											
$^{1}\iota^{hh'}$	3	0.208	1.246	0.492	0.497	0.383	0.350	2.529	1.923	0.100	0.000	0.050
	9	1.274	1.070	0.399	0.494	0.429	0.161	3.399	0.000	0.040	10.000	0.100
	11	0.027	0.161	0.064	0.064	0.050	0.046	0.332	0.250	0.013	0.000	0.000
ICOR *) for new fixed capital formation		1.509	2.477	0.955	1.055	0.862	0.557	6.260	2.173	0.153	10.000	0.157
Total ICOR *)		1.902	2.713	1.339	1.583	1.098	0.917	6.389	2.192	0.222	10.000	0.165

*) Incremental capital–output ratio.
Source: tables 3–8 and 3–11 in [4, Volume II].

References

[1] T. Balogh, 'Multilateral v. Bilateral Aid', *Oxford Economic Papers*, Vol. 19, no. 3 (1967), pp. 328–344.

[2] A. Carlin, 'Project Versus Programme Aid: From the Donor's Viewpoint', *The Economic Journal*, 305 (1967), pp. 48–58.

[3] H. B. Chenery, 'The effectiveness of foreign assistance' in H. B. Chenery et al., *Towards a Strategy for Development Co-operation*. Rotterdam, Universitaire Pers Rotterdam, 1967.

[4] R. S. Eckaus and K. S. Parikh, *Planning for Growth. Multi-sectoral, Intertemporal Models applied to India* (Draft, For Discussion Only). Cambridge, Center for International Studies, Massachusetts Institute of Technology, 1966.

[5] I. M. D. Little and J. M. Clifford, *International Aid*. London, George Allen and Unwin Ltd., 1965.

[6] I. M. D. Little, 'Aid: project, programme, and procurement tying' in H. B. Chenery et al., *Towards a Strategy for Development Co-operation*. Rotterdam, Universitaire Pers Rotterdam, 1967.

[7] H. W. Singer, 'External Aid: For Plans or Projects?', *The Economic Journal*, 299 (1965), pp. 539–545.

[8] H. W. Singer, 'Project Versus Programme Aid: A Rejoinder', *The Economic Journal*, 308 (1967), pp. 963–964.

[9] J. Tinbergen, *Development Planning*. London, Weidenfeld and Nicolson Ltd., 1967, and New York, McGraw-Hill Book Company, 1967.

[10] J. Tinbergen, 'Some Refinements of the Semi-Input–Output Method', *The Pakistan Development Review*, Vol. VI, no. 2 (1966), pp. 243–247.

[11] J. Tinbergen, 'Balance of Payments and Project Appraisal', *mimeographed*.

[12] J. Tinbergen, 'Discussion' to [3] and 'Concluding remarks' in H. B. Chenery et al., *Towards a Strategy for Development Co-operation*. Rotterdam, Universitaire Pers Rotterdam, 1967.

[13] B. A. De Vries, 'External Aid: For Plans or Projects? An Alternative Approach', *The Economic Journal*, 307 (1967), pp. 653–655.

FROM MACRO TO MICRO – AND BACK*

SOME THOUGHTS OF A B.I.G. MAN WHO WENT INTO BIG BUSINESS**

J. C. RAMAER

Utterly Useless at first

Transferring from the macro-sphere into the micro-realm of an enterprise appears to be requiring quite some effort of adaptation from many economists. That at least was the author's experience, and it made him reflect on the reasons why. Those reasons may give some insight into the gap between the macro and the micro approach in development.

What explains that feeling of utter uselessness at first? The author was considered 'theoretical' and sometimes narrow-minded, and he had difficulties in making himself understood. Probably two reasons dominated.

Understanding and Jargon

In the first place the author discovered the big problem of making oneself understood to the many people in an enterprise who do not know economic jargon and who are not particularly interested in learning it, because they are busy enough doing their own job. This problem can be solved of course, especially when it has got to be solved. Why talk about 'inflation' when the term 'rising prices' can do the job in the context of the conversation or report? Why talk about 'deficit on the balance of payments' when 'shortage of foreign currency' is more clear and understandable? The art of making oneself understood to specialists of other disciplines has to be mastered

---

*) This article is a 'joint venture'. Prof. Dr. A. van Doorn, Drs. S. de Leve, Dr. J. van Rees and Dr. L. Traas supplied know-how on the subject matter by spending much time and patience on manuscripts. Mr. G. E. Luton and Mrs. E. A. Ramaer commented on the English, while Miss E. Enkelstroth did a considerable deal of typing. Without all this assistance the job could not have been finished in time.

**) B.I.G. stands for the Division of Balanced International Growth of the Netherlands Economic Institute.

if an inter-disciplinary team is ever to become a success, and in many ways an enterprise is such a team. Without that art, such a 'team' becomes a repetition of the old story of the tower of Babel.[1]) Unfortunately many people do not seem interested in trying to exercise the art of making themselves understood, often for snobbish reasons. Moreover, only very few listeners or readers will openly admit that they do not understand the jargon of another discipline because they are unwilling to confess their ignorance, which is a form of snobbism too.

Abstraction, a Luxury

In the second place the author discovered what an incredible luxury the high level of abstraction is to which he was accustomed in academic circles. Two forms of abstraction may be mentioned here:

(a) abstraction from the complexity of the real world, including the unpredictable performance of certain human beings whose role is vital to certain projects or other micro-economic achievements. These factors seem to cancel out in mathematical well-behaving closed functions with anonymous 'aggregates' or 'residual factors' in the case of macro-analysis[2]) due to the law of numbers;

(b) abstraction from the past and the present and a lack of foresight.

a. The complexity of the real world

Abstraction may cause irrelevant and therefore unnecessary thinking and research. An economic analysis of a country may show that it makes sense to establish a factory, but the analysis will prove to have been unnecessary after all if the technical man can show that a factory cannot be established

---

[1]) See '*Neue Zürcher Zeitung*', August 23, 1967. The article 'Forscher und Praktiker' by Edmond Tondeur offers some interesting views on the problem, leading to the conclusion that universities will have to pay more attention to this communication problem.

[2]) On pp. 547/8 of Moag [2] the problem is expressed as follows: 'Thus, although it is useful to think of a firm as a fixed system fully under the control of the models of its metasystem, the realities of economic and business activity seldom permit closed systems which fully account for all the significant activities of the firm. The model set, as a result, is most often ad hoc and variable. People change their preferences, new technologies evolve and environments change radically. The models of the metasystem are probabilistic; for information about the environment and the system is either partial or unreliable or both. In effect, as information develops or is corrected, the metasystem itself changes.'

In Chapter 3 Traas [6] explains the impossibility of formulating closed models that can produce operational conclusions.

for compelling reasons having to do with scale of production, power supply, etc. The man making the analysis of the country should, therefore, have some notion of what stumbling blocks there might be in other fields. Such notions may prevent him from starting a great deal of unnecessary work. They will enable him to develop a feeling about what people to contact before he proceeds. A sense for these things is characteristic of so-called 'practical people'.

Another and even greater danger of abstraction is that it can lead to inconsistencies – not to inconsistencies in the reasoning carried out in the sphere limited by the abstraction – but to inconsistencies when that reasoning is confronted with the conclusion drawn from fields beyond it. For instance, during an international conference the author heard a fine analysis of the market for glass in a certain area. The analysis showed a glass plant to be quite feasible. Returning home, he spoke to the manager of a glass plant, only to find out that one could lump together the demand for different types of glass in demand statistics, but not in the technical process of making the types of glass. Thus it happens to be a fact that the glass from which bottles are made is quite different from that used for making electric bulbs. The abstraction from these technical realities had made the conclusions of the analysis useless to anybody concerned with the real world of a glass plant and the responsibility of making it viable, both technically and economically.

Surprisingly enough one often sees an abstraction made from the performance of human being in the micro-realm. Proper attention to this factor is essential to the proper functioning of an enterprise. In a way the term 'technological gap' as used to express the backwardness of Europe in comparison with the U.S.A. is an example of this type of abstraction. A gap largely caused by a lack of creative management in political and business affairs in Western Europe is dubbed 'technological'.[3])

Another example of this abstraction: labour-intensive techniques are being propagated for developing countries, on the basis of well-known purely economic reasons. However, it is only too often forgotten in this connection

[3]) Discussing U.S. investments in Western Europe Servan-Schreiber [5] writes on page 23: 'Car nous n'assistons pas à un débordement de dollars qui ne trouveraient pas à s'employer aux Etats-Unis, et qu'une conjoncture plus ou moins passagère orienterait vers le Marché Commun, mais – ce qui est nouveau et autrement plus grave – au déploiement sur le sol européen d'un *art de l'organisation* auquel nous demeurons étrangers.'

that a labour-intensive production process may require more foremen and managerial staff. Such men may be even scarcer than capital. If they are not available in sufficient numbers, a labour-intensive plant may end up very capital-intensive due to the waste caused by a lack of available management.[4])

Again in propagating certain instruments of economic policy, economists seem to have little regard for the consequences in terms of work for the machinery of government and the administration of business enterprises. One example is the idea of subsidising labour employed in industry. In itself the economic logic is quite understandable. Such subsidies could lead to more labour-intensive production processes. However, what would such a scheme mean in terms of administration and consequently in staff required? That problem – crucial for both government and business in all developing countries – is only too often shelved away in the intellectual ice-box of abstraction. Of course it would de-freeze and come to life if an attempt were made to apply such a scheme in practice. By then it might prove to be rather awkward.

On similar grounds the advisability of propagating modern comprehensive planning methods in many developing countries can be questioned. A considerable degree of abstraction from personnel problems often seems to have led to a disappointing performance. To make a comparison: propagating sophisticated comprehensive planning in developing countries with a serious shortage of qualified personnel is like installing sophisticated machinery in a plant that has insufficient trained personnel to handle and repair it.[5])

---

[4]) On problems of labour-intensive and capital-intensive techniques Joan Robinson [3] makes some observations that seem refreshing: 'To find a way through the fog, we may first propose two simple rules which appeal to common sense. First, no equipment should be scrapped or methods of production rejected so long as the materials used with them and the labour operating them cannot find a better use elsewhere. The best techniques must be embodied in new investment, but the new does not replace the old; it works beside it. Until all workers are equipped with the best, inferior equipment is better than none. Second, no technique should be chosen just because it gives employment. The object of the operation is not to be able to count the largest total of statistical employment but to increase production. (It is misleading to state the question in terms of labour-intensive techniques. The advantage of the handicrafts lies in being capital-saving, not in being labour-using.)' (pp. 114–115).

[5]) Waterston [7] writes: 'A comprehensive plan can be, and often is, completed in less developed countries by a few technicians, especially when assisted by foreign experts, without much recourse to the governmental machinery. But it is usually impossible for a government to prepare and carry out numerous projects without heavy reliance on its

One may say: of course, but abstraction is only a first step. The boundaries of abstraction should be widened step by step. But all too often we stop after the first step or at least a number of steps before the last! This is something a manager *just cannot* afford. He is responsible for making his organization work. To him pure intellectual abstraction is therefore an exercise that serves little purpose. He must have concrete indications on the action to be taken and therefore he must have overall conclusions.

There is another reason why he tends to feel abstraction to be of little use to this problem. Eliminating abstraction is often a time-consuming process, even when this is done by an interdisciplinary team whose members are able to communicate effectively with each other. Discussions by such teams of a management decision often end by the responsible manager 'taking a plunge' on an intuitive basis. He cannot restrict himself to a discussion, he must take action, *and he must therefore come to operational conclusions before a certain date – he is usually short of time.* He has only one advantage: not all decisions have to be taken here and now. Many can be taken at a later date, when more information is available. A 'plunge' in coming to operational decisions is also inevitable for other reasons having to do with a lack of data on past and present and a lack of foresight.

b. Lack of data and foresight

There is always a lack of data – both about past and present. Very often statistics do not offer the break-down one needs, a well-known deficiency due to the fact that they were drawn up on the basis of past needs that have become obsolete in the meantime. It is not possible to regroup them, or even if it is, there is just no time to do it, or it is too expensive[6]).

Along with incomplete insight into past and present, perfect foresight into the future does not exist. Aggregates like national product or consumer expenditure may be predictable for a few years into the future within a certain margin of error. However, as soon as a forecast of a certain part of

---

administrative apparatus. The government may obtain foreign technicians and contractors to help, but because of the character, volume, and continuing nature of project preparation and execution, great reliance must be placed on the government services.' (p. 87).

[6]) The author recently heard one striking example of incomplete statistics for micro-purposes. Population statistics of some of the most developed Western European countries appeared insufficient to make an analysis of markets for certain products possible. Certain 'abstractions' had to be made in order to make an analysis possible at all. Further research and some samples produced results that proved valuable to the official statistical bureaux.

these aggregates has to be made, 100% deviations from predicted growth rates within two years are no exception. The reason for this is well-known. The law of numbers does not work in these cases.

The economist entering business may believe at first that technical processes are at least predictable. He will soon learn that this is the case only in too few instances. It is not only the technical evolution and the market that cause trouble, but also human factors like management, etc. These factors, often treated as a 'residual' in many macro-models may fool micro-predictions by factors of 100% within a few years, even in cases where the technical process was well-known when the design was made. In some cases it may make a very big difference: the difference between the life and death of a project or company.

In short, the hard facts prove that forecasts of specific aggregates of statistical series are of much less use in the micro-field than in the macro-field. Nevertheless this truth offers a challenge. There is first of all the game of narrowing down the margin of error. Incidentally, this term seems a bit euphemistic. Instead of narrowing down the margin of error, it would be more correct to speak of widening the margin of certainty, because that is generally the margin, and a very narrow one at that. Here, private enterprise and all others involved in micro-situations often extend a helping hand to official institutions. The more developed a country is the more opportunities there are to improve statistics. Unfortunately, as a rule the reverse is true also. As long as statistics remain poor, the gap of uncertainty has to be attacked with the only remaining weapon: intuition. This weapon may produce remarkable results.

Private versus Public Interest

It was the lack of data and foresight that, probably more than any other experience, caused the author to question some concepts that seemed acceptable to him before. One such concept is the question of private versus public interest. Some theories assume (a) that both can be determined in an exact way, and (b) that action based on private interest than has to be 'corrected' to serve the purpose of 'the public interest', deemed superior. Leaving the critical remarks that could be made on point (b), the author would like to restrict himself to point (a). In concrete cases, i.e. mostly in micro-situations, one can only determine such a difference of interests and take appropriate decisions on the basis of reasonably complete information about the past and perfect foresight into the future. Such situations are exceptional and usually restricted to cases obvious to everybody, such as air pollution produced by industries.

There is a simple reason why literature seldom or never illustrates the general theory in this field with concrete case studies beyond the obvious ones mentioned before: it is for want of data and foresight. Consequently, when certain decisions are propagated in concrete cases – often by politicians – the foundations of their reasoning usually look rather woolly. Let's face it: they are as woolly as the 'business feeling' of private entrepreneurs embarking upon a new initiative.

This reasoning seems to lead in an interesting direction: as soon as we descend from the macro-realm into the micro-underworld, the law of numbers starts letting us down, the mist engendered by a lack of data and foresight thickens, and in it the distinction between private and public interest disappears.

In this context something could be said on the inclination of public authorities and private business to take a long-term view. Supposedly, public authorities can afford to take the long-term view, while businessmen are said to be more or less forced to take a short-term view because they have to watch profits. In fact, however, one also sees a great deal of short-sightedness in government, especially where rather immediate 'political profits' seem to be at stake! At the same time business appears perfectly able to make a long-term view – in fact it has to do this for the sake of continuity in many cases. The actual world appears to be more complicated than some simplistic, but unfortunately wide-spread, theories suggest.

Because we meet people that have the imagination to look into the future, both in government and in business, we see a forecasting and planning effort going on in both circles. Let us delve into this somewhat further.

Forecasting, Planning and Communications

Why do we go on forecasting and basing plans on our forecasts – both in government and private circles? The reason was once mentioned to the author by an executive: 'We go on forecasting and planning to have a background for the decisions of to-day. However, we know beforehand that plans are there to be changed and also that many decisions can be taken later on the basis of information available by then. Consequently, we must be informed quickly about developments in the real world, so that we can adjust our plans accordingly. In other words, communications showing quickly what is happening are more important than forecasting and planning. Plans are useless unless there is fast feedback and information on changing external conditions.

In principle there are three ways to make lines of communications more efficient:

(a) shortening the lines of communication;
(b) simplifying information;
(c) reducing processing time.

a. Shortening the lines

(1) One method is to eliminate as many intermediate stations as possible, another is (2) to prevent information from going beyond the point where it cannot serve the real purpose it should serve: providing the feedback that enables those responsible for implementing the plans to adjust them in time.

If the information arrives too late due to too long lines of communication, it might as well have been ditched on the way. It is generally known that delayed feedback induces measures that aggravate a development already taking place but not yet reported back. A well-known example is a government reacting to previous deflation with measures that gather momentum during an ensuing inflationary period.

It is probably for this reason that decentralization has gained in importance in many big enterprises. When the levels of responsibility and decision are brought down from the centre towards levels away from it, the feedback and information on changing circumstances can take place quicker and become more relevant for the adjustment of the course set. The gain in flexibility thus realised often appears bigger than losses due to uncoordinated action of different centres of decision.

This may cause some reflection on the idea of fitting provincial plans into national programmes, the latter into regional plans and these again into an indicative world plan. Will the feedback really work in such a system? Conversely, it may be asked what maximum feedback time should be allowed to make such a structure useful.

b. Simplifying information

Simpler information can be processed more quickly, and that again results in shorter feedback time and quicker decisions on corrective measures.

Herein lies one strong point of the price mechanism. People are responsive to changes in prices, because they understand what they mean. Prices are simple indicators to watch: prices and price changes speak louder than a thousand words. More complicated forms of information are mostly contained in written documents. It often takes a great deal of trouble to make sure that the information contained in them really reaches those for whom it is meant.

c. Reducing processing time

It is only in this field that modern aids, including computers, can be of help – not in the 'final consumption' of information on which decisions have to be based. Only too often modern aids produce just a more massive flow of information. More time is then taken up in consuming information and less time remains for decision-taking, which is the real purpose of the exercise. Often managers simply skip part of a stream of information, because the human mind puts a limit to the number of points of view that can be taken into consideration. Thus, a wrong use of modern aids can either reduce productivity at managerial levels or simply be useless. Therefore the possibility of increasing the efficiency with which information is produced calls for greater selectivity and self-discipline, both on the part of those who can produce information and of those who ask for information. Only too often it happens that a certain type of information once asked for becomes 'institutionalised' into a regular flow. A rather amusing example comes to the author's mind. Part of the job of administering a local branch of a certain organization consisted of supplying information on certain forms that had to be filled out and mailed to a central office. Some thinking raised doubts as to the practical use of this information to the central administration. The theory was 'tested' by quietly throwing the forms into the wastepaper basket. No request ever reached the branch for the forms. The forms were the 'forgotten flow' in the administration, and they were forgotten because the information they contained was never needed anymore.

Communications, Psychology and Market Mechanism

A very efficient method of putting a stop to requests for non-essential information seems the introduction of the market mechanism. Anybody who has to pay the cost of certain information supplied to him will be a bit more careful about asking for it than when he gets it free. Suppose authorities had to pay for the hours worked in filling out forms for all sorts of purposes:

statistical, fiscal, legal, etc. They would probably reduce the 'needs' for information drastically. They would also reduce the staff required by offices, and release skilled labour for activities of a more direct character. The author saw the effects of a comparable operation within a business enterprise, and the results were rather surprising: the market mechanism proved to be a weapon against Parkinsonian tendencies. It may very well be that the biggest distortions in many economies are not created by imperfections in the sectors where the price mechanism functions, but in those sectors where the price mechanism does not function at all: i.e. where labour and other factors of production are not paid for by those asking for their services. Of course, one can define this as a special case in which certain prices are 0, while they should have a certain value, i.e. a maximum distortion of the price structure. Considered in this way, there is nothing wrong about a tollroad. It makes people realize that economic assets are scarce things, and people realizing this think twice before they take an economic decision. Conversely, it is an inescapable fact that something one has not paid for is generally felt to be more or less 'free' – even if one knows the price. In this way a more or less automatic mechanism is introduced that really brings economic information to those to whom it is relevant. Such a mechanism is often a great deal more efficient than most institutions supplying information in the form of documents, like most administrative measures of public authorities.

Of course one generally has to pay for something out of one's income. It is this that really makes people think twice before spending. A similar psychological effect is created by making somebody responsible for a budget in an organization that has to pay its own way. Mostly the inefficient spots of an enterprise are the departments in which the people working are farthest removed from the acute realization of personal responsibility for keeping within the lines set by a budget, because of the necessity to make the enterprise at least pay its own way.

The above-mentioned points lead towards the following conclusions. The market mechanism may be imperfect in many ways. However, it creates the psychological climate for efficient communication, and thereby it prompts decisions that are a condition for adaptation to changing circumstances. This system cannot be replaced by a system of communications based on other more formal and institutionalized methods except at a very high human and economic cost (as for example in centrally planned economies).

Amending somewhat Churchill's words on democracy one could say: 'The market mechanism is the worst mechanism on earth – excepting all others!'

Communications versus Institutions

If it is correct to say that efficient communications are necessary because of the limits of forecasting and planning, one question may be worth looking into somewhat more closely. We could call this the question of communications versus institutions. It is probably due to the abstract thinking that we often think in terms of institutions – preferably new ones – when a certain job has to be done. Or conversely, that many think of wiping out existing institutions in order to 'improve society', etc.[7]

The author remembers a discussion in which he was involved a number of years ago. Proposals were made to prepare an organization to take action in a certain direction. The creation of a coordinating committee was proposed 'to make appropriate action possible.' A senior manager looked at the proposals and started asking questions. What action had to be taken? Certain markets had to be approached in a new way and finance had to be made available for that purpose. Who would have to do all this? The approach to the markets: the managements of local companies. The creation of facilities for production: the relevant managements of technical departments. The provision of finance: the finance department, and especially its top staff.

It was found that all these people were in continuous touch with each other already, and that decisions and a clear explanation on the part of the board of management could set all these persons in motion. Some of them had to be convinced of the necessity of the new approach, of course. However, that could be done by means of personal talks with the relevant managers. For such talks persons would have to be selected to whom they were prepared to listen – who could communicate the new idea in an efficient way. The senior executive concluded that a new institution was unnecessary because the job could be done within the existing structure and via existing communications.

7) Cf. Waterston: 'There is a notable tendency in many countries to try to overcome administrative deficiencies, especially in agriculture, by creating new organizations. This solution often results in increasing the difficulties in the way of achieving proper co-ordination.' (p. 290). Waterston's statement seems to need two corrections. In the first place the tendency is unfortunately not restricted to countries, but it has also spread to the field of international organizations. In the second place the tendency seems equally strong outside agriculture.

Suppose the committee had been created. The secretary of that committee would have had to see to it that a number of strategically located staff-members met a number of times to look into the matter. Getting together such busy people is a problem in itself. Getting the information and feeding it to them, and making sure that they really looked at it would have been another tough problem. Supposing the committee had reached concrete conclusions on the action to be taken. Then the secretary would have been faced with the problem of communicating the findings of the committee to the relevant executives. That would in fact have meant creating another communications channel to the relevant executives. In other words: adding another flow of information to the flows existing. That new flow would have been competing with the other flows for the scarce time of the front-line men. These men would not have been very receptive to the new flow, because they would have been bothered with requests for information previously – often information they were already supplying to other institutions anyway. Consequently the added burden on communications created by the new institution would have caused the irritation which results in a poor reception of new ideas. Thus, the creation of a new institution would have led to a deterioration of communications, and to resistance to the acceptance of the ideas! The only advantage of the committee could have been a more detailed working out of the new ideas – but that in itself would probably also have led to irritation on the part of the front-line men! One thing was quite certain: the creation of the new institution would have led to more hours worked by expensive specialists and a considerable loss of time, i.e. a less flexible organization.

It was therefore quite understandable that the executive decided not to create a new institution, but to rely on existing lines of communication to make the new policy clear in principle, and to leave the front-line executives to work it out in detail. They, in turn, felt it was a stimulating experience to try something new, and the responsibility implied by that degree of autonomy made them do the job faster. It increased the flexibility of the organization. Of course, they made mistakes, but such mistakes – and perhaps many more – would also have been made in the case of the institutional approach. Apart from that, it would have been time-consuming – the best guarantee for a complete flop of the scheme.

The above-mentioned example seems to show that new institutions, centralizing certain functions, increase the number of communications channels and thereby reduce the action time of the executives on the spot – and often their willingness to take action. Consequently, the arguments in favour of new institutions have to be very powerful for them to produce a net benefit.

Of course, many newly created institutions do perform a function for which a need is felt outside their boundaries; in other words they are considered useful and so there appears to be a 'market' for their services. One example is committees that are created between departments to increase the understanding of each other's language and problems and consequently to improve the speed and quality of decisions. In such cases the creation of the committees is generally preceded by individual contacts that have made the need for the service clear. More generally, new bodies that prove successful are often an institutionalisation of communications and activities that already exist and function. The establishing of an institution is then formal proof of the success of what was happening already, and a stepping-stone for further growth of the activity.

National planning tries to avoid overcapacity or undercapacity in certain sectors and similar inconsistencies. On the other hand, however, it stimulates creation of centralised institutions, and thereby increases the risks of the above-mentioned communications troubles. This danger is especially acute in developing countries that often have a chronic shortage of experienced staff. Moreover central institutions tend to discourage the often scarce initiative that exists at the 'front-line' level where development really takes place.

Consequently existing channels of communications can often do the job of development and adjustment to changes more efficiently than new institutions and new channels. The change of attitudes often necessary for development may therefore very well take place within the framework of existing institutions. Attempts to eliminate the existing structure and to build new institutions and channels of communications may prove very time-consuming and also wasteful. The energy released for breaking down the existing structure may lead to a waste, neutralising its favourable effect.

One example of this phenomenon is given by Rostow when he compares Russian and American industrial growth largely on the basis of Warren Nutter's research. For our purpose the most interesting comparison, however, is not the one made between the United States and Russia, but that between pre-revolutionary Russia and Soviet Russia. The performance between 1880 and 1914 compares surprisingly well to that after 1930. The revolution and the collectivization period meant an incredible waste in human resources (especially trained people), which apparently neutralized the favourable effect of the energy released by the revolution, except in agriculture where the change did more harm than good.[8]) In short: organizational changes only make sense if they induce improvements in communications. Organizational changes for their own sake can do more harm than good.

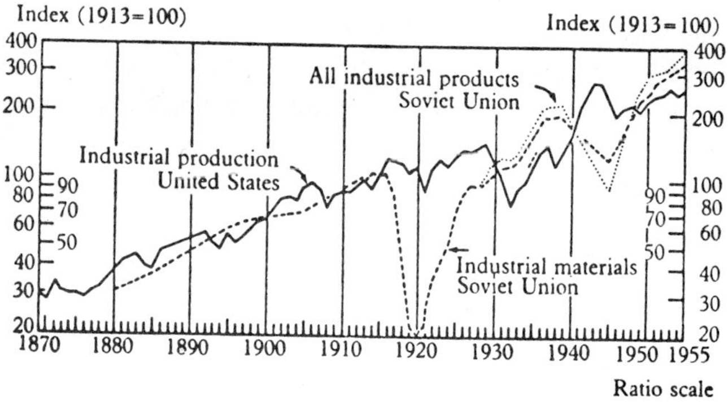

Fig. 1

The above reasoning implies that economic development can take place under a wide variety of institutional systems. History seems to confirm this – and especially recent history. What may be most important of all is that those

[8]) See p. 94 of Rostow [4] where Nutter's chart converting industrial output per head into an index, with 1913 equal to 100, is reproduced: 'It shows, therefore, comparative rates of growth in output per head, not absolute figures; and it should be read with an awareness that the median lag in 1955, for the thirty-seven industries involved, is fifty-six years of growth: in short the whole Soviet curve is set below the American by an amount that does not vary greatly, in terms of time-lag. What emerges is that, between the 1880's and the First World War, Russia, relatively, came forward during its take-off; it fell behind in the 1920's, when the United States enjoyed a boom, and Russia reorganized slowly after war and revolution; it came forward relatively during the first Five Year Plans of the 1930's, when the United States were gripped in a slump; and in its post-1945 phase Russia again came forward relatively, at a time when Russian output was more heavily concentrated in industry and American output was shifting structurally to housing and non-manufactured services.'

Note the curve for Russia before and after the revolution: the general trend seems to remain the same notwithstanding the draconic measures taken during and after the revolution.

in control of economic and political power become interested in developing production and succeed in inspiring increasing groups of the population to take part in the process. In other words, they should be able to communicate the necessary new ideas to groups of the population.

The crucial problem, in business and development alike is: how do people acquire an interest? How are they activated and kept alert to new possibilities? Clearly, people should be interested in receiving information, otherwise they cannot start thinking about taking action on the basis of it. This is true of a housewife buying daily needs on the market, of a farmer seeking to improve his output as well as of the entrepreneur and manager of an enterprise. Only people with such an inclination make modern economic development possible – irrespective of the institutional framework in which it takes place. The author would like to suggest a number of conditions that came to his mind as he enjoyed the stimulus of a big enterprise which itself takes a very active part in the process of development all over the world[9]):

The Fun of Making Choices

The first psychological condition for making people receptive to information is the realization that it is possible to choose between alternatives. Once this is realized, the urge is felt to acquire information about the different possibilities. Needless to say, extremely poor and extremely traditional societies often have a built-in resistance against the awakening of this urge. It may be that the much loathed 'demonstration effect' has a function after all! It breaks the crust and induces people to see new horizons. In this connection it seems appropriate to quote the very interesting inaugural address entitled 'Liberty Revisited' delivered by Dr. J. F. Glastra van Loon at the 14th Dies Natalis of the Institute of Social Studies in The Hague, October 10, 1966: 'Now it is obvious that life at or comparatively near subsistence level leaves only a narrow margin of liberty for raising questions as to what *ought* to be done as distinct from what *can* be done. This is not to say that those living at such levels of development are less guided by moral values and judgements than those living at higher ones, as defined in these economic terms. What it does mean is that in a society of people living at subsistence level there is little room for asking questions about the adequacy of their mores and

[9]) See also the extremely interesting chapter 'The General Theory of Motivation', pp. 128–140 in Galbraith [1]. Mr. Galbraith distinguishes four motivations: compulsion, pecuniary, identification and adaptation.

traditional standards of judgement. The same applies to the possibility of widening their scope of involvement beyond the limits of those to which they are related in their daily life and work. Not only, however, is there little room or possibility for doing these things but to do so even constitutes a serious threat to the survival of both the individual and the group. It is clear, therefore, that to raise their standard of living is one of the first conditions that must be fulfilled in order to increase their liberty. This is elementary. Beyond this point, however, everything becomes less simple. First of all, in order to raise the standard of living of a traditional society it is necessary to change deeply rooted ways of life. Now not only will this run up against resistance but it actually presupposes the existence of margins of liberty on the basis of which new possibilities of action can be envisaged as morally acceptable and upon which new and wider ranging social relations can be founded. Amongst the first things to be done, therefore, should *not only* be counted a determination of the economic and technological measures to be taken in view of available skills and resources and the conditions of the international market, but also an ascertainment of the nature and the scope of the liberty of the people as moral agents, of the distribution of that liberty in the society concerned, and of its accessibility in view of the political power structure of that society.'[10])

The Fun of Autonomy

Even if the means and the number of possible choices are limited, people must have a certain autonomy to choose. If that is abolished, the fun of choice disappears. What disappears also will be the urge to acquire more resources to continue and expand the game of choosing. Thus, the individual consumer will want autonomy to choose between different alternatives. The same goes for all people running enterprises of some sort to earn a living: farmers growing cash crops, traders and industrialists. All those entrepreneurs will be more receptive to information if they are autonomous. This is perhaps the fundamental reason why so many attempts at collectivization failed. People were less receptive to information because their autonomy has disappeared and with it the fun of choosing. And because they were less receptive, crude methods had to be followed to make them do what central

---

10) See: *Jaarverslag 1966 Stichting Internationaal Instituut voor Sociale Studies*, Annex pages 12 and 13.

institutions wanted them to do, i.e. to follow the choice that *was made for them.*

... and of Paying Your Own Way, or More if Possible

In the economic field, the vital condition for autonomy is to be able to pay one's own way. The person earning his or her own living is economically autonomous compared to the person being maintained by his family, his clan or the government. The enterprise that is able to pay its own way is autonomous. As the dependence upon outside sources of finance increases, the freedom of decision is reduced and thereby the range of choices. One of the basic rules the author heard proclaimed by an industrial entrepreneur was: 'Stay away from bankers and try to take care of your own financing!' Needless to say the author is convinced that the quest for autonomy is the strongest motive for making a profit. [11]) The other motives are: securing the continuity and growth of the enterprise.

... and of Inducing Change

Of course one way of securing continuity as an autonomous unit is to create financial reserves that can form a buffer against future uncertainty or pay for expansion. Another way is to be responsive to change, i.e. to take notice of indications of change and adjust accordingly. One step further lies in taking an active part in inducing change. That part may be small. It may mean a product or service at the same price considered superior by the consumer. How many simple new tools have been invented in recent years! Tools tackling simple jobs that have had to be tackled by human beings since time immemorial. The author (one of many 'do-it-yourself fanatics') has often found himself exclaiming in hardware stores: 'How simple, why didn't *I* think of this?' Of course such tiny innovations have to be put on the market by enterprises trying to pay their own way – they have little economic meaning when they stay in the one-person's workshop. The inventions made outside enterprises can reach the market if enterprises are eager to get information on new ideas that crop up. Here lies another communication problem: finding ideas that can bring about a change.

[11]) Viewed from this angle, the term 'profit motive' is misleading. It suggests that making a profit is an end in itself. This is not so, the urge to make a profit is derived from more fundamental motives: autonomy, the desire to increase strength and the desire to expand. These motives are healthy signs of life in any living organism. It is therefore understandable that public enterprises often also show a tendency to make a profit.

Back to Macro

With the gap between macro- and micro-economics, with the lack of facts and foresight and problems in communication, we economists seem to have little to offer towards solving the major problems of development. And yet, a great future lies ahead for humanity. More and more people are learning to see the fun of making choices and are seeking the autonomy they want for it. And with it comes the urge to pay one's way to take part in change and innovation. Even with the present unsatisfactory rates of growth in many developing countries, the growth that is taking place is producing margins for choice that will play a significant role in sparking off the process of change of mind that was mentioned in the previous pages.

Both in the micro- and macro-spheres economists will have to play their role in pointing out sets of alternatives. In that sense they can be compared with salesmen whose job it is to show the things that money can be spent on. There will, however, be one big difference between the two: the economists have the unpopular job of showing the limits of scarce resources. They will have to show that making a choice means foregoing something else. In that respect their job is the same in business or government, in macro and micro.

Macro will never be able to work without the assistance of micro – especially in the increasingly complex world with the proliferation of choices that can be made. Conversely, micro will need the framework of macro to an increasing extent not in forms that reduce initiative and resourcefulness, but in forms that can expand existing narrow margins of certainty – as e.g. by overall measures aimed at full employment, stability and growth: Balanced International Growth! There will be less and less uniformity in the micro-realm because 'Man is a pluralistic being – a complex household, not a maximizing unit – and he has the right to live in a pluralistic society'. [4, p. 167].

References

[1] John Kenneth GALBRAITH, *The New Industrial State*. London, Hamish Hamilton, 1967.

[2] Joseph S. MOAG, William T. CARLETON and Eugene M. LERNER, 'Defining the Finance Function: A Model-Systems Approach.' *The Journal of Finance*, December 1967.

[3] Joan ROBINSON, *Economic Philosophy*. London, Pelican Books, 1964.

[4] W. W. ROSTOW, *The Stages of Economic Growth*. Cambridge, Cambridge University Press, 1960.

[5] Jean-Jacques SERVAN-SCHREIBER, *Le Défi Américain*. Paris, Editions Denoël, 1967.

[6] L. TRAAS, *Het investerings- en financieringsplan van de onderneming*, Alphen aan de Rijn, N. Samson N.V., 1968.

[7] Albert WATERSTON, *Development Planning. Lessons of Experience*, London, Oxford University Press, 1966.

INDEX